HOLT McDOUGAL LITERATURE

Interactive Reader

GRADE 8

HOLT McDOUGAL
a division of Houghton Mifflin Harcourt

TABLE OF CONTENTS

How to Use This Book

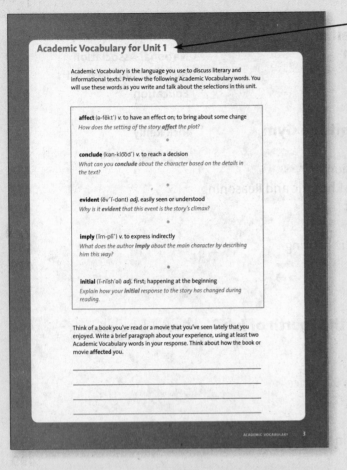

Academic Vocabulary for the Unit

Academic vocabulary is the language you use to talk and write about the subjects you are studying, including math, science, social studies, and language arts. It is the language you use in your classroom and the language you find in books, tests, and formal writing. Understanding and using academic vocabulary correctly will help you succeed in school and on assessments.

You will find five academic vocabulary words, defined for ready reference and use at the beginning of each unit. You will have the opportunity to practice using these words after each selection.

Before Reading

Before Reading pages introduce you to the text-analysis and reading skills you will practice as you read. Vocabulary words for the selection are introduced here as well.

Big Question

Each selection or group of selections begins with an activity that gets you thinking about the real-life questions that literature addresses. Sometimes you'll work in a group or with a partner to complete this activity. After reading, you'll return to this activity. Don't be surprised if you have a different perspective.

Text Analysis

This section presents a brief, easy-to-understand lesson that introduces an important literary element and explains what to look for in the selection you are about to read.

Reading Skill: Make Inferences

When you make an inference while reading, you use clues from the story and your own knowledge to guess about things the author doesn't say directly. As you read "Raymond's Run," notes in the side column will ask you to record your inferences in a chart like the one below.

Clue from the Story		My Experience		Inference
Squeaky says her dad is the only one faster than she is.	+	Kids like when their parents are talented.	=	Squeaky is proud of her father.

Vocabulary in Context

Note: Words are listed in the order in which they appear in the story.

relay (rē'lā) *n.* a race in which several team members take turns running to complete the race
A relay is usually made up of teams of three or four.

clutch (klŭch) *v.* to grasp and hold tightly
The winner might clutch the blue ribbon to her chest.

prodigy (prŏd'ə-jē) *n.* a person with an exceptional talent
The talented young sprinter was considered a track prodigy.

liable (lī'ə-bəl) *adj.* likely to
Ben is liable to get injured if he doesn't warm up before the race.

sidekick (sĭd'kĭk') *n.* a close friend
My sidekick and I spend most afternoons together.

crouch (krouch) *v.* to stoop with bent knees
At the start of a race, runners crouch close to the ground.

Vocabulary Practice

Review the vocabulary words and think about their meanings. Then, brainstorm with a partner what you think "Raymond's Run" will be about based on the list above. Write down your prediction.

_____

_____

_____

RAYMOND'S RUN   5

Reading Skill or Strategy

This lesson presents a reading skill or strategy that will help your reading comprehension, such as making inferences, making connections, or paraphrasing. You will have opportunities to practice these skills as you read the selection.

Vocabulary in Context

Vocabulary words for the selection are introduced before reading. Each entry gives the pronunciation and definition of the word as well as a context sentence. **Vocabulary Practice** activities give you an opportunity to use selection vocabulary.

Monitor Your Comprehension

SET A PURPOSE FOR READING
Read "Raymond's Run" to discover what Squeaky learns on the day of the big race.

RAYMOND'S RUN

Short Story by
TONI CADE BAMBARA

BACKGROUND A dialect is a way of speaking that is characteristic of a certain of a certain geographical area or group of people. Dialect can include special pronunciations, vocabulary, and grammar. In Raymond's Run," Toni Cade Bambara captures the voice of her characters by having them speak in a dialect used in 1970s Harlem, a neighborhood in New York City. Notice how the use of dialect makes the narrator sound unique.

ⓐ PLOT EXPOSITION
In lines 1–6, the narrator introduces herself. Circle the one thing she has to do in life. Who else is introduced in these lines?

_____
_____
_____
_____
_____
_____
_____
_____
_____
_____

I don't have much work to do around the house like some girls. My mother does that. And I don't have to earn my pocket money by hustling; George runs errands for the big boys and sells Christmas cards. And anything else that's got to get done, my father does. All I have to do in life is mind my brother Raymond, which is enough. ⓐ

Sometimes I slip and say my little brother Raymond. But as any fool can see he's much bigger and he's older too. But a lot of people call him my little brother cause he 10 needs looking after cause he's not quite right. And a lot of smart mouths got lots to say about that too, especially when George was minding him. But now, if anybody has anything to say to Raymond, anything to say about his big head,[1] they have to come by me. And I don't play the dozens[2] or believe in standing around with somebody in my face doing a lot of talking. I much rather just knock you down and take my chances even if I am a little girl

1. **big head:** a result of hydrocephalus, or fluid in parts of the brain, that causes enlargement of the skull.
2. **play the dozens:** exchange rhyming insults.

6   INTERACTIVE READER / UNIT 1: PLOT AND CONFLICT

Reading the Selection

Notes in the side columns guide your interaction with the selection. Many notes ask you to underline or circle in the text itself. Others provide lines on which you can write your responses.

Set a Purpose for Reading

This feature gives you a reason for reading the selection.

Background

This paragraph provides important information about the selection you are about to read. It helps you understand the context of the literature through additional information about the author, the subject, or the time period during which the selection was written.

How to Use This Book

with skinny arms and a squeaky voice, which is how I got the name Squeaky. And if things get too rough, I run. And
20 as anybody can tell you, I'm the fastest thing on two feet.

There is no track meet that I don't win the first place medal. I used to win the twenty-yard dash when I was a little kid in kindergarten. Nowadays, it's the fifty-yard dash. And tomorrow I'm subject to run the quarter-meter relay all by myself and come in first, second, and third. The big kids call me Mercury[3] cause I'm the swiftest thing in the neighborhood. Everybody knows that—except two people who know better, my father and me. He can beat me to Amsterdam Avenue with me having a two fire
30 hydrant headstart and him running with his hands in his pockets and whistling. But that's private information. Cause can you imagine some thirty-five-year-old man stuffing himself into PAL shorts to race little kids? So as far as everyone's concerned, I'm the fastest and that goes for Gretchen, too, who has put out the tale that she is going to win the first-place medal this year. Ridiculous. In the second place, she's got short legs. In the third place, she's got freckles. In the first place, no one can beat me and that's all there is to it. **PAUSE & REFLECT**

40 I'm standing on the corner admiring the weather and about to take a stroll down Broadway so I can practice my breathing exercises, and I've got Raymond walking on the inside close to the buildings, cause he's subject to fits of fantasy and starts thinking he's a circus performer and that the curb is a tightrope strung high in the air. And sometimes after a rain he likes to step down off his tightrope right into the gutter and slosh around getting his shoes and cuffs wet. Then I get hit when I get home. Or sometimes if you don't watch him he'll dash across traffic to
50 the island in the middle of Broadway and give the pigeons

3. **Mercury:** in Roman mythology, the swift messenger of the gods.

RAYMOND'S RUN 7

○ PLOT EXPOSITION
Reread lines 7–20. Circle the reason Raymond needs to be cared for. Circle three things you learn about Squeaky.

relay (rē'lā) *n.* a race in which several team members take turns running to complete the race

Why do you think Squeaky runs the relay all by herself?

PAUSE & REFLECT
Explain whether you believe all of Squeaky's claims.

Side notes provide a variety of activities for you to complete as you read the selection.

Text Analysis or Reading Skill or Strategy

These notes help you identify and analyze the literary element or reading skill you learned about on the **Before Reading** pages.

Vocabulary words

Vocabulary words introduced on the **Before Reading** page are defined in the side column and appear underlined in blue within the selection, allowing you to see them in context.

Pause & Reflect

These notes give you a chance to stop reading and take time to think about what you have just read.

Additional Side Note

Visual Vocabulary provides photographs in addition to definitions, to illustrate the meaning of words when it helps to picture a word's meaning.

After Reading

Text Analysis: Plot
The plot of "Raymond's Run" revolves around Squeaky's desire to win the May Day race. In each box of the chart below, write down the events that happen at each stage of the plot.

PLOT STRUCTURE OF "RAYMOND'S RUN"

2. RISING ACTION

3. CLIMAX

4. FALLING ACTION

1. EXPOSITION

5. RESOLUTION

Review your notes for "Raymond's Run" and your completed plot diagram. What do you think is the most important conflict in the story? Explain whether or not this conflict is resolved, or settled, by the end of the story.

RAYMOND'S RUN 17

After Reading

After Reading pages feature graphic organizers to reinforce the skills you have practiced throughout the selection.

Text Analysis

Here you demonstrate your knowledge of the literary element you examined before and during reading by completing a graphic organizer. You will often cite details from the selection as you complete your text analysis.

Reading Skill: Make Inferences

Make an inference about each character based on details from the story.

SQUEAKY	Detail: She is serious about running and doesn't care who knows it (lines 58–59).
My Inference:	_____
	_____
GRETCHEN	Detail: During the race, she juts out her chin as if that would win the race (lines 275-276).
My Inference:	_____
	_____
MR. PEARSON	Detail: He is always dropping his clipboard, pencils, whistles, and other things (lines 192–195).
My Inference:	_____
	_____

What's worth the EFFORT?

Do you think that Squeaky believes that taking care of her brother Raymond is worth the effort? Support your answer with evidence from the text.

_____

_____

Vocabulary Practice

Circle the part of each sentence that answers the question.

1. Is a sidekick likely to be a friend or someone you just met?

2. If you were to clutch something, would you be tossing it away or holding it close?

3. Which would you expect a sports prodigy to be—clumsy or talented?

4. When are you more likely to crouch—picking a flower from the garden or reaching for a glass of water?

5. What's more important in a relay race—one good runner or team effort?

Reading Skill or Strategy

The Reading Skill or Strategy activity follows up on the skill you used to help you understand the text.

Big Question

Here's a chance to think again about the Big Question you examined before reading. It offers an opportunity to consider whether your viewpoint has changed now that you have read the selection.

Vocabulary Practice

This activity helps you assess your understanding of the selection vocabulary words.

Academic Vocabulary in Writing

affect	conclude	evident	imply	initial

How does Squeaky's attitude toward Gretchen change over the course of the story? Compare Squeaky's initial reaction to Gretchen to her feelings at the end of the story. Use at least one Academic Vocabulary word in your response. Definitions of these words are on page 3.

_____

_____

_____

_____

Assessment Practice

DIRECTIONS Use "Raymond's Run" to answer questions 1–6.

1 Who does Squeaky race against?
  A Rosie
  B Raymond
  C Gretchen
  D Mary Louise

2 The conflict in this story begins when—
  A Squeaky sees Gretchen on the street
  B Squeaky wins a spelling bee
  C Gretchen makes fun of Squeaky's brother
  D Gretchen tells everyone she will win the race

3 The event that occurs first in the story is—
  A Squeaky decides to teach Raymond how to become a runner
  B Squeaky develops some respect for Gretchen
  C the announcer gives the winner's name.
  D Squeaky tells off Gretchen and her friends

4 Which event in the plot is not part of the story's rising action?
  A Squeaky practices her breathing exercises.
  B Squeaky and Gretchen smile at each other.
  C Mr. Pearson pins on Squeaky's race number.
  D Squeaky argues with Gretchen and her friends.

5 What word best describes how Squeaky feels when she notices Raymond running during the race?
  A angry
  B happy
  C jealous
  D embarrassed

6 How does Squeaky change by the end of the story?
  A She is embarrassed by her brother.
  B She doesn't care anymore about winning the race.
  C She drops out of the race.
  D She thinks that Gretchen may not be so bad after all.

Academic Vocabulary

In this activity, you use the academic vocabulary words for the unit in a speaking or writing activity about the selection.

Assessment Practice

Finally, after each selection, multiple-choice questions assess your knowledge of the selection and the skill taught with it.

UNIT 1

The Main Events

PLOT AND CONFLICT

Be sure to read the Text Analysis Workshop on pp. 28–33 in *Holt McDougal Literature*.

Academic Vocabulary for Unit 1

Academic Vocabulary is the language you use to discuss literary and informational texts. Preview the following Academic Vocabulary words. You will use these words as you write and talk about the selections in this unit.

affect (ə-fĕkt′) *v.* to have an effect on; to bring about some change
*How does the setting of the story **affect** the plot?*

●

conclude (kən-klōōd′) *v.* to reach a decision
*What can you **conclude** about the character based on the details in the text?*

●

evident (ĕv′ĭ-dənt) *adj.* easily seen or understood
*Why is it **evident** that this event is the story's climax?*

●

imply (ĭm-plī′) *v.* to express indirectly
*What does the author **imply** about the main character by describing him this way?*

●

initial (ĭ-nĭsh′əl) *adj.* first; happening at the beginning
*Explain how your **initial** response to the story has changed during reading.*

Think of a book you've read or a movie that you've seen lately that you enjoyed. Write a brief paragraph about your experience, using at least two Academic Vocabulary words in your response. Think about how the book or movie **affected** you.

_____

_____

_____

_____

Raymond's Run

Short Story by Toni Cade Bambara

What's worth the EFFORT?

Have you ever wanted something so badly you'd do anything to achieve it? If so, you've felt motivation, the drive that causes people to strive toward a goal. In the story you are about to read, a spunky young girl does what it takes to be the fastest runner in her neighborhood.

QUICKWRITE Make a list of three things you've been willing to work for. Make a check next to your favorite, and then in a sentence or two, explain what motivates you.

Text Analysis: Plot

A **plot,** or the series of events in a story, typically includes five stages of development. In a linear plot, the order in which these stages occur follows a pattern, as shown in the graphic.

What I am willing to work for

1. Hold record for most chin-ups

2. Learn new dance

3. _____

What Motivates Me

PLOT STRUCTURE AT A GLANCE

2. RISING ACTION
- Introduces obstacles that make the conflict more complicated
- Builds suspense as "the plot thickens"

3. CLIMAX
- Is the turning point in the story and the moment of greatest suspense
- Presents the conflict at its most intense and dramatic

4. FALLING ACTION
- Reveals the outcome of the story's climax
- Eases the tension
- Shows how the main character resolves the conflict

1. EXPOSITION
- Introduces the setting and the characters
- Reveals the conflict or sets the stage for it

5. RESOLUTION
- Reveals the story's final outcome
- Ties up any loose ends

Reading Skill: Make Inferences

When you make an inference while reading, you use clues from the story and your own knowledge to guess about things the author doesn't say directly. As you read "Raymond's Run," notes in the side column will ask you to record your inferences in a chart like the one below.

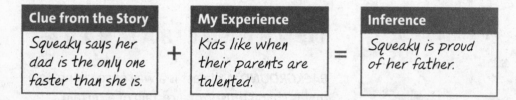

Clue from the Story		My Experience		Inference
Squeaky says her dad is the only one faster than she is.	+	Kids like when their parents are talented.	=	Squeaky is proud of her father.

Vocabulary in Context

Note: Words are listed in the order in which they appear in the story.

relay (rē′lā) *n.* a race in which several team members take turns running to complete the race
  *A **relay** is usually made up of teams of three or four.*

clutch (klŭch) *v.* to grasp and hold tightly
  *The winner might **clutch** the blue ribbon to her chest.*

prodigy (prŏd′ə-jē) *n.* a person with an exceptional talent
  *The talented young sprinter was considered a track **prodigy.***

liable (lī′ə-bəl) *adj.* likely to
  *Ben is **liable** to get injured if he doesn't warm up before the race.*

sidekick (sīd′kĭk′) *n.* a close friend
  *My **sidekick** and I spend most afternoons together.*

crouch (krouch) *v.* to stoop with bent knees
  *At the start of a race, runners **crouch** close to the ground.*

Vocabulary Practice

Review the vocabulary words and think about their meanings. Then, brainstorm with a partner what you think "Raymond's Run" will be about based on the list above. Write down your prediction.

_____

_____

_____

SET A PURPOSE
FOR READING

Read "Raymond's Run" to discover what Squeaky learns on the day of the big race.

A PLOT EXPOSITION
In lines 1–6, the narrator introduces herself. Circle the one thing she has to do in life. Who else is introduced in these lines?

_____

_____

_____

_____

_____

_____

_____

_____

_____

RAYMOND'S RUN

Short Story by
TONI CADE BAMBARA

BACKGROUND A dialect is a way of speaking that is characteristic of a certain of a certain geographical area or group of people. Dialect can include special pronunciations, vocabulary, and grammar. In Raymond's Run," Toni Cade Bambara captures the voice of her characters by having them speak in a dialect used in 1970s Harlem, a neighborhood in New York City. Notice how the use of dialect makes the narrator sound unique.

I don't have much work to do around the house like some girls. My mother does that. And I don't have to earn my pocket money by hustling; George runs errands for the big boys and sells Christmas cards. And anything else that's got to get done, my father does. All I have to do in life is mind my brother Raymond, which is enough. **A**

Sometimes I slip and say my little brother Raymond. But as any fool can see he's much bigger and he's older too. But a lot of people call him my little brother cause he
10 needs looking after cause he's not quite right. And a lot of smart mouths got lots to say about that too, especially when George was minding him. But now, if anybody has anything to say to Raymond, anything to say about his big head,[1] they have to come by me. And I don't play the dozens[2] or believe in standing around with somebody in my face doing a lot of talking. I much rather just knock you down and take my chances even if I am a little girl

---

1. **big head:** a result of hydrocephalus, or fluid in parts of the brain, that causes enlargement of the skull.
2. **play the dozens:** exchange rhyming insults.

with skinny arms and a squeaky voice, which is how I got the name Squeaky. And if things get too rough, I run. And
20 as anybody can tell you, I'm the fastest thing on two feet. **B**

There is no track meet that I don't win the first place medal. I used to win the twenty-yard dash when I was a little kid in kindergarten. Nowadays, it's the fifty-yard dash. And tomorrow I'm subject to run the quarter-meter **relay** all by myself and come in first, second, and third. The big kids call me Mercury[3] cause I'm the swiftest thing in the neighborhood. Everybody knows that—except two people who know better, my father and me. He can beat me to Amsterdam Avenue with me having a two fire
30 hydrant headstart and him running with his hands in his pockets and whistling. But that's private information. Cause can you imagine some thirty-five-year-old man stuffing himself into PAL shorts to race little kids? So as far as everyone's concerned, I'm the fastest and that goes for Gretchen, too, who has put out the tale that she is going to win the first-place medal this year. Ridiculous. In the second place, she's got short legs. In the third place, she's got freckles. In the first place, no one can beat me and that's all there is to it. **PAUSE & REFLECT**

40 I'm standing on the corner admiring the weather and about to take a stroll down Broadway so I can practice my breathing exercises, and I've got Raymond walking on the inside close to the buildings, cause he's subject to fits of fantasy and starts thinking he's a circus performer and that the curb is a tightrope strung high in the air. And sometimes after a rain he likes to step down off his tightrope right into the gutter and slosh around getting his shoes and cuffs wet. Then I get hit when I get home. Or sometimes if you don't watch him he'll dash across traffic to
50 the island in the middle of Broadway and give the pigeons

---

3. **Mercury:** in Roman mythology, the swift messenger of the gods.

B PLOT EXPOSITION
Reread lines 7–20. Circle the reason Raymond needs to be cared for. Circle three things you learn about Squeaky.

relay (rē′lā) *n.* a race in which several team members take turns running to complete the race

Why do you think Squeaky runs the **relay** all by herself?

PAUSE & REFLECT
Explain whether you believe all of Squeaky's claims.

C MAKE INFERENCES
Reread lines 40–59. Circle three
details that Squeaky uses to
explain what it is like to care
for Raymond. Complete the
organizer by making an inference
about how Squeaky feels about
taking care of Raymond.

Clues from Story

↓

My Experience

↓

Inference

clutch (klŭch) *v.* to grasp and
hold tightly

a fit. Then I have to go behind him apologizing to all the
old people sitting around trying to get some sun and getting
all upset with the pigeons fluttering around them, scattering
their newspapers and upsetting the waxpaper lunches[4] in
their laps. So I keep Raymond on the inside of me, and he
plays like he's driving a stage coach which is O.K. by me so
long as he doesn't run me over or interrupt my breathing
exercises, which I have to do on account of I'm serious about
my running, and I don't care who knows it. **C**

60 Now some people like to act like things come easy
to them, won't let on that they practice. Not me. I'll
high-prance down 34th Street like a rodeo pony to keep my
knees strong even if it does get my mother uptight so that
she walks ahead like she's not with me, don't know me, is
all by herself on a shopping trip, and I am somebody else's
crazy child. Now you take Cynthia Procter for instance.
She's just the opposite. If there's a test tomorrow, she'll
say something like, "Oh, I guess I'll play handball this
afternoon and watch television tonight," just to let you
70 know she ain't thinking about the test. Or like last week
when she won the spelling bee for the millionth time, "A
good thing you got 'receive,' Squeaky, cause I would have
got it wrong. I completely forgot about the spelling bee."
And she'll **clutch** the lace on her blouse like it was a narrow
escape. Oh, brother. But of course when I pass her house on
my early morning trots around the block, she is practicing
the scales on the piano over and over and over and over.
Then in music class she always lets herself get bumped
around so she falls accidentally on purpose onto the piano
80 stool and is so surprised to find herself sitting there that she
decides just for fun to try out the ole keys. And what do you
know—Chopin's waltzes[5] just spring out of her fingertips
and she's the most surprised thing in the world. A regular

---

4. **waxpaper lunches:** sandwiches wrapped in wax paper.
5. **Chopin's** (shō'pănz') **waltzes:** music by composer Frédéric Chopin.

prodigy. I could kill people like that. I stay up all night studying the words for the spelling bee. And you can see me any time of day practicing running. I never walk if I can trot, and shame on Raymond if he can't keep up. But of course he does, cause if he hangs back someone's **liable** to walk up to him and get smart, or take his allowance from him, or ask him where he got that great big pumpkin head. People are so stupid sometimes. **PAUSE & REFLECT**

So I'm strolling down Broadway breathing out and breathing in on counts of seven, which is my lucky number, and here comes Gretchen and her **sidekicks**: Mary Louise, who used to be a friend of mine when she first moved to Harlem from Baltimore and got beat up by everybody till I took up for her on account of her mother and my mother used to sing in the same choir when they were young girls, but people ain't grateful, so now she hangs out with the new girl Gretchen and talks about me like a dog; and Rosie, who is as fat as I am skinny and has a big mouth where Raymond is concerned and is too stupid to know that there is not a big deal of difference between herself and Raymond and that she can't afford to throw stones. So they are steady coming up Broadway and I see right away that it's going to be one of those Dodge City[6] scenes cause the street ain't that big and they're close to the buildings just as we are. First I think I'll step into the candy store and look over the new comics and let them pass. But that's chicken and I've got a reputation to consider. So then I think I'll just walk straight on through them or even over them if necessary. But as they get to me, they slow down. I'm ready to fight, cause like I said I don't feature a whole lot of chit-chat, I much prefer to just knock you down right from the jump and save everybody a lotta precious time. **D**

---

6. **Dodge City:** an Old West town, famous for showdowns between outlaws and lawmen.

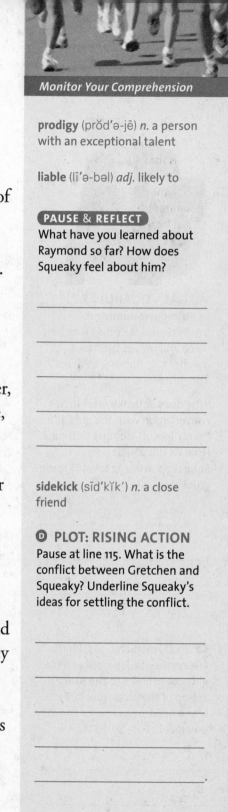

prodigy (prŏd′ə-jē) *n.* a person with an exceptional talent

liable (lī′ə-bəl) *adj.* likely to

PAUSE & REFLECT
What have you learned about Raymond so far? How does Squeaky feel about him?

_____

_____

_____

_____

sidekick (sīd′kĭk′) *n.* a close friend

D PLOT: RISING ACTION
Pause at line 115. What is the conflict between Gretchen and Squeaky? Underline Squeaky's ideas for settling the conflict.

_____

_____

_____

_____

_____

_____

_____

_____

_____

_____

VISUAL VOCABULARY
ventriloquist-dummy *n.* A ventriloquist controls his or her voice and moves the mouth of a puppet, or dummy, to make it appear to be talking.

Why does Squeaky refer to her conversation with the girls as a "ventriloquist-dummy routine"? How would you describe Squeaky's attitude toward these girls?

_____

_____

_____

E PLOT: RISING ACTION
The confrontation between the girls contributes to the rising action of the plot. How does the scene build suspense for the May Day race?

_____

_____

_____

_____

_____

_____

_____

"You signing up for the May Day races?" smiles Mary Louise, only it's not a smile at all. A dumb question like that doesn't deserve an answer. Besides, there's just me and Gretchen standing there really, so no use wasting my
120 breath talking to shadows.

"I don't think you're going to win this time," says Rosie, trying to signify with her hands on her hips all salty, completely forgetting that I have whupped her behind many times for less salt than that.

"I always win cause I'm the best," I say straight at Gretchen who is, as far as I'm concerned, the only one talking in this **ventriloquist-dummy** routine. Gretchen smiles, but it's not a smile, and I'm thinking that girls never really smile at each other because they don't know how
130 and don't want to know how and there's probably no one to teach us how, cause grown-up girls don't know either. Then they all look at Raymond who has just brought his mule team to a standstill. And they're about to see what trouble they can get into through him.

"What grade you in now, Raymond?"

"You got anything to say to my brother, you say it to me, Mary Louise Williams of Raggedy Town, Baltimore." **E**

"What are you, his mother?" sasses Rosie.

"That's right, Fatso. And the next word out of anybody
140 and I'll be *their* mother too." So they just stand there and Gretchen shifts from one leg to the other and so do they. Then Gretchen puts her hands on her hips and is about to say something with her freckle-face self but doesn't. Then she walks around me looking me up and down but keeps walking up Broadway, and her sidekicks follow her. So me and Raymond smile at each other and he says, "Gidyap" to his team and I continue with my breathing exercises, strolling down Broadway toward the ice man on 145th with not a care in the world cause I am Miss Quicksilver[7] herself.

7. **Miss Quicksilver:** a reference to how fast quicksilver (mercury) flows.

150　　I take my time getting to the park on May Day because the track meet is the last thing on the program. The biggest thing on the program is the May Pole dancing, which I can do without, thank you, even if my mother thinks it's a shame I don't take part and act like a girl for a change. You'd think my mother'd be grateful not to have to make me a white organdy dress with a big satin sash and buy me new white baby-doll shoes that can't be taken out of the box till the big day. You'd think she'd be glad her daughter ain't out there prancing around a May Pole getting the new
160 clothes all dirty and sweaty and trying to act like a fairy or a flower or whatever you're supposed to be when you should be trying to be yourself, whatever that is, which is, as far as I am concerned, a poor Black girl who really can't afford to buy shoes and a new dress you only wear once a lifetime cause it won't fit next year. **F**

　　I was once a strawberry in a Hansel and Gretel pageant when I was in nursery school and didn't have no better sense than to dance on tiptoe with my arms in a circle over my head doing umbrella steps and being a perfect fool just
170 so my mother and father could come dressed up and clap. You'd think they'd know better than to encourage that kind of nonsense. I am not a strawberry. I do not dance on my toes. I run. That is what I am all about. So I always come late to the May Day program, just in time to get my number pinned on and lay in the grass till they announce the fifty-yard dash.

　　I put Raymond in the little swings, which is a tight squeeze this year and will be impossible next year. Then I look around for Mr. Pearson, who pins the numbers on. I'm
180 really looking for Gretchen, if you want to know the truth, but she's not around. The park is jam-packed. Parents in hats and corsages and breast-pocket handkerchiefs peeking up. Kids in white dresses and light-blue suits. The parkees[8]

F MAKE INFERENCES
Reread lines 150–165. Underline at least one example of what Squeaky's mother wants and one example of what Squeaky wants. Then make an inference about Squeaky's relationship with her mother. Cite evidence from the text in your response.

_____

_____

_____

_____

_____

_____

_____

_____

_____

_____

_____

---

8. **parkees:** people who regularly gather in the park.

ⓖ MAKE INFERENCES
Pause at line 191. How do you think Squeaky feels about the people in the May Day crowd?

_____

_____

_____

_____

_____

_____

_____

_____

_____

ⓗ MAKE INFERENCES
What nice gesture is Mr. Pearson referring to in lines 213–214?

_____

_____

_____

_____

_____

_____

_____

_____

_____

_____

unfolding chairs and chasing the rowdy kids from Lenox[9] as if they had no right to be there. The big guys with their caps on backwards, leaning against the fence swirling the basketballs on the tips of their fingers, waiting for all these crazy people to clear out the park so they can play. Most of the kids in my class are carrying bass drums and
190 glockenspiels[10] and flutes. You'd think they'd put in a few bongos or something for real like that. ⓖ

Then here comes Mr. Pearson with his clipboard and his cards and pencils and whistles and safety pins and 50 million other things he's always dropping all over the place with his clumsy self. He sticks out in a crowd because he's on stilts. We used to call him Jack and the Beanstalk to get him mad. But I'm the only one that can outrun him and get away, and I'm too grown for that silliness now.

"Well, Squeaky," he says, checking my name off the
200 list and handing me number seven and two pins. And I'm thinking he's got no right to call me Squeaky, if I can't call him Beanstalk.

"Hazel Elizabeth Deborah Parker," I correct him and tell him to write it down on his board.

"Well, Hazel Elizabeth Deborah Parker, going to give someone else a break this year?" I squint at him real hard to see if he is seriously thinking I should lose the race on purpose just to give someone else a break. "Only six girls running this time," he continues, shaking his head
210 sadly like it's my fault all of New York didn't turn out in sneakers. "That new girl should give you a run for your money." He looks around the park for Gretchen like a periscope[11] in a submarine movie. "Wouldn't it be a nice gesture if you were . . . to ahhh . . ." ⓗ

---

9. **Lenox:** street in Harlem in New York City.
10. **glockenspiels** (glŏk'ən-spēlz'): musical instruments with tuned metal bars played with light hammers.
11. **periscope:** a tube with mirrors or prisms inside through which a person can see the reflection of an object at the other end.

I give him such a look he couldn't finish putting that idea into words. Grownups got a lot of nerve sometimes. I pin number seven to myself and stomp away, I'm so burnt. And I go straight for the track and stretch out on the grass while the band winds up with "Oh, the Monkey Wrapped
220 His Tail Around the Flag Pole," which my teacher calls by some other name. The man on the loudspeaker is calling everyone over to the track and I'm on my back looking at the sky, trying to pretend I'm in the country, but I can't, because even grass in the city feels hard as sidewalk, and there's just no pretending you are anywhere but in a "concrete jungle" as my grandfather says. **PAUSE & REFLECT**

The twenty-yard dash takes all of two minutes cause most of the little kids don't know no better than to run off the track or run the wrong way or run smack into the
230 fence and fall down and cry. One little kid, though, has got the good sense to run straight for the white ribbon up ahead so he wins. Then the second-graders line up for the thirty-yard dash and I don't even bother to turn my head to watch cause Raphael Perez always wins. He wins before he even begins by psyching the runners, telling them they're going to trip on their shoelaces and fall on their faces or lose their shorts or something, which he doesn't really have to do since he is very fast, almost as fast as I am. After that is the forty-yard dash which I used to run when
240 I was in first grade. Raymond is hollering from the swings cause he knows I'm about to do my thing cause the man on the loudspeaker has just announced the fifty-yard dash, although he might just as well be giving a recipe for angel food cake cause you can hardly make out what he's sayin for the static. I get up and slip off my sweat pants and then I see Gretchen standing at the starting line, kicking her

❶ PLOT: RISING ACTION
Reread lines 227–251. Underline the details that increase excitement and tension.

crouch (krouch) *v.* to stoop with bent knees

legs out like a pro. Then as I get into place I see that ole Raymond is on line on the other side of the fence, bending down with his fingers on the ground just like he knew
250 what he was doing. I was going to yell at him but then I didn't. It burns up your energy to holler. ❶

Every time, just before I take off in a race, I always feel like I'm in a dream, the kind of dream you have when you're sick with fever and feel all hot and weightless. I dream I'm flying over a sandy beach in the early morning sun, kissing the leaves of the trees as I fly by. And there's always the smell of apples, just like in the country when I was little and used to think I was a choo-choo train, running through the fields of corn and chugging up the
260 hill to the orchard. And all the time I'm dreaming this, I get lighter and lighter until I'm flying over the beach again, getting blown through the sky like a feather that weighs nothing at all. But once I spread my fingers in the dirt and **crouch** over the Get on Your Mark, the dream goes and I am solid again and am telling myself, Squeaky you must win, you must win, you are the fastest thing in the world, you can even beat your father up Amsterdam if you really try. And then I feel my weight coming back just behind my knees then down to my feet then into the
270 earth and the pistol shot explodes in my blood and I am off and weightless again, flying past the other runners, my arms pumping up and down and the whole world is quiet except for the crunch as I zoom over the gravel in the track. I glance to my left and there is no one. To the right, a blurred Gretchen, who's got her chin jutting out as if it would win the race all by itself. And on the other side of the fence is Raymond with his arms down to his side and the palms tucked up behind him, running in his very own style, and it's the first time I ever saw that and I almost

stop to watch my brother Raymond on his first run. But the white ribbon is bouncing toward me and I tear past it, racing into the distance till my feet with a mind of their own start digging up footfuls of dirt and brake me short. Then all the kids standing on the side pile on me, banging me on the back and slapping my head with their May Day programs, for I have won again and everybody on 151st Street can walk tall for another year. **J**

"In first place . . ." the man on the loudspeaker is clear as a bell now. But then he pauses and the loudspeaker starts to whine. Then static. And I lean down to catch my breath and here comes Gretchen walking back, for she's overshot the finish line too, huffing and puffing with her hands on her hips taking it slow, breathing in steady time like a real pro and I sort of like her a little for the first time. "In first place . . ." and then three or four voices get all mixed up on the loudspeaker and I dig my sneaker into the grass and stare at Gretchen who's staring back, we both wondering just who did win. I can hear old Beanstalk arguing with the man on the loudspeaker and then a few others running their mouths about what the stopwatches say. Then I hear Raymond yanking at the fence to call me and I wave to shush him, but he keeps rattling the fence like a gorilla in a cage like in them gorilla movies, but then like a dancer or something he starts climbing up nice and easy but very fast. And it occurs to me, watching how smoothly he climbs hand over hand and remembering how he looked running with his arms down to his side and with the wind pulling his mouth back and his teeth showing and all, it occurred to me that Raymond would make a very fine runner. Doesn't he always keep up with me on my trots? And he surely knows how to breathe in counts of seven cause he's always doing it at the dinner table, which drives

J **MAKE INFERENCES**
What does Raymond do for the first time in this race? What do you think made Squeaky keep running?

_____

_____

_____

_____

_____

_____

_____

_____

_____

_____

_____

_____

_____

_____

_____

_____

Ⓚ PLOT: CLIMAX
Pause at line 322. Explain how Squeaky's thoughts about Raymond represent a turning point in the story.

_____

_____

_____

_____

_____

_____

_____

Ⓛ PLOT: FALLING ACTION AND RESOLUTION
What is surprising about the story's resolution?

_____

_____

_____

_____

_____

_____

my brother George up the wall. And I'm smiling to beat the band cause if I've lost this race, or if me and Gretchen tied, or even if I've won, I can always retire as a runner and begin a whole new career as a coach with Raymond as my champion. After all, with a little more study I can beat Cynthia and her phony self at the spelling bee. And if I bugged my mother, I could get piano lessons and become
320 a star. And I have a big rep as the baddest thing around. And I've got a roomful of ribbons and medals and awards. But what has Raymond got to call his own? Ⓚ

So I stand there with my new plans, laughing out loud by this time as Raymond jumps down from the fence and runs over with his teeth showing and his arms down to the side, which no one before him has quite mastered as a running style. And by the time he comes over I'm jumping up and down so glad to see him—my brother Raymond, a great runner in the family tradition. But of
330 course everyone thinks I'm jumping up and down because the men on the loudspeaker have finally gotten themselves together and compared notes and are announcing, "In first place—Miss Hazel Elizabeth Deborah Parker." (Dig that.) "In second place—Miss Gretchen P. Lewis." And I look over at Gretchen wondering what the "P" stands for. And I smile. Cause she's good, no doubt about it. Maybe she'd like to help me coach Raymond; she obviously is serious about running, as any fool can see. And she nods to congratulate me and then she smiles. And I smile. We
340 stand there with this big smile of respect between us. It's about as real a smile as girls can do for each other, considering we don't practice real smiling every day, you know, cause maybe we too busy being flowers or fairies or strawberries instead of something honest and worthy of respect . . . you know . . . like being people. Ⓛ

Text Analysis: Plot

The plot of "Raymond's Run" revolves around Squeaky's desire to win the May Day race. In each box of the chart below, write down the events that happen at each stage of the plot.

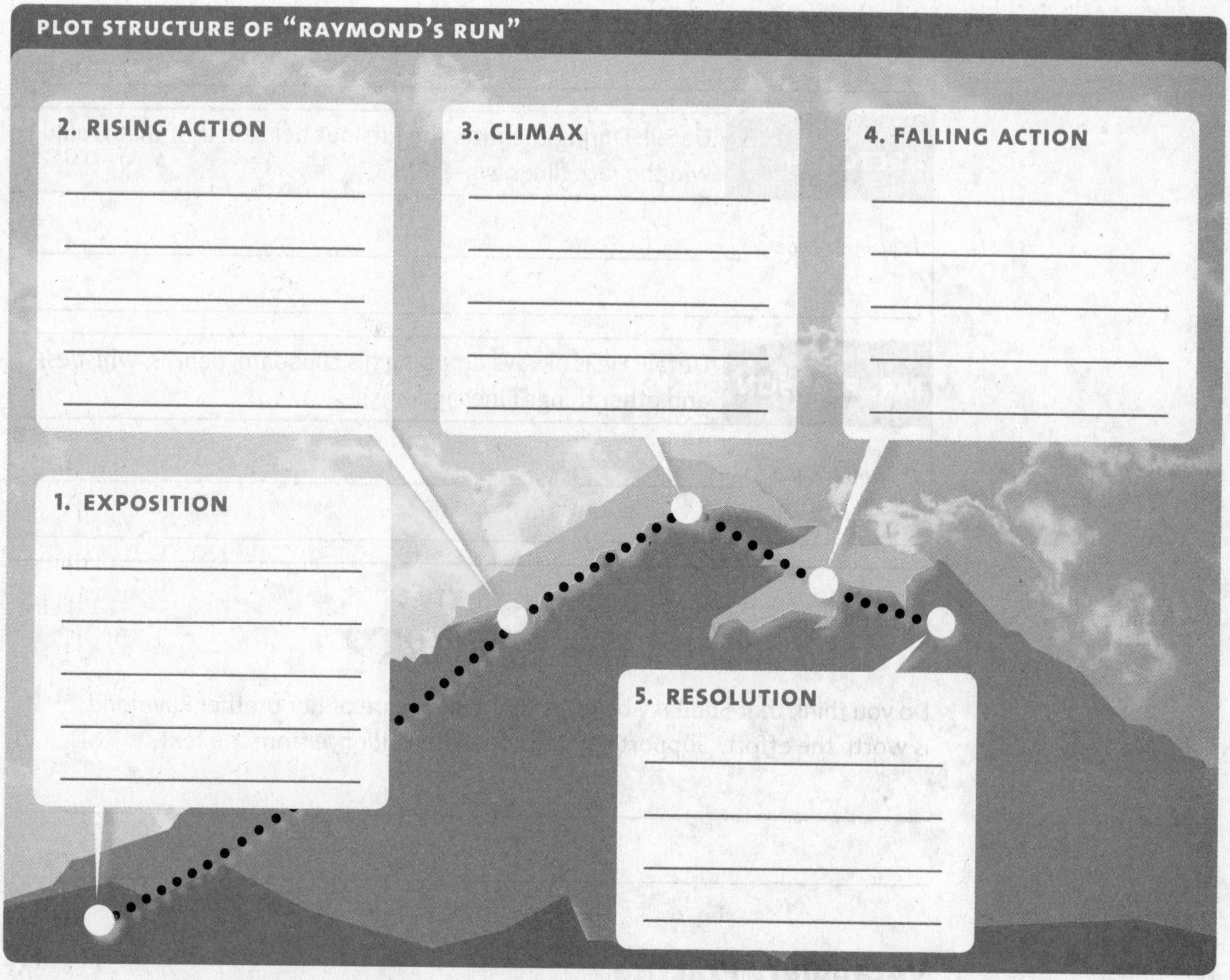

PLOT STRUCTURE OF "RAYMOND'S RUN"

2. RISING ACTION

_____
_____
_____
_____
_____

3. CLIMAX

_____
_____
_____
_____
_____

4. FALLING ACTION

_____
_____
_____
_____
_____

1. EXPOSITION

_____
_____
_____
_____
_____

5. RESOLUTION

_____
_____
_____
_____

Review your notes for "Raymond's Run" and your completed plot diagram. What do you think is the most important conflict in the story? Explain whether or not this conflict is resolved, or settled, by the end of the story.

_____
_____
_____

Reading Skill: Make Inferences

Make an inference about each character based on details from the story.

SQUEAKY	Detail: She is serious about running and doesn't care who knows it (lines 58–59).
My Inference: _____ _____	
GRETCHEN	Detail: During the race, she juts out her chin as if that would win the race (lines 275–276).
My Inference: _____ _____	
MR. PEARSON	Detail: He is always dropping his clipboard, pencils, whistles, and other things (lines 192–195).
My Inference: _____ _____	

What's worth the EFFORT?

Do you think that Squeaky believes that taking care of her brother Raymond is worth the effort? Support your answer with evidence from the text.

_____

_____

Vocabulary Practice

Circle the part of each sentence that answers the question.

1. Is a sidekick likely to be a friend or someone you just met?

2. If you were to clutch something, would you be tossing it away or holding it close?

3. Which would you expect a sports prodigy to be—clumsy or talented?

4. When are you more likely to crouch—picking a flower from the garden or reaching for a glass of water?

5. What's more important in a relay race—one good runner or team effort?

Academic Vocabulary in Writing

affect	conclude	evident	imply	initial

How does Squeaky's attitude toward Gretchen change over the course of the story? Compare Squeaky's initial reaction to Gretchen to her feelings at the end of the story. Use at least one Academic Vocabulary word in your response. Definitions of these words are on page 3.

_____

_____

_____

_____

Assessment Practice

DIRECTIONS Use "Raymond's Run" to answer questions 1–6.

1 Who does Squeaky race against?

- Ⓐ Rosie
- Ⓑ Raymond
- Ⓒ Gretchen
- Ⓓ Mary Louise

2 The conflict in this story begins when—

- Ⓐ Squeaky sees Gretchen on the street
- Ⓑ Squeaky wins a spelling bee
- Ⓒ Gretchen makes fun of Squeaky's brother
- Ⓓ Gretchen tells everyone she will win the race

3 The event that occurs first in the story is—

- Ⓐ Squeaky decides to teach Raymond how to become a runner
- Ⓑ Squeaky develops some respect for Gretchen
- Ⓒ the announcer gives the winner's name.
- Ⓓ Squeaky tells off Gretchen and her friends

4 Which event in the plot is not part of the story's rising action?

- Ⓐ Squeaky practices her breathing exercises.
- Ⓑ Squeaky and Gretchen smile at each other.
- Ⓒ Mr. Pearson pins on Squeaky's race number.
- Ⓓ Squeaky argues with Gretchen and her friends.

5 What word best describes how Squeaky feels when she notices Raymond running during the race?

- Ⓐ angry
- Ⓑ happy
- Ⓒ jealous
- Ⓓ embarrassed

6 How does Squeaky change by the end of the story?

- Ⓐ She is embarrassed by her brother.
- Ⓑ She doesn't care anymore about winning the race.
- Ⓒ She drops out of the race.
- Ⓓ She thinks that Gretchen may not be so bad after all.

The Ransom of Red Chief

Short Story by **O. Henry**

Is any plan FOOLPROOF?

You can make a list. You can check it twice. You can go over every last detail of a plan in your mind. But even when you think you've thought of everything, something unexpected can change the result in surprising, terrible, or sometimes hysterically funny ways. In the story you are about to read, the main characters have a plan for making some quick money, but things don't work out the way they had hoped.

DISCUSS IT With a partner, plan a surprise party for a friend by making a list of what you need to do. Then, write down an unexpected event that could spoil each part of the plan.

Text Analysis: Conflict and Resolution

A story's plot centers on **conflicts,** or struggles between opposing forces. By the end of the story, the conflicts are usually **resolved,** or settled. The chart below explains the conflicts and resolutions in a story.

Conflict and Resolution		Example
Conflict A struggle between two opposing forces in a story.	→	Two characters face each other in a fight for the championship.
Resolution The moment that reveals the outcome of the conflict.	→	One character defeats the other to become champion.

As you read "The Ransom of Red Chief," try to identify the conflicts and explain how they are resolved.

Our Plans for Lu's Party!

1. E-mail our group to invite them.

2. _____

    _____

3. _____

    _____

Unexpected Event

1. Forget to take Lu off the mailing list.

2. _____

    _____

3. _____

    _____

Reading Strategy: Predict

One way to monitor your understanding of a story is by making **predictions**. Use text clues and your own common sense to predict likely events. As you read, you'll use a chart like the one below to record your predictions and keep track of whether you predicted accurately or were surprised by the way events unfolded.

My Prediction	Actual Event	Correct or Surprised?
The boy will fight back when kidnapped.	The boy fights back.	correct

Vocabulary in Context

Note: Words are listed in the order in which they appear in the story.

diatribe (dī′ə-trīb′) *n.* bitter, abusive criticism
*The speaker delivered an angry **diatribe** against crime.*

ransom (răn′səm) *n.* payment demanded for the release of a person or property
*The kidnappers would not release the child until the **ransom** was paid.*

provisions (prə-vĭzh′ənz) *n.* necessary supplies; food
*The outlaws stored their **provisions** in a secret cave.*

collaborate (kə-lăb′ə-rāt′) *v.* to work together on a project
*The partners will **collaborate** and write the letter together.*

comply (kəm-plī′) *v.* to act according to a command or request
*The kidnappers insisted that we **comply** with their demand.*

proposition (prŏp′ə-zĭsh′ən) *n.* a suggested plan
*We expect that you will agree with our **proposition**.*

commend (kə-mĕnd′) *v.* to speak highly of; to praise; to recommend
*I **commend** you for your brilliant plan.*

impudent (ĭm′pyə-dənt) *adj.* bold and disrespectful
*The child's **impudent** remark shocked the adults.*

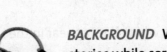

THE RANSOM OF RED CHIEF

Short Story by

O. HENRY

BACKGROUND William Sydney Porter began writing stories while serving a prison sentence. Upon his release, he changed his name to O. Henry, and grew into one of the country's best-loved fiction writers. O. Henry's stories often have surprise endings. Today, stories that end with an unexpected twist are said to be written in the "O. Henry style."

It looked like a good thing; but wait till I tell you. We were down South, in Alabama—Bill Driscoll and myself—when this kidnapping idea struck us. It was, as Bill afterward expressed it, "during a moment of temporary mental apparition";[1] but we didn't find that out till later.

There was a town down there, as flat as a flannel-cake, and called Summit, of course. It contained inhabitants of as undeleterious[2] and self-satisfied a class of peasantry as ever clustered around a Maypole.

10   Bill and me had a joint capital of about six hundred dollars, and we needed just two thousand dollars more to pull off a fraudulent town-lot scheme in Western Illinois with. We talked it over on the front steps of the hotel. Philoprogenitiveness,[3] says we, is strong in semi-rural communities; therefore, and for other reasons, a kidnapping

---

1. **apparition** (ăp'ə-rĭsh'ən): a sudden or unusual sight.
2. **undeleterious** (ŭn-dĕl'ĭ-tîr'ē-əs): harmless.
3. **philoprogenitiveness** (fĭl'ō-prō-jĕn'ĭ-tĭv-nĕs): love for one's own children.

project ought to do better there than in the radius of newspapers that send reporters out in plain clothes to stir up talk about such things. We knew that Summit couldn't get after us with anything stronger than constables, and, maybe, some lackadaisical bloodhounds and a <u>diatribe</u> or two in the *Weekly Farmers' Budget*. So, it looked good.

We selected for our victim the only child of a prominent citizen named Ebenezer Dorset. The father was respectable and tight, a mortgage fancier and a stern, upright collection-plate passer and forecloser. The kid was a boy of ten, with bas-relief[4] freckles, and hair the color of the cover of the magazine you buy at the news-stand when you want to catch a train. Bill and me figured that Ebenezer would melt down for a <u>ransom</u> of two thousand dollars to a cent. But wait till I tell you. **Ⓐ**

About two miles from Summit was a little mountain, covered with a dense cedar brake.[5] On the rear elevation of this mountain was a cave. There we stored <u>provisions</u>.

One evening after sundown, we drove in a buggy past old Dorset's house. The kid was in the street, throwing rocks at a kitten on the opposite fence.

"Hey, little boy!" says Bill, "would you like to have a bag of candy and a nice ride?"

The boy catches Bill neatly in the eye with a piece of brick.

"That will cost the old man an extra five hundred dollars," says Bill, climbing over the wheel.

That boy put up a fight like a welter-weight cinnamon bear; but, at last, we got him down in the bottom of the buggy and drove away. We took him up to the cave, and I hitched the horse in the cedar brake. After dark I drove the buggy to the little village, three miles away, where we had hired it, and walked back to the mountain. **Ⓑ**

Bill was pasting court plaster[6] over the scratches and bruises on his features. There was a fire burning behind

20

30

40

4. **bas-relief** (bä′rĭ-lĕf′): slightly raised.
5. **brake:** a thick grouping of trees.
6. **court plaster:** adhesive cloth for covering cuts and scratches.

diatribe (dī′ə-trīb′) *n.* bitter, abusive criticism

ransom (răn′səm) *n.* payment demanded for the release of a person or property

Ⓐ PREDICT
Reread lines 22–30. Make a prediction about whether you think the men's plan will be successful. Underline the details that support your prediction.

_____

_____

_____

_____

_____

provisions (prə-vĭzh′ənz) *n.* necessary supplies; food

Ⓑ CONFLICT
Which characters are in conflict at this point in the story? How can you tell?

_____

_____

_____

_____

_____

_____

● PREDICT
How do you think the boy will respond to being held in captivity?

_____

_____

_____

_____

_____

_____

_____

_____

_____

_____

_____

_____

_____

_____

_____

_____

50 the big rock at the entrance of the cave, and the boy was watching a pot of boiling coffee, with two buzzard tail feathers stuck in his red hair. He points a stick at me when I come up, and says:

"Ha! cursed paleface, do you dare to enter the camp of Red Chief, the terror of the plains?" **●**

"He's all right now," says Bill, rolling up his trousers and examining some bruises on his shins. "We're playing Indian. We're making Buffalo Bill's show look like magic-lantern views[7] of Palestine in the town hall. I'm Old Hank,
60 the Trapper, Red Chief's captive, and I'm to be scalped at daybreak. By Geronimo! that kid can kick hard."

Yes, sir, that boy seemed to be having the time of his life. The fun of camping out in a cave had made him forget that he was a captive himself. He immediately christened me Snake-eye, the Spy, and announced that, when his braves returned from the warpath, I was to be broiled at the stake at the rising of the sun.

Then we had supper; and he filled his mouth full of bacon and bread and gravy, and began to talk. He made a
70 during-dinner speech something like this:

"I like this fine. I never camped out before; but I had a pet 'possum once, and I was nine last birthday. I hate to go to school. Rats ate up sixteen of Jimmy Talbot's aunt's speckled hen's eggs. Are there any real Indians in these woods? I want some more gravy. Does the trees moving make the wind blow? We had five puppies. What makes your nose so red, Hank? My father has lots of money. Are the stars hot? I whipped Ed Walker twice, Saturday. I don't like girls. You dassent[8] catch toads unless with a string. Do
80 oxen make any noise? Why are oranges round? Have you got beds to sleep on in this cave? Amos Murray has got six toes. A parrot can talk, but a monkey or a fish can't. How many does it take to make twelve?"

---

7. **magic-lantern views**: slides.
8. **dassent**: dare not.

Every few minutes he would remember that he was an Indian, and pick up his stick rifle and tiptoe to the mouth of the cave to search for the scouts of the hated paleface. Now and then he would let out a war whoop that made Old Hank the Trapper shiver. That boy had Bill terrorized from the start. **PAUSE & REFLECT**

90   "Red Chief," says I to the kid, "would you like to go home?"

"Aw, what for?" says he. "I don't have any fun at home. I hate to go to school. I like to camp out. You won't take me back home again, Snake-eye, will you?"

"Not right away," says I. "We'll stay here in the cave awhile."

"All right!" says he. "That'll be fine. I never had such fun in all my life."

We went to bed about eleven o'clock. We spread down
100 some wide blankets and quilts and put Red Chief between us. We weren't afraid he'd run away. He kept us awake for three hours, jumping up and reaching for his rifle and screeching: "Hist! pard," in mine and Bill's ears, as the fancied crackle of a twig or the rustle of a leaf revealed to his young imagination the stealthy approach of the outlaw band. At last, I fell into a troubled sleep, and dreamed that I had been kidnapped and chained to a tree by a ferocious pirate with red hair.

Just at daybreak, I was awakened by a series of awful
110 screams from Bill. They weren't yells, or howls, or shouts, or whoops, or yawps, such as you'd expect from a manly set of vocal organs—they were simply indecent, terrifying, humiliating screams, such as women emit when they see ghosts or caterpillars. It's an awful thing to hear a strong, desperate, fat man scream incontinently in a cave at daybreak.

I jumped up to see what the matter was. Red Chief was sitting on Bill's chest, with one hand twined in Bill's hair. In the other he had the sharp case-knife we used for slicing

PAUSE & REFLECT
How is the boy's behavior different from what the two men probably expected?

_____

_____

_____

_____

_____

_____

_____

_____

_____

_____

_____

_____

_____

_____

_____

D CONFLICT
Reread lines 109–129. Underline the words that help you picture the conflict between the boy and Bill. In what way has the confrontation with the boy affected Bill?

_____

_____

_____

_____

_____

_____

_____

_____

_____

_____

_____

_____

bacon; and he was industriously and realistically trying to
120 take Bill's scalp, according to the sentence that had been pronounced upon him the evening before.

I got the knife away from the kid and made him lie down again. But, from that moment, Bill's spirit was broken. He laid down on his side of the bed, but he never closed an eye again in sleep as long as that boy was with us. I dozed off for a while, but along toward sun-up I remembered that Red Chief had said I was to be burned at the stake at the rising of the sun. I wasn't nervous or afraid; but I sat up and leaned against a rock. **D**

130 "What you getting up so soon for, Sam?" asked Bill.

"Me?" says I. "Oh, I got a kind of a pain in my shoulder. I thought sitting up would rest it."

"You're a liar!" says Bill. "You're afraid. You was to be burned at sunrise, and you was afraid he'd do it. And he would, too, if he could find a match. Ain't it awful, Sam? Do you think anybody will pay out money to get a little imp like that back home?"

"Sure," said I. "A rowdy kid like that is just the kind that parents dote on. Now, you and the Chief get up and cook
140 breakfast, while I go up on the top of this mountain and reconnoiter."[9]

I went up on the peak of the little mountain and ran my eye over the contiguous vicinity. Over toward Summit I expected to see the sturdy yeomanry of the village armed with scythes and pitchforks beating the countryside for the dastardly kidnappers. But what I saw was a peaceful landscape dotted with one man plowing with a dun mule. Nobody was dragging the creek; no couriers dashed hither and yon, bringing tidings of no news to the distracted
150 parents. There was a sylvan[10] attitude of somnolent sleepiness pervading that section of the external outward surface of Alabama that lay exposed to my view. "Perhaps,"

9. **reconnoiter** (rē′kə-noi′tər): to seek information about an enemy's whereabouts.

10. **sylvan** (sĭl′vən): like woods or forests.

says I to myself, "it has not yet been discovered that the wolves have borne away the tender lambkin from the fold. Heaven help the wolves!" says I, and I went down the mountain to breakfast.

When I got to the cave I found Bill backed up against the side of it, breathing hard, and the boy threatening to smash him with a rock half as big as a coconut.

160 "He put a red-hot boiled potato down my back," explained Bill, "and then mashed it with his foot; and I boxed his ears. Have you got a gun about you, Sam?"

I took the rock away from the boy and kind of patched up the argument. "I'll fix you," says the kid to Bill. "No man ever yet struck the Red Chief but what he got paid for it. You better beware!"

After breakfast the kid takes a piece of leather with strings wrapped around it out of his pocket and goes outside the cave unwinding it.

170 "What's he up to now?" says Bill anxiously. "You don't think he'll run away, do you, Sam?"

"No fear of it," says I. "He don't seem to be much of a homebody. But we've got to fix up some plan about the ransom. There don't seem to be much excitement around Summit on account of his disappearance; but maybe they haven't realized yet that he's gone. His folks may think he's spending the night with Aunt Jane or one of the neighbors. Anyhow, he'll be missed today. Tonight we must get a message to his father demanding the two thousand dollars

180 for his return."

Just then we heard a kind of war whoop, such as David might have emitted when he knocked out the champion Goliath. It was a sling that Red Chief had pulled out of his pocket, and he was whirling it around his head.

I dodged, and heard a heavy thud and a kind of a sigh from Bill, like a horse gives out when you take his saddle off. A rock the size of an egg had caught Bill just behind his left

E PREDICT
What do you predict from the boy's remark at the end of line 166? Write your prediction in the top row of this chart. Complete the remainder of the chart as you read.

My Prediction:

↓

Actual Event:

↓

Correct or Surprised?:

F PREDICT
Reread lines 198–203. Do you expect that the boy will behave better from now on?

_____
_____
_____
_____
_____
_____

G CONFLICT
Go back to the start of the story to reread lines 42–47. In what ways has the conflict changed since the beginning of the story?

_____
_____
_____
_____
_____
_____
_____
_____
_____

ear. He loosened himself all over and fell in the fire across the frying pan of hot water for washing the dishes. I dragged
190 him out and poured cold water on his head for half an hour.

By and by, Bill sits up and feels behind his ear and says: "Sam, do you know who my favorite Biblical character is?"

"Take it easy," says I. "You'll come to your senses presently."

"King Herod,"[11] says he. "You won't go away and leave me here alone, will you, Sam?"

I went out and caught that boy and shook him until his freckles rattled.

"If you don't behave," says I, "I'll take you straight home. Now, are you going to be good, or not?"
200 "I was only funning," says he, sullenly. "I didn't mean to hurt Old Hank. But what did he hit me for? I'll behave, Snake-eye, if you won't send me home, and if you'll let me play the Scout today." **F**

"I don't know the game," says I. "That's for you and Mr. Bill to decide. He's your playmate for the day. I'm going away for a while, on business. Now, you come in and make friends with him and say you are sorry for hurting him, or home you go, at once." **G**

I made him and Bill shake hands, and then I took Bill
210 aside and told him I was going to Poplar Cove, a little village three miles from the cave, and find out what I could about how the kidnapping had been regarded in Summit. Also, I thought it best to send a peremptory letter to old man Dorset that day, demanding the ransom and dictating how it should be paid.

"You know, Sam," says Bill, "I've stood by you without batting an eye in earthquakes, fire, and flood—in poker games, dynamite outrages, police raids, train robberies, and cyclones. I never lost my nerve yet till we kidnapped
220 that two-legged skyrocket of a kid. He's got me going. You won't leave me long with him, will you, Sam?"

---

11. **King Herod:** an ancient king of Judea who once ordered the execution of all Bethlehem boys under the age of two.

"I'll be back sometime this afternoon," says I. "You must keep the boy amused and quiet till I return. And now we'll write the letter to old Dorset."

Bill and I got paper and pencil and worked on the letter while Red Chief, with a blanket wrapped around him, strutted up and down, guarding the mouth of the cave. Bill begged me tearfully to make the ransom fifteen hundred dollars instead of two thousand. "I ain't attempting," says 230 he, "to decry[12] the celebrated moral aspect of parental affection, but we're dealing with humans, and it ain't human for anybody to give up two thousand dollars for that forty-pound chunk of freckled wildcat. I'm willing to take a chance at fifteen hundred dollars. You can charge the difference up to me." **PAUSE & REFLECT**

So, to relieve Bill, I acceded, and we <u>collaborated</u> a letter that ran this way:

EBENEZER DORSET, ESQ.:

We have your boy concealed in a place far from Summit.
240 It is useless for you or the most skillful detectives to attempt to find him. Absolutely, the only terms on which you can have him restored to you are these: We demand fifteen hundred dollars in large bills for his return: the money to be left at midnight at the same spot and in the same box as your reply—as hereinafter described. If you agree to these terms, send your answer in writing by a solitary messenger tonight at half-past eight o'clock. After crossing Owl Creek on the road to Poplar Cove, there are three large trees about a hundred yards apart, close to the fence of the wheat field
250 on the right-hand side. At the bottom of the fence post, opposite the third tree, will be found a small pasteboard box.

The messenger will place the answer in this box and return immediately to Summit.

---

12. **decry**: to criticize.

PAUSE & REFLECT
In lines 225–235, what is the unexpected decision that Bill and Sam make? Is there any way they could have anticipated their struggles with the boy?

_____

_____

_____

_____

_____

_____

_____

_____

_____

_____

_____

_____

_____

_____

_____

collaborate (kə-lăb′ə-rāt′) v. to work together on a project

comply (kəm-plīˈ) v. to act according to a command or request

What actions Ebenezer Dorset must take to show that he is complying?

_____

_____

_____

ⓗ PREDICT
How do you think the boy's father will respond to the men's demands?

_____

_____

_____

_____

ⓘ CONFLICT
Reread lines 272–289. Underline details that show the conflict between Bill and the boy. Who seems to be winning the struggle?

_____

_____

_____

_____

If you attempt any treachery or fail to **comply** with our demand as stated, you will never see your boy again.

If you pay the money as demanded, he will be returned to you safe and well within three hours. These terms are final, and if you do not accede to them no further communication will be attempted.

260   TWO DESPERATE MEN. ⓗ

I addressed this letter to Dorset and put it in my pocket. As I was about to start, the kid comes up to me and says:

"Aw, Snake-eye, you said I could play the Scout while you was gone."

"Play it, of course," says I. "Mr. Bill will play with you. What kind of a game is it?"

"I'm the Scout," says Red Chief, "and I have to ride to the stockade to warn the settlers that the Indians are coming. I'm tired of playing Indian myself. I want to be the Scout."

270   "All right," says I. "It sounds harmless to me. I guess Mr. Bill will help you foil the enemy."

"What am I to do?" asks Bill, looking at the kid suspiciously.

"You are the hoss," says Scout. "Get down on your hands and knees. How can I ride to the stockade without a hoss?"

"You'd better keep him interested," said I, "till we get the scheme going. Loosen up."

Bill gets down on his all fours, and a look comes in his eye like a rabbit's when you catch it in a trap.

280   "How far is it to the stockade, kid?" he asks, in a husky manner of voice.

"Ninety miles," says the Scout. "And you have to hurry to get there on time. Whoa, now!"

The Scout jumps on Bill's back and digs his heels in his side.

"For Heaven's sake," says Bill, "hurry back, Sam, as soon as you can. I wish we hadn't made the ransom more than a thousand. Say, you quit kicking me or I'll get up and warm you good." ⓘ

290   I walked over to Poplar Cove and sat around the post office and store, talking with the chawbacons that came in to trade. One whiskerando says that he hears Summit is all upset on account of Elder Ebenezer Dorset's boy having been lost or stolen. That was all I wanted to know. I referred casually to the price of black-eyed peas, posted my letter surreptitiously and came away. The postmaster said the mail carrier would come by in an hour to take the mail on to Summit.

    When I got back to the cave Bill and the boy were not to be found. I explored the vicinity of the cave, and risked a
300 yodel or two, but there was no response.

    So I sat down on a mossy bank to await developments.

    In about half an hour I heard the bushes rustle, and Bill wabbled out into the little glade in front of the cave. Behind him was the kid, stepping softly like a scout, with a broad grin on his face. Bill stopped, took off his hat and wiped his face with a red handkerchief. The kid stopped about eight feet behind him.

    "Sam," says Bill, "I suppose you think I'm a renegade, but I couldn't help it. I'm a grown person with masculine
310 proclivities and habits of self-defense, but there is a time when all systems of egotism and predominance fail. The boy is gone. I have sent him home. All is off. There was martyrs in old times," goes on Bill, "that suffered death rather than give up the particular graft they enjoyed. None of 'em ever was subjugated to such supernatural tortures as I have been. I tried to be faithful to our articles of depredation;[13] but there came a limit." **J**

    "What's the trouble, Bill?" I asks him.

    "I was rode," says Bill, "the ninety miles to the stockade,
320 not barring an inch. Then, when the settlers was rescued, I was given oats. Sand ain't a palatable substitute. And then, for an hour I had to try to explain to him why there was nothin' in holes, how a road can run both ways and what makes the grass green. I tell you, Sam, a human can only

J CONFLICT
Reread lines 301–317. Bill thinks the conflict has been resolved. Circle the details that tell you Bill is mistaken.

---

13. **depredation** (dĕp'rĭ-dā'shən): robbery.

K **PREDICT**

What do you think Bill will do when he learns the truth? Add your prediction to your chart.

My Prediction:
_____
_____
_____

↓

Actual Event:
_____
_____
_____

↓

Correct or Surprised?:

proposition (prŏp′ə-zĭsh′ən) *n.* a suggested plan

commend (kə-mĕnd′) *v.* to speak highly of; to praise; to recommend

stand so much. I takes him by the neck of his clothes and drags him down the mountain. On the way he kicks my legs black and blue from the knees down; and I've got to have two or three bites on my thumb and hand cauterized.[14]

"But he's gone"—continues Bill—"gone home. I showed 330 him the road to Summit and kicked him about eight feet nearer there at one kick. I'm sorry we lose the ransom; but it was either that or Bill Driscoll to the madhouse." **K**

Bill is puffing and blowing, but there is a look of ineffable peace and growing content on his rose-pink features.

"Bill," says I, "there isn't any heart disease in your family, is there?"

"No," says Bill, "nothing chronic except malaria and accidents. Why?"

"Then you might turn around," says I, "and have a look 340 behind you."

Bill turns and sees the boy, and loses his complexion and sits down plump on the ground and begins to pluck aimlessly at grass and little sticks. For an hour I was afraid of his mind. And then I told him that my scheme was to put the whole job through immediately and that we would get the ransom and be off with it by midnight if old Dorset fell in with our **proposition**. So Bill braced up enough to give the kid a weak sort of a smile and a promise to play the Russian in a Japanese war with him as soon as he felt a little better.

350 I had a scheme for collecting that ransom without danger of being caught by counterplots that ought to **commend** itself to professional kidnappers. The tree under which the answer was to be left—and the money later on—was close to the road fence with big, bare fields on all sides. If a gang of constables should be watching for anyone to come for the note they could see him a long way off crossing the fields or in the road. But no, sirree! At

14. **cauterized** (kô′tə-rīzd′): burned a wound to stop bleeding.

half-past eight I was up in that tree as well hidden as a tree toad, waiting for the messenger to arrive. PAUSE & REFLECT

PAUSE & REFLECT
Reread lines 350–359. How does the narrator feel about his skills as a kidnapper? What does he expect will happen?

_____

_____

_____

_____

_____

_____

_____

_____

_____

_____

_____

_____

360   Exactly on time, a half-grown boy rides up the road on a bicycle, locates the pasteboard box at the foot of the fence post, slips a folded piece of paper into it and pedals away again back toward Summit.

I waited an hour and then concluded the thing was square. I slid down the tree, got the note, slipped along the fence till I struck the woods, and was back at the cave in another half an hour. I opened the note, got near the lantern, and read it to Bill. It was written with a pen in a crabbed hand, and the sum and substance of it
370 was this:

TWO DESPERATE MEN.
GENTLEMEN: I received your letter today by post, in regard to the ransom you ask for the return of my son. I think you are a little high in your demands, and I hereby make you a counter-proposition, which I am inclined to believe you will accept. You bring Johnny home and pay me two hundred and fifty dollars in cash, and I agree to take him off your hands. You had better come at night, for the neighbors believe he is lost, and I couldn't be
380 responsible for what they would do to anybody they saw bringing him back.

Very respectfully,
EBENEZER DORSET.

"Great Pirates of Penzance!" says I; "of all the **impudent**—"
But I glanced at Bill, and hesitated. He had the most appealing look in his eyes I ever saw on the face of a dumb or a talking brute.

impudent (ĭm′pyə-dənt) *adj.* bold and disrespectful

L CONFLICT AND
RESOLUTION
Who wins out in the conflict
between the kidnappers and the
boy's father?

_____

_____

_____

_____

_____

_____

_____

_____

M CONFLICT AND
RESOLUTION
How is the conflict between
the men and the boy finally
resolved?

_____

_____

_____

_____

_____

_____

_____

_____

390 "Sam," says he, "what's two hundred and fifty dollars, after all? We've got the money. One more night of this kid will send me to bed in Bedlam.[15] Besides being a thorough gentleman, I think Mr. Dorset is a spendthrift for making us such a liberal offer. You ain't going to let the chance go, are you?"

"Tell you the truth, Bill," says I, "this little he ewe lamb has somewhat got on my nerves, too. We'll take him home, pay the ransom, and make our getaway." **L**

We took him home that night. We got him to go by telling him that his father had bought a silver-mounted

400 rifle and a pair of moccasins for him, and we were going to hunt bears the next day.

It was just twelve o'clock when we knocked at Ebenezer's front door. Just at the moment when I should have been abstracting the fifteen hundred dollars from the box under the tree, according to the original proposition, Bill was counting out two hundred and fifty dollars into Dorset's hand.

When the kid found out we were going to leave him at home he started up a howl like a calliope[16] and fastened

410 himself as tight as a leech to Bill's leg. His father peeled him away gradually, like a porous plaster.

"How long can you hold him?" asks Bill.

"I'm not as strong as I used to be," says old Dorset, "but I think I can promise you ten minutes."

"Enough," says Bill. "In ten minutes I shall cross the Central, Southern, and Middle Western States, and be legging it trippingly for the Canadian border."

And, as dark as it was, and as fat as Bill was, and as good a runner as I am, he was a good mile and a half out of

420 Summit before I could catch up with him. **M**

---

15. **Bedlam:** an insane asylum.
16. **calliope** (kə-lī'ə-pē'): an instrument with steam whistles.

Text Analysis: Conflict and Resolution

The characters in "The Ransom of Red Chief" have opposite goals, and their conflicts fuel the story. Fill out the chart to tell about the conflicts and their resolutions.

	Kidnappers vs. Boy	Kidnappers vs. Mr. Dorset
Reason for Conflict	Sam and Bill kidnap the boy and bring him to their hideaway.	
Description of Conflict		
Resolution of Conflict		

Review your notes from "The Ransom of Red Chief" and your completed chart. How are the resolutions of the conflicts different from what the kidnappers expected?

_____

_____

_____

Reading Strategy: Predict

Review the predictions you made as you read. Then explain whether you were surprised by each of the story events below. Include details from the text in your explanation.

Story Event		Surprised?
The boy terrorizes the men who kidnapped him.	→	
People seem unconcerned about the boy's disappearance.	→	
Mr. Dorset demands money from the kidnappers.	→	
Bill and Sam pay money Mr. Dorset to take back the boy.	→	

Is any plan FOOLPROOF?

What could Bill and Sam have done to make their plan more likely to succeed?

_____

_____

_____

Vocabulary Practice

Write an *S* next to the pairs of words that are synonyms (words with similar meanings). Write an *A* if they are antonyms (words with opposite meanings).

1. diatribe/approval _____

2. proposition/offer _____

3. ransom/payment _____

4. comply/refuse _____

5. collaborate/contradict _____

6. impudent/polite _____

7. commend/praise _____

8. provisions/supplies _____

Academic Vocabulary in Speaking

affect	conclude	evident	imply	initial

TURN AND TALK Reread the letter from Mr. Dorset that appears on page 33. What does the letter **imply** about how he and his neighbors feel about his son? Use the Academic Vocabulary words in a discussion with a partner. Definitions of these words are on page 3.

Assessment Practice

DIRECTIONS Use "The Ransom of Red Chief" to answer questions 1–6.

1 What event happens first in the story?

  (A) Bill and Sam set up a mountain camp.

  (B) Bill and Sam arrive in Summit.

  (C) Bill and Sam see a boy throwing rocks at a kitten.

  (D) Bill plays the role of Red Chief's captive.

2 The conflict of this story begins when —

  (A) Bill and Sam learn that Ebenezer Dorset is a prominent citizen

  (B) the boy says he's having a fine time in the mountain camp

  (C) the boy throws a piece of brick at Bill

  (D) the kidnappers write a ransom note

3 Which word best describes Bill?

  (A) clever

  (B) defeated

  (C) brave

  (D) mean-spirited

4 The conflict is shown with descriptions of —

  (A) the games that Bill and the boy play

  (B) the citizens of the town

  (C) the kidnappers' previous crimes

  (D) the setting

5 Why are Mr. Dorset and the kidnappers in conflict?

  (A) He wants them to be punished.

  (B) He feels sorry for them.

  (C) He won't pay the ransom.

  (D) He understands his son.

6 The story conflict is resolved because —

  (A) kidnapping is a crime

  (B) the kidnappers are glad to be rid of the boy

  (C) the boy's father is wealthy and can pay a large ransom

  (D) the boy is happy to go home

Clean Sweep

Short Story by **Joan Bauer**

When does trash become TREASURE?

There is an old saying, "One man's trash is another man's treasure." A scrap of cloth, a wrinkled photo, or a worn, torn book can have great value to a person if there are special memories attached. In "Clean Sweep," a girl finds out not only that a simple object can hold memories, but also that those memories can heal.

LIST IT What do you value that someone else might be tempted to throw away? List a few special objects. Then circle one and explain why it means so much to you. You might include some memories connected to the special object.

Text Analysis: Conflicts and Subplots

There are two basic kinds of conflicts in stories: external conflicts and internal conflicts.

- **External conflicts** are struggles between a character and an outside force. The outside force could be another character, a society, or a force of nature.

- **Internal conflicts** are struggles within a character. This type of conflict may occur when the character has to make a difficult decision or deal with opposing feelings.

A story may develop more than one kind of conflict. Sometimes, an additional conflict is worked out in a subplot. A **subplot** is minor plot that is related to the main story. For instance, in "Raymond's Run," the main plot centers on Squeaky's race with Gretchen. Squeaky's concern with her brother Raymond is a subplot.

As you read "Clean Sweep," notice how a past event causes both an internal and an external conflict. Also, see if you can spot a subplot.

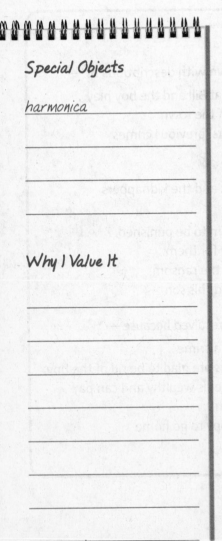

Special Objects

harmonica

_____

_____

_____

Why I Value It

_____

_____

_____

_____

_____

_____

_____

Reading Skill: Sequence

To follow a story, you must pay attention to the **sequence,** or order, of events. Writers often present events in the order in which they happen, but they may also interrupt the action to show or explain earlier events. The earlier scene is called a **flashback.** Look for words and phrases that signal sequence, such as *four years ago, moments later,* and *while.* Keep track of the sequence of important events by recording them in a sequence chart.

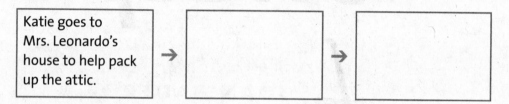

| Katie goes to Mrs. Leonardo's house to help pack up the attic. | → | | → | |

Vocabulary in Context

Note: Words are listed in the order in which they appear in the story.

minuscule (mĭn′ə-skyōol′) *adj.* very small; tiny
*A **minuscule** amount of light came through the window.*

vileness (vīl′nəs) *n.* unpleasantness; disgusting quality
*I can't stand the **vileness** of rotten eggs.*

dingy (dĭn′jē) *adj.* dirty or discolored
*The room was dark and **dingy.***

propriety (prə-prī′ĭ-tē) *n.* the quality of being proper; appropriateness
*Her sense of **propriety** kept her from interrupting him.*

aberration (ăb′ə-rā′shən) *n.* an abnormal alteration
*It was an **aberration,** not what she usually sees.*

turmoil (tûr′moil′) *n.* a state of extreme confusion or agitation
*She hid her feeling of **turmoil** as she spoke in front of the class.*

Vocabulary Practice

Review the vocabulary words and think about their meanings. Then use at least two of the words to describe an unpleasant setting or job.

_____

_____

_____

_____

**SET A PURPOSE
FOR READING**

Read "Clean Sweep" to find
out what Katie learns from
Mrs. Leonardo.

Clean Sweep

Short Story by
JOAN BAUER

BACKGROUND As a child, Joan Bauer
dreamed of becoming a comedian or
comedy writer when she grew up. However,
she also faced troubles, including the
divorce of her parents. She continued
to write, finding that it helped ease her
pain. Bauer often draws from difficult life
experiences to create touching, amusing
stories.

minuscule (mĭn'ə-skyōōl') *adj.*
very small; tiny

"HAVE YOU EVER SEEN A DUST MITE?"
My mother always lowers her voice when she asks
this; it adds to the emotional impact. Never in the four
years since she's had the cleaning business has anyone ever
said they've seen one. That's because the only people who
have seen dust mites are scientists who put dust balls on
slides and look at them under microscopes. Personally I
have better things to do than look at **minuscule** animals
who cause great torture among the allergic, but my mother
10 has a photo of a dust mite blown up to ten gazillion times
its size—she is holding it up now, as she always does in
this part of her presentation—and the two women who sit
on the floral couch before her gasp appropriately and shut

their eyes, because dust mites, trust me, are ugly. Think *Invasion of the Body Snatchers* meets *The Hunchback of Notre Dame,* and you're just beginning to enter into the **vileness** of this creature. Ⓐ

"They're everywhere," Mom says to the women. "Under the bed, on the sheets, clinging to the blinds; hiding, 20 waiting. And at Clean Sweep," she offers quietly, but dramatically, "we *kill* them for you. We hate them even more than you do. *This* is why we're in business."

The two women look at each other and say *yes,* they want the cleaning service to start immediately.

Mom tells them our price. One woman, as expected, says, "That sounds a little high." People are so cheap. Everyone wants quality, no one wants to pay for it. Here's the suburban dream—to hire great workers who are such meek morons that they don't have the guts to ask for a 30 living wage. Ⓑ

This is not my mother's problem. She holds up the dust mite enlargement to make the point. "We cost more because we know where he and his army are hiding."

She used to say "we know where he and his friends are hiding," but "army" sounds more fierce, and when you are serious about eliminating dust, you'd better let everyone know it's war.

"Well . . . ," the other woman says, unsure.

Mom presses in. "We suggest two cleanings per week 40 for one month to achieve total elimination. Then weekly cleanings should do, unless you have special needs."

Special needs in the cleaning world range from cleaning out attics to detoxification[1] of teenage bedrooms. I am a specialist in cleaning rooms of kids who have just gone off to college. It takes nerves of steel. And I have them.

My brother Benjamin doesn't. To begin with, he's allergic to dust—bad news when the family business is

---

1. **detoxification** (dē-tŏk′sə-fĭ-kā′shən): the process of removing toxic substances.

vileness (vīl′nəs) *n.* unpleasantness; disgusting quality

Ⓐ **SEQUENCE**
The narrator is describing the present scene. She also tells about an earlier event. Underline the words and phrases that signal **sequence**—the time order of events.

Then add two events from lines 2–17 to the chart below.

↓

Ⓑ **CONFLICTS AND SUBPLOTS**
Reread lines 25–30. What conflicts do the main character and her family face with each job?

_____

_____

_____

_____

_____

C **CONFLICTS AND SUBPLOTS**
Reread lines 46–61. Underline the details that help you picture Benjamin. How does the narrator feel about her brother's behavior? How does she handle it?

_____

_____

_____

_____

_____

_____

dedicated to eliminating it. To end with, he's a devoted underachiever, in stark contrast to myself. And Benjamin 50 knows how to get out of work—he could give seminars on this. He gets the perfect look of abject2 pain over his face, says he's not feeling too well, he's sorry, he doesn't want to be a *burden*. He talks about the pain moving across his back, down his leg, and into his ankle. Then he gets dizzy and has to sit down; lying down comes moments later after his face gets a little pale (I don't know how he does this) and his hand touches his forehead which, I swear, has small drops of sweat on it. Then he'll try to get up and help, but by this time, you feel like such a snake that a sick person is 60 going to get sicker because of your insensitive demands that you say, no, you rest, I'll do it. **C**

This is what he's done to me today, and I'm not in the mood for the game. He tells me, groaning, he'll *try* to make it to Mrs. Leonardo's today to help her pack up her attic, but he's not sure he can even sit. He's lying on the couch in misery saying if he can sit, he will try to stand, and if he attempts standing, he will attempt actual walking—Mrs. Leonardo's house being four houses down the street. I throw my book bag at him. Suggest he *crawl* 70 to Mrs. Leonardo's house and he says, "Thanks, Katie. Just thanks." To which I reply, "Look, Benny Boy, I'm getting sick of carrying your weight around here. If you think I'm going to do your job and mine until I die, think again." Benjamin groans deep, turns off the light, closes his eyes and says his headache is cosmic and could I please go get him some aspirin. **D**

I don't get the aspirin. It's a big bad world out there and he needs to find it out now, at fourteen. This is what big sisters are for.

D **SEQUENCE**
Reread lines 62–65. Circle the word that shows that the specific events of this story are beginning. Add the event to the chart below.

```
┌─────────────────────┐
│                     │
│                     │
│                     │
│                     │
│                     │
└─────────────────────┘
```

2. **abject** (ăb′jĕkt): of the most miserable kind; wretched.

80　So I'm basically crabby and bitter all day; taking it out on random people. After school I have mounds of homework. You wonder what teachers are thinking—I have three hundred pages of reading in three textbooks plus a paper due on Friday. Have you ever noticed that it takes a textbook dozens of pages to say what normal people can cover fast?

Example:

What was the full impact of World War II?

Clear-cut teenage answer: We won.

90　So I'm close to dying young from excessive homework, and I have to help Mrs. Leonardo clean out her attic. She is paying big bucks for this, and, believe me, my family needs the money.

Mrs. Leonardo wants people there on time and working like ants. Ants carry their weight on their backs and are thrilled as anything to be abused. But that is the insect world; I am not one of them. I'm not in the mood to sit with her in her **dingy** attic and lug tons of garbage down the stairs and listen to her stories of how her family

100　deserted her. I know that sounds mean, but Mrs. Leonardo is a mean person. It's easy to see why she's alone. The big joke is that when her husband died, he had a big smile on his face in the casket that he'd never had in real life. The funeral director said they tried to wipe that grin off his face, but they couldn't do it. ⓔ

So I'm on my knees in the dust, putting things in bags, while Mrs. Leonardo tells me about her selfish brother Horace who deserted her, and her uncaring, money-grubbing cousin Cynthia who backed out of the

110　driveway eight years ago and never came back. She tells me how she helped them and loaned them money which they never paid back. She's going on and on about how the world is a dark, dark place. I clear my throat: "Boy,

dingy (dĭn′jē) *adj.* dirty or discolored

ⓔ **CONFLICTS AND SUBPLOTS**
How can you tell that there may be conflict between Katie and Mrs. Leonardo?

_____

_____

_____

_____

_____

_____

_____

_____

_____

_____

F SEQUENCE

Reread lines 106–115. Underline
the words that signal that the
narrator, Katie, is returning to
the main story she is telling. Add
this event to the sequence chart
below.

propriety (prə-prī′ĭ-tē) n.
the quality of being proper;
appropriateness

Mrs. Leonardo, you've got a lot of stuff up here. Are you
sure you want to keep it all?" **F**

This is the wrong thing to say. Mrs. Leonardo's gray eyes
get spitting mad and she says, *well,* she's seventy-six years
old and she's had a *very* interesting life and she doesn't want
to throw out anything of value. I look in a box with IRS
120 tax forms dating back to 1955.

"Mrs. Leonardo, the IRS says you only need to keep
tax records from the last three years. We could dump this
whole box . . ." My mother told me this.

She lunges as much as a seventy-six-year-old person can
and says she isn't giving her tax records to anyone so they
can steal her secrets. Like tons of thieves are out there ready
to pounce on this.

But at twenty-five dollars per hour, you learn to be
patient. "Think of the money," my mother always says,
130 "and the graciousness will come." So I'm taping the box
and writing IMPORTANT PAPERS 1955–1963. Maybe
she could turn this attic into a museum and people could
walk through and learn all the things you should never
hold on to.

Benjamin would have cracked under this pressure.
Mrs. Leonardo is kneeling by a huge trunk, saying how
the younger generation (mine) doesn't understand about
manners, **propriety**, or simple human decency. Her
grandniece, Veronica, walks around with her belly button
140 showing. She pulls old clothes out of the trunk and yanks
this old lace tablecloth out and just looks at it. Finally,
she says she got it when she was married and she's only
used it once. She waited for a special occasion and only
one came—her twentieth anniversary. No other occasion
was special enough, and then her husband died right
before their twenty-fifth anniversary and the tablecloth

has been in this trunk ever since—only used once, she keeps saying—beautiful Egyptian linen. She looks kind of sad, though stiff. I say, "You could start using it now, 150 Mrs. Leonardo," which is the wrong thing to say. She shuts that trunk and asks me just who do I think she's going to invite to dinner since everyone she's ever done anything for has either deserted her or died. **G**

I don't know how to answer a question like this. My mother didn't cover it during Clean Sweep boot camp training where I learned how to scour a bathtub that a toddler spilled ink in, how to clean pet stains from any carpet known to man, how to wash windows and not leave streaks, how to open a refrigerator with year-old meat and 160 not gag in front of the client. I pledged that the customer was always right and I, the lowly dust eliminator, was always, always wrong. **H**

But I'm not sure what to do. If I agree with her, I'm not helping, and if I listen, I won't get the job done. The truth is, I don't like Mrs. Leonardo—so there's a big part of me that doesn't care—even though I know this is probably inhumane because she's a sad person, really. Kneeling there in the dust, surrounded by the boxes of her so-called interesting life, going on and on about people 170 who are gone. I'm thinking about the next stage of the job—the actual cleaning of the attic which is going to take two people, and I know Benjamin will be hurled into monumental physical **aberrations** up here.

I'm tired, too, and my paper is late on King Lear who, in my opinion, thought too much and couldn't deliver. I'm thinking about my personal life—yes, dust eliminators have them. We have feelings; we have needs, dreams. I'm feeling that I work too much and I wish my mom had another business because what I do all day at school is

G CONFLICTS AND SUBPLOTS

What causes Mrs. Leonardo to be upset with Katie?

_____

_____

_____

_____

_____

_____

H SEQUENCE

Fill out the sequence chart below with three events having to do with Mrs. Leonardo's tablecloth.

```
┌─────────────────────┐
│                     │
│                     │
└─────────────────────┘
          ↓
┌─────────────────────┐
│                     │
│                     │
└─────────────────────┘
          ↓
┌─────────────────────┐
│                     │
│                     │
└─────────────────────┘
```

aberration (ăb′ə-rā′shən) *n.* an abnormal alteration

180 exhausting enough without having to do heavy lifting after school and on the weekends. I think about when my dad died four years ago, and because of disorganization—that is, getting behind on paying his life insurance premiums—his insurance policy was cancelled and we got no insurance money when he died. He never meant to hurt us, but it was so scary not knowing if we could keep the house mixed with all the pain of losing him. We never got a regular time of mourning because we were fighting to stay afloat. Mom was trying to sort through Dad's huge piles of papers. We 190 loved him so much, but he could never get rid of what Mom called his "clutter demons." ❶

❶ CONFLICTS AND SUBPLOTS
What internal and external conflicts does Katie face as a result of her dad's death?

Internal Conflict:

_____

_____

_____

_____

_____

External Conflict:

_____

_____

_____

_____

_____

It took several months, but we got his papers sorted. We learned firsthand how you get organized, clean up, and obliterate dust. We became total aces at it; learned how widespread the problem truly is. We knew then we needed to share what we'd learned with others who were suffering, and felt that twenty-five dollars an hour was reasonable.

I'm not sure if Mrs. Leonardo wants someone to help or someone to complain to. Between you and me, I feel 200 that listening to complaining *and* busting dust should earn thirty-five dollars per hour. But, I'm remembering being in our attic after my dad died; trying to go through his things. He had a trunk that his grandfather had given him—inside were all his photos and papers from school. I remember reading some of his essays from high school and just crying. I couldn't throw those out. Mom said going through all that was therapeutic[3] for me because it was like being with him, kind of. He was forty-one years old when he died. Had a heart attack at work and was dead by the 210 time the ambulance came.

Just thinking about the day makes me shaky. Over the years I've dissected every last thing I remember about

---

3. **therapeutic** (thĕr′ə-pyōō′tĭk): having healing powers.

the last morning I saw him. I should have made him breakfast—I knew how much he liked it when I did. I should have hugged him when he went out the door, but I was on the phone with Roger Rugsby who was my biology partner who needed me to go over my lab notes or he would fail. I missed the bus and Dad missed his train and he took me to school. I was late, so I hurled myself out
220 of the car and he said, "Go get 'em, kiddo." That's the last thing he ever said to me. But I did better than Benjamin who overslept and didn't even see Dad that morning. ❶

   Mrs. Leonardo leans over a trunk like the one my father had. I want to say something encouraging to her, like, "Gee, Mrs. Leonardo, I know how hard it must be going through all these memories," or, "I hope sorting through all this is helping you the way it helped me." Memories are the only things we have left sometimes. You can hold a photo of a person you loved who's gone, but it isn't alive.
230 Memories—the best ones—are filled with sights, smells, love, and happiness. I try to hold some of those in my heart for my dad each day.

   She goes through the trunk, stony-faced. I can't tell what she's found, can't tell if she's going to torch the contents or hold them to her heart. I lug a big bag over and throw old newspapers inside. Mrs. Leonardo stops going through the trunk. She's holding something in her hands, not moving. I look at her stiff face and for a moment in the weird light of the attic, she looks like she's going to cry. But that's
240 impossible. Then I hear a sniff and she says softly, "My mother read this book to my sister and me every night before bed."

   I look at the book—a well-worn brown leather cover. Doesn't look like much.

   "I thought she had it," Mrs. Leonardo says sadly.

❶ **SEQUENCE**
Underline the words in lines 211–222 that signal a **flashback**. Record the event below.

"Who had it?"

"My sister, Helen. I thought she had the book. She always wanted it."

In these situations it's best to say, "Oh."

250 "I thought . . . I thought I'd sent it to her after Mother died." She looks down.

I say, "It's hard to remember what you've done after someone important dies."

"But, she'd asked me for it. It was the one thing she'd wanted."

"Well . . ."

"I haven't talked to her since Mother died. I thought she . . ." **K**

I'm not sure how to ask this. Is Helen still alive?

260 I dance around it. "What do you think you should do with the book, Mrs. Leonardo?" She doesn't answer.

I try again. "Why did Helen want it so bad?"

She hands me the book. "She said these stories were her best memories of childhood." I look through it. "The Naughty Little Frog," "The Little Lost Tulip," "Spanky, the Black Sheep." It's amazing what we put up with as children. But then I remember my favorite bedtime story—"Rupert, the Church Mouse"—about this little mouse who lives in a church and polishes all the stained glass windows every 270 night before he goes to sleep so the light can come forth every morning.

"I know she lives in Vermont," Mrs. Leonardo offers. "I heard from a cousin a while ago . . ." Her voice trails off.

"I think you should call her, Mrs. Leonardo."

She shakes her old head. No—she couldn't possibly.

"I think you should call her and tell her you've got the book."

She glares at me. "I believe we're done for today." She grabs the book from my hands, puts it back in the trunk.

K CONFLICTS AND SUBPLOTS
A **subplot** often follows the same pattern as a main plot. Reread lines 233–258. Tell who is involved in the subplot and what the central conflict seems to be.

_____

_____

_____

_____

_____

_____

_____

_____

_____

_____

280 "Sorry, ma'am. I didn't mean . . ."

She heads down the attic stairs.

I tell Benjamin that I don't want to hear about his problems, that his back looks strong to me, the shooting pain in his leg will go away eventually, and his headache is just a reflection of his deep, inner **turmoil**. I say this as we're walking to Mrs. Leonardo's house.

"I think my whole left side is going numb," he whispers pitifully as we walk up her steps.

"Deal with it."

290 Mrs. Leonardo is waiting for us. We're late. I don't mention that having to drag a hypochondriac[4] four doors down the street takes time. Great food smells swirl from her kitchen. **①**

Mrs. Leonardo looks Benjamin up and down, not impressed. "You've not been here before," she says. Benjamin half smiles and rubs his tennis elbow,[5] which makes me nuts because he doesn't play tennis.

I introduce them. Tell her Benjamin is here to help with dust elimination and heavy lifting, at which point 300 Benjamin leans painfully against the wall and closes his eyes.

"He's a very dedicated worker once he gets started, Mrs. Leonardo."

I jam my elbow into his side.

Okay, so we're cleaning this cavernous[6] attic like there's no tomorrow. We've got all the trunks and boxes wiped down and pushed to the far side. We're running the turbo-charged Clean Sweep Frankenstein portable vacuum that is so powerful it can suck up pets and small children 310 if they get too close. Benjamin is wearing a dust mask over

---

4. **hypochondriac** (hī'pə-kŏn'drē-ăk'): a person who continually thinks he or she is ill or about to become ill.

5. **tennis elbow**: pain around the elbow, often caused from playing tennis or similar activities.

6. **cavernous** (kăv'ər-nəs): filled with caverns; like a cave.

turmoil (tûr'moil') *n.* a state of extreme confusion or agitation

What does Katie mean when she tells Benjamin that his headache reflects his inner **turmoil**?

_____

_____

_____

_____

_____

① CONFLICTS AND SUBPLOTS
In what ways is Katie responsible for her brother?

_____

_____

_____

_____

_____

_____

_____

_____

_____

_____

his nose and mouth—he wrote *The Terminator* over it. This boy is appropriately miserable, pulling down spiders' webs, sucking up dust mites. I can almost hear their little screams of terror. Almost, but not quite. My mother claims she can hear dust mites shrieking for mercy and uses this in her presentation if she thinks potential clients can handle it. **PAUSE & REFLECT**

PAUSE & REFLECT

How is Katie's relationship with Benjamin different from Mrs. Leonardo's relationship with her sister?

_____

_____

_____

_____

_____

_____

_____

_____

_____

_____

_____

_____

_____

_____

"Get the lace tablecloth from the trunk!" Mrs. Leonardo shouts from downstairs.

320   What's she want with that?

"And bring the book, too," she hollers impatiently.

I don't mention that we've shoved everything in the corner like she said to, that I'll have to move it all to get to the trunk, and, by the way, I'm going as fast as I can. I get the book and the lace tablecloth that's been folded in very old plastic. I look at the book—reddish brown leather— *Aunt Goody's Good Night Stories*, it's called. Benjamin comes over looking like some kind of cosmic alien with his mask, takes the book, starts laughing.

330   "The Naughty Little Frog," he says reading. "Once upon a time there was a naughty little frog named Edmond. Edmond was so naughty that he never, ever cleaned his lily pad. It got so dirty that his mother had to make him stay on that lily pad several times each day to—"

"You're going to have to wait for the end." I yank the book from his hands and head down the creaky attic stairs with the tablecloth. Mrs. Leonardo is in the kitchen wearing a frilly apron, stirring a pot of something that smells beyond great.

340   She turns to look at me, puts her wooden spoon down.

"Help me put it on the table," she orders.

I'm smiling a little now because I know this tablecloth's history. I'm wondering who's coming to dinner.

"Looks like you're having a party," I offer as we get the tablecloth squared perfectly on the table.

Mrs. Leonardo says nothing, sets the table for two with what looks like the good silverware, the good napkins. Then she puts the storybook in front of one of the place settings.

350 "My sister, you see . . ." She pauses emotionally. "Well, she's . . . coming to dinner."

"You mean the one you haven't seen for a long time?"

"I only have *one* sister."

I'm just grinning now and I tell her I hope they have the best dinner in the world.

"Well, I do too." She looks nervously out the window and says whatever work we haven't finished can be done tomorrow. "You were right about . . . calling her, Katie." Ⓜ

I smile brightly, wondering if she's going to offer me
360 some of her great-smelling food to show her gratitude. She doesn't. I head up the attic stairs and drag Benjamin to safety. He's sneezing like he's going to die. I take off his Terminator dust mask and lean him against a wall. Half of me wants to give Mrs. Leonardo a little hug of encouragement, but the other half warns, *Don't touch clients because they can turn on you.*

"Whatever you're cooking, Mrs. Leonardo, it sure smells good," I shout. "Your sister's going to love it." I'm not sure she hears all of that. Benjamin is into his fifth
370 sneezing attack.

She nods from the kitchen; I push Benjamin out on the street.

"I could have died up there," he shouts, blowing his nose.

"But you didn't."

And I remember the book my dad would read to us when we were little about the baby animals and their

Ⓜ **CONFLICTS AND SUBPLOTS**
Has the conflict between Katie and Mrs. Leonardo been fully resolved? Use story details to explain your answer.

_____

_____

_____

_____

_____

_____

_____

_____

_____

_____

parents and how each mother and father animal kissed their babies good night. That book was chewed to death, ripped, stained, and missing the last two pages, but I 380 wouldn't give it up for anything.

We walk back home almost silently, except for Benjamin's sniffs, sneezes, and groans. People just don't understand what important things can be hiding in the dust.

Mom says that all the time in her presentation.

PAUSE & REFLECT

PAUSE & REFLECT

What has Katie learned from Mrs. Leonardo?

_____

_____

_____

_____

_____

_____

_____

_____

_____

_____

_____

_____

_____

_____

_____

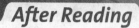

Text Analysis: Conflicts and Subplots

In "Clean Sweep" the author describes the conflicts characters experience in the main plot and in a subplot. Fill out the chart to tell about these conflicts and how they are resolved.

	Katie's Story (plot)	Mrs. Leonardo's Story (subplot)
Characters Involved		
Conflicts		
Resolution (Is every conflict resolved?)		

Review your notes from "Clean Sweep" and your completed chart. Think about the connections between the subplot and the main plot. How does the conflict in the subplot influence the main character?

_____

_____

_____

_____

_____

_____

_____

_____

Reading Skill: Sequence

The author of "Clean Sweep" takes the reader from the present to the past and back again. Two story events are shown in the frame below. Review your reading notes, and fill in important missing events in the correct sequence.

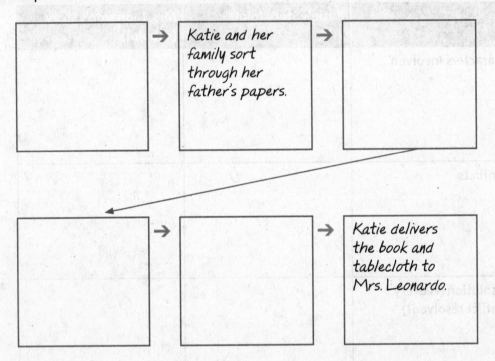

| | → | Katie and her family sort through her father's papers. | → | |

| | → | | → | Katie delivers the book and tablecloth to Mrs. Leonardo. |

When does trash become TREASURE?

Look again at the List It activity on page 38. Imagine you are Katie, and her treasure is the book she mentions on page 52, lines 378–380. What good memories might Katie connect to the book?

_____

_____

_____

_____

Vocabulary Practice

Circle the word that is a synonym for the vocabulary word.

1. vileness (niceness/nastiness)

2. propriety (decency/ownership)

3. dingy (angry/shabby)

4. minuscule (strong/tiny)

5. turmoil (confusion/hope)

6. aberration (refusal/change)

Academic Vocabulary in Writing

affect	conclude	evident	imply	initial

How did the death of the narrator's father **affect** the remaining family members? In a paragraph, explain how the narrator, her mother, and her brother appear to have coped with their loss. Use at least one Academic Vocabulary word in your response. Definitions of the words are on page 3.

_____

_____

_____

_____

Assessment Practice

DIRECTIONS Use "Clean Sweep" to answer questions 1–6.

1 Which event happens first?

- **A** Mrs. Leonardo stops talking to her sister.
- **B** Mrs. Leonardo hires Clean Sweep to clean out the attic.
- **C** Katie listens to Mrs. Leonardo's complaints.
- **D** Katie watches her mother give a presentation on dust mites.

2 The conflict in this story begins when —

- **A** Katie's mother tries to talk customers into using her cleaning service
- **B** Mrs. Leonardo complains about her family
- **C** Katie is both proud of her work and resentful that she has to do it
- **D** Katie's father dies

3 The author uses Katie's memory of her father to show why Katie —

- **A** feels guilty and responsible for his death
- **B** understands that old things in an attic can have special meaning
- **C** is a hard worker who meets goals
- **D** and her brother often argue

4 How does the narrator's view of Mrs. Leonardo change at the end of the story?

- **A** Katie admires her.
- **B** Katie loses respect for her.
- **C** Katie feels sympathy for her.
- **D** Katie feels grateful toward her.

5 Which of these conflicts is NOT part of the story?

- **A** conflict between Katie and Benjamin
- **B** conflict between Katie and Mrs. Leonardo
- **C** conflict between Mrs. Leonardo and Katie's mother
- **D** conflict between grief and acceptance.

6 By telling this story from Katie's point of view, the author helps the reader understand —

- **A** the narrator's internal conflicts
- **B** the sequence of events
- **C** the subplot
- **D** the conflicts revealed through dialogue

The Tell-Tale Heart
Short Story by **Edgar Allan Poe**

What makes you SUSPICIOUS?

Has something or someone ever seemed dangerous or untrustworthy to you? The feeling you had was suspicion. While suspicion might come from a misunderstanding, it can also be a warning that something is very wrong. In this story, you'll meet a man whose own suspicions are his downfall.

DISCUSS With a small group, discuss suspicious characters you've read about or seen on television shows. In what ways did these characters look or act differently from other characters? Continue your discussion by creating a list of warning signs that make a person suspicious.

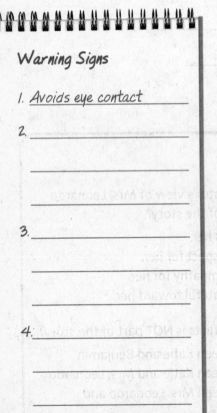

Warning Signs

1. *Avoids eye contact*

2. _____

   _____

3. _____

   _____

   _____

4. _____

   _____

   _____

Text Analysis: Suspense

You know a story is exciting when you are so anxious to find out what happens that you can't put it down. Writers often "hook" readers by creating a sense of excitement, tension, dread, or fear about what will happen next. This feeling is called **suspense.**

Edgar Allan Poe uses the following techniques to develop suspense:

- describing a character's anxiety or fear
- relating vivid descriptions of dramatic sights and sounds
- repeating words, phrases, or characters' actions

As you read "The Tell-Tale Heart," notice how the writer uses these techniques to create suspense.

Reading Skill: Evaluate Narrator

Just as you can't trust every person you meet, you can't trust every **narrator,** or character who tells a story. To evaluate a narrator's **reliability,** or trustworthiness, pay attention to his or her actions, attitudes, and statements. Do any raise your suspicions? As you read "The Tell-Tale Heart," use a chart like the one below to record clues that reveal whether the narrator is reliable or not.

Narrator's Reliability	
Makes Me Suspicious	**Makes Me Trust Him**
denies that he is mad	

Vocabulary in Context

Note: Words are listed in the order in which they appear in the story.

acute (ə-kyōōt') *adj.* sharp, keen
*My hearing is **acute,** so I know what you whispered.*

conceive (kən-sēv') *v.* to think of
*After thinking for a while, **I conceived** a brilliant plan.*

vex (věks) *v.* to disturb; to annoy
*My worries and concerns continued to **vex** me.*

stifled (stī'fəld) *adj.* smothered **stifle** *v.*
*I heard the faint sound of a **stifled** yawn.*

crevice (krěv'ĭs) *n.* crack
*Light filtered through a **crevice** in the wall.*

stealthily (stěl'thə-lē) *adv.* cautiously; secretly
*I moved **stealthily** so that he would not hear me approach.*

audacity (ô-dăs'ĭ-tē) *n.* shameless daring or boldness
*With a show of **audacity,** I barged into the room.*

vehemently (vē'ə-mənt-lē) *adv.* with intense emotion
*I **vehemently** proclaimed my innocence.*

derision (dĭ-rĭzh'ən) *n.* ridicule
*Nobody likes being an object of **derision.***

hypocritical (hĭp'ə-krĭt'ĭ-kəl) *adj.* false or deceptive
*I decided to distrust him when he flashed a **hypocritical** smile.*

The Tell-Tale Heart

Short Story by

EDGAR ALLAN POE

BACKGROUND Edgar Allan Poe is often credited with having invented the modern horror or suspense story. Many of the familiar elements from today's horror movies are found in this story—fury, murder, blood, and madness. Poe was also one of the first writers to explore science fiction and detective styles.

acute (ə-kyōōt′) *adj.* sharp; keen

Why does the narrator think that his hearing is **acute**?

_____

_____

_____

_____

conceive (kən-sēv′) *v.* to think of

True!—nervous—very, very dreadfully nervous I had been and am! but why *will* you say that I am mad? The disease had sharpened my senses—not destroyed—not dulled them. Above all was the sense of hearing **acute**. I heard all things in the heaven and in the earth. I heard many things in hell. How, then, am I mad? Hearken! and observe how healthily—how calmly I can tell you the whole story.

It is impossible to say how first the idea entered my
10 brain; but once **conceived**, it haunted me day and night. Object there was none. Passion there was none. I loved the

old man. He had never wronged me. He had never given me insult. For his gold I had no desire. I think it was his eye! yes, it was this! He had the eye of a vulture—a pale blue eye, with a film over it. Whenever it fell upon me, my blood ran cold; and so by degrees—very gradually—I made up my mind to take the life of the old man, and thus rid myself of the eye forever.

Now this is the point. You fancy me mad. Madmen know
20 nothing. But you should have seen *me*. You should have seen how wisely I proceeded—with what caution—with what foresight—with what dissimulation[1] I went to work! Ⓐ

I was never kinder to the old man than during the whole week before I killed him. And every night, about midnight, I turned the latch of his door and opened it—oh, so gently! And then, when I had made an opening sufficient for my head, I put in a dark lantern, all closed, closed, so that no light shone out, and then I thrust in my head. Oh, you would have laughed to see how cunningly I thrust it in!
30 I moved it slowly—very, very slowly, so that I might not disturb the old man's sleep. It took me an hour to place my whole head within the opening so far that I could see him as he lay upon his bed. Ha!—would a madman have been so wise as this? And then, when my head was well in the room, I undid the lantern cautiously—oh, so cautiously—cautiously (for the hinges creaked)—I undid it just so much that a single thin ray fell upon the vulture eye. And this I did for seven long nights—every night just at midnight—but I found the eye always closed; and so it
40 was impossible to do the work; for it was not the old man who **vexed** me, but his Evil Eye. And every morning, when the day broke, I went boldly into the chamber, and spoke courageously to him, calling him by name in a hearty tone, and inquiring how he had passed the night. So you see

Ⓐ **EVALUATE NARRATOR**
Reread lines 1–22. Underline the words that the narrator uses to convince you that he is not mad. Does the narrator's opinion of himself make you trust him more or less? Why?

_____

_____

_____

_____

_____

_____

_____

vex (vĕks) *v.* to disturb; to annoy

---

1. **dissimulation** (dĭ-sĭm′yə-lā′shən): a hiding of one's true feelings.

B SUSPENSE
In lines 23–47, the narrator describes what he does repeatedly, night after night. Why does this repetition create a sense of dread?

_____

_____

_____

_____

_____

_____

C SUSPENSE
Reread lines 62–69. In what way does the characters' inaction create tension?

_____

_____

_____

_____

_____

_____

_____

stifled (stī′fəld) *adj.* smothered
stifle *v.*

he would have been a very profound old man, indeed, to suspect that every night, just at twelve, I looked in upon him while he slept. **B**

Upon the eighth night I was more than usually cautious in opening the door. A watch's minute hand moves more
50 quickly than did mine. Never before that night had I *felt* the extent of my own powers—of my sagacity.[2] I could scarcely contain my feelings of triumph. To think that there I was, opening the door, little by little, and he not even to dream of my secret deeds or thoughts. I fairly chuckled at the idea; and perhaps he heard me; for he moved on the bed suddenly, as if startled. Now you may think that I drew back—but no. His room was as black as pitch with the thick darkness (for the shutters were close fastened, through fear of robbers), and so I knew that he
60 could not see the opening of the door, and I kept pushing it on steadily, steadily.

I had my head in, and was about to open the lantern, when my thumb slipped upon the tin fastening, and the old man sprang up in the bed, crying out—"Who's there?"

I kept quite still and said nothing. For a whole hour I did not move a muscle, and in the meantime I did not hear him lie down. He was still sitting up in the bed listening,—just as I have done, night after night, hearkening to the death watches[3] in the wall. **C**
70 Presently I heard a slight groan, and I knew it was the groan of mortal terror. It was not a groan of pain or grief—oh, no!—it was the low, stifled sound that arises from the bottom of the soul when overcharged with awe. I knew the sound well. Many a night, just at midnight, when all the world slept, it has welled up from my own bosom, deepening, with its dreadful echo, the terrors that distracted me. I say I knew it well. I knew what the old

---

2. **sagacity** (sə-găs′ĭ-tē): sound judgment.
3. **death watches**: deathwatch beetles—insects that make a tapping sound with their heads.

man felt, and pitied him, although I chuckled at heart.
I knew that he had been lying awake ever since the first
80 slight noise, when he had turned in the bed. His fears had
been ever since growing upon him. He had been trying to
fancy them causeless, but could not. He had been saying to
himself—"It is nothing but the wind in the chimney—it
is only a mouse crossing the floor," or "it is merely a cricket
which has made a single chirp." Yes, he has been trying to
comfort himself with these suppositions; but he had found
all in vain. *All in vain;* because Death, in approaching
him, had stalked with his black shadow before him, and
enveloped the victim. And it was the mournful influence of
90 the unperceived shadow that caused him to feel—although
he neither saw nor heard—to *feel* the presence of my head
within the room.

When I had waited a long time, very patiently, without
hearing him lie down, I resolved to open a little—a very,
very little **crevice** in the lantern. So I opened it—you
cannot imagine how **stealthily**, stealthily—until, at length,
a single dim ray, like the thread of the spider, shot from out
the crevice and fell full upon the vulture eye.

It was open—wide, wide open—and I grew furious as
100 I gazed upon it. I saw it with perfect distinctness—all a
dull blue, with a hideous veil over it that chilled the very
marrow in my bones; but I could see nothing else of the
old man's face or person: for I had directed the ray as if by
instinct, precisely upon the damned spot.

And now have I not told you that what you mistake
for madness is but over-acuteness of the senses?—now,
I say, there came to my ears a low, dull, quick sound, such
as a watch makes when enveloped in cotton. I knew *that*
sound well too. It was the beating of the old man's heart.
110 It increased my fury, as the beating of a drum stimulates
the soldier into courage. **D**

crevice (krĕv′ĭs) *n.* crack

stealthily (stĕl′thə-lē) *adv.* cautiously; secretly

D EVALUATE NARRATOR
Reread lines 105–111. Underline
what the narrator claims to be
hearing. What do you think of
that claim? Does it make you
suspicious of the narrator or
does it make you trust him? Add
your idea to your chart.

Makes Me Suspicious

Makes Me Trust Him

E SUSPENSE
Reread lines 112–137. What is the scariest or most exciting part of this paragraph? Circle details contribute to this feeling.

_____

_____

_____

_____

_____

_____

_____

_____

_____

_____

_____

_____

_____

_____

_____

_____

_____

But even yet I refrained and kept still. I scarcely breathed. I held the lantern motionless. I tried how steadily I could maintain the ray upon the eye. Meantime the hellish tattoo[4] of the heart increased. It grew quicker and quicker, and louder and louder every instant. The old man's terror *must* have been extreme! It grew louder, I say, louder every moment!—do you mark me well? I have told you that I am nervous: so I am. And now at the dead hour

120 of the night, amid the dreadful silence of that old house, so strange a noise as this excited me to uncontrollable terror. Yet, for some minutes longer I refrained and stood still. But the beating grew louder, louder! I thought the heart must burst. And now a new anxiety seized me—the sound would be heard by a neighbor! The old man's hour had come! With a loud yell, I threw open the lantern and leaped into the room. He shrieked once—once only. In an instant I dragged him to the floor, and pulled the heavy bed over him. I then smiled gaily, to find the deed so far

130 done. But, for many minutes, the heart beat on with a muffled sound. This, however, did not vex me; it would not be heard through the wall. At length it ceased. The old man was dead. I removed the bed and examined the corpse. Yes, he was stone, stone dead. I placed my hand upon the heart and held it there many minutes. There was no pulsation. He was stone dead. His eye would trouble me no more. **E**

If still you think me mad, you will think so no longer when I describe the wise precautions I took for the

140 concealment of the body. The night waned,[5] and I worked hastily, but in silence. First of all I dismembered the corpse. I cut off the head and the arms and the legs.

I then took up three planks from the flooring of the chamber, and deposited all between the scantlings.[6] I then

---

4. **hellish tattoo:** awful drumming.
5. **waned:** approached its end.
6. **scantlings:** small wooden beams supporting the floor.

replaced the boards so cleverly, so cunningly, that no human eye—not even *his*—could have detected anything wrong. There was nothing to wash out—no stain of any kind—no blood-spot whatever. I had been too wary for that. A tub had caught all—ha! ha!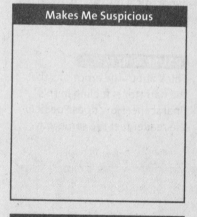

150   When I made an end of these labors, it was four o'clock—still dark as midnight. As the bell sounded the hour, there came a knocking at the street door. I went down to open it with a light heart,—for what had I *now* to fear? There entered three men, who introduced themselves, with perfect suavity,[7] as officers of the police. A shriek had been heard by a neighbor during the night: suspicion of foul play had been aroused; information had been lodged at the police office, and they (the officers) had been deputed[8] to search the premises.

160   I smiled,—for *what* had I to fear? I bade the gentlemen welcome. The shriek, I said, was my own in a dream. The old man, I mentioned, was absent in the country. I took my visitors all over the house. I bade them search—search *well*. I led them, at length, to *his* chamber. I showed them his treasures, secure, undisturbed. In the enthusiasm of my confidence, I brought chairs into the room, and desired them *here* to rest from their fatigues, while I myself, in the wild **audacity** of my perfect triumph, placed my own seat upon the very spot beneath which reposed[9] the corpse of
170 the victim.

   The officers were satisfied. My *manner* had convinced them. I was singularly at ease. They sat, and while I answered cheerily, they chatted of familiar things. But, ere long, I felt myself getting pale and wished them gone. My head ached, and I fancied a ringing in my ears: but still they sat and still chatted. The ringing became more

F EVALUATE NARRATOR
Reread lines 138–149. Underline the words the narrator uses to describe himself and his actions. How does narrator's view of himself affect your evaluation of him? Add your ideas to the chart.

Makes Me Suspicious

Makes Me Trust Him

audacity (ô-dăs′ĭ-tē) *n.* shameless daring or boldness

---

7. **suavity** (swä′vĭ-tē): graceful politeness.
8. **deputed**: appointed as a representative.
9. **reposed**: rested.

vehemently (vē'ə-mənt-lē) *adv.*
with intense emotion

derision (dĭ-rĭzh'ən) *n.* ridicule

hypocritical (hĭp'ə-krĭt'ĭ-kəl) *adj.*
false or deceptive

PAUSE & REFLECT
Think about the emotions that
the narrator is feeling in this
final scene. How does Poe help
the reader feel the same way?

_____

_____

_____

_____

_____

_____

_____

_____

_____

_____

_____

_____

distinct:—it continued and became more distinct: I talked
more freely to get rid of the feeling: but it continued and
gained definitiveness—until at length, I found that the
180 noise was *not* within my ears.

No doubt I now grew *very* pale;—but I talked more
fluently, and with a heightened voice. Yet the sound
increased—and what could I do? It was *a low, dull, quick
sound—much such a sound as a watch makes when enveloped
in cotton.* I gasped for breath—and yet the officers heard
it not. I talked more quickly—more **vehemently**; but the
noise steadily increased. I arose and argued about trifles, in
a high key and with violent gesticulations,[10] but the noise
steadily increased. Why *would* they not be gone? I paced
190 the floor to and fro with heavy strides, as if excited to fury
by the observation of the men—but the noise steadily
increased. What *could* I do? I foamed—I raved—I swore.
I swung the chair upon which I had been sitting, and
grated it upon the boards, but the noise arose over all and
continually increased. It grew louder—louder—*louder!*
And still the men chatted pleasantly, and smiled. Was
it possible they heard not?—no, no! They heard!—they
suspected!—they *knew!*—they were making a *mockery* of
my horror!—this I thought, and this I think. But anything
200 was better than this agony! Anything was more tolerable
than this **derision**! I could bear those **hypocritical** smiles
no longer! I felt that I must scream or die!—and now—
again!—hark! louder! louder! *louder!*—

"Villains!" I shrieked, "dissemble[11] no more! I admit the
deed!—tear up the planks!—here, here!—it is the beating
of his hideous heart!" **PAUSE & REFLECT**

---

10. **gesticulations** (jĕ-stĭk'yə-lā'shəns): energetic gestures of the hands or arms.
11. **dissemble:** pretend.

Text Analysis: Suspense

Review the story sections shown in the chart. Then list an appropriate example of a technique Poe uses to build suspense. Finally, rank the sections from 1–3, with 1 being the most suspenseful.

Lines	Examples of Techniques	Rank
1–104	1. repeated words and actions: 2. description of fear:	
105–149	1. repeated sounds: 2. vivid description of event:	
150–206	1. description of anxiety: 2. vivid description of event:	

How did you choose the section that you ranked as 1, most suspenseful? Which of Poe's techniques for creating suspense were most effective for you?

_____

_____

_____

_____

_____

_____

Reading Skill: Evaluate Narrator

Evaluate the narrator of "The Tell-Tale Heart" by analyzing the following quotations from the story. How reliable is the narrator? Do you believe what he says? List your ideas in the chart.

Detail: "Madmen know nothing. But you should have seen *me*. You should have seen how wisely I proceeded." (lines 19–21)
My Evaluation: _____ _____
Detail: "Never before that night had I *felt* the extent of my own powers—of my sagacity." (lines 50–51)
My Evaluation: _____ _____
Detail: "And now have I not told you that what you mistake for madness is but over-acuteness of the senses?" (lines 105–106)
My Evaluation: _____ _____

What makes you SUSPICIOUS?

Review your list of warning signs that make someone suspicious. Which of these warning signs did the narrator show while talking to the police?

_____

_____

Vocabulary Practice

Write *S* if both words are synonyms (words with similar meanings). Write *A* if they are antonyms (words with opposite meanings).

1. hypocritical/genuine _____   6. stifled/crushed _____

2. stealthily/boldly _____   7. conceived/thought _____

3. acute/dull _____   8. crevice/crack _____

4. derision/praise _____   9. audacity/caution _____

5. vex/bother _____   10. vehemently/strongly _____

Academic Vocabulary in Writing

affect	conclude	evident	imply	initial

At what point in "The Tell-Tale Heart," did it become **evident** to you that the narrator was mad, or insane? Write a short paragraph explaining your answer. Use at least one Academic Vocabulary word in your response. Definitions of these words are on page 3.

_____

_____

_____

_____

_____

Assessment Practice

DIRECTIONS Use "The Tell-Tale Heart" to answer questions 1–4.

1 In line 10, what does the narrator mean when he says, "it haunted me day and night"?

   (A) The old man's pale blue eye sent a chill through him.

   (B) The narrator was always troubled by his fear of ghosts.

   (C) The narrator's acute sense of hearing frightened him all the time.

   (D) The narrator couldn't rid himself of the idea of killing the old man.

2 The author builds suspense by—

   (A) not revealing what the crime will be

   (B) having the narrator watch the sleeping victim for seven nights in a row

   (C) having the narrator explain how clever he thinks he is

   (D) describing what is done with the victim's body

3 In his description of the murder, the narrator reveals that he—

   (A) had not thought of killing the man before

   (B) is overcome by guilt

   (C) feels a thrill

   (D) performs the act with perfect calmness

4 By telling this story from the murderer's point of view, the author helps the reader —

   (A) recognize the narrator's insanity

   (B) feel compassion for the narrator

   (C) realize that the murderer is pretending to be insane

   (D) understand why the police have come

UNIT

2

Through Different Eyes

CHARACTER AND POINT OF VIEW

Be sure to read the Text Analysis Workshop on pp. 170–175 in *Holt McDougal Literature*.

Academic Vocabulary for Unit 2

Academic Vocabulary is the language you use to discuss literary and informational texts. Preview the following Academic Vocabulary words. You will use these words as you write and talk about the selections in this unit.

appropriate (ə-prō′prē-ĭt) *adj.* fitting for the purpose; suitable

*Is it **appropriate** for the character to use her wealth to win the game?*

•

assess (ə-sĕs′) *v.* to determine the value or significance of something

*How would you **assess** the value of the clue the characters discover?*

•

intelligence (ĭn-tĕl′ə-jəns) *n.* the ability to learn, understand, and solve problems

*How does the character's **intelligence** affect her attempts to resolve the conflict?*

•

motive (mō′tĭv) *n.* emotion, desire, or need that compels one to take a certain action

*What is the character's **motive** for lying about his actions?*

•

role (rōl) *n.* a character or part played by a performer; a function or position

*Describe the main character's **role** in solving the mystery.*

Think of a dislikable character in a book you've read or a movie you've seen. Describe the actions that made the character disagreeable, using at least two Academic Vocabulary words in your response. What is the character's **motive** for acting as he or she did?

_____

_____

_____

The Treasure of Lemon Brown
Short Story by Walter Dean Myers

What do you CHERISH?

Think of what you most cherish, or hold dear. Is it worth a lot of money, or is it valuable because of a memory that is important only to you? In the story you're about to read, a boy's encounter with an old blues musician helps him discover what he treasures most.

LIST IT Make a list of five things that you cherish. They might be tangible (things you can touch, such as a pair of jeans or a pet) or intangible (things you cannot touch, such as a memory or an idea like freedom). Choose one thing on your list and explain why it is important to you.

Things I cherish

1. _____

2. _____

3. _____

4. _____

5. _____

Why _____ is
important to me

_____

_____

_____

_____

_____

Text Analysis: Third-Person Point of View

In the **third-person omniscient point of view,** the narrator is an outside observer who can see into the minds of all the characters. A **third-person limited** narrator is also an outside observer, but this point of view focuses on what one character sees, thinks, and feels. Look at the example in the graphic below.

Report cards were due in a week, and Greg had been hoping for the best.	←	The narrator: • is an outside observer • tells readers how Greg feels about the report card he's about to receive

As you read, pay attention to how much the narrator allows you to know about each character's thoughts and feelings.

Reading Skill: Infer Characters' Motivations

To fully understand the characters in a story, you need to think about their **motivations,** or the reasons for their actions. Sometimes a narrator will actually state a character's motives, but more often you need to **infer,** or guess, them. To infer a character's motives, notice his or her words, thoughts, and reactions, and ask yourself what you would do in a similar situation. As you read, you will make inferences about motivations in a chart like the one shown.

Details About Character	What I Infer About Motives
Greg's father lectures him about his poor effort in math.	Greg's father wants his son to succeed in life.

Vocabulary in Context

Note: Words are listed in the order in which they appear in the story.

ajar (ə-jär') *adj.* partially open
*The door was **ajar** and let in a small amount of light.*

tentatively (tĕn'tə-tĭv-lē) *adv.* uncertainly or hesitantly
*The hallway was dark, so he moved **tentatively.***

tremor (trĕm'ər) *n.* nervous trembling
*There was a **tremor** in his voice as he told the sad tale.*

commence (kə-mĕns') *v.* to begin
*He would **commence** his trip when the rain stopped.*

gnarled (närld) *adj.* roughened, as from age or work
*Years of hard work left him with **gnarled** hands.*

ominous (ŏm'ə-nəs) *adj.* threatening
*The silence was **ominous** and scary.*

Vocabulary Practice

Review the vocabulary words and think about their meanings. Then use at least two words to describe a suspenseful scene.

_____

_____

_____

SET A PURPOSE FOR READING

Read "The Treasure of Lemon Brown" to discover what the treasure is and why it is valuable.

THE TREASURE OF LEMON BROWN

Short Story by

WALTER DEAN MYERS

BACKGROUND "The Treasure of Lemon Brown" is set in Harlem, a neighborhood in New York City. After World War I, Harlem was the center of an African American literary explosion called the Harlem Renaissance. Important writers such as Langston Hughes and Zora Neal Hurston lived in Harlem during this time. Though Harlem has always been a vibrant place, many of its buildings were not maintained for many years and were abandoned. Recently, however, Harlem has enjoyed a new wave of development and restoration.

Ⓐ POINT OF VIEW
Reread lines 1–8. Whose thoughts and feelings is the narrator describing?

The dark sky, filled with angry, swirling clouds, reflected Greg Ridley's mood as he sat on the stoop[1] of his building. His father's voice came to him again, first reading the letter the principal had sent to the house, then lecturing endlessly about his poor efforts in math.

"I had to leave school when I was 13," his father had said, "that's a year younger than you are now. If I'd had half the chances that you have, I'd . . ." Ⓐ

---

1. **stoop:** a porch or staircase at the entrance of a building.

Greg had sat in the small, pale green kitchen listening, knowing the lecture would end with his father saying he couldn't play ball with the Scorpions. He had asked his father the week before, and his father had said it depended on his next report card. It wasn't often the Scorpions took on new players, especially 14-year-olds, and this was a chance of a lifetime for Greg. He hadn't been allowed to play high school ball, which he had really wanted to do, but playing for the Community Center team was the next best thing. Report cards were due in a week, and Greg had been hoping for the best. But the principal had ended the suspense early when she sent that letter saying Greg would probably fail math if he didn't spend more time studying.

"And you want to play *basketball*?" His father's brows knitted over deep brown eyes. "That must be some kind of a joke. Now you just get into your room and hit those books." **B**

That had been two nights before. His father's words, like the distant thunder that now echoed through the streets of Harlem, still rumbled softly in his ears.

It was beginning to cool. Gusts of wind made bits of paper dance between the parked cars. There was a flash of nearby lightning, and soon large drops of rain splashed onto his jeans. He stood to go upstairs, thought of the lecture that probably awaited him if he did anything except shut himself in his room with his math book, and started walking down the street instead. Down the block there was an old tenement that had been abandoned for some months. Some of the guys had held an impromptu checker tournament there the week before, and Greg had noticed that the door, once boarded over, had been slightly **ajar**.

Pulling his collar up as high as he could, he checked for traffic and made a dash across the street. He reached the

B INFER CHARACTERS' MOTIVATION
Why is Greg's father so upset about Greg's poor math grades?

_____

_____

_____

_____

_____

_____

ajar (ə-jär´) *adj.* partially open

tentatively (tĕn′tə-tĭv-lē) *adv.*
uncertainly or hesitantly

house just as another flash of lightning changed the night to day for an instant, then returned the graffiti-scarred building to the grim shadows. He vaulted over the outer stairs and pushed **tentatively** on the door. It was open, and he let himself in.

The inside of the building was dark except for the dim light that filtered through the dirty windows from the streetlamps. There was a room a few feet from the door, and from where he stood at the entrance, Greg could see a squarish patch of light on the floor. He entered the room, frowning at the musty smell. It was a large room that might have been someone's parlor at one time. Squinting, Greg could see an old table on its side against one wall, what looked like a pile of rags or a torn mattress in the corner, and a couch, with one side broken, in front of the window.

He went to the couch. The side that wasn't broken was comfortable enough, though a little creaky. From this spot he could see the blinking neon sign over the bodega[2] on the corner. He sat a while, watching the sign blink first green then red, allowing his mind to drift to the Scorpions, then to his father. His father had been a postal worker for all Greg's life, and was proud of it, often telling Greg how hard he had worked to pass the test. Greg had heard the story too many times to be interested now. **C**

For a moment Greg thought he heard something that sounded like a scraping against the wall. He listened carefully, but it was gone.

Outside the wind had picked up, sending the rain against the window with a force that shook the glass in its frame. A car passed, its tires hissing over the wet street and its red tail lights glowing in the darkness.

C INFER CHARACTERS' MOTIVATIONS
Reread lines 32–35 and 63–66. From Greg's thoughts, what can you infer about his reasons for not going home?

_____

_____

_____

_____

_____

_____

_____

2. **bodega** (bō-dä′gə): a small grocery store.

Greg thought he heard the noise again. His stomach tightened as he held himself still and listened intently. There weren't any more scraping noises, but he was sure he had heard something in the darkness—something breathing!

80 He tried to figure out just where the breathing was coming from; he knew it was in the room with him. Slowly he stood, tensing. As he turned, a flash of lightning lit up the room, frightening him with its sudden brilliance. He saw nothing, just the overturned table, the pile of rags and an old newspaper on the floor. Could he have been imagining the sounds? He continued listening, but heard nothing and thought that it might have just been rats. Still, he thought, as soon as the rain let up he would leave. He went to the window and was about to look out when he heard a voice behind him.

90 "Don't try nothin' 'cause I got a razor here sharp enough to cut a week into nine days!"

Greg, except for an involuntary **tremor** in his knees, stood stock still. The voice was high and brittle, like dry twigs being broken, surely not one he had ever heard before. There was a shuffling sound as the person who had been speaking moved a step closer. Greg turned, holding his breath, his eyes straining to see in the dark room.

The upper part of the figure before him was still in darkness. The lower half was in the dim rectangle of light

100 that fell unevenly from the window. There were two feet, in cracked, dirty shoes from which rose legs that were wrapped in rags.

"Who are you?" Greg hardly recognized his own voice.

"I'm Lemon Brown," came the answer. "Who're you?"

"Greg Ridley."

"What you doing here?" The figure shuffled forward again, and Greg took a small step backward.

tremor (trĕm′ər) *n.* nervous trembling

What can you tell about Greg from the **tremor** he feels in his knees?

_____

_____

_____

_____

_____

"It's raining," Greg said.

"I can see that," the figure said.

110 The person who called himself Lemon Brown peered forward, and Greg could see him clearly. He was an old man. His black, heavily wrinkled face was surrounded by a halo of crinkly white hair and whiskers that seemed to separate his head from the layers of dirty coats piled on his smallish frame. His pants were bagged to the knee, where they were met with rags that went down to the old shoes. The rags were held on with strings, and there was a rope around his middle. Greg relaxed. He had seen the man before, picking through the trash on the corner and pulling 120 clothes out of a Salvation Army box. There was no sign of the razor that could "cut a week into nine days." **D**

"What are you doing here?" Greg asked.

"This is where I'm staying," Lemon Brown said. "What you here for?"

"Told you it was raining out," Greg said, leaning against the back of the couch until he felt it give slightly.

"Ain't you got no home?"

"I got a home," Greg answered.

"You ain't one of them bad boys looking for my treasure, 130 is you?" Lemon Brown cocked his head to one side and squinted one eye. "Because I told you I got me a razor."

"I'm not looking for your treasure," Greg answered, smiling. "*If* you have one."

"What you mean, *if* I have one," Lemon Brown said. "Every man got a treasure. You don't know that, you must be a fool!"

"Sure," Greg said as he sat on the sofa and put one leg over the back. "What do you have, gold coins?"

"Don't worry none about what I got," Lemon Brown 140 said. "You know who I am?"

D POINT OF VIEW
In lines 110–121, the narrator describes Greg's view of Lemon Brown. How does knowing Greg's thoughts and actions affect your impression of Lemon Brown?

_____

_____

_____

_____

_____

_____

_____

_____

_____

"You told me your name was orange or lemon or something like that."

"Lemon Brown," the old man said, pulling back his shoulders as he did so, "they used to call me Sweet Lemon Brown." **E**

"Sweet Lemon?" Greg asked.

"Yessir. Sweet Lemon Brown. They used to say I sung the blues[3] so sweet that if I sang at a funeral, the dead would **commence** to rocking with the beat. Used to travel
150 all over Mississippi and as far as Monroe, Louisiana, and east on over to Macon, Georgia. You mean you ain't never heard of Sweet Lemon Brown?"

"Afraid not," Greg said. "What . . . what happened to you?"

"Hard times, boy. Hard times always after a poor man. One day I got tired, sat down to rest a spell and felt a tap on my shoulder. Hard times caught up with me."

"Sorry about that."

"What you doing here? How come you didn't go on
160 home when the rain come? Rain don't bother you young folks none."

"Just didn't." Greg looked away.

"I used to have a knotty-headed boy just like you." Lemon Brown had half walked, half shuffled back to the corner and sat down against the wall. "Had them big eyes like you got. I used to call them moon eyes. Look into them moon eyes and see anything you want."

"How come you gave up singing the blues?" Greg asked.

"Didn't give it up," Lemon Brown said. "You don't give
170 up the blues; they give you up. After a while you do good for yourself, and it ain't nothing but foolishness singing about how hard you got it. Ain't that right?"

"I guess so."

---

3. **blues:** a style of music developed from southern African-American songs.

E INFER CHARACTERS' MOTIVATIONS

Reread lines 143–145. Underline the action that the man performs as he says his name. Then use the chart below to make an inference about Lemon Brown.

Details About Lemon Brown
Pulls back his shoulders as he says his name.

↓

What I Infer

commence (kə-mĕns') *v.* to begin

"What's that noise?" Lemon Brown asked, suddenly sitting upright.

Greg listened, and he heard a noise outside. He looked at Lemon Brown and saw the old man was pointing toward the window.

Greg went to the window and saw three men, 180 neighborhood thugs, on the stoop. One was carrying a length of pipe. Greg looked back toward Lemon Brown, who moved quietly across the room to the window. The old man looked out, then beckoned frantically for Greg to follow him. For a moment Greg couldn't move. Then he found himself following Lemon Brown into the hallway and up darkened stairs. Greg followed as closely as he could. They reached the top of the stairs, and Greg felt Lemon Brown's hand first lying on his shoulder, then probing down his arm until he finally took Greg's hand 190 into his own as they crouched in the darkness. **F**

"They's bad men," Lemon Brown whispered. His breath was warm against Greg's skin.

"Hey! Rag man!" a voice called. "We know you in here. What you got up under them rags? You got any money?"

Silence.

"We don't want to have to come in and hurt you, old man, but we don't mind if we have to."

Lemon Brown squeezed Greg's hand in his own hard, **gnarled** fist.

200 There was a banging downstairs and a light as the men entered. They banged around noisily, calling for the rag man.

"We heard you talking about your treasure." The voice was slurred. "We just want to see it, that's all."

"You sure he's here?" One voice seemed to come from the room with the sofa.

"Yeah, he stays here every night."

F INFER CHARACTERS' MOTIVATION
Why does Lemon Brown hold Greg's hand?

_____

_____

_____

_____

gnarled (närld) *adj.* roughened, as from age or work

"There's another room over there; I'm going to take a look. You got that flashlight?"

210 "Yeah, here, take the pipe too."

Greg opened his mouth to quiet the sound of his breath as he sucked it in uneasily. A beam of light hit the wall a few feet opposite him, then went out.

"Ain't nobody in that room," a voice said. "You think he gone or something?"

"I don't know," came the answer. "All I know is that I heard him talking about some kind of treasure. You know they found that shopping bag lady with that money in her bags."

220 "Yeah. You think he's upstairs?"

"HEY, OLD MAN, ARE YOU UP THERE?"

Silence.

"Watch my back. I'm going up."

There was a footstep on the stairs, and the beam from the flashlight danced crazily along the peeling wallpaper. Greg held his breath. There was another step and a loud crashing noise as the man banged the pipe against the wooden banister. Greg could feel his temples throb as the man slowly neared them. Greg thought about the pipe,
230 wondering what he would do when the man reached them—what he *could* do. **G**

Then Lemon Brown released his hand and moved toward the top of the stairs. Greg looked around and saw stairs going up to the next floor. He tried waving to Lemon Brown, hoping the old man would see him in the dim light and follow him to the next floor. Maybe, Greg thought, the man wouldn't follow them up there. Suddenly, though, Lemon Brown stood at the top of the stairs, both arms raised high above his head.

240 "There he is!" a voice cried from below.

G POINT OF VIEW
A third-person limited narrator helps you understand what a character sees, thinks, and feels. Underline details in lines 224–231 that help you understand Greg's experience.

_____

_____

_____

_____

_____

_____

_____

❶ POINT OF VIEW
Reread lines 253–258. How does
the use of the third-person
limited narrator make you more
concerned for Lemon Brown?

_____

_____

_____

_____

_____

_____

_____

ominous (ŏm′ə-nəs) *adj.*
threatening

**❶ INFER CHARACTERS'
MOTIVATIONS**
What might Greg's motivation
be for leaving?

_____

_____

_____

_____

_____

_____

_____

"Throw down your money, old man, so I won't have to
bash your head in!"

Lemon Brown didn't move. Greg felt himself near panic.
The steps came closer, and still Lemon Brown didn't move.
He was an eerie sight, a bundle of rags standing at the top
of the stairs, his shadow on the wall looming over him.
Maybe, the thought came to Greg, the scene could be even
eerier.

Greg wet his lips, put his hands to his mouth and tried
250 to make a sound. Nothing came out. He swallowed hard,
wet his lips once more and howled as evenly as he could.

"What's that?"

As Greg howled, the light moved away from Lemon
Brown, but not before Greg saw him hurl his body down
the stairs at the men who had come to take his treasure.
There was a crashing noise, and then footsteps. A rush of
warm air came in as the downstairs door opened, then
there was only an **ominous** silence. **❶**

Greg stood on the landing. He listened, and after a while
260 there was another sound on the staircase.

"Mr. Brown?" he called.

"Yeah, it's me," came the answer. "I got their flashlight."

Greg exhaled in relief as Lemon Brown made his way
slowly back up the stairs.

"You O.K.?"

"Few bumps and bruises," Lemon Brown said.

"I think I'd better be going," Greg said, his breath
returning to normal. "You'd better leave, too, before they
come back."**❶**

270 "They may hang around outside for a while," Lemon
Brown said, "but they ain't getting their nerve up to come
in here again. Not with crazy old rag men and howling
spooks. Best you stay awhile till the coast is clear. I'm
heading out West tomorrow, out to east St. Louis."

"They were talking about treasures," Greg said. "You
really have a treasure?"

"What I tell you? Didn't I tell you every man got a
treasure?" Lemon Brown said. "You want to see mine?"

"If you want to show it to me," Greg shrugged.

280 "Let's look out the window first, see what them
scoundrels be doing," Lemon Brown said.

They followed the oval beam of the flashlight into one
of the rooms and looked out the window. They saw the
men who had tried to take the treasure sitting on the curb
near the corner. One of them had his pants leg up, looking
at his knee.

"You sure you're not hurt?" Greg asked Lemon Brown.

"Nothing that ain't been hurt before," Lemon Brown
said. "When you get as old as me all you say when
290 something hurts is 'Howdy, Mr. Pain, sees you back again.'
Then when Mr. Pain see he can't worry you none, he go on
mess with somebody else."

Greg smiled. PAUSE & REFLECT

"Here, you hold this." Lemon Brown gave Greg the
flashlight.

PAUSE & REFLECT
How has Greg's attitude toward
Lemon Brown changed? What
events may have caused this
change?

_____

_____

_____

_____

_____

_____

_____

_____

_____

_____

J INFER CHARACTERS' MOTIVATIONS

Reread lines 312–319. Complete the chart to tell why Lemon Brown gave his son his old newspaper clippings and harmonica.

Details About Character
Lemon gives his son his old newspaper clippings and his harmonica.

↓

What I Infer
_____
_____
_____
_____
_____
_____
_____
_____

He sat on the floor near Greg and carefully untied the strings that held the rags on his right leg. When he took the rags away, Greg saw a piece of plastic. The old man carefully took off the plastic and unfolded it. He 300 revealed some yellowed newspaper clippings and a battered harmonica.

"There it be," he said, nodding his head. "There it be."

Greg looked at the old man, saw the distant look in his eye, then turned to the clippings. They told of Sweet Lemon Brown, a blues singer and harmonica player who was appearing at different theaters in the South. One of the clippings said he had been the hit of the show, although not the headliner. All of the clippings were reviews of shows Lemon Brown had been in more than 50 years ago. Greg 310 looked at the harmonica. It was dented badly on one side, with the reed holes on one end nearly closed.

"I used to travel around and make money for to feed my wife and Jesse—that's my boy's name. Used to feed them good, too. Then his mama died, and he stayed with his mama's sister. He growed up to be a man, and when the war come he saw fit to go off and fight in it. I didn't have nothing to give him except these things that told him who I was, and what he come from. If you know your pappy did something, you know you can do something too. **J**

320 "Anyway, he went off to war, and I went off still playing and singing. 'Course by then I wasn't as much as I used to be, not without somebody to make it worth the while. You know what I mean?"

"Yeah," Greg nodded, not quite really knowing.

"I traveled around, and one time I come home, and there was this letter saying Jesse got killed in the war. Broke my heart, it truly did.

"They sent back what he had with him over there, and what it was is this old mouth fiddle and these clippings. Him carrying it around with him like that told me it meant something to him. That was my treasure, and when I give it to him he treated it just like that, a treasure. Ain't that something?"

"Yeah, I guess so," Greg said.

"You *guess* so?" Lemon Brown's voice rose an octave as he started to put his treasure back into the plastic. "Well, you got to guess 'cause you sure don't know nothing. Don't know enough to get home when it's raining."

"I guess . . . I mean, you're right."

"You O.K. for a youngster," the old man said as he tied the strings around his leg, "better than those scalawags[4] what come here looking for my treasure. That's for sure."

"You really think that treasure of yours was worth fighting for?" Greg asked. "Against a pipe?" (K)

"What else a man got 'cepting what he can pass on to his son, or his daughter, if she be his oldest?" Lemon Brown said. "For a big-headed boy you sure do ask the foolishest questions."

Lemon Brown got up after patting his rags in place and looked out the window again.

"Looks like they're gone. You get on out of here and get yourself home. I'll be watching from the window so you'll be all right."

Lemon Brown went down the stairs behind Greg. When they reached the front door the old man looked out first, saw the street was clear and told Greg to scoot on home.

"You sure you'll be O.K.?" Greg asked.

"Now didn't I tell you I was going to east St. Louis in the morning?" Lemon Brown asked. "Don't that sound O.K. to you?"

4. **scalawags** (skăl'ə-wăgz'): rascals.

Monitor Your Comprehension

(K) POINT OF VIEW

Reread lines 328–344. What does Greg think about Lemon Brown's treasure? Underline the details that tell you.

360   "Sure it does," Greg said. "Sure it does. And you take care of that treasure of yours."

"That I'll do," Lemon said, the wrinkles about his eyes suggesting a smile. "That I'll do."

The night had warmed and the rain had stopped, leaving puddles at the curbs. Greg didn't even want to think how late it was. He thought ahead of what his father would say and wondered if he should tell him about Lemon Brown. He thought about it until he reached his stoop, and decided against it. Lemon Brown would be O.K., Greg

370 thought, with his memories and his treasure.

Greg pushed the button over the bell marked Ridley, thought of the lecture he knew his father would give him, and smiled. ⬤

⬤ INFER CHARACTERS' MOTIVATIONS

Why does the thought of his father's lecture make Greg smile?

_____

_____

_____

_____

_____

_____

_____

_____

_____

_____

_____

_____

_____

_____

_____

Text Analysis: Third-Person Point of View

To examine the use of third-person point of view in "The Treasure of Lemon Brown," revisit the sections of the story listed below. Then complete the chart by answering the questions.

Lines 79–140: Greg encounters Lemon Brown.	**Whose feelings or actions are described?** *Greg's*
How does the character feel or act? *He is scared, but later decides Lemon is harmless and gently teases him.*	

Lines 179–287: Thugs enter the building and Lemon acts.	**Whose feelings/actions are described?** _____
How does the character feel/act? _____	

Lines 303–334: Lemon shows his treasure to Greg.	**Whose feelings/actions are described** _____
How does the character feel/act? _____	

Lines 358–374: Greg says goodbye to Lemon.	**Whose feelings/actions are described** _____
How does the character feel/act? _____	

How might the story have been different if readers knew more about the thoughts of other characters?

_____

_____

_____

Reading Skill: Infer Characters' Motivations

At the beginning of "The Treasure of Lemon Brown," Greg recalls conversations with his father. Make an inference about Greg's father's motivations based on what you read about the discussions.

Detail: Greg's father tells Greg that he had to leave school when he was 13. (line 6)
My Inference:
Detail: Greg's father remarks that Greg's desire to play basketball "must be some kind of a joke." (lines 22–25)
My Inference:
Detail: Greg's father has told him many times how hard he worked to pass the test to become a postal worker. (lines 63–66)
My Inference:

What do you CHERISH?

Review the list you made on page 70 of things you cherish. How has reading this story influenced your ideas about the things you value?

_____

_____

_____

Vocabulary Practice

Decide whether the words in each of the following pairs are synonyms (words that have the same meaning) or antonyms (words that have the opposite meaning)

1. tentatively/cautiously _____   **4.** ajar/open _____

2. ominous/haunting _____   **5.** tremor/stillness _____

3. gnarled/smooth _____   **6.** commence/stop _____

Academic Vocabulary in Writing

appropriate	assess	intelligence	motive	role

In a paragraph, **assess** the value of Lemon Brown's "treasure." What is it worth to him? What would it be worth to the boys who try to steal it from him? Use at least one Academic Vocabulary word in your response. Definitions of these words are on page 69.

_____

_____

_____

_____

Assessment Practice

DIRECTIONS Use "The Treasure of Lemon Brown" to answer questions 1–4.

1 You can tell that this story is told from a third-person limited point of view because the narrator—

- (A) is a character in the story
- (B) explains the thoughts and feelings of all of the characters
- (C) describes his or her own thoughts
- (D) tells what one character sees, thinks, and feels

2 The story's point of view helps you understand—

- (A) how Greg came to love basketball
- (B) that things that appear to be worthless may be invaluable
- (C) why the treasure is worth stealing
- (D) why family is important to Greg's father

3 In the old building, Greg's motivation for making a howling sound is to—

- (A) help frighten off the would-be robbers
- (B) express he feels lonely
- (C) alert Lemon Brown to danger
- (D) scare Lemon Brown

4 In what way are Lemon Brown and Greg's father alike?

- (A) They had careers as blues musicians when they were younger.
- (B) Their children do not care deeply about what they have done.
- (C) They want to set examples for their children.
- (D) They are disappointed in their children.

Rules of the Game
Short Story by Amy Tan

Can allies be OPPONENTS?

Family, friends, coaches—these are people who usually want the best for you. Then why can it feel like they're always giving you a hard time? Understanding people's good intentions can be challenging, and it may even feel like people who support you aren't on your side. In the story you're about to read, find out why a young girl sees her mother—who is her biggest fan—as her main opponent.

QUICKWRITE Think of one or two people in your life who want you to be the best you can be. Make a list of the ways in which their support helps you. Then list the ways that their support makes things harder for you.

Ways they help me:

Encourage me to work hard

_____

_____

_____

Ways they make things difficult:

_____

_____

_____

_____

_____

Text Analysis: First-Person Point of View

When a writer uses the **first-person point of view,** the narrator is a character in the story—usually the main character. Use the information in the graphic to help you identify characteristics of the first-person point of view.

```
                    A FIRST-PERSON NARRATOR
                    ↙                    ↘
DOES                              DOES NOT
• use the pronouns I and me       • know the inner thoughts
• describe people and events        and feelings of other
  as he or she experiences          characters
  them
```

As you read, notice how the narrator's **subjective,** or personal, observations affect your understanding of the story.

Reading Skill: Draw Conclusions

When you read, you often **draw conclusions,** or make logical judgments, about things that are not directly stated. To draw conclusions, you gather evidence from the text, consider your own experience and knowledge, and then combine all that information to make a judgment. Notes in the text will ask you to draw conclusions as you read.

Vocabulary in Context

Note: Words are listed in the order in which they appear in the story.

impart (ĭm-pärt´) *v.* to make known; reveal
*My aunt was happy to **impart** secrets to winning at chess.*

pungent (pŭn´jənt) *adj.* sharp or intense
*The **pungent** aromas of exotic foods cooking filled the kitchen.*

benefactor (bĕn´ə-făk´tər) *n.* a person who gives monetary or other aid
*An unknown **benefactor** made a generous donation to the club.*

tactic (tăk´tĭk) *n.* a maneuver to achieve a goal
*The team huddled to discuss what might be the best **tactic.***

adversary (ăd´vər-sĕr´ē) *n.* an opponent
*Tom was nervous about playing against a far superior **adversary.***

foresight (fôr´sīt) *n.* perception of the significance of events before they have occurred
*She wished he'd had the **foresight** to predict his next move.*

retort (rĭ-tôrt´) *n.* a quick, sharp, witty reply
*Tea answered Jack's simple question with a sarcastic **retort.***

malodorous (măl-ō´dər-əs) *adj.* having a bad odor
*The alley was **malodorous** from the trashcans full of rotting food.*

concession (kən-sĕsh´ən) *n.* the act of yielding or conceding
*My **concession** to let Jill move first may have cost me the game.*

ponder (pŏn´dər) *v.* to think or consider carefully
*There was no time to **ponder** our options—we had to move fast.*

SET A PURPOSE FOR READING

Read "Rules of the Game" to learn about an ongoing conflict between a young girl and her mother.

Rules of the Game

Short Story by
AMY TAN

BACKGROUND The game of chess is hundreds of years old, and competitive chess remains a popular pastime today. A special class of players strives for the title of grand master, which only the top 0.02% of tournament players worldwide earn. A player must accumulate at least 2,500 points in tournament play to be recognized as a grand master by the World Chess Federation.

I was six when my mother taught me the art of invisible strength. It was a strategy for winning arguments, respect from others, and eventually, though neither of us knew it at the time, chess games.

"Bite back your tongue," scolded my mother when I cried loudly, yanking her hand toward the store that sold bags of salted plums. At home, she said, "Wise guy, he not go against wind. In Chinese we say, Come from South, blow with wind—poom!—North will follow. Strongest 10 wind cannot be seen."

The next week I bit back my tongue as we entered the store with the forbidden candies. When my mother finished her shopping, she quietly plucked a small bag of plums from the rack and put it on the counter with the rest of the items. **Ⓐ**

My mother **imparted** her daily truths so she could help my older brothers and me rise above our circumstances. We lived in San Francisco's Chinatown. Like most of the other Chinese children who played in the back alleys of
20 restaurants and curio shops,[1] I didn't think we were poor. My bowl was always full, three five-course meals every day, beginning with a soup full of mysterious things I didn't want to know the names of.

We lived on Waverly Place, in a warm, clean, two-bedroom flat that sat above a small Chinese bakery specializing in steamed pastries and dim sum.[2] In the early morning, when the alley was still quiet, I could smell fragrant red beans as they were cooked down to a pasty sweetness. By daybreak, our flat was heavy with the odor
30 of fried sesame balls and sweet curried chicken crescents. From my bed, I would listen as my father got ready for work, then locked the door behind him, one-two-three clicks.

At the end of our two-block alley was a small sandlot playground with swings and slides well-shined down the middle with use. The play area was bordered by wood-slat benches where old-country people sat cracking roasted watermelon seeds with their golden teeth and scattering the husks to an impatient gathering of gurgling pigeons.
40 The best playground, however, was the dark alley itself. It was crammed with daily mysteries and adventures. My brothers and I would peer into the medicinal herb shop, watching old Li[3] dole out onto a stiff sheet of white paper

Ⓐ **POINT OF VIEW**
The narrator of this story is a Chinese-American girl. What has she suggested about her relationship with her mother so far?

_____

_____

_____

_____

_____

_____

_____

_____

_____

_____

_____

impart (ĭm-pürt') v. to make known; reveal

---

1. **curio shops:** shops that sell curious or unusual objects.
2. **dim sum:** small portions of a variety of Chinese foods and dumplings.
3. **Li** (lē).

pungent (pŭn′jənt) *adj.* sharp or intense

Ⓑ DRAW CONCLUSIONS
Why do you think the narrator's mother told the story of the careless girl who was crushed by a cab?

_____

_____

_____

_____

_____

_____

_____

_____

_____

_____

_____

_____

_____

_____

the right amount of insect shells, saffron-colored seeds, and **pungent** leaves for his ailing customers. It was said that he once cured a woman dying of an ancestral curse that had eluded the best of American doctors. Next to the pharmacy was a printer who specialized in gold-embossed wedding invitations and festive red banners.

50   Farther down the street was Ping Yuen[4] Fish Market. The front window displayed a tank crowded with doomed fish and turtles struggling to gain footing on the slimy green-tiled sides. A hand-written sign informed tourists, "Within this store, is all for food, not for pet." Inside, the butchers with their bloodstained white smocks deftly gutted the fish while customers cried out their orders and shouted, "Give me your freshest," to which the butchers always protested, "All are freshest." On less crowded market days, we would inspect the crates of live frogs and
60 crabs which we were warned not to poke, boxes of dried cuttlefish, and row upon row of iced prawns, squid, and slippery fish. The sanddabs made me shiver each time; their eyes lay on one flattened side and reminded me of my mother's story of a careless girl who ran into a crowded street and was crushed by a cab. "Was smash flat," reported my mother. **Ⓑ**

At the corner of the alley was Hong Sing's, a four-table café with a recessed stairwell in front that led to a door marked "Tradesmen." My brothers and I believed the bad
70 people emerged from this door at night. Tourists never went to Hong Sing's, since the menu was printed only in Chinese. A Caucasian man with a big camera once posed me and my playmates in front of the restaurant. He had us move to the side of the picture window so the photo would capture the roasted duck with its head dangling from a juice-covered rope. After he took the picture, I told him he should go into Hong Sing's and eat dinner. When he

4. **Ping Yuen** (bǐng yü′ěn).

smiled and asked me what they served, I shouted, "Guts
and duck's feet and octopus gizzards!" Then I ran off with
80 my friends, shrieking with laughter as we scampered across
the alley and hid in the entryway grotto[5] of the China Gem
Company, my heart pounding with hope that he would
chase us. **C**

My mother named me after the street that we lived on:
Waverly Place Jong, my official name for important
American documents. But my family called me Meimei,[6]
"Little Sister." I was the youngest, the only daughter. Each
morning before school, my mother would twist and yank
on my thick black hair until she had formed two tightly
90 wound pigtails. One day, as she struggled to weave a
hard-toothed comb through my disobedient hair, I had a
sly thought.

I asked her, "Ma, what is Chinese torture?" My mother
shook her head. A bobby pin was wedged between her lips.
She wetted her palm and smoothed the hair above my ear,
then pushed the pin in so that it nicked sharply against
my scalp.

"Who say this word?" she asked without a trace of
knowing how wicked I was being. I shrugged my shoulders
100 and said, "Some boy in my class said Chinese people do
Chinese torture."

"Chinese people do many things," she said simply.
"Chinese people do business, do medicine, do painting.
Not lazy like American people. We do torture. Best
torture." **D**

My older brother Vincent was the one who actually got
the chess set. We had gone to the annual Christmas party
held at the First Chinese Baptist Church at the end of the
alley. The missionary ladies had put together a Santa bag
110 of gifts donated by members of another church. None of

---

5. **grotto** (grŏt′ō): an artificial structure made to resemble a cave or cavern.
6. **Meimei** (mā′mā).

C POINT OF VIEW
Reread lines 67–83. What do the narrator's words and actions tell you about her attitude toward taking risks?

D DRAW CONCLUSIONS
Reread lines 87–105. How does Waverly feel about her mother fixing her hair? Underline evidence that supports your conclusion.

the gifts had names on them. There were separate sacks for boys and girls of different ages.

One of the Chinese parishioners had donned a Santa Claus costume and a stiff paper beard with cotton balls glued to it. I think the only children who thought he was the real thing were too young to know that Santa Claus was not Chinese. When my turn came up, the Santa man asked me how old I was. I thought it was a trick question; I was seven according to the American formula and eight by 120 the Chinese calendar. I said I was born on March 17, 1951. That seemed to satisfy him. He then solemnly asked if I had been a very, very good girl this year and did I believe in Jesus Christ and obey my parents. I knew the only answer to that. I nodded back with equal solemnity.

Having watched the other children opening their gifts, I already knew that the big gifts were not necessarily the nicest ones. One girl my age got a large coloring book of biblical characters, while a less greedy girl who selected a smaller box received a glass vial of lavender toilet water. 130 The sound of the box was also important. A ten-year-old boy had chosen a box that jangled when he shook it. It was a tin globe of the world with a slit for inserting money. He must have thought it was full of dimes and nickels, because when he saw that it had just ten pennies, his face fell with such undisguised disappointment that his mother slapped the side of his head and led him out of the church hall, apologizing to the crowd for her son who had such bad manners he couldn't appreciate such a fine gift. **PAUSE & REFLECT**

As I peered into the sack, I quickly fingered the 140 remaining presents, testing their weight, imagining what they contained. I chose a heavy, compact one that was wrapped in shiny silver foil and a red satin ribbon. It was a twelve-pack of Life Savers and I spent the rest of the party arranging and rearranging the candy tubes in the order of

PAUSE & REFLECT
What do you learn about Waverly from her observations of the other people at the Christmas party? Explain whether any of Waverly's observations are surprising.

_____

_____

_____

_____

_____

_____

_____

_____

_____

_____

my favorites. My brother Winston chose wisely as well. His present turned out to be a box of intricate plastic parts; the instructions on the box proclaimed that when they were properly assembled he would have an authentic miniature replica of a World War II submarine.

150   Vincent got the chess set, which would have been a very decent present to get at a church Christmas party, except it was obviously used and, as we discovered later, it was missing a black pawn and a white knight. My mother graciously thanked the unknown **benefactor**, saying, "Too good. Cost too much." At which point, an old lady with fine white, wispy hair nodded toward our family and said with a whistling whisper, "Merry, merry Christmas."

     When we got home, my mother told Vincent to throw the chess set away. "She not want it. We not want it,"
160 she said, tossing her head stiffly to the side with a tight, proud smile. My brothers had deaf ears. They were already lining up the chess pieces and reading from the dog-eared instruction book. **E**

     I watched Vincent and Winston play during Christmas week. The chessboard seemed to hold elaborate secrets waiting to be untangled. The chessmen were more powerful than Old Li's magic herbs that cured ancestral curses. And my brothers wore such serious faces that I was sure something was at stake that was greater than avoiding
170 the tradesmen's door to Hong Sing's.

     "Let me! Let me!" I begged between games when one brother or the other would sit back with a deep sigh of relief and victory, the other annoyed, unable to let go of the outcome. Vincent at first refused to let me play, but when I offered my Life Savers as replacements for the buttons that filled in for the missing pieces, he relented. He chose the flavors: wild cherry for the black pawn and peppermint for the white knight. Winner could eat both.

benefactor (bĕn′ə-făk′tər) *n.* a person who gives monetary or other aid

E **DRAW CONCLUSIONS**
Use the chart below to draw a conclusion about why Mrs. Jong wants Vincent to throw away his chess set? Identify **evidence** in lines 158–163 that tells what she thinks. Then combine this information with your own experience to draw a conclusion about why she feels this way.

Evidence

+

My Thoughts

↓

Conclusion

F DRAW CONCLUSIONS
Reread lines 189–198. What conclusion can you draw about Waverly from her questions about the rules of chess?

_____

_____

_____

_____

_____

_____

_____

_____

_____

_____

_____

_____

_____

_____

_____

_____

As our mother sprinkled flour and rolled out small
180 doughy circles for the steamed dumplings that would
be our dinner that night, Vincent explained the rules,
pointing to each piece. "You have sixteen pieces and so
do I. One king and queen, two bishops, two knights,
two castles, and eight pawns. The pawns can only move
forward one step, except on the first move. Then they
can move two. But they can only take men by moving
crossways like this, except in the beginning, when you can
move ahead and take another pawn."

"Why?" I asked as I moved my pawn. "Why can't they
190 move more steps?"

"Because they're pawns," he said.

"But why do they go crossways to take other men? Why
aren't there any women and children?"

"Why is the sky blue? Why must you always ask stupid
questions?" asked Vincent. "This is a game. These are the
rules. I didn't make them up. See. Here. In the book." He
jabbed a page with a pawn in his hand. "Pawn. P-A-W-N.
Pawn. Read it yourself." **F**

My mother patted the flour off her hands. "Let me see
200 book," she said quietly. She scanned the pages quickly, not
reading the foreign English symbols, seeming to search
deliberately for nothing in particular.

"This American rules," she concluded at last. "Every
time people come out from foreign country, must know
rules. You not know, judge say, Too bad, go back. They
not telling you why so you can use their way go forward.
They say, Don't know why, you find out yourself. But they
knowing all the time. Better you take it, find out why
yourself." She tossed her head back with a satisfied smile.

210 I found out about all the whys later. I read the rules and
looked up all the big words in a dictionary. I borrowed

books from the Chinatown library. I studied each chess piece, trying to absorb the power each contained.

I learned about opening moves and why it's important to control the center early on; the shortest distance between two points is straight down the middle. I learned about the middle game and why <u>tactics</u> between two <u>adversaries</u> are like clashing ideas; the one who plays better has the clearest plans for both attacking and getting out of traps. I learned

220 why it is essential in the endgame to have <u>foresight</u>, a mathematical understanding of all possible moves, and patience; all weaknesses and advantages become evident to a strong adversary and are obscured to a tiring opponent. I discovered that for the whole game one must gather invisible strengths and see the endgame before the game begins.

I also found out why I should never reveal "why" to others. A little knowledge withheld is a great advantage one should store for future use. That is the power of chess. It is

230 a game of secrets in which one must show and never tell.

I loved the secrets I found within the sixty-four black and white squares. I carefully drew a handmade chessboard and pinned it to the wall next to my bed, where at night I would stare for hours at imaginary battles. Soon I no longer lost any games or Life Savers, but I lost my adversaries. Winston and Vincent decided they were more interested in roaming the streets after school in their Hopalong Cassidy cowboy hats.

On a cold spring afternoon, while walking home from

240 school, I detoured through the playground at the end of our alley. I saw a group of old men, two seated across a folding table playing a game of chess, others smoking pipes, eating peanuts, and watching. I ran home and grabbed Vincent's chess set, which was bound in a cardboard box with rubber bands. I also carefully selected two prized rolls

tactic (tăk′tĭk) *n.* a maneuver to achieve a goal

adversary (ăd′vər-sĕr′ē) *n.* an opponent

foresight (fôr′sīt) *n.* perception of the significance of events before they have occurred

Why is having foresight an important skill for a chess player?

_____

_____

_____

_____

_____

retort (rĭ-tôrt') *n.* a quick, sharp, witty reply

G DRAW CONCLUSIONS
Reread lines 254–271. Why does Waverly start winning more chess games? Complete the chart by recording evidence that tells about her progress, your own thoughts, and a conclusion you've drawn.

Evidence

+

My Thoughts

↓

Conclusion

of Life Savers. I came back to the park and approached a man who was observing the game.

"Want to play?" I asked him. His face widened with surprise and he grinned as he looked at the box under
250 my arm.

"Little sister, been a long time since I play with dolls," he said, smiling benevolently. I quickly put the box down next to him on the bench and displayed my **retort**.

Lau Po,[7] as he allowed me to call him, turned out to be a much better player than my brothers. I lost many games and many Life Savers. But over the weeks, with each diminishing roll of candies, I added new secrets. Lau Po gave me the names. The Double Attack from the East and West Shores. Throwing Stones on the Drowning Man.
260 The Sudden Meeting of the Clan. The Surprise from the Sleeping Guard. The Humble Servant Who Kills the King. Sand in the Eyes of Advancing Forces. A Double Killing Without Blood.

There were also the fine points of chess etiquette. Keep captured men in neat rows, as well-tended prisoners. Never announce "Check"[8] with vanity, lest someone with an unseen sword slit your throat. Never hurl pieces into the sandbox after you have lost a game, because then you must find them again, by yourself, after apologizing to all
270 around you. By the end of the summer, Lau Po had taught me all he knew, and I had become a better chess player. **G**

A small weekend crowd of Chinese people and tourists would gather as I played and defeated my opponents one by one. My mother would join the crowds during these outdoor exhibition games.[9] She sat proudly on the bench, telling my admirers with proper Chinese humility, "Is luck."

---

7. **Lau Po** (lou bō).

8. **check:** a move in chess that places an opponent's king under direct attack.

9. **exhibition games:** public showings or demonstrations.

A man who watched me play in the park suggested that my mother allow me to play in local chess tournaments. My mother smiled graciously, an answer that meant nothing. I desperately wanted to go, but I bit back my tongue. I knew she would not let me play among strangers. So as we walked home I said in a small voice that I didn't want to play in the local tournament. They would have American rules. If I lost, I would bring shame on my family. Ⓗ

"Is shame you fall down nobody push you," said my mother.

During my first tournament, my mother sat with me in the front row as I waited for my turn. I frequently bounced my legs to unstick them from the cold metal seat of the folding chair. When my name was called, I leapt up. My mother unwrapped something in her lap. It was her *chang*, a small tablet of red jade which held the sun's fire. "Is luck," she whispered, and tucked it into my dress pocket. I turned to my opponent, a fifteen-year-old boy from Oakland. He looked at me, wrinkling his nose.

As I began to play, the boy disappeared, the color ran out of the room, and I saw only my white pieces and his black ones waiting on the other side. A light wind began blowing past my ears. It whispered secrets only I could hear.

"Blow from the South," it murmured. "The wind leaves no trail." I saw a clear path, the traps to avoid. The crowd rustled. "Shhh! Shhh!" said the corners of the room. The wind blew stronger. "Throw sand from the East to distract him." The knight came forward ready for the sacrifice. The wind hissed, louder and louder. "Blow, blow, blow. He cannot see. He is blind now. Make him lean away from the wind so he is easier to knock down."

Monitor Your Comprehension

Ⓗ **POINT OF VIEW**
Reread lines 278–286. Underline the strategy Waverly uses to get permission to play in the chess tournament. What does Waverly reveal about herself in these lines?

_____
_____
_____
_____
_____
_____
_____
_____
_____
_____
_____
_____
_____
_____

"Check," I said, as the wind roared with laughter. The wind died down to little puffs, my own breath.

My mother placed my first trophy next to a new plastic chess set that the neighborhood Tao society had given to me. As she wiped each piece with a soft cloth, she said, "Next time win more, lose less."

"Ma, it's not how many pieces you lose," I said. "Sometimes you need to lose pieces to get ahead."

"Better to lose less, see if you really need."

320   At the next tournament, I won again, but it was my mother who wore the triumphant grin.

"Lost eight pieces this time. Last time was eleven. What I tell you? Better off lose less!" I was annoyed, but I couldn't say anything. ❶

I attended more tournaments, each one farther away from home. I won all games, in all divisions. The Chinese bakery downstairs from our flat displayed my growing collection of trophies in its window, amidst the dust-covered cakes that were never picked up. The day after

330 I won an important regional tournament, the window encased a fresh sheet cake with whipped-cream frosting and red script saying, "Congratulations, Waverly Jong, Chinatown Chess Champion." Soon after that, a flower shop, headstone engraver, and funeral parlor offered to sponsor me in national tournaments. That's when my mother decided I no longer had to do the dishes. Winston and Vincent had to do my chores.

"Why does she get to play and we do all the work?" complained Vincent.

340   "Is new American rules," said my mother. "Meimei play, squeeze all her brains out for win chess. You play, worth squeeze towel."

By my ninth birthday, I was a national chess champion. I was still some 429 points away from grand-master status,

❶ DRAW CONCLUSIONS
Reread lines 313–324. Why does Waverly feel she can't correct her mother?

but I was touted as the Great American Hope, a child prodigy and a girl to boot. They ran a photo of me in *Life* magazine next to a quote in which Bobby Fischer[10] said, "There will never be a woman grand master." "Your move, Bobby," said the caption. PAUSE & REFLECT

350   The day they took the magazine picture I wore neatly plaited braids clipped with plastic barrettes trimmed with rhinestones. I was playing in a large high school auditorium that echoed with phlegmy coughs and the squeaky rubber knobs of chair legs sliding across freshly waxed wooden floors. Seated across from me was an American man, about the same age as Lau Po, maybe fifty. I remember that his sweaty brow seemed to weep at my every move. He wore a dark, **malodorous** suit. One of his pockets was stuffed with a great white kerchief on which he wiped his palm
360   before sweeping his hand over the chosen chess piece with great flourish.

       In my crisp pink-and-white dress with scratchy lace at the neck, one of two my mother had sewn for these special occasions, I would clasp my hands under my chin, the delicate points of my elbows poised lightly on the table in the manner my mother had shown me for posing for the press. I would swing my patent leather shoes back and forth like an impatient child riding on a school bus. Then I would pause, suck in my lips, twirl my chosen piece in
370   midair as if undecided, and then firmly plant it in its new threatening place, with a triumphant smile thrown back at my opponent for good measure.

       I no longer played in the alley of Waverly Place. I never visited the playground where the pigeons and old men gathered. I went to school, then directly home to learn new chess secrets, cleverly concealed advantages, more escape routes.

---

10. **Bobby Fischer:** a well-known chess player who, at 15, was the world's youngest grand master.

PAUSE & REFLECT
In lines 343–349, Waverly mentions that she was featured in *Life* magazine. How do you think she feels about the photo of herself and the magazine's challenge to Bobby Fischer?

_____

_____

_____

_____

_____

_____

_____

_____

_____

_____

_____

malodorous (măl-ō′dər-əs) *adj.* having a bad odor

❶ POINT OF VIEW
Reread lines 378–388. How does knowing only Waverly's point of view affect your impression of her mother?

_____

_____

_____

_____

_____

_____

_____

_____

_____

concession (kən-sĕsh′ən) *n.* the act of yielding or conceding

But I found it difficult to concentrate at home. My mother had a habit of standing over me while I plotted out my games. I think she thought of herself as my protective ally. Her lips would be sealed tight, and after each move I made, a soft "Hmmmmph" would escape from her nose.

"Ma, I can't practice when you stand there like that," I said one day. She retreated to the kitchen and made loud noises with the pots and pans. When the crashing stopped, I could see out of the corner of my eye that she was standing in the doorway. "Hmmmph!" Only this one came out of her tight throat. ❶

My parents made many **concessions** to allow me to practice. One time I complained that the bedroom I shared was so noisy that I couldn't think. Thereafter, my brothers slept in a bed in the living room facing the street. I said I couldn't finish my rice; my head didn't work right when my stomach was too full. I left the table with half-finished bowls and nobody complained. But there was one duty I couldn't avoid. I had to accompany my mother on Saturday market days when I had no tournament to play. My mother would proudly walk with me, visiting many shops, buying very little. "This my daughter Wave-ly Jong," she said to whoever looked her way.

One day, after we left a shop I said under my breath, "I wish you wouldn't do that, telling everybody I'm your daughter." My mother stopped walking. Crowds of people with heavy bags pushed past us on the sidewalk, bumping into first one shoulder, then another.

"Aiii-ya. So shame be with mother?" She grasped my hand even tighter as she glared at me.

I looked down. "It's not that, it's just so obvious. It's just so embarrassing."

"Embarrass you be my daughter?" Her voice was cracking with anger.

"That's not what I meant. That's not what I said."

"What you say?"

I knew it was a mistake to say anything more, but I heard my voice speaking. "Why do you have to use me to show off? If you want to show off, then why don't you learn to play chess." ⓚ

My mother's eyes turned into dangerous black slits. She had no words for me, just sharp silence.

420   I felt the wind rushing around my hot ears. I jerked my hand out of my mother's tight grasp and spun around, knocking into an old woman. Her bag of groceries spilled to the ground.

"Aii-ya! Stupid girl!" my mother and the woman cried. Oranges and tin cans careened down the sidewalk. As my mother stooped to help the old woman pick up the escaping food, I took off.

I raced down the street, dashing between people, not looking back as my mother screamed shrilly, "Meimei!

430 Meimei!" I fled down an alley, past dark curtained shops and merchants washing the grime off their windows. I sped into the sunlight, into a large street crowded with tourists examining trinkets and souvenirs. I ducked into another dark alley, down another street, up another alley. I ran until it hurt and I realized I had nowhere to go, that I was not running from anything. The alleys contained no escape routes.

My breath came out like angry smoke. It was cold. I sat down on an upturned plastic pail next to a stack of empty

440 boxes, cupping my chin with my hands, thinking hard. I imagined my mother, first walking briskly down one street or another looking for me, then giving up and returning home to await my arrival. After two hours, I stood up on creaking legs and slowly walked home.

ⓚ **DRAW CONCLUSIONS**
Reread lines 389–417. Why is Waverly embarrassed by her mother's behavior?

ponder (pŏn′dər) *v.* to think or consider carefully

PAUSE & REFLECT

Think about the story's ending. Would you prefer to know what happens next? Why or why not?

_____

_____

_____

_____

_____

_____

_____

_____

_____

_____

_____

_____

_____

_____

The alley was quiet and I could see the yellow lights shining from our flat like two tiger's eyes in the night. I climbed the sixteen steps to the door, advancing quietly up each so as not to make any warning sounds. I turned the knob; the door was locked. I heard a chair moving, quick 450 steps, the locks turning—click! click! click!—and then the door opened.

"About time you got home," said Vincent. "Boy, are you in trouble."

He slid back to the dinner table. On a platter were the remains of a large fish, its fleshy head still connected to bones swimming upstream in vain escape. Standing there waiting for my punishment, I heard my mother speak in a dry voice.

"We not concerning this girl. This girl not have 460 concerning for us."

Nobody looked at me. Bone chopsticks clinked against the insides of bowls being emptied into hungry mouths.

I walked into my room, closed the door, and lay down on my bed. The room was dark, the ceiling filled with shadows from the dinnertime lights of neighboring flats.

In my head, I saw a chessboard with sixty-four black and white squares. Opposite me was my opponent, two angry black slits. She wore a triumphant smile. "Strongest wind cannot be seen," she said.

470 Her black men advanced across the plane, slowly marching to each successive level as a single unit. My white pieces screamed as they scurried and fell off the board one by one. As her men drew closer to my edge, I felt myself growing light. I rose up into the air and flew out the window. Higher and higher, above the alley, over the tops of tiled roofs, where I was gathered up by the wind and pushed up toward the night sky until everything below me disappeared and I was alone.

I closed my eyes and **pondered** my next move.

PAUSE & REFLECT

Text Analysis: First-Person Point of View

The use of first-person point of view in "Rules of the Game" shapes the reader's impressions of Mrs. Jong. Readers know only what her daughter Waverly chooses to share. Read the first entry in the chart below. Then revisit the story and identify two more scenes in which Waverly affects your impression of Mrs. Jong.

Lines 150–163: *Vincent gets a chess set at the church Christmas party.*
What the reader learns about Mrs. Jong: *She thanks the woman graciously, but at home, she wants to throw the set away. Waverly shows the reader that her mother is complicated. She acts one way in a public setting, but at home, she is proud and opinionated.*

Lines:
What the reader learns about Mrs. Jong:

Lines:
What the reader learns about Mrs. Jong:

How would the story be different if you knew what Waverly's mother was thinking? Explain your ideas.

_____

_____

_____

_____

Reading Skill: Draw Conclusions

List some of the positive ways Waverly's mother supports her. Next, list things about Mrs. Jong that Waverly sees as negative or causing conflict. Then use these ideas and your own knowledge and experiences to draw a conclusion about why Waverly views her mother as her opponent.

Positives	Negatives
• teaches Waverly the "art of invisible strength" • •	• • •

My conclusion:

Can allies be OPPONENTS?

Do you think that Waverly and her mother will soon end their quarrel and become allies again? Why or why not?

_____

_____

_____

Vocabulary Practice

Write the letter of the item you might associate with each word.

_____ concession	**A.** think long and carefully
_____ tactic	**B.** a sharp scent
_____ impart	**C.** a smart move
_____ foresight	**D.** planning ahead
_____ retort	**E.** giving in
_____ pungent	**F.** share wisdom
_____ ponder	**G.** an unpleasant smell
_____ adversary	**H.** a generous person
_____ malodorous	**I.** a sharp reply
_____ benefactor	**J.** an opponent

Academic Vocabulary in Speaking

| appropriate | assess | intelligence | motive | role |

TURN AND TALK Is it **appropriate** for Mrs. Jong to show off her daughter in public? Explain why or why not in a discussion with your classmates. Use at least one Academic Vocabulary word in your response. Definitions of these terms are listed on page 69.

Assessment Practice

DIRECTIONS Use "Rules of the Game" to answer questions 1–6.

1 You can tell that this story is told from a first-person point of view because the narrator—

　Ⓐ is a minor character in the story who reveals some information

　Ⓑ tells about the thoughts and feelings of all of the characters

　Ⓒ describes people and events as she experiences them

　Ⓓ is outside the story and tells what one character sees, thinks, and feels

2 Which character has the strongest influence on Waverly?

　Ⓐ her brother Vincent

　Ⓑ her mother

　Ⓒ her father

　Ⓓ the older chess player in the park

3 Waverly gets permission from her mother to play in local chess tournaments by —

　Ⓐ explaining why she enjoys chess

　Ⓑ running away

　Ⓒ teaching her the rules of the game

　Ⓓ telling her that she does not want to enter them

4 Which words best describe the way Waverly's mother makes her feel?

　Ⓐ frustrated and pressured

　Ⓑ secure and clever

　Ⓒ competent and optimistic

　Ⓓ sad and ashamed

5 Why does Waverly run away at the market?

　Ⓐ She is flustered by the community's support for her.

　Ⓑ She is angry that her mother does not support her.

　Ⓒ She thinks she should be at a tournament.

　Ⓓ She is embarrassed by the way her mother shows her off.

6 Which best describes the story's ending?

　Ⓐ Waverly comes to appreciate that her mother is right and she is wrong.

　Ⓑ The conflict between Waverly and her mother remains unresolved.

　Ⓒ Waverly's family insists that she must change her ways.

　Ⓓ Waverly's mother realizes that she does not always support her in a positive way.

The Medicine Bag
Short Story by **Virginia Driving Hawk Sneve**

Who Are You Today, María?
Vignette by **Judith Ortiz Cofer**

Parts of My Identity

1. _____
   _____
   _____

2. _____
   _____
   _____

3. _____
   _____
   _____

4. _____
   _____
   _____

5. _____
   _____
   _____

What shows others WHO we are?

Our clothes, our families, and the cultural traditions we follow are all parts of our identity, the way we see ourselves and how we want others to see us. In the stories you're about to read, two young people must decide which parts of their identities they want to share with the world.

DISCUSS Make a list of essential parts of your identity, such as important beliefs and meaningful activities. How do you reflect your beliefs in your behavior? Share your ideas with a partner.

Text Analysis: Central Character

Short stories usually focus on one **central character.** The plot and central conflict of the story generally revolve around this person. Ask yourself questions like these to get to know the central character of a story.

- Where does the character live? How does that place affect him or her?
- With whom does the character have important relationships?
- What conflicts develop in these relationships?
- What is the character's social background or cultural heritage?
- How does the character feel about who he or she is?

Keep these questions in mind as you read "The Medicine Bag" and "Who Are You Today, María?"

Reading Strategy: Set a Purpose for Reading

In this lesson, your **purpose** for reading is to compare two central characters. As you read, notes in the side column will ask you to record ideas in a chart similar to the one below.

	Martin	María
How does the character's environment affect him or her?	*doesn't think his grandfather fits in.*	
What is his or her relationship with grandparent like?		
What is his or her attitude toward cultural heritage?		

Vocabulary in Context

Note: Words are listed in the order in which they appear in the selections.

authentic (ô-thĕn′tĭk) *adj.* having a verifiable origin; not counterfeit
*The factory-made trinkets in the gift shop are not **authentic**.*

commotion (kə-mō′shən) *n.* a disturbance
*The **commotion** on the crowded bus made it hard to think.*

unseemly (ŭn-sēm′lē) *adj.* inappropriate
*His behavior appears **unseemly** to one unfamiliar with the culture.*

descendant (dĭ-sĕn′dənt) *n.* a person whose descent can be traced to an individual or group
***Descendants** of Sioux tribes now live throughout the country.*

sheepishly (shē′pĭsh-lē) *adv.* meekly; with embarrassment
*The boy **sheepishly** apologized to his classmates.*

conspiracy (kən-spîr′ə-sē) *n.* an agreement to perform together an illegal or wrongful act
*They formed a **conspiracy** to overthrow the government.*

SET A PURPOSE FOR READING

Read "The Medicine Bag" to discover what a boy learns about his cultural identity.

The Medicine Bag

Short Story by
VIRGINIA DRIVING HAWK SNEVE

BACKGROUND The passage into adulthood in some cultures and families is marked by a ritual such as the Jewish bar mitzvah or bat mitzvah ceremony or the Mexican American quinceañera. This is a story about a similar ritual for young people of a Native American background.

My kid sister Cheryl and I always bragged about our Sioux grandpa, Joe Iron Shell. Our friends, who had always lived in the city and only knew about Indians from movies and TV, were impressed by our stories. Maybe we exaggerated and made Grandpa and the reservation sound glamorous, but when we'd return home to Iowa after our yearly summer visit to Grandpa we always had some exciting tale to tell.

We always had some **authentic** Sioux article to show
10 our listeners. One year Cheryl had new moccasins that Grandpa had made. On another visit he gave me a small,

authentic (ô-thĕn′tĭk) *adj.* having a verifiable origin; not counterfeit

round, flat, rawhide drum which was decorated with
a painting of a warrior riding a horse. He taught me a
real Sioux chant to sing while I beat the drum with a
leather-covered stick that had a feather on the end. Man,
that really made an impression.

We never showed our friends Grandpa's picture. Not
that we were ashamed of him, but because we knew that
the glamorous tales we told didn't go with the real thing.
20 Our friends would have laughed at the picture, because
Grandpa wasn't tall and stately like TV Indians. His hair
wasn't in braids, but hung in stringy, gray strands on
his neck and he was old. He was our great-grandfather,
and he didn't live in a tipi, but all by himself in a part
log, part tar-paper shack on the Rosebud Reservation in
South Dakota. So when Grandpa came to visit us, I was so
ashamed and embarrassed I could've died. **Ⓐ**

There are a lot of yippy poodles and other fancy little
dogs in our neighborhood, but they usually barked singly
30 at the mailman from the safety of their own yards. Now it
sounded as if a whole pack of mutts were barking together
in one place. **Ⓑ**

I got up and walked to the curb to see what the
commotion was. About a block away I saw a crowd of little
kids yelling, with the dogs yipping and growling around
someone who was walking down the middle of the street.

I watched the group as it slowly came closer and saw
that in the center of the strange procession was a man
wearing a tall black hat. He'd pause now and then to
40 peer at something in his hand and then at the houses on
either side of the street. I felt cold and hot at the same
time as I recognized the man. "Oh, no!" I whispered. "It's
Grandpa!"

Ⓐ CENTRAL CHARACTER
Pause at line 27. What have you
learned about the narrator's
relationship with his grandfather
so far?

_____

_____

_____

_____

_____

_____

_____

_____

Ⓑ CENTRAL CHARACTER
Underline the details in
lines 28–32 that tell you
where the narrator lives.

commotion (kə-mō′shən) *n.* a
disturbance

I stood on the curb, unable to move even though I wanted to run and hide. Then I got mad when I saw how the yippy dogs were growling and nipping at the old man's baggy pant legs and how wearily he poked them away with his cane. "Stupid mutts," I said as I ran to rescue Grandpa.

50 When I kicked and hollered at the dogs to get away, they put their tails between their legs and scattered. The kids ran to the curb where they watched me and the old man.

"Grandpa," I said and felt pretty dumb when my voice cracked. I reached for his beat-up old tin suitcase, which was tied shut with a rope. But he set it down right in the street and shook my hand.

"*Hau*,[1] *Takoza*, Grandchild," he greeted me formally in Sioux.

All I could do was stand there with the whole neighborhood watching and shake the hand of the leather-
60 brown old man. I saw how his gray hair straggled from under his big black hat, which had a drooping feather in its crown. His rumpled black suit hung like a sack over his stooped frame. As he shook my hand, his coat fell open to expose a bright-red, satin shirt with a beaded bolo tie under the collar. His getup wasn't out of place on the reservation, but it sure was here, and I wanted to sink right through the pavement. **C**

"Hi," I muttered with my head down. I tried to pull my hand away when I felt his bony hand trembling, and
70 looked up to see fatigue in his face. I felt like crying. I couldn't think of anything to say so I picked up Grandpa's suitcase, took his arm, and guided him up the driveway to our house.

Mom was standing on the steps. I don't know how long she'd been watching, but her hand was over her mouth and

C CENTRAL CHARACTER
How does Martin feel about his grandfather's outfit? Explain.

_____

_____

_____

_____

_____

_____

_____

_____

_____

_____

_____

_____

_____

1. *Hau Sioux:* hello.

she looked as if she couldn't believe what she saw. Then she ran to us.

"Grandpa," she gasped. "How in the world did you get here?"

80 She checked her move to embrace Grandpa and I remembered that such a display of affection is **unseemly** to the Sioux and would embarrass him.

"*Hau*, Marie," he said as he shook Mom's hand. She smiled and took his other arm.

As we supported him up the steps the door banged open and Cheryl came bursting out of the house. She was all smiles and was so obviously glad to see Grandpa that I was ashamed of how I felt. ⓓ

"Grandpa!" she yelled happily. "You came to see us!"

90 Grandpa smiled and Mom and I let go of him as he stretched out his arms to my 10-year-old sister, who was still young enough to be hugged.

"*Wicincala*,[2] little girl," he greeted her and then collapsed.

He had fainted. Mom and I carried him into her sewing room, where we had a spare bed.

After we had Grandpa on the bed Mom stood there helplessly patting his shoulder.

"Shouldn't we call the doctor, Mom?" I suggested, since 100 she didn't seem to know what to do.

"Yes," she agreed with a sigh. "You make Grandpa comfortable, Martin."

I reluctantly moved to the bed. I knew Grandpa wouldn't want to have Mom undress him, but I didn't want to, either. He was so skinny and frail that his coat slipped off easily. When I loosened his tie and opened his shirt collar, I felt a small leather pouch that hung from a thong around his neck. I left it alone and moved to remove his

---

2. *Wicincala* Sioux: girl.

unseemly (ŭn-sēm′lē) *adj.* inappropriate

ⓓ **SET A PURPOSE FOR READING**
Reread lines 68–88. Then complete the chart below to answer the question about Martin. Cite details in the text in your answer.

Martin
What is his relationship with his grandfather like?

↓

boots. The scuffed old cowboy boots were tight and he
110 moaned as I put pressure on his legs to jerk them off.

I put the boots on the floor and saw why they fit so
tight. Each one was stuffed with money. I looked at the
bills that lined the boots and started to ask about them, but
Grandpa's eyes were closed again.

Mom came back with a basin of water. "The doctor
thinks Grandpa is suffering from heat exhaustion," she
explained as she bathed Grandpa's face. Mom gave a big
sigh, "*Oh hinh*, Martin. How do you suppose he got here?"

We found out after the doctor's visit. Grandpa was
120 angrily sitting up in bed while Mom tried to feed him
some soup.

"Tonight you let Marie feed you, Grandpa," spoke my
dad, who had gotten home from work just as the doctor
was leaving. "You're not really sick," he said as he gently
pushed Grandpa back against the pillows. "The doctor said
you just got too tired and hot after your long trip."

Grandpa relaxed, and between sips of soup, he told us of
his journey. Soon after our visit to him Grandpa decided
that he would like to see where his only living **descendants**
130 lived and what our home was like. Besides, he admitted
sheepishly, he was lonesome after we left.

I knew everybody felt as guilty as I did—especially
Mom. Mom was all Grandpa had left. So even after she
married my dad, who's a white man and teaches in the
college in our city, and after Cheryl and I were born,
Mom made sure that every summer we spent a week with
Grandpa.

I never thought that Grandpa would be lonely after our
visits, and none of us noticed how old and weak he had
140 become. But Grandpa knew and so he came to us. He had
ridden on buses for two and a half days. When he arrived

descendant (dĭ-sĕn'dənt) *n.* a
person whose descent can be
traced to an individual or group

sheepishly (shē'pĭsh-lē) *adv.*
meekly; with embarrassment

Why does Grandpa **sheepishly**
say that he is lonely?

_____

_____

_____

_____

_____

in the city, tired and stiff from sitting for so long, he set out, walking, to find us.

He had stopped to rest on the steps of some building downtown and a policeman found him. The cop, according to Grandpa, was a good man who took him to the bus stop and waited until the bus came and told the driver to let Grandpa out at Bell View Drive. After Grandpa got off the bus, he started walking again. But

150 he couldn't see the house numbers on the other side when he walked on the sidewalk so he walked in the middle of the street. That's when all the little kids and dogs followed him.

I knew everybody felt as bad as I did. Yet I was proud of this 86-year-old man, who had never been away from the reservation, having the courage to travel so far alone. **E**

"You found the money in my boots?" he asked Mom.

"Martin did," she answered, and roused herself to scold. "Grandpa, you shouldn't have carried so much money.

160 What if someone had stolen it from you?"

Grandpa laughed. "I would've known if anyone tried to take the boots off my feet. The money is what I've saved for a long time—a hundred dollars—for my funeral. But you take it now to buy groceries so that I won't be a burden to you while I am here."

"That won't be necessary, Grandpa," Dad said. "We are honored to have you with us and you will never be a burden. I am only sorry that we never thought to bring you home with us this summer and spare you the discomfort of

170 a long trip."

Grandpa was pleased. "Thank you," he answered. "But do not feel bad that you didn't bring me with you for I would not have come then. It was not time." He said this in such a way that no one could argue with him. To Grandpa

E CENTRAL CHARACTER
How has the story of Grandpa's journey affected the way Martin sees him?

_____

_____

_____

_____

_____

_____

_____

_____

_____

_____

and the Sioux, he once told me, a thing would be done when it was the right time to do it and that's the way it was.

"Also," Grandpa went on, looking at me, "I have come because it is soon time for Martin to have the medicine bag."

We all knew what that meant. Grandpa thought he was going to die and he had to follow the tradition of his family to pass the medicine bag, along with its history, to the oldest male child.

"Even though the boy," he said still looking at me, "bears a white man's name, the medicine bag will be his."

I didn't know what to say. I had the same hot and cold feeling that I had when I first saw Grandpa in the street. The medicine bag was the dirty leather pouch I had found around his neck. "I could never wear such a thing," I almost said aloud. I thought of having my friends see it in gym class, at the swimming pool, and could imagine the smart things they would say. But I just swallowed hard and took a step toward the bed. I knew I would have to take it. **F**

But Grandpa was tired. "Not now, Martin," he said, waving his hand in dismissal, "it is not time. Now I will sleep."

So that's how Grandpa came to be with us for two months. My friends kept asking to come see the old man, but I put them off. I told myself that I didn't want them laughing at Grandpa. But even as I made excuses I knew it wasn't Grandpa that I was afraid they'd laugh at.

Nothing bothered Cheryl about bringing her friends to see Grandpa. Every day after school started there'd be a crew of giggling little girls or round-eyed little boys crowded around the old man on the patio, where he'd gotten in the habit of sitting every afternoon.

Grandpa would smile in his gentle way and patiently answer their questions, or he'd tell them stories of brave
210 warriors, ghosts, animals, and the kids listened in awed silence. Those little guys thought Grandpa was great.

Finally, one day after school, my friends came home with me because nothing I said stopped them. "We're going to see the great Indian of Bell View Drive," said Hank, who was supposed to be my best friend. "My brother has seen him three times so he oughta be well enough to see us." **G**

When we got to my house Grandpa was sitting on the patio. He had on his red shirt, but today he also wore a
220 fringed leather vest that was decorated with beads. Instead of his usual cowboy boots he had solidly beaded moccasins on his feet that stuck out of his black trousers. Of course, he had his old black hat on—he was seldom without it. But it had been brushed and the feather in the beaded headband was proudly erect, its tip a brighter white. His hair lay in silver strands over the red shirt collar.

I stared just as my friends did and I heard one of them murmur, "Wow!"

Grandpa looked up and when his eyes met mine they
230 twinkled as if he were laughing inside. He nodded to me and my face got all hot. I could tell that he had known all along I was afraid he'd embarrass me in front of my friends.

"*Hau, hoksilas,* boys," he greeted and held out his hand.

My buddies passed in a single file and shook his hand as I introduced them. They were so polite I almost laughed. "How, there, Grandpa," and even a "How-do-you-do, sir."

"You look fine, Grandpa," I said as the guys sat on the lawn chairs or on the patio floor.

G CENTRAL CHARACTER
Why is Martin concerned about bringing his friends to meet his grandfather?

H CENTRAL CHARACTER
Reread lines 240–255. Why is
Martin proud of his grandfather?

_____

_____

_____

_____

_____

_____

_____

_____

I CENTRAL CHARACTER
Reread 259–268. How has
Martin's attitude about the
medicine bag changed?

_____

_____

_____

_____

_____

_____

_____

_____

240 "*Hanh*, yes," he agreed. "When I woke up this morning it seemed the right time to dress in the good clothes. I knew that my grandson would be bringing his friends."

"You guys want some lemonade or something?" I offered. No one answered. They were listening to Grandpa as he started telling how he'd killed the deer from which his vest was made.

Grandpa did most of the talking while my friends were there. I was so proud of him and amazed at how respectfully quiet my buddies were. Mom had to chase 250 them home at supper time. As they left they shook Grandpa's hand again and said to me:

"Martin, he's really great!"

"Yeah, man! Don't blame you for keeping him to yourself."

"Can we come back?" **H**

But after they left, Mom said, "No more visitors for a while, Martin. Grandpa won't admit it, but his strength hasn't returned. He likes having company, but it tires him."

That evening Grandpa called me to his room before he 260 went to sleep. "Tomorrow," he said, "when you come home, it will be time to give you the medicine bag."

I felt a hard squeeze from where my heart is supposed to be and was scared, but I answered, "OK, Grandpa."

All night I had weird dreams about thunder and lightning on a high hill. From a distance I heard the slow beat of a drum. When I woke up in the morning I felt as if I hadn't slept at all. At school it seemed as if the day would never end and, when it finally did, I ran home. **I**

Grandpa was in his room, sitting on the bed. The shades 270 were down and the place was dim and cool. I sat on the floor in front of Grandpa, but he didn't even look at me. After what seemed a long time he spoke.

"I sent your mother and sister away. What you will hear today is only for a man's ears. What you will receive is only for a man's hands." He fell silent and I felt shivers down my back.

"My father in his early manhood," Grandpa began, "made a vision quest to find a spirit guide for his life. You cannot understand how it was in that time, when the great
280 Teton Sioux were first made to stay on the reservation. There was a strong need for guidance from *Wakantanka,* the Great Spirit. But too many of the young men were filled with despair and hatred. They thought it was hopeless to search for a vision when the glorious life was gone and only the hated confines of a reservation lay ahead. But my father held to the old ways.

"He carefully prepared for his quest with a purifying sweat bath and then he went alone to a high butte[3] top to fast and pray. After three days he received his sacred
290 dream—in which he found, after long searching, the white man's iron. He did not understand his vision of finding something belonging to the white people, for in that time they were the enemy. When he came down from the butte to cleanse himself at the stream below, he found the remains of a campfire and the broken shell of an iron kettle. This was a sign which reinforced his dream. He took a piece of the iron for his medicine bag, which he had made of elk skin years before, to prepare for his quest.

"He returned to his village, where he told his dream to
300 the wise old men of the tribe. They gave him the name *Iron Shell,* but neither did they understand the meaning of the dream. This first Iron Shell kept the piece of iron with him at all times and believed it gave him protection from the evils of those unhappy days. **PAUSE & REFLECT**

---

3. **butte** (byo͞ot): an abruptly rising hill with sloping sides and a flat top.

⬤ CENTRAL CHARACTER
Reread lines 305–328. What
is Martin learning about his
heritage?

_____

_____

_____

_____

_____

_____

_____

_____

_____

_____

_____

_____

_____

_____

_____

_____

_____

_____

_____

_____

_____

"Then a terrible thing happened to Iron Shell. He and
several other young men were taken from their homes by
the soldiers and sent far away to a white man's boarding
school. He was angry and lonesome for his parents and the
young girl he had wed before he was taken away. At first
310 Iron Shell resisted the teachers' attempts to change him and
he did not try to learn. One day it was his turn to work in
the school's blacksmith shop. As he walked into the place
he knew that his medicine had brought him there to learn
and work with the white man's iron.

"Iron Shell became a blacksmith and worked at the
trade when he returned to the reservation. All of his life he
treasured the medicine bag. When he was old, and I was
a man, he gave it to me, for no one made the vision quest
any more."

320 Grandpa quit talking and I stared in disbelief as he
covered his face with his hands. His shoulders were shaking
with quiet sobs and I looked away until he began to
speak again.

"I kept the bag until my son, your mother's father, was
a man and had to leave us to fight in the war across the
ocean. I gave him the bag, for I believed it would protect
him in battle, but he did not take it with him. He was ·
afraid that he would lose it. He died in a faraway place." **⬤**

Again Grandpa was still and I felt his grief around me.

330 "My son," he went on after clearing his throat, "had only
a daughter and it is not proper for her to know of these
things."

He unbuttoned his shirt, pulled out the leather pouch,
and lifted it over his head. He held it in his hand, turning
it over and over as if memorizing how it looked.

"In the bag," he said as he opened it and removed
two objects, "is the broken shell of the iron kettle, a pebble

from the butte, and a piece of the sacred sage." He held the pouch upside down and dust drifted down.

340   "After the bag is yours you must put a piece of prairie sage within and never open it again until you pass it on to your son." He replaced the pebble and the piece of iron and tied the bag.

I stood up, somehow knowing I should. Grandpa slowly rose from the bed and stood upright in front of me holding the bag before my face. I closed my eyes and waited for him to slip it over my head. But he spoke.

"No, you need not wear it." He placed the soft leather bag in my right hand and closed my other hand over it. "It
350 would not be right to wear it in this time and place where no one will understand. Put it safely away until you are again on the reservation. Wear it then, when you replace the sacred sage."

Grandpa turned and sat again on the bed. Wearily he leaned his head against the pillow. "Go," he said. "I will sleep now."

"Thank you, Grandpa," I said softly and left with the bag in my hands.

That night Mom and Dad took Grandpa to the hospital.
360 Two weeks later I stood alone on the lonely prairie of the reservation and put the sacred sage in my medicine bag. **K**

K SET A PURPOSE FOR READING
Why does Martin return to the reservation? How has his attitude toward his cultural heritage changed?

Who Are You Today, María?

Vignette by

JUDITH ORTIZ COFER

BACKGROUND Judith Ortiz Cofer was born
in Puerto Rico, but she spent much of her
childhood in New Jersey after her father
joined the U.S. Navy. When her father was
at sea, the family returned to Puerto Rico for
extended visits with Cofer's grandfather.

Ⓛ CENTRAL CHARACTER
Which of María's relationships
do you learn about in lines 1–9?
Which relationship do you think
will be most important?

_____

_____

_____

_____

_____

_____

_____

_____

Abuela[1] knocks on my bedroom door. She has come to
my room this morning to watch me choose my outfit
for Who You Are Day at school. This is a day when we are
allowed to dress in clothes that we think tell the world who
we really are. (Within reason, our principal warned—no
extremes will be tolerated. I hope that her definition of the
word *extreme* is the same as my friend Whoopee's. Nothing
that she will put on this morning has ever been seen on this
planet, much less at school.) Ⓛ

10 Abuela makes herself comfortable on my bed as I put on
my costume of myself made up of pieces of my life. I thought
about my Who You Are Day outfit a lot. Mr. Golden told
us in English class to think about our choices: are you going
to walk around as a joke or as a poem? I have a suspicion
that our teachers have allowed us this chance to dress up as
ourselves for a reason. Our school is already a united nations,
a carnival, and a parade all at once. There are students
from dozens of different countries, and we do not always
get along. Most of us are too shy to talk to others outside

---

1. **Abuela** (ä-bwä'lä) *Spanish:* grandmother.

20 our little circles, and so misunderstandings come up. The principal has tried almost everything. The Who You Are Day is another of her crazy ideas to get us to communicate. In each of my classes, the teacher said, let us know something about what has made you who you are by what you wear to school tomorrow. It all sounds like a **conspiracy** to me. But I like dressing up so I do not complain like the boys have been doing. Most of them hate the idea! ⓜ

Abuela looks at my choices hanging on the door and shakes her head, smiling, like she did when we went to 30 see *Cats*. It is a smile that says, I do not understand, but if it is important to María, I will bear it the best I can. She is elegant even at 7:00 A.M. in her embroidered silk robe and red velvet slippers. She has wrapped a shawl over her shoulders because she is always cold in our cueva,[2] as she calls the apartment. The shawl was handmade by her mother and it is Abuela's most prized possession. As a little girl, I liked to put it over my head because the pattern of sequins made a night sky full of stars and because it smelled like Abuela. ⓝ

Abuela sips from her cup of café con leche[3] as she 40 watches me.

I feel a little strange about being in my underwear in front of her and go in my closet with my choices, which are:

My mother's red skirt that she wore when she had a part in a musical play on the Island. I have played dress-up with it since I was five years old, but it finally fits me perfectly. It is the kind of skirt that opens like an umbrella when you turn in circles.

A top I sewed together from an old sari[4] Uma's mother was going to throw away. It is turquoise blue with silver edges.

50 And finally, over my sari, I will wear my father's sharkskin[5] suit jacket—it's big on me but I can roll up the

---

2. *cueva* (kwä'vä) *Spanish:* cave.
3. **café con leche** (kă-fä kŏn lĕch'ā) *Spanish:* coffee with milk.
4. **sari** (sä'rē): a traditional Indian women's garment.
5. **sharkskin:** a synthetic fabric with a smooth, shiny surface.

conspiracy (kən-spîr'ə-sē) *n.* an agreement to perform together an illegal or wrongful act

ⓜ **CENTRAL CHARACTER**
Reread lines 10–27. What have you learned about where María lives?

_____

_____

_____

_____

_____

_____

ⓝ **CENTRAL CHARACTER**
What can you infer about María's relationship with her grandmother?

_____

_____

_____

_____

_____

_____

_____

_____

Ⓟ SET A PURPOSE FOR READING
Reread lines 70–79. What is María's attitude toward her grandmother's Puerto Rican customs and clothing?

_____

_____

_____

_____

_____

_____

_____

_____

_____

_____

_____

_____

_____

_____

_____

_____

_____

_____

_____

sleeves. It is what he likes to wear when he sings at rent parties. Under the light, it changes colors and seems to come alive as the design shifts and moves. Papi says it is great for dancing; you don't even need a partner.

And finally, tall platform shoes we found buried deep in Whoopee's closet, circa 1974, she told me. Whoopee collects antique shoes to go with her science fiction outfits. It is a fashion statement; she will tell anyone who asks. No 60 one knows what the statement means, and that is just fine with Whoopee.

When I part the clothes in my closet and come out like an actor in a play, Abuela's eyes open wide. Before she can say anything, I point to each piece of my outfit and say a name: Mami, Papi, Uma, and Whoopee.

Abuela's face changes as she begins to understand the meaning of my fashion statement.

"Ahora sé quién eres, María, y quién puedes ser, si quieres. Ven acá, mi amor."

70 Abuela says that she knows who I am and who I may be if I choose. I have heard those words before but I don't remember when or where. Abuela embraces me and kisses my face several times. This is a Puerto Rican thing. It goes on for a while. I close my eyes to wait it out and I suddenly inhale a familiar scent. When I open my eyes, I see a starry sky. Abuela has put her shawl over my head.

"Algo mío para tu día de ser quien eres, mi hija," she tells me. *Something of mine for your day of being who you are.* She is letting me borrow her mother's beautiful shawl! Ⓟ

80 All day at school, I feel elegant. Whenever anyone tries to make fun of my costume, I think of the words my grandmother quoted to me: *I know who you are and who you may be if you choose.* And when I go into Mr. Golden's class and his eyes ask me, *Who are you today, María?* I will say by the way I walk in, head held high, that today I am a poem.

Text Analysis: Central Character

Use the charts below to analyze Martin's relationship with Grandpa and María's relationship with Abuela. First explain how each relationship changes over the course of the story. Use details from the text in your response. Then answer the question that follows.

Martin's relationship with Grandpa	
In the beginning of the story:	**At the end of the story:**

María's relationship with Abuela	
In the beginning of the story:	**At the end of the story:**

How is Martin's relationship with his grandfather similar to María's relationship with Abuela. How is it different?

_____

_____

_____

_____

_____

_____

Reading Strategy: Set a Purpose for Reading

How does each character's attitude toward cultural heritage change over the course of the story? Support your response with details from the text.

_____

_____

_____

_____

_____

_____

_____

_____

_____

What shows others WHO we are?

Think about your relationships with family members. How has reading these two stories influenced your ideas about your identity?

_____

_____

_____

Vocabulary Practice

For each item, circle the word that differs most in meaning from the other words. Refer to a dictionary if you need help.

1. uprising, commotion, calmness, racket

2. unseemly, crude, rude, proper

3. phony, factual, real, authentic

4. heir, descendant, parent, child

5. shyly, self-consciously, sheepishly, boldly

6. conspiracy, loyalty, plot, trickery

Academic Vocabulary in Writing

appropriate	assess	intelligence	motive	role

What is Joe Iron Shell's **motive** for coming to visit Martin's family in Iowa? In a paragraph, write your response to this question. Include at least one Academic Vocabulary word in your response. Definitions of these words are on page 69.

_____

_____

_____

_____

Assessment Practice

DIRECTIONS Use the two selections you have just read to answer questions 1–4.

1 Which statement best describes Martin, the central character in "The Medicine Bag"?

  (A) He gains a deeper understanding of himself after he spends time with his grandfather.

  (B) He travels a long distance to spend time with his descendants.

  (C) He learns to respect his cultural identity because of his friends' response to his great-grandfather.

  (D) He exaggerates the importance of his cultural heritage.

2 The medicine bag —

  (A) represents Martin's future

  (B) contains healing agents to be used in times of poor health

  (C) contains items that link the wearer to his cultural roots

  (D) can be worn only by its maker

3 In "Who Are You Today, María?" what does Mr. Golden mean when he asks, "Are you going to walk around as a joke or as a poem?"

  (A) He expects students to recite a joke or a poem as they enter the classroom.

  (B) He hopes students have a sense of humor.

  (C) He wants students to take the assignment seriously.

  (D) He is warning students to behave.

4 Which is true of the central characters in both selections?

  (A) They feel embarrassed by their relatives.

  (B) They express pride in their cultural heritage.

  (C) Cultural diversity is celebrated in their environments.

  (D) They worry about what their closest friends think of them.

UNIT 3

The Place to Be

SETTING AND MOOD

Be sure to read the Text Analysis Workshop on pp. 322–327 in *Holt McDougal Literature*.

Academic Vocabulary for Unit 3

Academic Vocabulary is the language you use to discuss literary and informational texts. Preview the following Academic Vocabulary words. You will use these words as you write and talk about the selections in this unit.

circumstance (sûr'kəm-stăns') *n.* an event or fact having some bearing on a particular situation; a determining factor

*What **circumstances** led to the main character's injury?*

•

emerge (ĭ-mûrj') *v.* to appear; to come into view or existence

*What information **emerged** to change your view of the main character?*

•

predominant (prĭ-dŏm'ə-nənt) *adj.* to have great importance, influence, or power

*What is the **predominant** mood at the beginning of the story?*

•

rely (rĭ-lī') *v.* to be dependent on for help or support; to have confidence in

*Can you **rely** on the first-person narrator's view of story events? Why?*

•

technology (tĕk-nŏl'ə-jē) *n.* science as it is applied to practical use and work

*How does the use of **technology** affect the story's conflict?*

Recall a book you've read or a movie you've seen. How did the setting affect the way the characters behaved? Describe the **circumstances** that bring about the conflict. Use at least two Academic Vocabulary words in your response.

_____

_____

_____

Hallucination

Short Story by **Isaac Asimov**

from **Ellis Island and I**

Personal Essay by **Isaac Asimov**

How do you find your PURPOSE?

Maybe you've heard about a pop star who began performing onstage at the age of three. Most of us, however, have to search, question, and take a few wrong turns before we discover our talents. In the story you are about to read, a 15-year-old boy discovers his purpose by traveling to an unusual place. What is the best way for you to put your talents to use?

LIST IT List five activities you enjoy participating in. Then, discuss with a partner the ways in which you might put these talents to use.

Text Analysis: Setting

The **setting** of a story is the time and place in which the action occurs. As shown in the graphic, in some stories, the details of setting do more than create a backdrop for events.

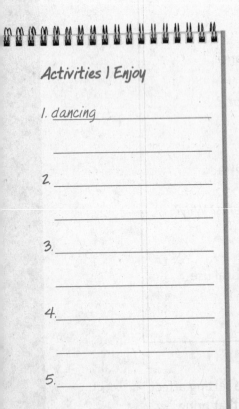

Activities I Enjoy

1. dancing
2.
3.
4.
5.

SETTING
Can affect characters by • determining jobs and living conditions • influencing values, beliefs, customs, and actions
Can create conflict • by exposing the characters to dangerous weather or natural disasters • having characters live difficult time periods or situations

As you read "Hallucination," look for ways the story's setting creates conflict and influences the characters' values and beliefs.

Reading Strategy: Reading Science Fiction

Science fiction stories are narratives that typically involve fantastical settings, characters, or events. Writers of science fiction often use their stories to comment upon emerging technologies, contemporary society, and human nature. Use a chart like the one shown to keep track of the technologies, customs, and beliefs that exist in the story. Jot down what you think Asimov might be saying about current technology, society, or human nature by making these elements ordinary in a future world.

Details	What Asimov Might Be Saying
A Central computer decides people's careers, and the characters just accept that.	• People want big decisions made for them. • Computers may one day run our lives.

Vocabulary in Context

Note: Words are listed in the order in which they appear in the story.

opposition (ŏp′ə-zĭsh′ən) *n.* the act of opposing or resisting
  Those in **opposition** *to the plan were told to keep quiet.*

inertia (ĭ-nûr′shə) *n.* resistance to motion, action, or change
  She overcame her **inertia** *and began seeking a cure.*

diminish (dĭ-mĭn′ĭsh′) *v.* to become smaller or less
  His desire to travel did not **diminish** *over time.*

conviction (kən-vĭk′shən) *n.* a strong belief
  He held a strong **conviction** *that something wasn't right.*

insolent (ĭn′sə-lənt) *adj.* insulting; arrogant
  The boy wasn't **insolent;** *he tried hard to be respectful.*

refrain (rĭ-frān′) *v.* to hold oneself back; to stop
  It's difficult to **refrain** *from doing something you enjoy.*

Vocabulary Practice

Review the vocabulary words and their meanings. With a partner, discuss what might happen to a boy who works on a faraway planet. Use at least two vocabulary words in your discussion.

HALLUCINATION

Short Story by
ISAAC ASIMOV

BACKGROUND "Hallucination" was first
published in 1985. In the two decades before
its publication, people in the United States
were losing faith in the government and
growing concerned about the environment.
At the same time, great advances were
being made in space exploration and
computer technology. The developments in
computer technology would soon lead to the
widespread use of computers in government
and business operations—and, eventually, to
the development of the personal computer.

PART ONE

Sam Chase arrived on Energy Planet on his fifteenth
birthday.

It was a great achievement, he had been told, to have
been assigned there, but he wasn't at all sure he felt that at
the moment.

It meant a three-year separation from Earth and from
his family, while he continued a specialized education in
the field, and that was a sobering thought. It was not the
field of education in which he was interested, and he could
10 not understand why Central Computer had assigned him
to this project, and that was downright depressing. **ⓐ**

He looked at the transparent dome overhead. It was
quite high, perhaps a thousand meters high, and it
stretched in all directions farther than he could clearly
see. He asked, "Is it true that this is the only Dome on the
planet, sir?"

The information-films he had studied on the spaceship that had carried him here had described only one Dome, but they might have been out-of-date.

20 Donald Gentry, to whom the question had been addressed, smiled. He was a large man, a little chubby, with dark brown, good-natured eyes, not much hair, and a short, graying beard.

He said, "The only one, Sam. It's quite large, though, and most of the housing facilities are underground, where you'll find no lack of space. Besides, once your basic training is done, you'll be spending most of your time in space. This is just our planetary base." **B**

"I see, sir," said Sam, a little troubled.

30 Gentry said, "I am in charge of our basic trainees so I have to study their records carefully. It seems clear to me that this assignment was not your first choice. Am I right?"

Sam hesitated, and then decided he didn't have much choice but to be honest about it. He said, "I'm not sure that I'll do as well as I would like to in gravitational engineering."

"Why not? Surely the Central Computer, which evaluated your scholastic record and your social and personal background can be trusted in its judgments. And 40 if you do well, it will be a great achievement for you, for right here we are on the cutting edge of a new technology."

"I know that, sir," said Sam. "Back on Earth, everyone is very excited about it. No one before has ever tried to get close to a neutron star and make use of its energy."

"Yes?" said Gentry. "I haven't been on Earth for two years. What else do they say about it? I understand there's considerable **opposition**?"

His eyes probed the boy.

Sam shifted uneasily, aware he was being tested. He said, 50 "There are people on Earth who say it's all too dangerous and might be a waste of money."

B SETTING
Reread lines 1–28 and underline details that describe the setting. What have you learned so far about where and when the story takes place?

_____

_____

_____

_____

_____

_____

_____

opposition (ŏp'ə-zĭsh'ən) *n.* the act of opposing or resisting

C **READING SCIENCE FICTION**

Reread lines 37–55. How are career decisions made in this future world? What idea might Asimov be expressing about society in these lines? Write your thoughts in the chart.

Details

↓

What Asimov Might Be Saying

VISUAL VOCABULARY

corridor (kôr′ĭ-dôr′) *n.* a narrow hallway, often with rooms opening onto it

---

"Do you believe that?"

"It might be so, but most new technologies have their dangers and many are worth doing despite that. This one is, I think." **C**

"Very good. What else do they say on Earth?"

Sam said, "They say the Commander isn't well and that the project might fail without him." When Gentry didn't respond, Sam said, hastily, "That's what they say."

60 Gentry acted as though he did not hear. He put his hand on Sam's shoulder and said, "Come, I've got to show you to your **Corridor**, introduce you to your roommate, and explain what your initial duties will be." As they walked toward the elevator that would take them downward, he said, "What was your first choice in assignment, Chase?"

"Neurophysiology,[1] sir."

"Not a bad choice. Even today, the human brain continues to be a mystery. We know more about neutron stars than we do about the brain, as we found out when 70 this project first began."

"Oh?"

"Indeed! At the start, various people at the base—it was much smaller and more primitive then—reported having experienced hallucinations.[2] They never caused any bad effects, and after a while, there were no further reports. We never found out the cause."

Sam stopped, and looked up and about again, "Was that why the Dome was built, Dr. Gentry?"

"No, not at all. We needed a place with a completely 80 Earth-like environment, for various reasons, but we haven't isolated ourselves. People can go outside freely. There are no hallucinations being reported now."

---

1. **neurophysiology** (nŏŏr′ō-fĭz′ē-ŏl′ə-jē): the study of the functions of the nervous system.

2. **hallucination** (hə-lŏŏ′sə-nā′shən): a perception of objects that don't really exist.

Sam said, "The information I was given about Energy Planet is that there is no life on it except for plants and insects, and that they're harmless."

"That's right, but they're also inedible, so we grow our own vegetables, and keep some small animals, right here under the Dome. Still, we've found nothing hallucinogenic about the planetary life." **D**

90 "Anything unusual about the atmosphere, sir?"

Gentry looked down from his only slightly greater height and said, "Not at all. People have camped in the open overnight on occasion and nothing has happened. It is a pleasant world. There are streams but no fish, just algae and water-insects. There is nothing to sting you or poison you. There are yellow berries that look delicious and taste terrible but do no other harm. The weather's pretty nearly always good. There are frequent light rains and it is sometimes windy, but there are no extremes of heat and cold." **E**

100 "And no hallucinations anymore, Dr. Gentry?"

"You sound disappointed," said Gentry, smiling.

Sam took a chance. "Does the Commander's trouble have anything to do with the hallucinations, sir?"

The good nature vanished from Gentry's eyes for a moment, and he frowned. He said, "What trouble do you refer to?"

Sam flushed and they proceeded in silence.

Sam found few others in the Corridor he had been assigned to, but Gentry explained it was a busy time at the forward
110 station, where the power system was being built in a ring around the neutron star—the tiny object less than ten miles across that had all the mass of a normal star, and a magnetic field of incredible power.

It was the magnetic field that would be tapped. Energy would be led away in enormous amounts and yet it would

D SETTING
Underline details about the unusal setting in lines 83–89. How does the setting affect the characters' living conditions?

_____

_____

_____

_____

E READING SCIENCE FICTION
Reread lines 83–99. Consider the planet's name and the mission of the people stationed on it. What might Asimov be saying about our energy supply and the way we are using it?

_____

_____

_____

_____

_____

_____

_____

_____

_____

_____

_____

all be a pinprick, less than a pinprick, to the star's rotational energy, which was the ultimate source. It would take billions of years to bleed off all that energy, and in that time, dozens of populated planets, fed the energy through hyperspace, 120 would have all they needed for an indefinite time.

Sharing his room was Robert Gillette, a dark-haired, unhappy-looking young man. After cautious greetings had been exchanged, Robert revealed the fact that he was sixteen and had been "grounded" with a broken arm, though the fact didn't show since it had been pinned internally.

Robert said, ruefully, "It takes a while before you learn to handle things in space. They may not have weight, but they have **inertia** and you have to allow for that."

130 Sam said, "They always teach you that in—" He was going to say that it was taught in fourth-grade science, but realized that would be insulting, and stopped himself.

Robert caught the implication, however, and flushed. He said, "It's easy to know it in your head. It doesn't mean you get the proper reflexes, till you've practiced quite a bit. You'll find out."

Sam said, "Is it very complicated to get to go outside?"

"No, but why do you want to go? There's nothing there."

"Have you ever been outside?"

140 "Sure," but he shrugged, and volunteered nothing else.

Sam took a chance. He said, very casually, "Did you ever see one of these hallucinations they talk about?"

Robert said, "*Who* talks about?"

Sam didn't answer directly. He said, "A lot of people used to see them, but they don't anymore. Or so they say."

"So *who* say?"

Sam took another chance. "Or if they see them, they keep quiet about them."

Robert said gruffly, "Listen, let me give you some advice. 150 Don't get interested in these—whatever they are. If you

---

inertia (ĭ-nûr'shə) *n.* resistance to motion, action, or change

F SETTING
Explain whether people on Energy Planet value nature and the outdoors. Support your answer with details from the text.

_____

_____

_____

_____

_____

_____

_____

_____

_____

_____

start telling yourself you see—uh—something, you might be sent back. You'll lose your chance at a good education and an important career."

Robert's eyes shifted to a direct stare as he said that.

Sam shrugged and sat down on the unused bunk. "All right for this to be my bed?"

"It's the only other bed here," said Robert, still staring. "The bathroom's to your right. There's your closet, your bureau. You get half the room. There's a gym here, a
160 library, a dining area." He paused and then, as though to let bygones be bygones,[3] said, "I'll show you around later."

"Thanks," said Sam. "What kind of a guy is the Commander?"

"He's aces. We wouldn't be here without him. He knows more about hyperspatial technology than anyone, and he's got pull with the Space Agency, so we get the money and equipment we need."

Sam opened his trunk and, with his back to Robert, said casually, "I understand he's not well."

170 "Things get him down. We're behind schedule, there are cost overruns, and things like that. Enough to get anyone down."

"Depression, huh? Any connection, you suppose, with—"

Robert stirred impatiently in his seat, "Say, why are you so interested in all this?"

"Energy physics isn't really my deal. Coming here—"

"Well, here's where you are, mister, and you better make up your mind to it, or you'll get sent home, and then you
180 won't be anywhere. I'm going to the library."

Sam remained in the room alone, with his thoughts.

PAUSE & REFLECT

PAUSE & REFLECT
Underline Robert's description of the Commander and his depression. Why do you think Sam continues to ask probing questions about the project?

_____

_____

_____

_____

_____

_____

_____

_____

_____

_____

_____

_____

_____

_____

3. **let bygones be bygones:** decide to forget past disagreements.

G READING SCIENCE FICTION
Reread lines 186–199 and identify two routine practices that occur in this future world. What might Asimov be saying about the present by making these practices commonplace in the future?

_____

_____

_____

_____

_____

_____

_____

_____

H SETTING
Reread lines 204–216. What creatures are part of this setting? How does Sam react to them?

_____

_____

_____

_____

_____

_____

_____

It was not at all difficult for Sam to get permission to leave the Dome. The Corridor-Master didn't even ask the reason until after he had checked him off.

"I want to get a feel for the planet, sir."

The Corridor-Master nodded. "Fair enough, but you only get three hours, you know. And don't wander out of sight of the Dome. If we have to look for you, we'll find you, because you'll be wearing this," and he held out a
190 transmitter which Sam knew had been tuned to his own personal wavelength, one which had been assigned him at birth. "But if we have to go to that trouble, you won't be allowed out again for a pretty long time. And it won't look good on your record, either. You understand?"

It won't look good on your record. Any reasonable career these days had to include experience and education in space, so it was an effective warning. No wonder people might have stopped reporting hallucinations, even if they saw them. **G**

200   Even so, Sam was going to have to take his chances. After all, the Central Computer *couldn't* have sent him here just to do energy physics. There was nothing in his record that made sense out of that.

As far as looks were concerned, the planet might have been Earth, some part of Earth anyway, some place where there were a few trees and low bushes and lots of tall grass.

There were no paths and with every cautious step, the grass swayed, and tiny flying creatures whirred upward with a soft, hissing noise of wings.
210   One of them landed on his finger and Sam looked at it curiously. It was very small and, therefore, hard to see in detail, but it seemed hexagonal, bulging above and concave below. There were many short, small legs so that when it moved it almost seemed to do so on tiny wheels. There were no signs of wings till it suddenly took off, and then four tiny, feathery objects unfurled. **H**

What made the planet different from Earth, though, was the smell. It wasn't unpleasant, it was just different. The plants must have had an entirely different chemistry
220 from those on Earth; that's why they tasted bad and were inedible. It was just luck they weren't poisonous.

The smell **diminished** with time, however, as it saturated Sam's nostrils. He found an exposed bit of rocky ledge he could sit on and considered the prospect. The sky was filled with lines of clouds, and the Sun was periodically obscured, but the temperature was pleasant and there was only a light wind. The air felt a bit damp, as though it might rain in a few hours.

Sam had brought a small hamper with him and he
230 placed it in his lap and opened it. He had brought along two sandwiches and a canned drink so that he could make rather a picnic of it.

He chewed away and thought: Why should there be hallucinations?

Surely those accepted for a job as important as that of taming a neutron star would have been selected for mental stability. It would be surprising to have even one person hallucinating, let alone a number of them. Was it a matter of chemical influences on the brain?

240 They would surely have checked that out.

Sam plucked a leaf, tore it in two and squeezed. He then put the torn edge to his nose cautiously, and took it away again. A very acrid, unpleasant smell. He tried a blade of grass. Much the same.

Was the smell enough? It hadn't made him feel dizzy or in any way peculiar. **PAUSE & REFLECT**

He used a bit of his water to rinse off the fingers that had held the plants and then rubbed them on his trouser leg. He finished his sandwiches slowly, and tried to see if anything
250 else might be considered unnatural about the planet.

diminish (dĭ-mĭn'ĭsh) *v.* to become smaller or less

PAUSE & REFLECT
Why do you think Sam rips and then sniffs a leaf and a blade of grass?

All that greenery. There ought to be animals eating it, rabbits, cows, whatever. Not just insects, innumerable insects, or whatever those little things might be, with the gentle sighing of their tiny feathery wings and the very soft crackle of their munch, munch, munchings of leaves and stalks. ❶

What if there were a cow—a big, fat cow—doing the munching? And with the last mouthful of his second sandwich between his teeth, his own munching stopped.

260   There was a kind of smoke in the air between himself and a line of hedges. It waved, billowed, and altered: a very thin smoke. He blinked his eyes, then shook his head, but it was still there.

He swallowed hastily, closed his lunch box, and slung it over his shoulder by its strap. He stood up.

He felt no fear. He was only excited—and curious.

The smoke was growing thicker, and taking on a shape. Vaguely, it looked like a cow, a smoky, insubstantial shape that he could see through. Was it a hallucination? A

270   creation of his mind? He had just been thinking of a cow.

Hallucination or not, he was going to investigate.

With determination, he stepped toward the shape.

PART TWO

Sam Chase stepped toward the cow outlined in smoke on the strange, far planet on which his education and career were to be advanced.

He was convinced there was nothing wrong with his mind. It was the "hallucination" that Dr. Gentry had mentioned, but it was no hallucination. Even as he pushed his way through the tall rank⁴ grasslike greenery, he noted

280   the silence, and knew not only that it was no hallucination, but what it really *was*.

---

4. **rank:** yielding an excessive crop.

The smoke seemed to condense and grow darker, outlining the cow more sharply. It was as though the cow were being painted in the air.

Sam laughed, and shouted, "Stop! Stop! Don't use me. I don't know a cow well enough. I've only seen pictures. You're getting it all wrong." **PAUSE & REFLECT**

It looked more like a caricature[5] than a real animal and, as he cried out, the outline wavered and thinned. The 290 smoke remained but it was as though an unseen hand had passed across the air to erase what had been written.

Then a new shape began to take form. At first, Sam couldn't quite make out what it was intended to represent, but it changed and sharpened quickly. He stared in surprise, his mouth hanging open and his hamper bumping emptily against his shoulder blade.

The smoke was forming a human being. There was no mistake about it. It was forming accurately, as though it had a model it could imitate, and of course it did have one, 300 for Sam was standing there.

It was becoming Sam, clothes and all, even the outline of the hamper and the strap over his shoulder. It was another Sam Chase.

It was still a little vague, wavering a bit, insubstantial, but it firmed as though it were correcting itself, and then, finally, it was steady.

It never became entirely solid. Sam could see the vegetation dimly through it, and when a gust of wind caught it, it moved a bit as if it were a tethered balloon. ❶

310 But it was real. It was no creation of his mind. Sam was sure of that.

But he couldn't just stand there, simply facing it. Diffidently, he said, "Hello, there."

---

5. **caricature** (kăr′ĭ-kə-chŏŏr′): a comic or exaggerated picture.

PAUSE & REFLECT
Why do you suppose Sam feels free to laugh and criticize whoever—or whatever—is making the "cow"?

_____

_____

_____

_____

_____

_____

_____

❶ **SETTING**
What is the smoke becoming now? Underline the answer. Explain whether you think that what Sam sees is a real part of the planet, or a hallucination.

_____

_____

_____

_____

_____

_____

_____

conviction (kən-vĭk´shən) *n.* a strong belief

What **conviction** does Sam have about the creatures that make up the "Other Sam"?

_____

_____

_____

_____

_____

_____

_____

_____

_____

_____

_____

_____

_____

_____

Somehow, he expected the Other Sam to speak, too, and, indeed, its mouth opened and closed, but no sound came out. It might just have been imitating the motion of Sam's mouth.

Sam said, again, "Hello, can you speak?"

There was no sound but his own voice, and yet there 320 was a tickling in his mind, a **conviction** that they could communicate.

Sam frowned. What made him so sure of that? The thought seemed to pop into his mind.

He said, "Is this what has appeared to other people, human people—my kind—on this world?"

No answering sound, but he was quite sure what the answer to his question was. This had appeared to other people, not necessarily in their own shape, but *something*. And it hadn't worked.

330 What made him so sure of *that*? Where did these convictions come from in answer to his questions?

Yes, of course, they *were* the answers to his questions. The Other Sam was putting thoughts into his mind. It was adjusting the tiny electric currents in his brain cells so that the proper thoughts would arise.

He nodded thoughtfully at *that* thought, and the Other Sam must have caught the significance of the gesture, for it nodded, too.

It had to be so. First a cow had formed, when Sam had 340 thought of a cow, and then it had shifted when Sam had said the cow was imperfect. The Other Sam could grasp his thoughts somehow, and if it could grasp them, then it could modify them, too, perhaps.

Was this what telepathy[6] was like, then? It was not like talking. It was having thoughts, except that the thoughts originated elsewhere and were not created entirely of one's

---

6. **telepathy** (tə-lĕp´ə-thē): communication directly from one person's mind to another.

own mental operations. But how could you tell your own thoughts from thoughts imposed from outside?

350 Sam knew the answer to that at once. Right now, he was unused to the process. He had never had practice. With time, as he grew more skilled at it, he would be able to tell one kind of thought from another without trouble.

In fact, he could do it now, if he thought about it. Wasn't he carrying on a conversation in a way? He was wondering, and then knowing. The wondering was his own question, the knowing was the Other Sam's answer. Of course it was.

There! The "of course it was," just now, was an answer.

"Not so fast, Other Sam," said Sam, aloud. "Don't go 360 too quickly. Give me a chance to sort things out, or I'll just get confused."

He sat down suddenly on the grass, which bent away from him in all directions. **K**

The Other Sam slowly tried to sit down as well.

Sam laughed. "Your legs are bending in the wrong place."

That was corrected at once. The Other Sam sat down, but remained very stiff from the waist up.

"Relax," said Sam.

370 Slowly, the Other Sam slumped, flopping a bit to one side, then correcting that.

Sam was relieved. With the Other Sam so willing to follow his lead, he was sure good will was involved. It was! Exactly!

"No," said Sam. "I said, not so fast. Don't go by my thoughts. Let me speak out loud, even if you can't hear me. *Then* adjust my thoughts, so I'll know it's an adjustment. Do you understand?"

He waited a moment and was then sure the Other 380 Sam understood.

Ah, the answer had come, but not right away. Good!

"Why do you appear to people?" asked Sam.

K SETTING
What is unusual about the grass Sam sits on?

_____

_____

_____

_____

_____

_____

_____

_____

_____

_____

_____

He stared earnestly at the Other Sam, and knew that the Other Sam wanted to communicate with people, but had failed.

No answer to that question had really been required. The answer was obvious. But then, *why* had they failed?

He put it in words. "Why did you fail? You are successfully communicating with me."

390 Sam was beginning to learn how to understand the alien manifestation.[7] It was as if his mind were adapting itself to a new technique of communication, just as it would adapt itself to a new language. Or was Other Sam influencing Sam's mind and teaching him the method without Sam even knowing it was being done?

Sam found himself emptying his mind of immediate thoughts. After he asked his question, he just let his eyes focus at nothing and his eyelids droop, as though he were about to drop off to sleep, and then he knew the answer. 400 There was a little clicking, or something, in his mind, a signal that showed him something had been put in from outside. **L**

He now knew, for instance, that the Other Sam's previous attempts at communication had failed because the people to whom it had appeared had been frightened. They had doubted their own sanity. And because they feared, their minds . . . tightened. Their minds would not receive. The attempts at communication gradually diminished, though they had never entirely stopped.

410 "But you're communicating with me," said Sam.

Sam was different from all the rest. He had not been afraid.

"Couldn't you have made them not afraid first? Then talked to them?"

It wouldn't work. The fear-filled mind resisted all. An attempt to change might damage. It would be wrong

L SETTING
How is the setting of the story affecting Sam's behavior?

_____

_____

_____

_____

_____

_____

_____

_____

_____

_____

_____

_____

_____

---

7. **manifestation** (măn′ə-fĕ-stā′shən): an indication of the presence of something.

to damage a thinking mind. There had been one such attempt, but it had not worked. **Ⓜ**

"What is it you are trying to communicate, 420 Other Sam?"

A wish to be left alone. *Despair*!

Despair was more than a thought; it was an emotion; it was a frightening sensation. Sam felt despair wash over him intensely, heavily—and yet it was not part of himself. He felt despair on the surface of his mind, keenly, but underneath it, where his own mind was, he was free of it.

Sam said, wonderingly, "It seems to me as though you're giving up. Why? We're not interfering with you?"

Human beings had built the Dome, cleared a large 430 area of all planetary life and substituted their own. And once the neutron star had its power station—once floods of energy moved outward through hyperspace to power-thirsty worlds—more power stations would be built and still more. Then what would happen to *Home*. (There must be a name for the planet that the Other Sam used but the only thought Sam found in his mind was *Home* and, underneath that, the thought: *ours—ours—ours—*)

This planet was the nearest convenient base to the neutron star. It would be flooded with more and more 440 people, more and more Domes, and their Home would be destroyed. **Ⓝ**

"But you could change our minds if you had to, even if you damaged a few, couldn't you?"

If they tried, people would find them dangerous. People would work out what was happening. Ships would approach, and from a distance, use weapons to destroy the life on Home, and then bring in People-life instead. This could be seen in the people's minds. People had a violent history; they would stop at nothing.

Ⓜ SETTING
Reread lines 403–418 and explain how the setting has affected communication between the characters.

_____
_____
_____
_____
_____
_____
_____
_____
_____
_____
_____

Ⓝ SETTING
Pause at line 441. What aspect of the setting makes humans such a threat to the planet's inhabitants?

_____
_____
_____
_____
_____
_____

PAUSE & REFLECT

Why do you think Sam is feeling frustrated right now?

_____

_____

_____

_____

_____

_____

⊙ SETTING

Underline key words Sam uses when thinking about the creatures. What have you discovered about the beings who inhabit this planet?

_____

_____

_____

_____

_____

_____

_____

_____

_____

_____

_____

450   "But what can I do?" said Sam. "I'm just an apprentice. I've just been here a few days. What can I do?" **PAUSE & REFLECT**

Fear. Despair.

There were no thoughts that Sam could work out, just the numbing layer of fear and despair.

He felt moved. It was such a peaceful world. They threatened nobody. They didn't even hurt minds when they could. **⊙**

It wasn't their fault they were conveniently near a neutron star. It wasn't their fault they were in the way of
460   expanding humanity.

He said, "Let me think."

He thought, and there was the feeling of another mind watching. Sometimes his thoughts skipped forward and he recognized a suggestion from outside.

There came the beginning of hope. Sam felt it, but wasn't certain.

He said doubtfully, "I'll try."

He looked at the time-strip[8] on his wrist and jumped a little. Far more time had passed than he had realized. His
470   three hours were nearly up. "I must go back now," he said.

He opened his lunch hamper and removed the small thermos of water, drank from it thirstily, and emptied it. He placed the empty thermos under one arm. He removed the wrappings of the sandwich and stuffed it in his pocket.

The Other Sam wavered and turned smoky. The smoke thinned, dispersed and was gone.

Sam closed the hamper, swung its strap over his shoulder again and turned toward the Dome.

His heart was hammering. Would he have the courage
480   to go through with his plan? And if he did, would it work?

---

8. **time-strip:** watch.

When Sam entered the Dome, the Corridor-Master was waiting for him and said, as he looked ostentatiously at his own time-strip, "You shaved it rather fine, didn't you?"

Sam's lips tightened and he tried not to sound **insolent**. "I had three hours, sir."

insolent (ĭn′sə-lənt) *adj.* insulting; arrogant

"And you took two hours and fifty-eight minutes."

"That's less than three hours, sir."

"Hmm." The Corridor-Master was cold and unfriendly. "Dr. Gentry would like to see you."

490   "Yes, sir. What for?"

"He didn't tell me. But I don't like you cutting it that fine your first time out, Chase. And I don't like your attitude either, and I don't like an officer of the Dome wanting to see you. I'm just going to tell you once, Chase—if you're a troublemaker, I won't want you in this Corridor. Do you understand?"

"Yes, sir. But what trouble have I made?"

"We'll find that out soon enough." **PAUSE & REFLECT**

PAUSE & REFLECT
Why do you think the Corridor-Master believes that Sam is a troublemaker?

Sam had not seen Donald Gentry since their one and only
500 meeting the day the young apprentice had reached the Dome. Gentry still seemed good natured and kindly, and there was nothing in his voice to indicate anything else. He sat in a chair behind his desk, and Sam stood before it, his hamper still bumping his shoulder blade.

Gentry said, "How are you getting along, Sam? Having an interesting time?"

"Yes, sir," said Sam.

"Still feeling you'd rather be doing something else, working somewhere else?"

510   Sam said, earnestly, "No, sir. This is a good place for me."

"Because you're interested in hallucinations?"

"Yes, sir."

"You've been asking others about it, haven't you?"

P READING SCIENCE FICTION

Pause at line 545. Think about what Sam's supervisors did to keep an eye on him. What might Asimov be saying about authorities keeping watch over employees or citizens?

_____

_____

_____

_____

_____

_____

_____

_____

_____

_____

_____

"It's an interesting subject to me, sir."

"Because you want to study the human brain?"

"Any brain, sir."

"And you've been wandering about outside the Dome, haven't you?"

520   "I was told it was permitted, sir."

"It is. But few apprentices take advantage of that so soon. Did you see anything interesting?"

Sam hesitated, then said, "Yes, sir."

"A hallucination?"

"No, sir." He said it quite positively.

Gentry stared at him for a few moments, and there was a kind of speculative hardening of his eyes. "Would you care to tell me what you did see? Honestly."

Sam hesitated again. Then he said, "I saw and spoke to

530 an inhabitant of this planet, sir."

"An intelligent inhabitant, young man?"

"Yes, sir."

Gentry said, "Sam, we had reason to wonder about you when you came. The Central Computer's report on you did not match our needs, though it was favorable in many ways, so I took the opportunity to study you that first day. We kept our collective eye on you, and when you left to wander about the planet on your own, we kept you under observation."

540   "Sir," said Sam, indignantly. "That violates my right of privacy."

"Yes, it does, but this is a most vital project and we are sometimes driven to bend the rules a little. We saw you talking with considerable animation for a substantial period of time." **P**

"I just told you I was, sir."

"Yes, but you were talking to *nothing*, to empty air. You were experiencing a hallucination, Sam!"

PART THREE

Sam Chase was speechless. A hallucination? It couldn't be a
550 hallucination.

Less than half an hour ago, he had been speaking to
the Other Sam, had been experiencing the thoughts of the
Other Sam. He knew exactly what had happened then, and
he was still the same Sam Chase he had been during that
conversation and before. He put his elbow over his lunch
hamper as though it were a connection with the sandwiches
he had been eating when the Other Sam had appeared.

He said, with what was almost a stammer, "Sir—
Dr. Gentry—it wasn't a hallucination. It was real."

560 Gentry shook his head. "My boy, I saw you talking with
animation to nothing at all. I didn't hear what you said,
but you were talking. Nothing else was there except plants.
Nor was I the only one. There were two other witnesses,
and we have it all on record."

"On record?"

"On a television cassette. Why should we lie to you,
young man? This has happened before. At the start it
happened rather frequently. Now it happens only very
rarely. For one thing, we tell the new apprentices of the
570 hallucinations at the start, as I told you, and they generally
avoid the planet until they are more acclimated, and then it
doesn't happen to them."

"You mean you scare them," blurted out Sam, "so that
it's not likely to happen. And they don't tell you if it does
happen. But I wasn't scared." **Q**

Gentry shook his head. "I'm sorry you weren't, if
that was what it would have taken you to keep from
seeing things."

"I wasn't seeing things. At least, not things that
580 weren't there."

Q READING SCIENCE FICTION
Reread lines 560–575. List the details that tell you about the authorities' activities. What might Asimov suggesting about his own present-day government?

Details

↓

What Asimov Might Be Saying

"How do you intend to argue with a television cassette, which will show you staring at nothing?"

"Sir, what I saw was not opaque. It was smoky, actually; foggy, if you know what I mean."

"Yes, I do. It looked as a hallucination might look, not as reality. But the television set would have seen even smoke."

"Maybe not, sir. My mind must have been focused to see it more clearly. It was probably less clear to the camera than to me."

590   "It focused your mind, did it?" Gentry stood up, and he sounded rather sad. "That's an admission of hallucination. I'm really sorry, Sam, because you are clearly intelligent, and the Central Computer rated you highly, but we can't use you."

"Will you be sending me home, sir?"

"Yes, but why should that matter? You didn't particularly want to come here."

"I want to stay here now."

"But I'm afraid you cannot."

600   "You can't just send me home. Don't I get a hearing?"

"You certainly can, if you insist, but in that case, the proceedings will be official and will go on your record, so that you won't get another apprenticeship anywhere. As it is, if you are sent back unofficially, as better suited to an apprenticeship in neurophysiology, you might get that, and be better off, actually, than you are now."

"I don't want that. I want a hearing—before the Commander."

"Oh, no. Not the Commander. He can't be bothered
610 with that."

"It *must* be the Commander," said Sam, with desperate force, "or this Project will fail." ®

"Unless the Commander gives you a hearing? Why do you say that? Come, you are forcing me to think that you are unstable in ways other than those involved with hallucinations."

® **SETTING**
Why does Sam so badly want to stay on Energy Planet?

"Sir." The words were tumbling out of Sam's mouth now. "The Commander is ill—they know that even on Earth—and if he gets too ill to work, this Project will fail.
620 I did not see a hallucination and the proof is that I know why he is ill and how he can be cured."

"You're not helping yourself," said Gentry.

"If you send me away, I tell you the Project will fail. Can it hurt to let me see the Commander? All I ask is five minutes."

"Five minutes? What if he refuses?"

"Ask him, sir. Tell him that I say the same thing that caused his depression can remove it."

"No, I don't think I'll tell him that. But I'll ask him if
630 he'll see you."

The Commander was a thin man, not very tall. His eyes were a deep blue and they looked tired.

His voice was very soft, a little low-pitched, definitely weary.

"You're the one who saw the hallucination?"

"It was not a hallucination, Commander. It was real. So was the one you saw, Commander." If that did not get him thrown out, Sam thought, he might have a chance. He felt his elbow tightening on his hamper again. He still had it
640 with him.

The Commander seemed to wince. "The one *I* saw?"

"Yes, Commander. It said it had hurt one person. They had to try with you because you were the Commander, and they . . . did damage."

The Commander ignored that and said, "Did you ever have any mental problems before you came here?"

"No, Commander. You can consult my Central Computer record."

Sam thought: *He* must have had problems, but they let it
650 go because he's a genius and they had to have him. **S**

Then he thought: Was that my own idea? Or had it been put there?

The Commander was speaking. Sam had almost missed it. He said, "What you saw can't be real. There is no intelligent life-form on this planet."

"Yes, sir. There is."

"Oh? And no one ever discovered it till you came here, and in three days you did the job?" The Commander smiled very briefly. "I'm afraid I have no choice but to—"

660 "Wait, Commander," said Sam, in a strangled voice. "We know about the intelligent life-form. It's the insects, the little flying things."

"You say the insects are intelligent?"

"Not an individual insect by itself, but they fit together when they want to, like little jigsaw pieces. They can do it in any way they want. And when they do, their nervous systems fit together, too, and build up. A lot of them *together* are intelligent." **T**

The Commander's eyebrows lifted. "That's an 670 interesting idea, anyway. Almost crazy enough to be true. How did you come to that conclusion, young man?"

"By observation, sir. Everywhere I walked, I disturbed the insects in the grass and they flew about in all directions. But once the cow started to form, and I walked toward it, there was nothing to see or hear. The insects were gone. They had gathered together in front of me and they weren't in the grass anymore. That's how I knew."

"You talked with a cow?"

"It was a cow at first, because that's what I thought of. 680 But they had it wrong, so they switched and came together to form a human being—*me*."

"You?" And then, in a lower voice, "Well, that fits anyway."

"Did you see it that way, too, Commander?"

T SETTING
Reread lines 664–668. How do the insects communicate with humans?

_____

_____

_____

_____

_____

_____

_____

_____

_____

The Commander ignored that. "And when it shaped itself like you, it could talk as you did? Is that what you're telling me?"

"No, Commander. The talking was in my mind."

"Telepathy?"

690 "Sort of."

"And what did it say to you, or think to you?"

"It wanted us to **refrain** from disturbing this planet. It wanted us not to take it over." Sam was all but holding his breath. The interview had lasted more than five minutes already, and the Commander was making no move to put an end to it, to send him home.

"Quite impossible."

"Why, Commander?"

"Any other base will double and triple the expense. We're
700 having enough trouble getting grants as it is. Fortunately, it is all a hallucination, young man, and the problem does not arise." He closed his eyes, then opened them and looked at Sam without really focusing on him. "I'm sorry, young man. You will be sent back—officially." ⓤ

Sam gambled again. "We can't afford to ignore the insects, Commander. They have a lot to give us."

The Commander had raised his hand halfway as though about to give a signal. He paused long enough to say, "Really? What do they have that they can give us?"

710 "The one thing more important than energy, Commander. An understanding of the brain."

"How do you know that?"

"I can demonstrate it. I have them here." Sam seized his hamper and swung it forward onto the desk.

"What's that?"

Sam did not answer in words. He opened the hamper, and a softly whirring, smoky cloud appeared.

The Commander rose suddenly and cried out. He lifted his hand high and an alarm bell sounded.

refrain (rĭ-frān′) *v.* to hold oneself back; to stop

ⓤ SETTING
Why is it important to the Commander to remain on the planet?

_____

_____

_____

_____

_____

_____

_____

_____

_____

_____

_____

_____

◊ READING SCIENCE FICTION

Reread lines 720–730. How does Gentry explain the group's experience? What might Asimov be suggesting about government officials by his response?

_____

_____

_____

_____

_____

_____

_____

_____

_____

_____

_____

_____

_____

_____

_____

_____

_____

_____

720 Through the door came Gentry, and others behind him. Sam felt himself seized by the arms, and then a kind of stunned and motionless silence prevailed in the room.

The smoke was condensing, wavering, taking on the shape of a Head, a thin head, with high cheekbones, a smooth forehead and receding hairline. It had the appearance of the Commander.

"I'm seeing things," croaked the Commander.

Sam said, "We're all seeing the same thing, aren't we?" He wriggled and was released.

730 Gentry said in a low voice, "Mass hysteria." ◊

"No," said Sam, "it's real." He reached toward the Head in midair, and brought back his finger with a tiny insect on it. He flicked it and it could just barely be seen making its way back to its companions.

No one moved.

Sam said, "Head, do you see the problem with the Commander's mind?"

Sam had the brief vision of a snarl in an otherwise smooth curve, but it vanished and left nothing behind. It 740 was not something that could be easily put into human thought. He hoped the others experienced that quick snarl. Yes, they had. He knew it.

The Commander said, "There is no problem."

Sam said, "Can you adjust it, Head?"

Of course, they could not. It was not right to invade a mind.

Sam said, "Commander, give permission."

The Commander put his hands to his eyes and muttered something Sam did not make out. Then he said, clearly, 750 "It's a nightmare, but I've been in one since—Whatever must be done, I give permission."

Nothing happened.

Or nothing seemed to happen.

And then slowly, little by little, the Commander's face lit in a smile.

He said, just above a whisper, "Astonishing. I'm watching a sun rise. It's been cold night for so long, and now I feel the warmth again." His voice rose high. "I feel wonderful."

760 The Head deformed at that point, turned into a vague, pulsing fog, then formed a curving, narrowing arrow that sped into the hamper. Sam snapped it shut.

He said, "Commander, have I your permission to restore these little insect-things to their own world?"

"Yes, yes," said the Commander, dismissing that with a wave of his hand. "Gentry, call a meeting. We've got to change all our plans." **PAUSE & REFLECT**

Sam had been escorted outside the Dome by a stolid guard and had then been confined to his quarters for the 770 rest of the day.

It was late when Gentry entered, stared at him thoughtfully, and said, "That was an amazing demonstration of yours. The entire incident has been fed into the Central Computer and we now have a double project—neutron-star energy and neurophysiology. I doubt that there will be any question about pouring money into this project now. And we'll have a group of neurophysiologists arriving eventually. Until then you're going to be working with those little things and you'll 780 probably end up the most important person here."

Sam said, "But will we leave their world to them?"

Gentry said, "We'll have to if we expect to get anything out of them, won't we? The Commander thinks we're going to build elaborate settlements in orbit about this world and shift all operations to them except for a skeleton crew in this Dome to maintain direct contact with the insects—or whatever we'll decide to call them. It will cost a

PAUSE & REFLECT
Reread lines 747–767. What prompts the Commander to give his permission for the invasion? Explain whether you agree or disagree with his reasoning.

W SETTING
Reread lines 771–789. If the Commander's plans are accepted, what will change on Energy Planet?

_____

_____

_____

_____

_____

_____

_____

_____

_____

_____

_____

_____

_____

_____

_____

_____

_____

great deal of money, and take time and labor, but it's going to be worth it. No one will question that." **W**

790 Sam said, "Good!"

Gentry stared at him again, longer and more thoughtfully than before.

"My boy," he said, "it seems that what happened came about because you did not fear the supposed hallucination. Your mind remained open, and that was the whole difference. Why was that? Why weren't you afraid?"

Sam flushed. "I'm not sure, sir. As I look back on it, though, it seemed to me I was puzzled as to why I was sent here. I had been doing my best to study neurophysiology

800 through my computerized courses, and I knew very little about astrophysics. The Central Computer had my record, all of it, the full details of everything I had ever studied and I couldn't imagine why I had been sent here.

"Then, when you first mentioned the hallucinations, I thought, 'That must be it. I was sent here to look into it.' I just made up my mind that was the thing I had to do. I had no *time* to be afraid, Dr. Gentry. I had a problem to solve and I—I had faith in the Central Computer. It wouldn't have sent me here, if I weren't up to it."

810 Gentry shook his head. "I'm afraid I wouldn't have had that much faith in that machine. But they say faith can move mountains, and I guess it did in this case."

Ellis Island and I

Personal Essay by
ISAAC ASIMOV

**SET A PURPOSE
FOR READING**

Read the essay to discover
how Isaac Asimov began
writing science fiction
stories.

BACKGROUND Much like Sam Chase
in "Hallucination," Isaac Asimov
found his purpose in a place far from
where he was born. When Asimov
was 3 years old, he and his parents
emigrated from Russia to the U.S. His
father never fully mastered English,
and both father and son wanted the
boy to succeed at reading and writing.

**❌ READING SCIENCE
FICTION**
How did science fiction stories
create a conflict between
Asimov and his father?

_____

_____

_____

_____

_____

_____

_____

_____

_____

_____

_____

_____

_____

Only in one point did we clash in this matter of
reading, and that was over the newsstand in the
candy store. I wanted to read the magazines and my father
was unalterably opposed. He felt that I would be reading
trash and contaminating what he obviously was beginning
to think was going to be a first-class mind.

For a while all my arguments fell on deaf ears, and
then I discovered science-fiction magazines, which I took
surreptitious peeks at while my father was taking his
10 afternoon nap. In particular, I found one called *Science
Wonder Stories*, and I pointed out to my father that
since the stories were about science, they were bound to
be educational. ❌

It was a good time to attack, for my mother was
pregnant with what turned out to be my younger brother,
and my father was feeling as though he had a lot more

PAUSE & REFLECT
What got Asimov first interested in writing science fiction? What other events motivated him?

on his mind than questions over whether I could read a magazine or not. He gave in.

That started me, at the age of nine, on my career as
20 a science-fiction reader. By the time I was eleven, I felt that I just could not get enough science fiction from the magazines (there were only three, and they came out only once a month), and it struck me that I might write my own.

I didn't quite write science fiction at first, but I managed to get to it when I was fifteen, and by the time I was eighteen I sold a story to one of the magazines and was off and running.

I cannot say how things would have been for me had I
30 not come into the United States as an immigrant. I can't go back and live life over under changed circumstances. Still, as I think about it, it seems to me I needed something to rise above.

To be brief, I'm glad I came here—and I'm glad I had to come here. Life might have been too easy for me if my ancestors had beat me to the punch and had come here on the Mayflower. **PAUSE & REFLECT**

Text Analysis: Setting

In the chart below, describe the setting of this story and explain how it affects the characters (how they live and what they do, value, and believe) and how it creates conflict.

Setting:

↓   ↓

How It Affects Characters:	How It Creates Conflict:

Imagine that the setting was less hospitable to humans. How would this change affect the characters and conflict in the story?

_____

_____

_____

_____

_____

_____

_____

Reading Strategy: Read Science Fiction

In the chart below, identify one message about contemporary life that Asimov might have been expressing in "Hallucination." Give three details from the story that support this message.

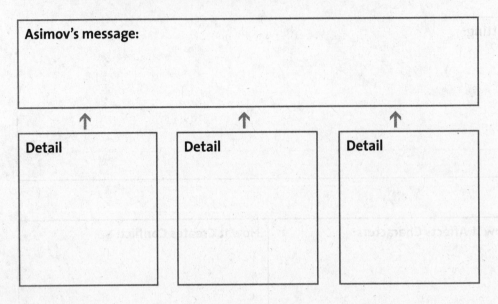

Asimov's message:

| Detail | Detail | Detail |

How do you find your PURPOSE?

Would you like to live in a society in which a Central Computer like the one in "Hallucination" identified each person's career, or purpose, in life? Why or why not?

_____

_____

_____

Vocabulary Practice

Write an *S* next to each pair of words that are synonyms (words that mean the same) and an *A* next to each pair that are antonyms (words that mean the opposite).

_____ 1. refrain/persist

_____ 2. opposition/resistance

_____ 3. inertia/activity

_____ 4. diminish/decrease

_____ 5. insolent/insulting

_____ 6. conviction/doubt

Academic Vocabulary in Writing

circumstance	emerge	predominant	rely	technology

Imagine you are the Commander, writing a report about the new information that has **emerged** since Sam's arrival on Energy Planet. Use two Academic Vocabulary words to write your one-paragraph report. Definitions for the words are on page 129.

_____

_____

_____

Assessment Practice

DIRECTIONS Use "Hallucination" and "*from* Ellis Island and I" to answer questions 1–6.

1 Why does Sam succeed in communicating with the life forms on Energy Planet?

  (A) The insects have chosen to communicate only with Sam.

  (B) Sam is smarter than the other scientists.

  (C) Sam is not afraid of the insects.

  (D) The insects use Sam.

2 The insects feel despair because —

  (A) humans may destroy the planet

  (B) the scientists' work is causing them pain

  (C) they can't communicate with the humans

  (D) the Commander wants to exterminate them

3 Why does Sam bring his lunchbox to his meeting with the Commander?

  (A) He forgot to return it to his room.

  (B) It holds the insects, proof that he did not hallucinate.

  (C) He wants to demonstrate how he captured the insects.

  (D) It was with him when he communicated with the insects.

4 What characteristics do Isaac Asimov and Sam share?

  (A) They are both writers.

  (B) They are both scientists.

  (C) They are both impulsive and observant.

  (D) They are both inquisitive and confident.

5 Which of the following lines describes the setting of "Hallucination"?

  (A) *It was no creation of his mind.*

  (B) *I want to get a feel for the planet, sir.*

  (C) *There were a few trees and low bushes and lots of tall grass.*

  (D) *At the start, various people at the base . . . reported having experienced hallucinations.*

6 Which modern technology does Asimov warn might be misused?

  (A) surveillance cameras

  (B) personal computers

  (C) space stations

  (D) the internet

The Monkey's Paw
Short Story by W. W. Jacobs

Are you SUPERSTITIOUS?

Many people are superstitious. They might own a lucky charm or get nervous on Friday the 13th. Usually these superstitions are harmless, but sometimes they can interfere with a person's life. In the selection you are about to read, curiosity about the power of an unusual object brings unexpected consequences.

DISCUSS What kinds of superstitious behaviors do you or people you know believe in? In a small group, brainstorm a list of common superstitions. Then discuss which you think are harmless, and which might cause problems or interfere with someone's life.

Text Analysis: Mood

Mood is the feeling or atmosphere the writer creates for the reader. A work's mood can usually be described in one or two adjectives, such as cheerful, gloomy, or anxious. Writers create mood through the use of the following elements. To analyze mood, ask yourself questions about these elements.

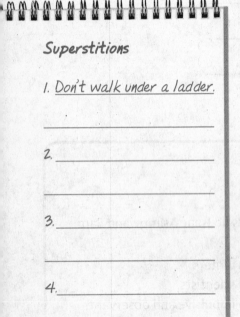

Superstitions

1. *Don't walk under a ladder.*

2. _____

3. _____

4. _____

5. _____

Element of Mood	Ask Yourself . . .
Description of setting	What mood does the time and place of story events create? Does the story take place in a cheerful café or a dark forest at midnight?
Imagery	What language appeals to the senses? Is there a mood of danger in images such as crashing waves and thunderous clouds?
Conversations between characters	How do characters feel about the setting and conflict? Are they scared, joyful, or depressed?

As you read "The Monkey's Paw," notice the way these elements create a particular mood.

Reading Skill: Identify Type of Narrator

A **narrator** is the voice that tells a story. A third-person narrator is not a character in the story, but rather an outside voice. This kind of narrator may be objective or subjective. An **objective narrator** reports events in a factual way, without sharing any characters' hidden thoughts or feelings. A **subjective narrator** recounts events including a character's thoughts, feelings, and observations.

As you read "The Monkey's Paw," try to determine whether the narrator is objective or subjective. Use a chart like this one to record the narrator's observations.

Event	Narrator's Description
A father and son play chess.	"Mr. White … was amiably desirous of preventing his son from seeing it." (lines 8–10)

Vocabulary in Context

Note: Words are listed in the order in which they appear in the story.

peril (pĕr′əl) *n.* danger
  *Mr. White enjoyed chess, but he often put his king in **peril**.*

grimace (grĭm′ĭs) *n.* a facial expression of pain or disgust
  *Mr. White **grimaced** upon seeing the cursed monkey's paw.*

fate (fāt) *n.* a power that is thought to determine the course of events
  *He was indifferent, as though **fate** determined what was going to happen next.*

credulity (krĭ-dōō′lĭ-tē) *n.* a disposition to believe to readily
  *The woman's **credulity** allowed the stranger to trick her.*

compensation (kŏm′pən-sā′shən) *n.* something, such as money, received as payment
  *People should receive **compensation** for their losses.*

resignation (rĕz′ĭg-nā′shən) *n.* acceptance of something that is inescapable
  *She could hope no more; she felt only **resignation**.*

Vocabulary Practice

Review the vocabulary words and their meanings. Then, predict what you think "The Monkey's Paw" will be about based on the list above. Discuss your prediction with a partner.

SET A PURPOSE FOR READING

Read "The Monkey's Paw" to find out what happens when a man is given three wishes.

THE MONKEY'S PAW

Short Story by

W. W. JACOBS

BACKGROUND One of the characters in "The Monkey's Paw" is an officer in the British Army who served in India during the British occupation of that country. The British first arrived in India in the 1600s, when the British East India Company established trading. Their role changed after the Sepoy Munity of 1857–1858, in which Indian soldiers of the British Army revolted. British rule of India ended in 1947, and today India is an independent nation.

peril (pĕr'əl) *n.* danger

Ⓐ IDENTIFY TYPE OF NARRATOR

What have you learned from the narrator so far? Explain whether you believe the narrator will be objective or subjective.

_____

_____

_____

_____

_____

_____

_____

I

Without, the night was cold and wet, but in the small parlor of Laburnum Villa the blinds were drawn and the fire burned brightly. Father and son were at chess; the former, who possessed ideas about the game involving radical changes, putting his king into such sharp and unnecessary **perils** that it even provoked comment from the white-haired old lady knitting placidly by the fire.

"Hark at the wind," said Mr. White, who, having seen a fatal mistake after it was too late, was amiably[1] desirous of
10 preventing his son from seeing it. Ⓐ

"I'm listening," said the latter, grimly surveying the board as he stretched out his hand. "Check."

"I should hardly think that he'd come tonight," said his father, with his hand poised over the board.

---

1. **amiably** (ā'mē-ə-blē): in a friendly way.

"Mate," replied the son.

"That's the worst of living so far out," bawled Mr. White, with sudden and unlooked-for violence; "of all the beastly, slushy, out-of-the-way places to live in, this is the worst. Pathway's a bog,[2] and the road's a torrent.[3]
20 I don't know what people are thinking about. I suppose because only two houses in the road are let,[4] they think it doesn't matter." **B**

"Never mind, dear," said his wife soothingly; "perhaps you'll win the next one."

Mr. White looked up sharply, just in time to intercept a knowing glance between mother and son. The words died away on his lips, and he hid a guilty grin in his thin gray beard.

"There he is," said Herbert White, as the gate banged
30 loudly and heavy footsteps came toward the door.

The old man rose with hospitable haste, and opening the door, was heard condoling[5] with the new arrival. The new arrival also condoled with himself, so that Mrs. White said, "Tut, tut!" and coughed gently as her husband entered the room, followed by a tall, burly man, beady of eye and rubicund of visage.[6]

"Sergeant-Major Morris," he said, introducing him.

The sergeant-major shook hands, and taking the proffered seat by the fire, watched contentedly while his
40 host brought out drinks and stood a small copper kettle on the fire.

He began to talk, the little family circle regarding with eager interest this visitor from distant parts, as he squared his broad shoulders in the chair and spoke of wild scenes and doughty[7] deeds; of wars and plagues and strange peoples.

---

2. **bog:** a swamp.
3. **torrent** (tôr′ənt): a swift-flowing stream.
4. **let:** rented.
5. **condoling** (kən-dōl′ing): expressing sympathy.
6. **rubicund** (roo′bĭ-kənd) **of visage** (vĭz′ĭj): with a ruddy complexion.
7. **doughty** (dou′tē): brave.

B MOOD

Reread lines 1–22. Underline words and phrases that describe the **setting**. What kind of **mood**, or atmosphere, do these details suggest?

_____

_____

_____

_____

_____

_____

_____

_____

_____

_____

_____

_____

_____

_____

_____

_____

_____

_____

VISUAL VOCABULARY

fakir (fə-kîr′) *n.* a Muslim or Hindu holy man

grimace (grĭm′ĭs) *n.* a facial expression of pain or disgust

Why might Mrs. White react with a grimace when she sees the monkey's paw?

_____

_____

_____

fate (fāt) *n.* a power that is thought to determine the course of events

⊙ MOOD
How does the characters' conversation in lines 65–82 cause the mood of the story to change?

_____

_____

_____

_____

_____

_____

"Twenty-one years of it," said Mr. White, nodding at his wife and son. "When he went away, he was a slip of a youth in the warehouse. Now look at him."

"He don't look to have taken much harm," said Mrs. White politely.

"I'd like to go to India myself," said the old man, "just to look round a bit, you know."

"Better where you are," said the sergeant-major, shaking his head. He put down the empty glass, and sighing softly, shook it again.

"I should like to see those old temples and **fakirs** and jugglers," said the old man. "What was that you started telling me the other day about a monkey's paw or something, Morris?"

"Nothing," said the soldier hastily. "Leastways nothing worth hearing."

"Monkey's paw?" said Mrs. White curiously.

"Well, it's just a bit of what you might call magic, perhaps," said the sergeant-major off-handedly.

His three listeners leaned forward eagerly. The visitor absent-mindedly put his empty glass to his lips and then set it down again. His host filled it for him.

"To look at," said the sergeant-major, fumbling in his pocket, "it's just an ordinary little paw, dried to a mummy."

He took something out of his pocket and proffered it. Mrs. White drew back with a **grimace,** but her son, taking it, examined it curiously.

"And what is there special about it?" inquired Mr. White as he took it from his son, and having examined it, placed it upon the table.

"It had a spell put on it by an old fakir," said the sergeant-major, "a very holy man. He wanted to show that **fate** ruled people's lives, and that those who interfered with it did so to their sorrow. He put a spell on it so that three separate men could each have three wishes from it."

His manner was so impressive that his hearers were conscious that their light laughter jarred somewhat. **⊙**

"Well, why don't you have three, sir?" said Herbert White cleverly.

The soldier regarded him in the way that middle age is wont to regard presumptuous youth. "I have," he said quietly, and his blotchy face whitened.

"And did you really have the three wishes granted?" asked Mrs. White.

90 "I did," said the sergeant-major, and his glass tapped against his strong teeth.

"And has anybody else wished?" persisted the old lady.

"The first man had his three wishes. Yes," was the reply; "I don't know what the first two were, but the third was for death. That's how I got the paw."

His tones were so grave that a hush fell upon the group.

"If you've had your three wishes, it's no good to you now, then, Morris," said the old man at last. "What do you keep it for?"

100 The soldier shook his head. "Fancy, I suppose," he said slowly. "I did have some idea of selling it, but I don't think I will. It has caused enough mischief already. Besides, people won't buy. They think it's a fairy tale, some of them; and those who do think anything of it want to try it first and pay me afterward."

"If you could have another three wishes," said the old man, eyeing him keenly, "would you have them?"

"I don't know," said the other. "I don't know."

He took the paw, and dangling it between his forefinger 110 and thumb, suddenly threw it upon the fire. White, with a slight cry, stooped down and snatched it off.

"Better let it burn," said the soldier solemnly.

"If you don't want it, Morris," said the other, "give it to me."

"I won't," said his friend doggedly. "I threw it on the fire. If you keep it, don't blame me for what happens. Pitch it on the fire again like a sensible man."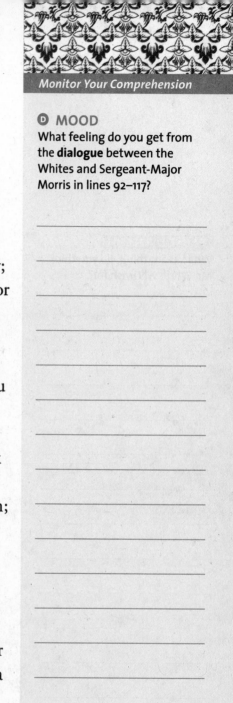

The other shook his head and examined his new 120 possession closely. "How do you do it?" he inquired.

"Hold it up in your right hand and wish aloud," said the sergeant-major, "but I warn you of the consequences."

ⅅ MOOD
What feeling do you get from the **dialogue** between the Whites and Sergeant-Major Morris in lines 92–117?

"Sounds like the *Arabian Nights*,"[8] said Mrs. White, as she rose and began to set the supper. "Don't you think you might wish for four pairs of hands for me?"

Her husband drew the talisman[9] from his pocket, and then all three burst into laughter as the sergeant-major, with a look of alarm on his face, caught him by the arm.

"If you must wish," he said gruffly, "wish for something sensible." **PAUSE & REFLECT**

PAUSE & REFLECT

What, if anything, do you think Mr. White will wish for?

_____

_____

_____

_____

_____

_____

_____

_____

_____

_____

_____

_____

_____

_____

_____

_____

_____

_____

130   Mr. White dropped it back in his pocket, and placing chairs, motioned his friend to the table. In the business of supper the talisman was partly forgotten, and afterward the three sat listening in an enthralled fashion to a second installment of the soldier's adventures in India.

"If the tale about the monkey's paw is not more truthful than those he has been telling us," said Herbert, as the door closed behind their guest, just in time for him to catch the last train, "we shan't make much out of it."

"Did you give him anything for it, Father?" inquired

140 Mrs. White, regarding her husband closely.

"A trifle," said he, coloring slightly. "He didn't want it, but I made him take it. And he pressed me again to throw it away."

"Likely," said Herbert, with pretended horror. "Why, we're going to be rich, and famous, and happy. Wish to be an emperor, Father, to begin with; then you can't be henpecked."

He darted round the table, pursued by the maligned Mrs. White armed with an antimacassar.[10]

150   Mr. White took the paw from his pocket and eyed it dubiously. "I don't know what to wish for, and that's a fact," he said slowly. "It seems to me I've got all I want."

"If you only cleared the house, you'd be quite happy, wouldn't you?" said Herbert, with his hand on his shoulder. "Well, wish for two hundred pounds, then; that'll just do it."

---

8. *Arabian Nights:* a famous collection of Asian stories.

9. **talisman** (tăl′ĭs-mən): an object thought to have magical powers.

10. **antimacassar** (ăn′tĭ-mə-kăs′ər): a cloth placed over an arm or back of a chair.

His father, smiling shamefacedly at his own <u>credulity</u>, held up the talisman, as his son, with a solemn face, somewhat marred by a wink at his mother, sat down at the
160 piano and struck a few impressive chords.

"I wish for two hundred pounds," said the old man distinctly.

A fine crash from the piano greeted the words, interrupted by a shuddering cry from the old man. His wife and son ran toward him.

"It moved," he cried, with a glance of disgust at the object as it lay on the floor. "As I wished, it twisted in my hand like a snake."

"Well, I don't see the money," said his son, as he picked
170 it up and placed it on the table, "and I bet I never shall."

"It must have been your fancy, father," said his wife, regarding him anxiously.

He shook his head. "Never mind, though; there's no harm done, but it gave me a shock all the same."

They sat down by the fire again. Outside, the wind was higher than ever, and the old man started nervously at the sound of a door banging upstairs. A silence unusual and depressing settled upon all three, which lasted until the old couple rose to retire for the night. **E**

180 "I expect you'll find the cash tied up in a big bag in the middle of your bed," said Herbert, as he bade them good-night, "and something horrible squatting up on top of the wardrobe[11] watching you as you pocket your ill-gotten gains."

He sat alone in the darkness, gazing at the dying fire, and seeing faces in it. The last face was so horrible and so simian[12] that he gazed at it in amazement. It got so vivid that, with a little uneasy laugh, he felt on the table for a glass containing a little water to throw over it. His hand
190 grasped the monkey's paw, and with a little shiver he wiped his hand on his coat and went up to bed. **F**

E MOOD
Reread lines 163–179. Underline the **imagery** in these lines. To what senses does it appeal? Explain how the imagery contributes to the mood.

_____

_____

_____

_____

F IDENTIFY TYPE OF NARRATOR
Mr. White sees something in the fire. Add this event—and the narrator's description of it—to your chart.

Event

↓

Narrator's Description

---

11. **wardrobe:** a piece of furniture that serves as a closet.
12. **simian** (sĭm′ē-ən): monkey- or ape-like.

II

In the brightness of the wintry sun next morning as it streamed over the breakfast table he laughed at his fears. There was an air of prosaic[13] wholesomeness about the room which it had lacked on the previous night, and the dirty, shriveled little paw was pitched on the sideboard[14] with a carelessness which betokened no great belief in its virtues.[15]

"I suppose all old soldiers are the same," said Mrs. White. "The idea of our listening to such nonsense! How could wishes be granted in these days? And if they could, how could two hundred pounds hurt you, father?"

"Might drop on his head from the sky," said the frivolous[16] Herbert.

"Morris said the things happened so naturally," said his father, "that you might if you so wished attribute it to coincidence."

"Well, don't break into the money before I come back," said Herbert as he rose from the table. "I'm afraid it'll turn you into a mean, avaricious[17] man, and we shall have to disown you."

His mother laughed, and following him to the door, watched him down the road; and returning to the breakfast table, was very happy at the expense of her husband's credulity. All of which did not prevent her from scurrying to the door at the postman's knock, when she found that the post brought a tailor's bill.

"Herbert will have some more of his funny remarks, I expect, when he comes home," she said, as they sat at dinner.

PAUSE & REFLECT

"I dare say," said Mr. White, "but for all that, the thing moved in my hand; that I'll swear to."

PAUSE & REFLECT

How would you describe the relationship between the Whites and their son?

---

13. **prosaic** (prō-zā′ĭk): ordinary.

14. **sideboard**: a piece of furniture used to store linens and dishes.

15. **virtues**: powers.

16. **frivolous** (frĭv′ə-ləs): inappropriately silly.

17. **avaricious** (ăv′ə-rĭsh′es): greedy.

"You thought it did," said the old lady soothingly.

"I say it did," replied the other. "There was no thought about it; I had just—What's the matter?"

His wife made no reply. She was watching the mysterious movements of a man outside, who, peering in an undecided fashion at the house, appeared to be trying to make up his mind to enter. In mental connection with the two hundred pounds, she noticed that the stranger was well dressed, and wore a silk hat of glossy newness. Three times he paused
230 at the gate, and then walked on again. The fourth time he stood with his hand upon it, and then with sudden resolution flung it open and walked up the path. Mrs. White at the same moment placed her hands behind her, and hurriedly unfastening the strings of her apron, put that useful article of apparel beneath the cushion of her chair.

She brought the stranger, who seemed ill at ease, into the room. He gazed at her furtively, and listened in a preoccupied fashion as the old lady apologized for the appearance of the room, and her husband's coat, a garment
240 which he usually reserved for the garden. She then waited patiently for him to broach his business, but he was at first strangely silent.

"I—was asked to call," he said at last, and stooped and picked a piece of cotton from his trousers. "I come from Maw and Meggins."

The old lady started. "Is anything the matter?" she asked breathlessly. "Has anything happened to Herbert? What is it? What is it?" **PAUSE & REFLECT**

Her husband interposed. "There, there, mother," he said
250 hastily. "Sit down, and don't jump to conclusions. You've not brought bad news, I'm sure, sir;" and he eyed the other wistfully.

"I'm sorry—" began the visitor.

"Is he hurt?" demanded the mother wildly.

The visitor bowed in assent. "Badly hurt," he said quietly, "but he is not in any pain."

PAUSE & REFLECT
Why do you think the stranger has arrived? What kind of news will he have about Robert?

_____

_____

_____

_____

_____

_____

_____

_____

_____

_____

_____

_____

_____

"Oh!" said the old woman, clasping her hands. "Thank goodness for that! Thank—"

She broke off suddenly as the sinister meaning of the assurance dawned upon her and she saw the awful confirmation of her fears in the other's averted face. She caught her breath, and turning to her slower-witted husband, laid her trembling old hand upon his. There was a long silence. **G**

"He was caught in the machinery," said the visitor at length in a low voice.

"Caught in the machinery," repeated Mr. White, in a dazed fashion, "yes."

He sat staring blankly out at the window, and taking his wife's hand between his own, pressed it as he had been wont to do in their old courting days nearly forty years before.

"He was the only one left to us," he said, turning gently to the visitor. "It is hard."

The other coughed, and rising, walked slowly to the window. "The firm wished me to convey their sincere sympathy with you in your great loss," he said, without looking round. "I beg that you will understand I am only their servant and merely obeying orders."

There was no reply; the old woman's face was white, her eyes staring, and her breath inaudible; on the husband's face was a look such as his friend the sergeant might have carried into his first action.

"I was to say that Maw and Meggins disclaim all responsibility," continued the other. "They admit no liability at all, but in consideration of your son's services, they wish to present you with a certain sum as **compensation**."

Mr. White dropped his wife's hand, and rising to his feet, gazed with a look of horror at his visitor. His dry lips shaped the words, "How much?"

"Two hundred pounds," was the answer.

G MOOD
Think about the news the stranger reveals during his conversation with the Whites. What feeling do you get as a result of this news?

_____

_____

_____

_____

_____

_____

_____

compensation (kŏm′pən-sā′shən) *n.* something, such as money, received as payment

Unconscious of his wife's shriek, the old man smiled faintly, put out his hands like a sightless man, and dropped, a senseless heap, to the floor.

III

In the huge new cemetery, some two miles distant, the old people buried their dead, and came back to a house steeped in shadow and silence. It was all over so quickly that at first they could hardly realize it, and remained in a state of expectation as though of something else to happen—something else which was to lighten this load, too heavy for old hearts to bear.

But the days passed, and expectation gave place to <u>resignation</u>—the hopeless resignation of the old, sometimes miscalled apathy. Sometimes they hardly exchanged a word, for now they had nothing to talk about, and their days were long to weariness. **H**

It was about a week after that the old man, waking suddenly in the night, stretched out his hand and found himself alone. The room was in darkness, and the sound of subdued weeping came from the window. He raised himself in bed and listened.

"Come back," he said tenderly. "You will be cold."

"It is colder for my son," said the old woman, and wept afresh.

The sound of her sobs died away on his ears. The bed was warm, and his eyes heavy with sleep. He dozed fitfully, and then slept until a sudden wild cry from his wife awoke him with a start.

"*The paw!*" she cried wildly. "The monkey's paw!"

He started up in alarm. "Where? Where is it? What's the matter?"

She came stumbling across the room toward him. "I want it," she said quietly. "You've not destroyed it?"

"It's in the parlor, on the bracket," he replied, marveling. "Why?"

resignation (rĕz′ ĭg-nā′shən) *n.* acceptance of something that is inescapable

H IDENTIFY TYPE OF NARRATOR
Does the narrator reveal the characters' thoughts and feelings about Herbert's death? Explain.

_____

_____

_____

_____

_____

_____

_____

❶ MOOD

Reread lines 312–335. How would you describe the mood in these lines? What helps create the mood—the setting, the imagery, or the characters' conversation?

_____

_____

_____

_____

_____

❷ MOOD

Reread lines 348–356. Underline the **imagery** the author uses to establish mood in this paragraph.

_____

_____

_____

_____

She cried and laughed together, and bending over, kissed his cheek.

"I only just thought of it," she said hysterically. "Why didn't I think of it before? Why didn't you think of it?"

330 "Think of what?" he questioned.

"The other two wishes," she replied rapidly. "We've only had one."

"Was not that enough?" he demanded fiercely.

"No," she cried triumphantly; "we'll have one more. Go down and get it quickly, and wish our boy alive again." ❶

The man sat up in bed and flung the bedclothes from his quaking limbs. "You are mad!" he cried, aghast.

"Get it," she panted; "get it quickly, and wish—Oh, my boy, my boy!"

340 Her husband struck a match and lit the candle. "Get back to bed," he said unsteadily. "You don't know what you are saying."

"We had the first wish granted," said the old woman feverishly; "why not the second?"

"A coincidence," stammered the old man.

"Go and get it and wish," cried his wife, quivering with excitement.

He went down in the darkness, and felt his way to the parlor, and then to the mantelpiece. The talisman was in 350 its place, and a horrible fear that the unspoken wish might bring his mutilated son before him ere he could escape from the room seized upon him, and he caught his breath as he found that he had lost the direction of the door. His brow cold with sweat, he felt his way round the table, and groped along the wall until he found himself in the small passage with the unwholesome thing in his hand. ❷

Even his wife's face seemed changed as he entered the room. It was white and expectant, and to his fears seemed to have an unnatural look upon it. He was afraid of her.

360 "*Wish!*" she cried, in a strong voice.

"It is foolish and wicked," he faltered.

"Wish!" repeated his wife.

He raised his hand. "I wish my son alive again."

PAUSE & REFLECT

The talisman fell to the floor, and he regarded it fearfully. Then he sank trembling into a chair as the old woman, with burning eyes, walked to the window and raised the blind.

He sat until he was chilled with the cold, glancing occasionally at the figure of the old woman peering
370 through the window. The candle-end, which had burned below the rim of the china candlestick, was throwing pulsating shadows on the ceiling and walls, until, with a flicker larger than the rest, it expired. The old man, with an unspeakable sense of relief at the failure of the talisman, crept back to his bed, and a minute or two afterward the old woman came silently and apathetically beside him.

Neither spoke, but lay silently listening to the ticking of the clock. A stair creaked, and a squeaky mouse scurried noisily through the wall. The darkness was oppressive, and
380 after lying for some time gathering up his courage, he took the box of matches, and striking one, went downstairs for a candle.

At the foot of the stairs the match went out, and he paused to strike another; and at the same moment a knock, so quiet and stealthy as to be scarcely audible, sounded on the front door. **K**

The matches fell from his hand. He stood motionless, his breath suspended until the knock was repeated. Then he turned and fled swiftly back to his room, and closed the
390 door behind him. A third knock sounded through the house.

"*What's that?*" cried the old woman, starting up.

"A rat," said the old man in shaking tones— "a rat. It passed me on the stairs."

His wife sat up in bed listening. A loud knock resounded through the house.

"It's Herbert!" she screamed. "It's Herbert!"

L IDENTIFY TYPE OF NARRATOR
Reread lines 383–429 to determine whether the narrator is objective or subjective. Explain your answer.

_____

_____

_____

_____

_____

_____

_____

_____

_____

_____

_____

_____

_____

_____

_____

_____

_____

_____

_____

_____

She ran to the door, but her husband was before her, and catching her by the arm, held her tightly.

"What are you going to do?" he whispered hoarsely.

400 "It's my boy; it's Herbert!" she cried, struggling mechanically. "I forgot it was two miles away. What are you holding me for? Let go. I must open the door."

"Don't let it in," cried the old man, trembling.

"You're afraid of your own son," she cried, struggling. "Let me go. I'm coming, Herbert; I'm coming."

There was another knock, and another. The old woman with a sudden wrench broke free and ran from the room. Her husband followed to the landing, and called after her appealingly as she hurried downstairs. He heard the chain
410 rattle back and the bottom bolt drawn slowly and stiffly from the socket. Then the old woman's voice, strained and panting.

"The bolt," she cried loudly. "Come down. I can't reach it."

But her husband was on his hands and knees groping wildly on the floor in search of the paw. If he could only find it before the thing outside got in. A perfect fusillade[18] of knocks reverberated through the house, and he heard the scraping of a chair as his wife put it down in the passage
420 against the door. He heard the creaking of the bolt as it came slowly back, and at the same moment he found the monkey's paw, and frantically breathed his third and last wish.

The knocking ceased suddenly, although the echoes of it were still in the house. He heard the chair drawn back, and the door opened. A cold wind rushed up the staircase, and a long loud wail of disappointment and misery from his wife gave him courage to run down to her side, and then to the gate beyond. The streetlamp flickering opposite shone on a quiet and deserted road. **L**

18. **fusillade** (fyoo′sə-läd′): discharge from many guns; a rapid outburst.

Text Analysis: Mood

In the chart below, give at least two examples of setting details, imagery, and conversations that helped create the mood of the story. Then describe the mood of the story in a sentence.

Setting Details	Imagery	Conversations

Mood: _____

_____

_____

Which of the elements—setting, imagery, or conversations—do you think was most effective in creating the overall mood of "The Monkey's Paw"? Explain your choice.

_____

_____

_____

_____

Reading Skill: Identify Type of Narrator

In the chart, identify whether the narrator of this story is objective or subjective. Provide two details from the story to support your response.

The narrator is (circle one)	
Objective	Subjective

Details:

1. _____

_____

_____

2. _____

_____

_____

Are you SUPERSTITIOUS?

Reread lines 204–206 of the story. After reading this story, are you more likely to believe in superstitions or coincidence? Why?

_____

_____

_____

Vocabulary Practice

Choose the word in each group that is most nearly opposite in meaning to the boldfaced word.

1. **peril:** **(a)** safety, **(b)** risk, **(c)** hazard

2. **credulity:** **(a)** simplicity, **(b)** doubt, **(c)** openness

3. **resignation:** **(a)** respect, **(b)** resistance, **(c)** acceptance

4. **compensation:** **(a)** consideration, **(b)** reward, **(c)** loss

5. **fate:** **(a)** choice, **(b)** destiny, **(c)** luck

6. **grimace:** **(a)** frown, **(b)** scowl, **(c)** grin

Academic Vocabulary in Writing

circumstance	emerge	predominant	rely	technology

Why do you suppose writers so often **rely** on stormy weather and night time to create a fearful or suspenseful mood? Use at least one Academic Vocabulary word in your response. Definitions of these words are on page 129.

_____

_____

_____

_____

Assessment Practice

DIRECTIONS Use "The Monkey's Paw" to answer questions 1–6.

1 Why does Sergeant-Major Morris throw the monkey's paw onto the fire?

- (A) It moved and startled him.
- (B) The fire is needed for the wishes to work.
- (C) He believes it will do harm and wants to destroy it.
- (D) He doesn't want someone else to get his three wishes.

2 Which of these lines from the story use setting details to create mood?

- (A) _the night was cold and wet_
- (B) _don't blame me for what happens_
- (C) _an ordinary little paw, dried to a mummy_
- (D) _The last face was so horrible and so simian_

3 How does the family's mood change after Mr. White makes his first wish?

- (A) They are no longer concerned.
- (B) They start to joke with one another.
- (C) They become nervous and depressed.
- (D) They start to feel excited about the possibilities.

4 When Morris says, "If you keep it, don't blame me for what happens," (line 116) it creates a mood of —

- (A) joy
- (B) hope
- (C) weariness
- (D) suspense

5 At the end of the story, the knocking stops suddenly because —

- (A) the knocking was only in Mr. White's imagination
- (B) Mr. White wishes Herbert back to his grave
- (C) Mrs. White has opened the door
- (D) Herbert has come alive

6 A narrator is subjective if his description includes —

- (A) facts
- (B) characters' thoughts
- (C) information about events
- (D) a physical description of the characters

The Story of an Eyewitness
Magazine Article by Jack London

Letter from New Orleans: Leaving Desire
Magazine Article by Jon Lee Anderson

Interview Questions

1. Where were you when the disaster struck?

2. _____

_____

_____

3. _____

_____

_____

4. _____

_____

5. _____

_____

_____

What is the role of a WITNESS?

When events such as natural disasters occur, a witness might describe what he or she saw so others can comprehend what happened. The authors of the following articles witnessed natural disasters. Their writing allows readers to share in their experiences.

ROLE-PLAY Imagine that a tornado, flood, or snow storm has just struck your community. With a partner, write five questions a reporter might ask an eyewitness. Then role-play a news broadcast on the disaster. Decide who will be the news reporter and who will be the eyewitness; then conduct the interview. Remember that your audience will want to know what the disaster looked, sounded, and felt like, as well as how people got hurt or stayed safe.

Text Analysis: Author's Purpose

Writers usually write for one or more of these purposes:

- to express thoughts or feelings
- to inform or explain
- to persuade
- to entertain

The authors of the following articles have the same main purpose: to inform readers about a disaster. However, each writer's purpose is actually more specific. London wants to explain that the earthquake caused widespread destruction. Anderson wants to explain the devastating effect a disaster has on people's lives. As you read their accounts, notice how the authors present and develop ideas to achieve their purposes.

Reading Strategy: Set a Purpose for Reading

Your **purpose** for reading the following articles is to compare and contrast how each author achieves his purpose. Use the side-column notes to help you complete this chart.

	"The Story of an Eyewitness"	"Letter from New Orleans"
What is the writer's main purpose?	to explain that the earthquake caused widespread destruction	to explain the devastating effect a disaster has people's lives
How broad or narrow is the writer's focus?		
Which events and people does the writer describe?		
Which details and images have a big impact on you?		

Vocabulary in Context

Note: Words are listed in the order in which they appear in the articles.

lavishly (lăv′ĭsh-lē) *adv.* extravagantly
*People tend not to behave **lavishly** after disaster strikes.*

menace (mĕn′ĭs) *n.* possible danger; threat
*The fire was a **menace** to all of the city's inhabitants.*

compel (kəm-pĕl′) *v.* to pressure by force
*The fire **compelled** families to leave all their belongings and flee.*

vigilantly (vĭj′ə-lənt-lē) *adv.* a state of alertness; watchfully
*Rescuers searched **vigilantly** for people stranded by the flood.*

intermittently (ĭn′tər-mĭt′nt-lē) *adv.* stopping and starting at intervals
***Intermittently** we saw signs that people remained in their homes.*

disconcert (dĭs′kən-sûrt′) *v.* to ruffle; to frustrate by throwing into disorder
*Many pets were seen looking **disconcerted** and distressed.*

SET A PURPOSE
FOR READING

Read this article to experience a first-hand account of the aftermath of a deadly earthquake.

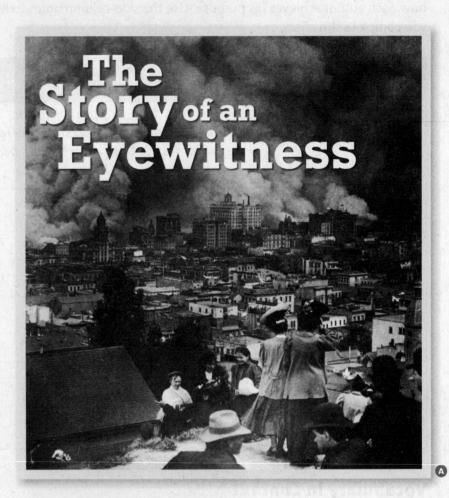

The Story of an Eyewitness

Magazine Article by Jack London

A AUTHOR'S PURPOSE

Based on this photograph, make a prediction about whether the focus of the article is going to be broad or narrow. Write your prediction in the chart on page 181.

BACKGROUND On April 18, 1906, a massive earthquake shook San Francisco, setting in motion events that would eventually destroy most of the city. Historians estimate that around 3,000 people died and 250,000 people were left homeless.

*U*pon receipt of the first news of the earthquake, *Collier's* telegraphed to Mr. Jack London—who lives only forty miles from San Francisco—requesting him to go to the scene of the disaster and write the story of what he saw. Mr. London started at once, and he sent *the following dramatic description of the tragic events he witnessed in the burning city.*

The earthquake shook down in San Francisco hundreds of thousands of dollars worth of walls and chimneys. But the conflagration[1] that followed burned up hundreds of millions of dollars' worth of property. There is no estimating within hundreds of millions the actual damage wrought. Not in history has a modern imperial city been so completely destroyed. San Francisco is gone. Nothing remains of it but memories and a fringe of dwelling houses on its outskirts. Its industrial section is wiped out. Its business section is wiped out. Its social and residential section is wiped out. The factories and warehouses, the great stores and newspaper buildings, the hotels and the palaces of the nabobs,[2] are all gone. Remains only the fringe of dwelling houses on the outskirts of what was once San Francisco. **B**

Within an hour after the earthquake shock the smoke of San Francisco's burning was a lurid[3] tower visible a hundred miles away. And for three days and nights this lurid tower swayed in the sky, reddening the sun, darkening the day, and filling the land with smoke.

On Wednesday morning at a quarter past five came the earthquake. A minute later the flames were leaping upward. In a dozen different quarters south of Market Street, in the working-class ghetto, and in the factories, fires started. There was no opposing the flames.

B **AUTHOR'S PURPOSE**
How much of the city is Jack London describing in this paragraph?

_____

_____

_____

_____

_____

_____

_____

_____

---

1. **conflagration** (kŏn'flə-grā'shən): a large destructive fire.
2. **nabobs** (nā'bŏbz'): people of wealth and prominence.
3. **lurid** (lŏŏr'ĭd): glowing with the glare of fire through a haze.

There was no organization, no communication. All the cunning adjustments of a twentieth century city had been smashed by the earthquake. The streets were humped into ridges and depressions, and piled with the debris of fallen walls. The steel rails were twisted into perpendicular and horizontal angles. The telephone and telegraph systems were disrupted. And the great
40 water-mains had burst. All the shrewd contrivances[4] and safeguards of man had been thrown out of gear by thirty seconds' twitching of the earth-crust. **C**

The Fire Made Its Own Draft

By Wednesday afternoon, inside of twelve hours, half the heart of the city was gone. At that time I watched the vast conflagration from out on the bay. It was dead calm. Not a flicker of wind stirred. Yet from every side wind was pouring in upon the city. East, west, north, and south, strong winds were blowing upon the doomed city. The heated air rising made an enormous
50 vacuum. Thus did the fire of itself build its own colossal chimney through the atmosphere. Day and night this dead calm continued, and yet, near to the flames, the wind was often half a gale, so mighty was the vacuum.

Wednesday night saw the destruction of the very heart of the city. Dynamite was __lavishly__ used, and many of San Francisco's proudest structures were crumbled by man himself into ruins, but there was no withstanding the onrush of the flames. Time and
60 again successful stands were made by the fire-fighters,

C AUTHOR'S PURPOSE
What people and events does London describe in lines 28–42? Why do you think he includes this information?

_____

_____

_____

_____

_____

_____

_____

lavishly (lăv′ĭsh-lē) *adv.* extravagantly

---

4. **contrivances** (kən-trī′vən-sĕz): acts of clever planning.

and every time the flames flanked[5] around on either side or came up from the rear, and turned to defeat the hard-won victory. An enumeration[6] of the buildings destroyed would be a directory of San Francisco. An enumeration of the buildings undestroyed would be a line and several addresses. An enumeration of the deeds of heroism would stock a library and bankrupt the Carnegie medal fund. An enumeration of the dead will never be made. All vestiges[7] of them were
70 destroyed by the flames. The number of the victims of the earthquake will never be known. South of Market Street, where the loss of life was particularly heavy, was the first to catch fire. **D**

Remarkable as it may seem, Wednesday night while the whole city crashed and roared into ruin, was a quiet night. There were no crowds. There was no shouting and yelling. There was no hysteria, no disorder. I passed Wednesday night in the path of the advancing flames, and in all those terrible hours I
80 saw not one woman who wept, not one man who was excited, not one person who was in the slightest degree panic stricken.

Before the flames, throughout the night, fled tens of thousands of homeless ones. Some were wrapped in blankets. Others carried bundles of bedding and dear household treasures. Sometimes a whole family was harnessed to a carriage or delivery wagon that was weighted down with their possessions. Baby

D AUTHOR'S PURPOSE
Reread lines 55–73. What aspects of the disaster is the writer describing?

_____

_____

_____

_____

_____

_____

_____

_____

_____

_____

---

5. **flanked** (flăngk'd): placed at the side of.
6. **enumeration** (ĭ-nōō′mə-rā′shŭn): the act of counting or listing one by one.
7. **vestiges** (věs′tĭj-əs): visible signs that something once existed.

E AUTHOR'S PURPOSE
Think about whether London has described individuals or crowds so far. Jot this information down in your chart.

The Story of an Eyewitness
Which events and people does the writer describe?

↓

_____
_____
_____
_____

Why might he have chosen to describe events and people in this way?

_____
_____
_____
_____
_____

menace (mĕn´ĭs) *n.* a possible danger; threat

compel (kəm-pĕl´) *v.* to pressure by force

buggies, toy wagons, and go-carts were used as trucks, while every other person was dragging a trunk. Yet everybody was gracious. The most perfect courtesy obtained. Never in all San Francisco's history were her people so kind and courteous as on this night of terror.

A Caravan of Trunks

All night these tens of thousands fled before the flames. Many of them, the poor people from the labor ghetto, had fled all day as well. They had left their homes burdened with possessions. Now and again they lightened up, flinging out upon the street clothing and treasures they had dragged for miles. **E**

They held on longest to their trunks, and over these trunks many a strong man broke his heart that night. The hills of San Francisco are steep, and up these hills, mile after mile, were the trunks dragged. Everywhere were trunks with across them lying their exhausted owners, men and women. Before the march of the flames were flung picket lines of soldiers. And a block at a time, as the flames advanced, these pickets retreated. One of their tasks was to keep the trunk-pullers moving. The exhausted creatures, stirred on by the **menace** of bayonets,[8] would arise and struggle up the steep pavements, pausing from weakness every five or ten feet.

Often, after surmounting a heart-breaking hill, they would find another wall of flame advancing upon them at right angles and be **compelled** to change anew the

---

8. **bayonets** (bā´ə-nĕts´): blades that fit on the end of rifles and are used as weapons.

line of their retreat. In the end, completely played out, after toiling for a dozen hours like giants, thousands of them were compelled to abandon their trunks. Here the shopkeepers and soft members of the middle class were
120 at a disadvantage. But the working-men dug holes in vacant lots and backyards and buried their trunks.

The Doomed City

At nine o'clock Wednesday evening I walked down through the very heart of the city. I walked through miles and miles of magnificent buildings and towering skyscrapers. Here was no fire. All was in perfect order. The police patrolled the streets. Every building had its watchman at the door. And yet it was doomed, all of it. There was no water. The dynamite was giving out. And at right angles two different conflagrations were
130 sweeping down upon it. Ⓕ

At one o'clock in the morning I walked down through the same section. Everything still stood intact. There was no fire. And yet there was a change. A rain of ashes was falling. The watchmen at the doors were gone. The police had been withdrawn. There were no firemen, no fire-engines, no men fighting with dynamite. The district had been absolutely abandoned. I stood at the corner of Kearney and Market, in the very innermost heart of San Francisco. Kearney Street
140 was deserted. Half a dozen blocks away it was burning on both sides. The street was a wall of flame. And against this wall of flame, silhouetted sharply, were two United States cavalrymen sitting on their horses,

Ⓕ **AUTHOR'S PURPOSE**
Reread lines 122–123. Underline the reference to what time it is when London makes his observations. As you continue reading, look for other references to the time.

G AUTHOR'S PURPOSE
Reread lines 122–146. What information does London hope to convey by describing the same section of downtown twice?

_____

_____

_____

_____

_____

H AUTHOR'S PURPOSE
Reread lines 157–170. Underline all the references to time of day. What do these references tell you about how quickly the flames were spreading?

_____

_____

_____

_____

_____

_____

_____

calmly watching. That was all. Not another person was in sight. In the intact heart of the city, two troopers sat [on] their horses and watched. **G**

Spread of the Conflagration

Surrender was complete. There was no water. The sewers had long since been pumped dry. There was no dynamite. Another fire had broken out further uptown, and now from three sides conflagrations were sweeping down. The fourth side had been burned earlier in the day. In that direction stood the tottering walls of the Examiner Building, the burned-out Call Building, the smoldering ruins of the Grand Hotel, and the gutted, devastated, dynamited Palace Hotel.

The following will illustrate the sweep of the flames and the inability of men to calculate their spread. At eight o'clock Wednesday evening I passed through Union Square. It was packed with refugees. Thousands of them had gone to bed on the grass. Government tents had been set up, supper was being cooked, and the refugees were lining up for free meals.

At half past one in the morning three sides of Union Square were in flames. The fourth side, where stood the great St. Francis Hotel, was still holding out. An hour later, ignited from top and sides the St. Francis was flaming heavenward. Union Square, heaped high with mountains of trunks, was deserted. Troops, refugees, and all had retreated. **H**

A Fortune for a Horse!

It was at Union Square that I saw a man offering a thousand dollars for a team of horses. He was in charge of a truck piled high with trunks from some hotel. It had been hauled here into what was considered safety, and the horses had been taken out. The flames were on three sides of the Square and there were no horses.

Also, at this time, standing beside the truck, I urged a man to seek safety in flight. He was all but hemmed in by several conflagrations. He was an old man and he was on crutches. Said he: "Today is my birthday. Last night I was worth thirty thousand dollars. I bought some delicate fish and other things for my birthday dinner. I have had no dinner, and all I own are these crutches." **PAUSE & REFLECT**

I convinced him of his danger and started him limping on his way. An hour later, from a distance, I saw the truck-load of trunks burning merrily in the middle of the street.

On Thursday morning at a quarter past five, just twenty-four hours after the earthquake, I sat on the steps of a small residence on Nob Hill. With me sat Japanese, Italians, Chinese, and negroes—a bit of the cosmopolitan flotsam[9] of the wreck of the city. All about were the palaces of the nabob pioneers of Forty-nine.[10] To the east and south at right angles, were advancing two mighty walls of flame.

---

9. **flotsam** (flŏt′səm): floating wreckage after a ship has sunk.
10. **pioneers of Forty-nine:** reference to the pioneers who came to San Francisco during the California gold rush in 1849.

PAUSE & REFLECT
Reread lines 171–184. What do these anecdotes tell you about how people were responding to the dangerous situation?

Which events and people does the writer describe?

↓

I went inside with the owner of the house on the steps of which I sat. He was cool and cheerful and hospitable. "Yesterday morning," he said, "I was worth six hundred thousand dollars. This morning this house is all I have left. It will go in fifteen minutes. He pointed to a large cabinet. "That is my wife's collection of china. This rug upon which we stand is a present. It cost fifteen hundred dollars. Try that piano. Listen to its tone. There are few like it. There are no horses. The flames will be here in fifteen minutes." ❶

Outside the old Mark Hopkins residence a palace was just catching fire. The troops were falling back and driving the refugees before them. From every side came the roaring of flames, the crashing of walls, and the detonations of dynamite.

The Dawn of the Second Day

I passed out of the house. Day was trying to dawn through the smoke-pall[11] A sickly light was creeping over the face of things. Once only the sun broke through the smoke-pall, blood-red, and showing a quarter its usual size. The smoke-pall itself, viewed from beneath, was a rose color that pulsed and fluttered with lavender shades. Then it turned to mauve and yellow and dun[12] There was no sun. And so dawned the second day on stricken San Francisco.

An hour later I was creeping past the shattered dome of the City Hall. Than it there was no better exhibit of the destructive force of the earthquake. Most of the stone had been shaken from the great dome, leaving

---

11. **pall** (pôl): a covering that darkens or covers.

standing the naked framework of steel. Market Street was piled high with the wreckage, and across the wreckage lay the overthrown pillars of the City Hall shattered into short crosswise sections.

230   This section of the city, with the exception of the Mint and the Post-Office, was already a waste of smoking ruins. Here and there through the smoke, creeping warily under the shadows of tottering walls, emerged occasional men and women. It was like the meeting of the handful of survivors after the day of the end of the world. **PAUSE & REFLECT**

Beeves Slaughtered and Roasted

On Mission Street lay a dozen steers, in a neat row stretching across the street just as they had been struck down by the flying ruins of the earthquake. The fire

---

12. **dun** (dŭn): dull brownish gray.

J AUTHOR'S PURPOSE
What event does London track from beginning to end? Why do you think he focuses on this event?

had passed through afterward and roasted them. The
240 human dead had been carried away before the fire
came. At another place on Mission Street I saw a milk
wagon. A steel telegraph pole had smashed down sheer
through the driver's seat and crushed the front wheels.
The milk cans lay scattered around.

All day Thursday and all Thursday night, all day
Friday and Friday night, the flames still raged on.

Friday night saw the flames finally conquered,
though not until Russian Hill and Telegraph Hill had
been swept and three-quarters of a mile of wharves and
250 docks had been licked up. **J**

The Last Stand

The great stand of the fire-fighters was made Thursday
night on Van Ness Avenue. Had they failed here, the
comparatively few remaining houses of the city would
have been swept. Here were the magnificent residences
of the second generation of San Francisco nabobs, and
these, in a solid zone, were dynamited down across the
path of the fire. Here and there the flames leaped the
zone, but these fires were beaten out, principally by
the use of wet blankets and rugs.

260 San Francisco, at the present time, is like the
crater of a volcano, around which are camped tens
of thousands of refugees. At the Presidio[13] alone are
at least twenty thousand. All the surrounding cities

---

13. **Presidio** (prĭ-sē′dē-ō′): a historic military post in San Francisco.

and towns are jammed with the homeless ones, where
they are being cared for by the relief committees.
The refugees were carried free by the railroads to any
point they wished to go, and it is estimated that over
one hundred thousand people have left the peninsula
on which San Francisco stood. The government has
270 the situation in hand, and, thanks to the immediate
relief given by the whole United States, there is not
the slightest possibility of a famine. The bankers
and business men have already set about making
preparations to rebuild San Francisco. **K**

K AUTHOR'S PURPOSE
What information about the
disaster does London provide in
this last paragraph?

_____

_____

_____

_____

_____

_____

_____

_____

_____

SET A PURPOSE
FOR READING
Read this article to discover the author's experiences during the flooding of New Orleans in 2005.

LETTER FROM NEW ORLEANS:

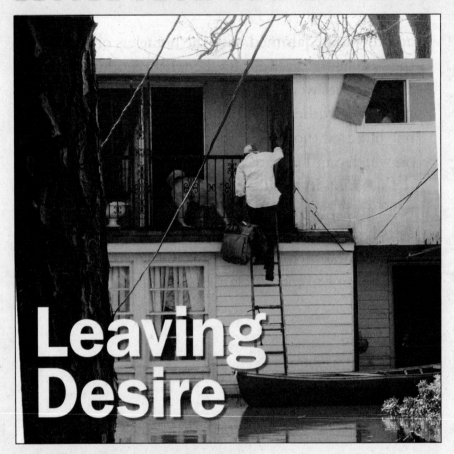

Leaving Desire

Magazine Article by Jon Lee Anderson

BACKGROUND Hurricane Katrina hit the Gulf Coast on the morning of August 29, 2005. New Orleans suffered some of the worst damage of the Gulf Coast cities. Heavy flooding there destroyed entire neighborhoods, forced thousands of people to flee the city, and stranded many others in dangerous and unsanitary conditions until they, too, could get out.

When I first saw Lionel Petrie, he was standing on the second-story porch of his house, at the junction of Desire Street and North Bunny Friend, in the Ninth Ward of New Orleans. The house was built

of wood, with white siding and peach trim. Petrie, an African-American with salt-and-pepper hair and a mustache, appeared to be in his sixties. A large Akita[1] was standing next to him, ears perked <u>vigilantly</u>. The two of them looked out from across the fenced-in
10 expanse of the front yard. Petrie was clearly an organized man: a painter's ladder was dangling from the railing of the porch, and a clutch of orange life vests hung within reach of a fibreglass canoe that was tethered to the house. The canoe bobbed on the surface of the stinking black water that filled the street and had engulfed most of the first floor of the house. The spiked parapet of a wrought-iron fence poked up about eight inches above the waterline, etching out a formal square that separated the house from the street. **L**

20   Petrie's house was different from those of his neighbors, most of which were small brick row houses, or rundown clapboard houses that had deep porches flush with the street. His was set far back in the lot, and had a self-possessed air about it. Near the fence, in what must have been the driveway, the hoods of two submerged cars and a truck could be seen.

I was seated in the back of a four-person Yamaha WaveRunner that was piloted by Shawn Alladio, an energetic woman in her forties, with long blond hair,
30 from Whittier, California. Eight days had passed since Hurricane Katrina made landfall, and Alladio was out on a search for trapped survivors and for what rescuers were calling "holdouts"—residents who didn't want to leave their homes—in one of the poorest and

vigilantly (vĭj'ə-lənt-lē) *adv.* in a state of alertness; watchfully

L **AUTHOR'S PURPOSE**
Reread lines 1–19. What kinds of details does the author include?

_____

_____

_____

_____

_____

_____

_____

_____

_____

_____

_____

---

1. **Akita** (ä-kē'tə): a breed of Japanese hunting dog.

worst-hit parts of the city, the Ninth Ward, in eastern
New Orleans.

   Alladio maneuvered the WaveRunner so that we
were alongside Petrie's fence, and, after calling out a
greeting to him, she asked him if he wanted to leave;
40 he waved politely in response, but shook his head. She
told him that the floodwater was toxic and that he
would soon become sick. He said something in reply,
but we couldn't hear him because of the rumble of
the WaveRunner's idling engine. Alladio turned the
ignition key off.

   Petrie explained that his wife and son and daughter
had left the city by car, heading for Baton Rouge,
the day before Katrina hit. He didn't know where his
family was now, and, if he left, they wouldn't know
50 where he was. He said that he intended to wait for
them to come back, and for the waters to go down.

   Alladio told him that the authorities were not
allowing people to return to this part of New Orleans,
and that it might be a month before the waters receded.
He listened carefully, nodded, and replied that he had
stocks of food and some water; that he'd be all right—
he'd wait. He patted his dog's head. "Thank you, but
I'll be fine," he said. Alladio tried again. "I can promise
you that you will *not* see your family if you stay here,"
60 she told him; it was much likelier that he would pass
out and die from the fumes from the water. Ⓜ

   He asked whether she would promise that he would
be able to join his family.

   Alladio paused, and said to me quietly, "I can't
promise him that. If I turn him over to the authorities,

Ⓜ **AUTHOR'S PURPOSE**
Reread lines 46–61. Underline
the details that tell you about
Petrie's situation. How would
you describe his attitude toward
his situation?

like the other evacuees, he could end up anywhere in the country."

Turning back to Petrie, she asked, "If I drive you to Baton Rouge myself, will you come with me?"

70 "You would take me yourself?" he asked.

"Yes," she said. "I promise. Today, when I am done with my work, I will take you there."

Petrie took a step back on his porch. He raised his head thoughtfully and asked, "Can I take my dog with me?"

"Oh, God," Alladio said under her breath. "I hate this." Then she said to him, "I am so sorry, Mr. Petrie, but, no, they won't allow us to take out animals. You will have to leave him here."

80 Petrie gripped the railing of the porch and leaned over again, in a kind of slow, sustained forward lurch, his head down. Then he nodded and said, "O.K."

Alladio told Petrie to prepare a small bag with his essential belongings, to say goodbye to his dog and, if he wanted, put out some food and water for him. She would be back in an hour to pick him up; in the meantime, she needed to see if there were more people who needed evacuating. He said, "O.K.," and waved, and went back inside the house. The dog followed him. **N**

90 Alladio had arrived in New Orleans on Saturday, September 3rd, with a team of California rescue workers and a small flotilla[2] of donated WaveRunners. She and her team were loosely attached to a task force sent by the State of California, but were mostly on

N AUTHOR'S PURPOSE
Why do you think the writer discusses the situation with Petrie and the dog in such detail?

_____

_____

_____

_____

_____

_____

_____

_____

---

2. **flotilla** (flō-tĭl′ə): a small fleet of ships.

⊙ **AUTHOR'S PURPOSE**
Why might the writer have
focused on Alladio and her team
of rescue workers? Write your
thoughts in the chart.

Letter from New Orleans
Which events and people does the writer describe?

↓

their own. We had met at a staging area underneath
an elevated section of Interstate 10. As I arrived,
evacuees were being brought out of the water to a
slightly raised stretch of land where railroad tracks
ran under the highway. A boat came up and deposited
100 an elderly black couple. Rescuers carried the woman,
who was wearing a denim skirt, a T-shirt, and gold
earrings, and sat her down on a fallen telephone pole.
She rocked back and forth, with one hand raised, and
murmured, "I just want to tell you—thank you, Jesus."
Her husband walked over unsteadily to join her. They
had stayed at home until just before the hurricane,
and then gone to their church. As the water rose, they
took refuge in the choir loft. They stayed there for
eight days, drinking the water the storm washed in.
110 "We were down to our last two crackers," she said.
Another man was brought over, shaking, and speaking
incoherently. The only words I could make out were
"I'm still alive." ⊙

After putting on chest waders to protect ourselves
from the fetid[3] floodwaters—which Alladio warned
me were "really gnarly"—we set off by boat from
Interstate 10. . . .

We passed cargo yards, electrical pylons,[4] and
houses with tar-paper roofs that had water halfway up
120 the windows, and other houses that were completely
submerged. When we came to the intersection of
Louisa Street and Higgins Boulevard, the street signs
were at eye level and the traffic lights were barely above
the surface of the water. We passed a house with a

---

3. **fetid** (fĕ′tĭd): having an offensive odor.
4. **electrical pylons** (pī′lŏnz′): steel towers supporting electrical wires.

shattered plate-glass window. Peering down into the living room, I saw a sofa floating near a framed photo of Muhammad Ali standing triumphantly over Sonny Liston. At a community swimming pool, a lifeguard seat poked just above the waters. We passed a rowboat
130　carrying two white men and being towed by a black man with dreadlocks, up to his neck in water. Later, we saw them again; all three were in the boat now, and were paddling with broken street signs.

It was a clear, hot day, and the floodwater smelled strongly of oil and raw sewage, and stung the eyes. There were other smells, from islands of rotting garbage, and, **intermittently,** as elsewhere in the city, the smell of death. Helicopters had been clattering overhead all morning, some of them dumping
140　buckets of water on house fires that had broken out everywhere. Scudding[5] columns of brown and gray smoke shot up from half a dozen points around the city. The towers of downtown New Orleans were visible in the distance. **P**

Until the nineteenth century, the Ninth Ward was a swamp, and, even after it became home to a black and immigrant white community, and was drained (in that order), it was periodically devastated by flooding. During Hurricane Betsy, in 1965, it was hit harder
150　than most of the city, and was underwater for days. The neglect of the Ninth Ward by the city government was notorious; well into the twentieth century, it lacked adequate sewers and clean water. The Norman Rockwell image that the Ninth Ward inspired was

intermittently (ĭn′tər-mĭt′nt-lē) *adv.* stopping and starting at intervals

P AUTHOR'S PURPOSE
Think about the sights, sounds, and smells the author describes in this paragraph. Circle at least two images in the paragraph that have a big impact on you.

---

5. **scudding** (skŭ′dĭng): skimming along swiftly.

that of the first grader Ruby Bridges, a tiny black girl in a white dress, who was led to school by federal marshals past jeering white crowds—a chapter in a violent desegregation struggle that divided the city in the nineteen-sixties. In the next decades, many of the
160 white residents of the Ninth Ward left; by the time Katrina hit, almost all the students in the school that Ruby Bridges integrated were black. **PAUSE & REFLECT**

PAUSE & REFLECT
Reread lines 145–162. What have you learned about the history of the Ninth Ward?

At 2037 Desire, a block past Petrie's home, three people stood on the second-floor porch of a large wooden house: a bulky young woman in a white blouse, with dyed orange hair, and tattoos on one arm; a young man with copper skin in a lilac polo shirt . . . and an old man who was bare-chested except for a pair of red suspenders. The ground floor was flooded
170 and a sign above it said, "Winner Supermarket— ATM Inside." Alladio hailed them and repeated the argument that she had made to Petrie. The young man said that his name was Theron Green, and that he and his father, Alfred Green, the old man, and his fiancée—Trinell Sanson, the tattooed woman—were fine, and were planning to stay. They also had a friend inside the house, they said. Theron Green spoke in a thick local accent, and his eyes were alert and suspicious. He was clearly anxious for us to leave. "We
180 feel comfortable, safe in our own house here," he said. "Anyway, I don't want no looters coming here." Alladio told him that there would soon be forced evacuations, but Green was adamant. "I'll wait till they force me

out, then," he said. Trinell Sanson said, "We're fine. If it gets too bad, we'll catch the helicopter." . . .

Alladio warned me not to get spattered by the floodwater. "The people who have been in this are going to get sick," she said. The Environmental Protection Agency had teams out taking water samples to check for toxins, and the rumor—apparently unfounded—was that entire districts were so contaminated that they would have to be razed, along with hundreds of thousands of vehicles. The people who lived there might not realize it, she said, "but once they leave they are never going to see their homes again." . . .

When we returned to Petrie's house, he was packed and waiting for us on the second-floor porch, dressed in slacks, a fresh unbuttoned shirt over a T-shirt, and a Marine Corps baseball cap. He leaned down to his dog, took both its ears in his hands and caressed them, and then told the dog to go inside. Petrie climbed into the canoe and began paddling over to us. The dog reemerged on the balcony, appearing <u>disconcerted</u> and watchful. Petrie did not look back. He came alongside the fence and we helped him first with a bag and then with a little black case that he said had his wife's Bible in it. "I know she'd want me to bring that," he said. He climbed onto the WaveRunner behind me. Alladio gave the vessel a little power, and we began moving off. ◉

As we made our way down Desire, Petrie looked around him at the devastation, his neighbors' houses

disconcert (dĭsˈkən-sûrtʹ) *v.* to ruffle; to frustrate by throwing into disorder

◉ **AUTHOR'S PURPOSE**
What event has the article focused on so far?

submerged in water. He said, "Oh, my God. I had no idea."

I asked him why he hadn't left earlier. "You tell yourself that the waters are going to recede, and when they don't one day you say maybe they will the next," he answered.

The waters had subsided somewhat after the initial
220 surge, he said. Then he had noticed, as the days went by, that there was an ebb and flow to them, as if a tide were moving in and out. To his mind, the city had become part of Lake Pontchartrain. He had heard on the radio about the levees breaking. When the electricity went out, he had listened to the radio each night, but had turned it off after a little while, to save his batteries.

As we spoke, he seemed to be trying to make sense of his own reaction to the catastrophe. He had understood
230 logically that he was stranded and in danger, and yet he had decided that his first priority was to remain and prepare the house for his family's return: "Pretty crazy, huh? I even started repairing my roof." About a third of the roof had been torn away by the hurricane, and he had worked for several days patching it up while the city lay underwater. . . . **PAUSE & REFLECT**

When we passed Theron Green's house, he and his father and his fiancée waved and smiled at Petrie. . . .

Petrie told me that he was worried about his aunt
240 Willa Mae Butler: "She's about eighty-two, and lives

PAUSE & REFLECT
Reread lines 228–236. What do you learn about Petrie's priorities from his actions after the hurricane?

_____

_____

_____

_____

_____

_____

_____

_____

on Bartholomew Street. I'm worried that she's dead, because this time she said she wasn't going."

As we travelled slowly back toward Interstate 10, avoiding debris and downed electrical lines, Petrie began calling out landmarks. He had lived in the neighborhood his entire life. As a child, he had lived on Louisa Street. He pointed to a building that he said was the primary school he had attended from kindergarten through eighth grade. . . . ⓡ

250   By now, he was reconciled to his rescue. "I think the good Lord sent you to me," he said. "I am looking forward to seeing my wife!" Her name was Mildred. He was sixty-four and Mildred was sixty-one. They had married when she was seventeen and he was twenty. "Everyone said we wouldn't last, but we've been together forty-five years, and this is the first time we have been apart." . . .

After we landed, Shawn Alladio went out on one more tour of the neighborhood to see if there was anyone 260 else to bring in. While we waited for her to return, Petrie and I sat in my rented van in the shade under Interstate 10. Nearby, rescuers stripped down and washed in solutions of water and bleach. . . .

    Petrie told me about his own children. Lionel, his namesake, forty-three years old, had been in the Marine Corps for fifteen years and served in the first Gulf War. He had been an aviation mechanic, but when he got out he couldn't get a job, so he went back to school, at the University of New Orleans, where

ⓡ **AUTHOR'S PURPOSE**
Is the writer's focus on New Orleans narrow or broad? Explain.

_____

_____

_____

_____

_____

_____

_____

_____

_____

_____

_____

270 he was pursuing an undergraduate degree when the hurricane arrived. Lionel owned two houses, one just blocks away from Petrie's, which he rented out. Petrie's second son, Bruce, who was thirty-eight, had also been a marine, had an accounting degree, and worked as a shelter supervisor for Girls and Boys Town. Bruce had driven out of the city with his wife and children before Katrina. Petrie smiled when he spoke of his daughter, Crystal, who was twenty-one. She was studying nursing in New Orleans. Lionel had driven her and 280 their mother out of the city. **⑤**

Petrie hadn't gone to college; he got hired at a shipyard right after high school. After a couple of years, he decided to train as a welder. "For a year, I went to welders' school from 8 A.M. to noon and worked at American Marine from 6 P.M. until 6 A.M. Got my certificate as a certified welder around 1962. I went to several places looking for a job as a welder, but never got hired." When, in 1965, Petrie went to apply for a job at Equitable Equipment, near his home, he saw 290 white welders being hired even as he was told that the only openings were for laborers. He contacted the local N.A.A.C.P. and filed a complaint with the newly formed Equal Employment Opportunity Commission. "They took an interest in my case, and I was the first black to be hired as a skilled worker by Equitable," he said. "I would sit down to eat my lunch and the white guys would go sit somewhere else. I didn't care—I was just there to do my job." After working for a decade at Equitable, and then at Kaiser Aluminum until

⑤ AUTHOR'S PURPOSE
Think about what you learn about Petrie and his family from this paragraph. How do these details explain the devastating effect the distaster had on people's lives?

300 1983, when it shut down its Louisiana operations, he decided to set up his own business, Petrie Iron and Construction. He didn't have insurance, though, and he figured that he'd lost everything.

Later that evening, Alladio drove Petrie and me to Baton Rouge in a rented pickup, towing her WaveRunner behind her. She had been told that forced evacuations would begin soon, and that the operation would shift toward law enforcement. She was leaving the next day.

310 In his exhaustion, Petrie had not been able to remember any telephone numbers, but, as we drove along, cell-phone numbers for his son Bruce and his daughter came back to him. I handed him my phone, and a minute later I heard him say, "They're in Memphis!"

When he hung up, he said that his wife and daughter were staying in Memphis at a cousin's house. Lionel had already found some temporary factory work. Bruce was staying with his wife's family, in Kentucky. 320 Willa Mae Butler, Petrie's aunt, was alive and in Texas. Bruce was going to look on the Internet for a flight for his father from Baton Rouge to Memphis.

A little while later, as we drove into the night, Petrie said reflectively, "I don't know if I want to go back to New Orleans—seeing it how it was, I don't think I do." He doubted, from what he had seen, that much of it could ever be re-built. "The first thing I picture now is the water I saw when I was coming out," he said. **PAUSE & REFLECT**

PAUSE & REFLECT
Why does Petrie say he doesn't think he wants to return to New Orleans? Explain whether you find his reaction understandable.

_____

_____

_____

_____

_____

_____

_____

_____

330　　A few minutes afterward, Bruce called back to say that the next available flight was in three days' time. Alladio suggested that we try the Greyhound station instead. It was already late when we arrived at the scruffy little bus station in Baton Rouge, full of refugees from New Orleans. I joined a long line of people waiting for information and tickets. Half an hour later, it had barely moved. A man and a woman were arguing, and when the stationmaster called for passengers for Houston, I heard the man tell her,

340　"I don't care what you say—I'm getting on that bus." After he left, the woman leaned against a pillar and wiped her eyes. A tall man with a stack of religious tracts was reciting Psalms from memory, and a woman made subdued sounds of agreement or said, "That's right," in a rhythmic cadence. Two policemen patrolled the station; there were a number of young men who looked street-wise and seemed to be loitering among the waiting passengers.

　　Around midnight, Bruce called again. He had

350　resolved to drive down from Kentucky to get his father. He would leave shortly with his wife, Donna. Lionel Petrie would wait for them in the Greyhound station. Bruce thought that if he and Donna took turns driving they could make the trip in twelve hours. They were there by noon the next day. ○

○ AUTHOR'S PURPOSE
Over what span of time did the events in this account take place?

_____

_____

_____

_____

Text Analysis: Author's Purpose

In the chart below, give three details or images from each selection to show how the author achieved his specific purpose.

The Story of an Eyewitness	Letter from New Orleans: Leaving Desire
Main Purpose: to explain that the earthquake caused widespread destruction	**Main Purpose:** to explain the devastating effect a disaster has people's lives

↓   ↓

Example:	Example:
Example:	Example:
Example:	Example:

Reading Strategy: Set a Purpose for Reading

Which techniques did each author use most effectively to achieve his purpose: a narrow or broad focus, descriptions of events and people, or vivid details and images? Support your answer with specific examples from the texts.

_____

_____

_____

_____

_____

What is the role of a WITNESS?

Based on the accounts you just read, what do you think an eyewitness to a disaster should pay attention to and report on?

_____

_____

_____

Vocabulary Practice

Answer each question to show your understanding of these vocabulary words.

1. Would a **lavishly** decorated home be simple or elegant? _____

2. Is a **menace** something to avoid or to look forward to? _____

3. If you **disconcert** people, do you confuse them or calm them down? _____

4. If you **compel** people to do something, are you forcing them or inviting them? _____

5. Would a person who watches **vigilantly** be alert or distracted? _____

6. Which sound would be heard **intermittently**—thunder or a steady siren? _____

Academic Vocabulary in Writing

circumstance	emerge	predominant	rely	technology

Imagine you volunteered to help in New Orleans after the hurricane. Using at least two Academic Vocabulary words, describe the **circumstances** you might have encountered there. Definitions for these terms are listed on page 129.

_____

_____

_____

Assessment Practice

DIRECTIONS Use "The Story of an Eyewitness" and "Letter from New Orleans" to answer questions 1–6.

1 What span of time does London's account cover?
- **A** one day
- **B** three hours
- **C** three days
- **D** one week

2 What effect is created by the repetition in lines 16–18 of "The Story of an Eyewitness"?
- **A** It emphasizes the extent of the devastation.
- **B** It tells why the response was so inadequate.
- **C** It highlights the continuing danger.
- **D** It underscores the city inhabitants' personal losses.

3 Where did the refugees from San Francisco go?
- **A** They were moved by railroad to any point they wished to go.
- **B** They moved to a part of San Francisco that was not burned.
- **C** They stayed in hospitals and schools in the city center.
- **D** They moved to other parts of California.

4 At the beginning of "Letter from New Orleans," what do the details about Petrie's ladder, life vests, and canoe suggest about him?
- **A** He is afraid.
- **B** He is organized.
- **C** He has been rescuing people.
- **D** He hopes to get away from New Orleans.

5 Why hadn't Petrie left earlier?
- **A** He had no family to go to.
- **B** He was afraid he might drown.
- **C** He didn't want to leave his dog.
- **D** He was waiting for the floodwaters to recede.

6 Which of the following do both authors use to achieve their purpose?
- **A** quotations from disaster experts
- **B** vivid imagery of the disaster's aftermath
- **C** statistics about the number of buildings lost
- **D** flashbacks to the moment the disaster took place

Mi Madre
Poem by Pat Mora

Canyon de Chelly
Poem by Simon J. Ortiz

What gifts does the EARTH provide?

You probably appreciate nature when you're taking a walk on a sunny day or swimming at a scenic beach. But the earth provides us with more things than we might realize. The gas that warms our homes, the concrete we use to pave our sidewalks, even the paper we write on—these are all precious resources provided to us by the earth. The poets whose work you are about to read share their appreciation for the earth's gifts through words.

LIST IT The earth's resources can be used in multiple ways. In a small group, choose one of the following resources and brainstorm at least five ways we can use it: *dirt, plants, rocks, sunlight, trees, water, wind.*

Text Analysis: Imagery

Writers use **imagery** to help readers imagine places and characters. In poetry, images can also convey the speaker's feelings in imaginative and surprising ways. Poets create imagery by using words or phrases that appeal to our senses of sight, hearing, smell, taste, and touch. For example, read the following lines from "Mi Madre." The chart shows which senses these lines appeal to.

I say tease me.
She sprinkles raindrops in my face on a sunny day.

Sight	"sunny day"
Hearing	"I say tease me"
Smell	
Taste	
Touch	"sprinkles raindrops"

If you think about the poem's images, they almost create a picture in your mind. You can also discern that the speaker feels loved and comforted. As you read, pay attention to how imagery helps you experience each poem.

Resource: _____

How we use it:

1. _____

2. _____

3. _____

4. _____

5. _____

Reading Skill: Understand Speaker

In poetry, the **speaker** is the voice that "talks" to the reader and presents the ideas in the poem from a specific point of view. It is important to understand that the speaker is not the same as the poet. For example, a poet may choose to write about a subject from the perspective of a child. In that case, the ideas that are expressed are those of the child, not necessarily the poet.

To understand a poem, you have to determine who the speaker is and how he or she feels about the subject of the poem. As you read "Mi Madre" and "Canyon de Chelly," use a chart like this one to identify the characteristics of each speaker and how he or she feels about the subject of the poem.

	Mi Madre	Canyon de Chelly
Text from poem	I say feed me (line 1)	
Speaker's characteristics	The speaker is demanding	
Speaker's feelings		

SET A PURPOSE FOR READING

Read "Mi Madre" to discover the comparison the speaker makes.

Mi Madre¹

Poem by
PAT MORA

BACKGROUND The granddaughter of Mexican immigrants, Pat Mora realized early in her writing career that her cultural heritage was "a source of pride." Her work, including "Mi Madre," celebrates family, the desert in which she grew up, and the Mexican-American experience.

Ⓐ IMAGERY
Circle the striking images in lines 1–6. To what senses do these images appeal?

_____

_____

_____

_____

_____

_____

_____

_____

_____

I say feed me.
She serves red prickly pear on a spiked cactus.

I say tease me.
She sprinkles raindrops in my face on a sunny day.

5 I say frighten me.
She shouts thunder, flashes lightning. Ⓐ

I say comfort me.
She invites me to lay on her firm body.

---

1. **Mi Madre** (mē mä'drā) *Spanish:* my mother.

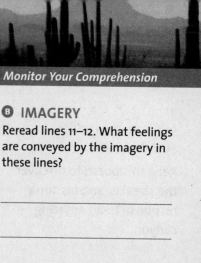

I say heal me.
10 She gives me *manzanilla, orégano, dormilón*.²

I say caress me.
She strokes my skin with her warm breath. **B**

I say make me beautiful.
She offers turquoise for my fingers, a pink blossom for
      my hair.

15 I say sing to me.
She chants lonely women's songs of femaleness.

I say teach me.
She endures: glaring heat
      numbing cold
20   frightening dryness.

She: the desert
She: strong mother. **C**

B IMAGERY
Reread lines 11–12. What feelings are conveyed by the imagery in these lines?

_____

_____

_____

_____

C SPEAKER
Underline the phrase the speaker uses to describe the desert. How does the speaker feel about nature? Write your thoughts in the chart.

Text from Poem
She: the desert
She: strong mother

↓

Speaker's Feelings
_____
_____
_____
_____
_____

2. *manzanilla, orégano, dormilón* (măn′zə-nē′yə, ə-rĕg′ə-nō′, dôr-mē-lŏn′)
Spanish: sweet-smelling herbs that can be used to make home medicines.

SET A PURPOSE FOR READING

Read this poem to discover the speaker and his son's response to an amazing canyon.

Canyon de Chelly

Poem by
SIMON J. ORTIZ

BACKGROUND Arizona's Canyon de Chelly (pronounced *sha*) is home to a Navajo tribal community that has preserved this sacred land for centuries. The canyon, now a national park, is known for its stunning landscapes, tribal artifacts, and rock paintings.

PAUSE & REFLECT
Reread lines 1–7. What gifts of the earth does the speaker appreciate?

_____

_____

_____

_____

_____

_____

_____

Lie on your back on stone,
the stone carved to fit
the shape of yourself.
Who made it like this,
5 knowing that I would be along
in a million years and look
at the sky being blue forever?   **PAUSE & REFLECT**

My son is near me. He sits
and turns on his butt
10 and crawls over to stones,
picks one up and holds it,
and then puts it into his mouth.
The taste of stone.
What is it but stone,
15 the earth in your mouth.
You, son, are tasting forever. **D**

We walk to the edge of cliff
and look down into the canyon.
On this side, we cannot see
20 the bottom cliff edge but looking
further out, we see fields,
sand furrows, cottonwoods.
In winter, they are softly gray.
The cliffs' shadows are distant,
25 hundreds of feet below;
we cannot see our own shadows.
The wind moves softly into us.
My son laughs with the wind;
he gasps and laughs. **E**

D SPEAKER
What do you know about
the speaker of the poem in
lines 14–16? Write your thoughts
in the chart.

Text from Poem
What is it but stone,
the earth in your mouth.
You, son, are tasting
forever.

↓

Speaker's Characteristics

E IMAGERY
Underline the images that
appeal to the senses of touch
and hearing in lines 27–29. What
feelings do they suggest?

30 We find gray root, old wood,
 so old, with curious twists
 in it, curving back into curves,
 juniper, piñon, or something
 with hard, red berries in spring.
35 You taste them, and they are sweet
 and bitter, the berries a delicacy
 for bluejays. The plant rooted
 fragilely into a sandy place
 by a canyon wall, the sun bathing
40 shiny, pointed leaves.

 My son touches the root carefully,
 aware of its ancient quality.
 He lays his soft, small fingers on it
 and looks at me for information.
45 I tell him: wood, an old root,
 and around it, the earth, ourselves. **PAUSE & REFLECT**

PAUSE & REFLECT
Reread lines 41–46. Why do you
think the speaker brings his son
to the canyon?

_____

_____

_____

_____

_____

_____

_____

Text Analysis: Imagery

Complete imagery charts for both poems below by recording at least one example of imagery in each box.

Mi Madre	
Sight	
Hearing	
Smell	
Taste	
Touch	

Canyon de Chelly	
Sight	
Hearing	
Smell	
Taste	
Touch	

Review your charts and explain which poem you think contains the most effective imagery.

_____

_____

_____

_____

_____

_____

Reading Skill: Understand Speaker

Compare and contrast the speakers of "Mi Madre" and "Canyon de Chelly." In the Y-chart, fill in the top part with details about each speaker. Consider each the speaker's characteristics and the feelings they express about the earth. In what ways are the speakers alike? Write the similarities in the bottom part.

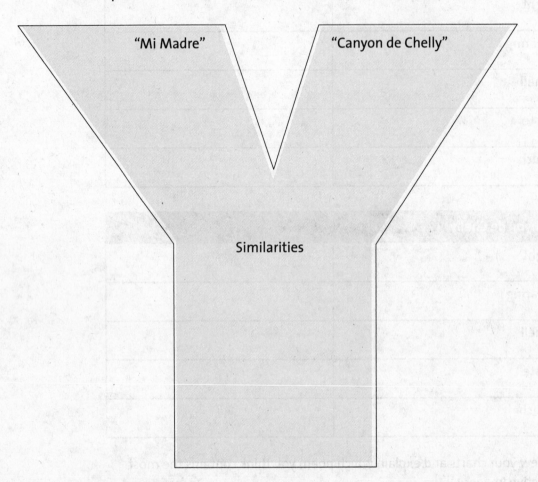

"Mi Madre"

"Canyon de Chelly"

Similarities

What gifts does the EARTH provide?

Now that you have read the poems, what other gifts from nature do you appreciate?

_____

_____

_____

Academic Vocabulary in Writing

circumstance	emerge	predominant	rely	technology

What is the **predominant** theme in these poems? How does the imagery in each poem allow the theme to **emerge**? Use at least two Academic Vocabulary words in your response. Definitions of these words are on page 129.

_____

_____

_____

Assessment Practice

DIRECTIONS Use "Mi Madre" and "Canyon de Chelly" to answer questions 1–6.

1 In "Mi Madre," line 6 is an example of —

- **A** a metaphor
- **B** repetition
- **C** hyperbole
- **D** an image

2 How does the desert heal the speaker?

- **A** The desert gives her a red prickly pear on a spiked cactus.
- **B** The desert gives her manzanilla, oregano, and dormilion.
- **C** The desert chants women's songs of femaleness.
- **D** The desert provides heat, cold, and dryness.

3 How is the desert like a mother?

- **A** The desert comforts and teaches her.
- **B** The desert asks for her loyalty.
- **C** The desert protects her.
- **D** The desert nurtures her.

4 In "Canyon de Chelly," what can you infer about the speaker's son?

- **A** He is shy and quiet.
- **B** He is from the city.
- **C** He is very young.
- **D** He is afraid.

5 To which sense does "the sky being blue forever" appeal?

- **A** sight
- **B** touch
- **C** taste
- **D** hearing

6 What two things does the speaker's son taste?

- **A** rocks and eternity
- **B** earth and freedom
- **C** stones and forever
- **D** grass and heritage

UNIT 4

A World of Meaning

THEME AND SYMBOL

Be sure to read the Text Analysis Workshop on pp. 462–467 in *Hòlt McDougal Literature*.

Academic Vocabulary for Unit 4

Academic Vocabulary is the language you use to discuss literary and informational texts. Preview the following Academic Vocabulary words. You will use these words as you write and talk about the selections in this unit.

comment (kŏm′ĕnt) *n.* a remark, written or spoken
*Which of the main character's **comments** created the conflict?*

●

community (kə-myōō′nĭ-tē) *n.* all people living in the same location under the same government
*How do the views of his **community** affect the main character?*

●

criteria (krī-tîr′ē-ə) *n.* standards or rules by which something can be judged; a measure of value
*What is one **criteria** you can use to judge the author's style?*

●

perspective (pər-spĕk′tĭv) *n.* a certain point of view; a subjective view of an issue
*Choose one character and retell the story from his or her **perspective**.*

●

technique (tĕk-nēk′) *n.* a systematic or especially organized way of completing a task; special skill related to completion of a task
*Describe the **technique** used to create a somber mood.*

Think of a movie you've seen that you really enjoyed. Explain why someone with another **perspective** might respond to the movie differently, using at least two Academic Vocabulary words in your response.

_____

_____

_____

_____

Pandora's Box
Greek Myth Retold by Louis Untermeyer

Loo-Wit, the Fire-Keeper
Native American Myth Retold by Joseph Bruchac

Why do we WANT what we don't have?

Why do people always seem to want what they don't have? In the myths you're about to read, individuals who aren't satisfied with what they have make serious trouble for everyone else.

DISCUSS What problems are caused by wanting things that are out of reach? What, if any, benefits might result? Jot down some ideas, and use your notes as you discuss the questions with your group.

Text Analysis: Theme

Writers often share messages, or **themes,** about life or human nature. Asking questions can help you identify a story's theme.

CLUES TO THEME	
1. Plot and Conflict **A story revolves around conflicts that are central to the theme. Ask:**	• What conflicts do the characters face? • How are the conflicts resolved?
2. Important Statements **The narrator or a character may make statements that hint at the theme. Ask:**	• What key statements are made in the story? • Could any statement be reworded as an overall theme?
3. Characters **Characters can hint at a theme by how they act or what they learn. Ask:**	• What do the main character's actions and thoughts tell you about him or her? • How does the character change? • What lesson does the character learn?

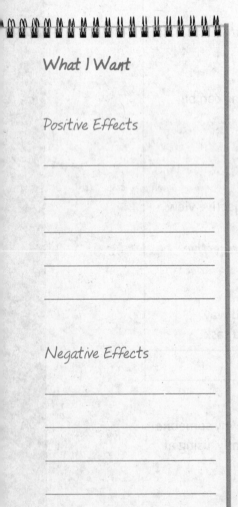

What I Want

Positive Effects

_____

_____

_____

_____

_____

Negative Effects

_____

_____

_____

_____

_____

4. Symbols	
A symbol can convey a theme because it stands for something beyond itself. Ask:	• What does the symbol usually stand for? • What might the symbol mean to the main characters? What might it represent to readers?

Reading Strategy: Reading a Myth

Myths are traditional stories that were passed along through word of mouth. They often feature gods or supernatural beings who show human characteristics such as anger and love. Myths may reveal the consequences of human errors, or explain how something came to be. As you read, use this chart to begin to compare and contrast the two myths.

	"Pandora's Box"	"Loo-Wit"
What qualities does the supreme god have?	Zeus — vengeful — wants to punish all humans — scheming	The Creator — generous — upset by human quarrels
What role does he play?		

Vocabulary in Context

Note: Words are listed in the order in which they appear in "Pandora's Box."

subtle (sŭt'l) *adj.* slight; difficult to detect
*Zeus' **subtle** punishment was not immediately obvious.*

adorn (ə-dôrn') *v.* to enhance or decorate
*The gods **adorn** her with special gifts.*

ensnare (ĕn-snâr') *v.* to take or catch in something
*Her beauty and charm helped **ensnare** his attention.*

restrain (rĭ-strān') *v.* to hold back; to control
*She could no longer **restrain** her curiosity.*

SET A PURPOSE FOR READING

Read "Pandora's Box" to learn about the cruelty humans suffer at the hands of the gods.

Pandora's BOX

Greek Myth retold by
LOUIS UNTERMEYER

BACKGROUND Greek myths are stories that explain mysterious forces of the universe, such as fire, drought, and seasonal changes. In the myth you are about to read, you will learn how the ancient Greeks explained the presence of another unwelcome force in the world.

Prometheus had thought about mankind with such sympathy that he had dared to steal the needed fire from Olympus,[1] and for this he was grievously punished by Zeus.[2] But the lord of Olympus did not think this cruelty was enough. Prometheus had a brother, Epimetheus, and though he was harmless and slow-witted, Zeus extended his displeasure to him. He did not punish Epimetheus as brutally as he had done his brother; he had a more **subtle** plan. It was a scheme which would not only affect
10 Epimetheus but also the whole race of human beings whom

subtle (sŭt′l) *adj.* slight; difficult to detect

---

1. **Olympus** (ə-lĭm′pəs): home of the mythical Greek gods.
2. **Zeus** (zōōs): father of the Greek gods; ruler of the heavens. **Prometheus,** a lesser god, gave humans fire against Zeus's will. Furious, Zeus condemned Prometheus to be chained to a rock for eternity.

Prometheus had dared to help and who were living happily and untroubled. **Ⓐ**

Zeus ordered Hephaestus, the smith and artisan of the gods, to make a woman out of the materials of earth. Hephaestus took some river clay that had flakes of gold in it and began to make a lovely girl. In with the clay he mixed the fragrance of a river rose, the sweetness of Hymettus[3] honey, the smoothness of a silver dolphin, the voices of larks and lake-water, the color of sunrise on
20 snow, the warmth of a sunny morning in May. Then he summoned the Four Winds to breathe life into the new creation. Finally he called upon the goddesses to complete the work and grant the glowing figure a touch of their own powers.

"Hephaestus has given her beauty," said Aphrodite,[4] "but I shall make her more beautiful by adding the spark of love. It will shine in her eyes, and everyone that looks on her will be enchanted."

"I shall make her wise," said Athene.[5] "She shall be able
30 to choose between false and true, between what men value and what she must know is worthless."

"I shall make her a woman, a puzzle to every man," said Hera, the wife of Zeus. "I shall make her a real woman, for I shall give her the gift of curiosity."

Smiling, the goddesses <u>adorned</u> her, and when Zeus beheld her grace, her garland of gold, and the glory of her endowments, he was as charmed as though he had been a mortal. "We will call her Pandora," he said, "Pandora, the All-Gifted. She shall become the bride of Epimetheus. But
40 she shall not go empty-handed. She shall bring with her a casket, a box of magic as her dowry.[6] And Hermes, my messenger, shall conduct her to earth." **Ⓑ**

---

3. **Hymettus** (hī-mĕt′əs): a mountain ridge near Athens, Greece.
4. **Aphrodite** (ăf′rə-dī′tē): Greek goddess of love and beauty.
5. **Athene** (ə-thē′nē): Greek goddess of wisdom; sometimes spelled Athena.
6. **dowry** (dou′rē): money or property a bride brings to a marriage.

Ⓐ READING A MYTH
Underline the words in lines 1–12 that describe Zeus and his actions. What qualities does he reveal? Add your ideas to your chart.

Zeus's Qualities

adorn (ə-dôrn′) v. to enhance or decorate

Ⓑ READING A MYTH
Reread lines 13–42. Underline the names of the gods and goddesses Zeus enlists in creating Pandora and bringing her to her new husband. Then circle the role each plays in her creation.

ensnare (ĕn-snâr') v. to take or catch in something

⊙ THEME
Reread lines 43–71. Circle the warning Prometheus gives Epimetheus and the warning Epimetheus gives Pandora. What does Pandora do with her box?

_____

_____

_____

_____

_____

restrain (rĭ-strān') v. to hold back; to control

Epimetheus could not understand why the gods had become concerned about him. He was dazzled by Hermes, and it was some time before he could believe that the exquisite creature brought by the messenger god was meant for him. Even after Hermes departed in a flashing cloud and Pandora stood blushing beside him, he was perturbed. He remembered how often his brother Prometheus had
50 warned him, "Do not trust the gods. And beware especially of Zeus and anything he may send you." However, when Pandora looked in his eyes and smiled, he was, as Aphrodite had predicted, enchanted and **ensnared**. Yet, even as he took her in his arms, he cautioned her.

"We have reason to fear the gods," said Epimetheus, "and also their gifts," he added, pointing to the casket.

"But this is my dowry," murmured Pandora. "Zeus himself filled it with magic as a present for us. See how beautifully it is carved and painted. Look at the silver
60 hinges and the great gold clasp that fastens it."

"Keep it well fastened," said Epimetheus, "otherwise I shall never rest easy. I do not know what the casket may contain, and I do not want to know. Promise me one thing. Never open the box. It is, I grant, a beautiful thing, too beautiful to destroy, and we will keep it. But hide it. Put it not only out of your sight but out of your mind. Then we shall both be content."

Happy that she could keep her dowry, Pandora put it under the bed and turned to her husband with love. And
70 so for a long time nothing disturbed their married life and their continual joy in each other. **⊙**

But, though Pandora benefited from the goddesses' gifts of beauty and wisdom, the gift of Hera had not been given in vain. For quite a while, Pandora **restrained** her curiosity about the wonderful casket. But with the passing of time

she could not help wondering what it might contain. After all, it was her dowry, and she had a right to see what the greatest of the gods had conferred upon her. Then, ashamed of her weakness, she put the idea from her, and
80 thought only of her delight in her home with Epimetheus.

One day, however, the curiosity, so long stifled, overmastered her. "I shall only lift the lid," she said to herself, "and snatch a moment's glimpse of what may be inside. No matter what I see, I won't touch a thing. Surely there can be no harm in that." **D**

Anxiously, as though she were being watched, she tiptoed to her room. Gently getting down on her hands and knees, she drew the casket from under the bed. Half fearfully and half eagerly she lifted the lid. It was only
90 a moment and the lid was up only an inch, but in that moment a swarm of horrible things flew out. They were noisome,[7] abominably colored, and evil-looking, for they were the spirits of all that was evil, sad, and hurtful. They were War and Famine, Crime and Pestilence, Spite and Cruelty, Sickness and Malice, Envy, Woe, Wickedness, and all the other disasters let loose in the world.

Hearing Pandora's scream, Epimetheus rushed in. But it was too late. He and Pandora were set upon and stung, and the evil spirits flew off to attack the rest of mankind. **E**
100 "It is all my fault," cried Pandora. "If I had thought more about your warning and less about my own desires, I could have controlled my curiosity."

"The fault is mine," said Epimetheus. "I should have burned the box." Then he added, for the poison of Malice was already taking effect, "After all, you are what you are—only a woman—and what else could one expect of a woman."

---

7. **noisome** (noi'səm): offensive.

D **READING A MYTH**
Reread lines 72–85. What prompts Pandora to look inside the box?

_____

_____

_____

_____

_____

_____

E **READING A MYTH**
Reread lines 86–99. Underline the descriptions of the things that fly out of the box. What do you think this myth will explain? Write your answer in your chart.

What the Myth Explains

F THEME
Reread lines 116–126. Underline the description of the thing left in the box. How does the winged creature relate to the other things in the box?

_____

_____

_____

_____

_____

_____

_____

Disconsolate[8] that she had brought so harmful a dowry to Epimetheus as well as to all other men and women, Pandora wept. It was hours before she let her husband comfort her. Finally, after she grew quiet, they heard a faint sound inside the box.

"Lift the lid again," said Epimetheus. "I think you have released the worst. Perhaps something else, something better, is still there."

He was right. At the bottom of the box was a quivering thing. Its body was small; its wings were frail; but there was a radiance about it. Somehow Pandora knew what it was, and she took it up, touched it carefully, and showed it to Epimetheus. "It is Hope," she said.

"Do you think it will live?" asked Epimetheus.

"Yes," answered Pandora. "I am sure it will. Somehow I know that it will outlive War and Sickness and all the other evils. And," she added, watching the shining thing rise and flutter about the room, "it will never leave us for long. Even if we lose sight of it, it will be there." **F**

She was no longer downhearted as Hope spread its wings and went out into the world.

---

8. **disconsolate** (dĭs-kŏn′sə-lĭt): gloomy.

Loo-Wit, THE Fire-Keeper

Native American Myth retold by

JOSEPH BRUCHAC

BACKGROUND An origin myth is a myth that explains how something began or was created. "Loo-Wit, the Fire-Keeper" explains the origin of some of the natural features of Washington and Oregon. The river gorges, mountains, and Native American peoples mentioned are all real.

SET A PURPOSE FOR READING

Read this myth to learn how the Creator deals with two quarreling brothers.

When the world was young, the Creator gave everyone all that was needed to be happy.

The weather was always pleasant. There was food for everyone and room for all the people. Despite this, though, two brothers began to quarrel over the land. Each wanted to control it. It reached a point where each brother gathered together a group of men to support his claim. Soon it appeared there would be war. **G**

The Creator saw this and was not pleased. He waited
10 until the two brothers were asleep one night and then carried them to a new country. There a beautiful river flowed and tall mountains rose into the clouds. He woke them just as the sun rose and they looked out from the mountaintop to the land below. They saw what a good place it was. It made their hearts good.

G THEME
Reread lines 1–8. What message about human nature is introduced at the start of this myth?

_____

_____

_____

_____

_____

_____

Ⓗ READING A MYTH

Think about all that the Creator has done in lines 1–32. What qualities do his actions reveal? List them in your chart.

The Creator's Qualities

Ⓘ THEME

Reread lines 33–40. The creator says the Great Stone Bridge is a sign of peace. Do the people stay peaceful? Why or why not?

_____

_____

_____

_____

_____

"Now," the Creator said, "this will be your land." Then he gave each of the brothers a bow and a single arrow. "Shoot your arrow into the air," the Creator said. "Where your arrow falls will be the land of you and your people, 20 and you shall be a great chief there."

The brothers did as they were told. The older brother shot his arrow. It arched over the river and landed to the south in the valley of the Willamette River.[1] There is where he and his people went, and they became the Multnomahs.[2] The younger brother shot his arrow. It flew to the north of the great river. He and his people went there and became the Klickitats.[3]

Then the Creator made a Great Stone Bridge across the river. "This bridge," the Creator said, "is a sign of peace. 30 You and your peoples can visit each other by crossing over this bridge. As long as you remain at peace, as long as your hearts are good, this bridge will stand." Ⓗ

For many seasons the two peoples remained at peace. They passed freely back and forth across the Great Stone Bridge. One day, though, the people to the north looked south toward the Willamette and said, "Their lands are better than ours." One day, though, the people to the south looked north toward the Klickitats and said, "Their lands are more beautiful than ours." Then, once again, the people 40 began to quarrel. Ⓘ

The Creator saw this and was not pleased.

The people were becoming greedy again. Their hearts were becoming bad. The Creator darkened the skies and took fire away. Now the people grew cold. The rains of autumn began and the people suffered greatly.

---

1. **Valley of the Willamette River:** a 30-mile-wide valley in Oregon, home today to a majority of Oregon's people.
2. **Multnomahs** (mult-no'mes): Native American group who lived in the area where Portland, Oregon, currently stands.
3. **Klickitats:** Native American group whose ancestral lands were situated north of the Columbia River in Washington.

"Give us back fire," they begged. "We wish to live again with each other in peace."

Their prayers reached the Creator's heart. There was only one place on Earth where fire still remained. An old
50 woman named Loo-Wit had stayed out of the quarreling and was not greedy. It was in her lodge only that fire still burned. So the Creator went to Loo-Wit.

"If you will share your fire with all the people," the Creator said, "I will give you whatever you wish. Tell me what you want."

"I want to be young and beautiful," Loo-Wit said.

"That is the way it will be," said the Creator. "Now take your fire to the Great Stone Bridge above the river. Let all the people come to you and get fire. You must keep the fire
60 burning there to remind people that their hearts must stay good." ❶

The next morning, the skies grew clear and the people saw the sun rise for the first time in many days. The sun shone on the Great Stone Bridge and there the people saw a young woman as beautiful as the sunshine itself. Before her, there on the bridge, burned a fire. The people came to the fire and ended their quarrels. Loo-Wit gave each of them fire. Now their homes again became warm and peace was everywhere.

70 One day, though, the chief of the people to the north came to Loo-Wit's fire. He saw how beautiful she was and wanted her to be his wife. At the same time, the chief of the people to the south also saw Loo-Wit's beauty. He, too, wanted to marry her. Loo-Wit could not decide which of the two she liked better. Then the chiefs began to quarrel. Their peoples took up the quarrel and fighting began.

When the Creator saw the fighting he became angry. He broke down the Great Stone Bridge. He took each of the two chiefs and changed them into mountains. The
80 chief of the Klickitat became the mountain we now know

 READING A MYTH

Reread lines 77–87. What does this myth explain? Add the answer to your chart.

What the Myth Explains

PAUSE & REFLECT

Reread the last paragraph. What do you think the reteller of this myth wants readers to understand?

_____

_____

_____

_____

_____

_____

_____

_____

_____

as Mount Adams. The chief of the Multnomahs became the mountain we now know as Mount Hood.[4] Even as mountains, they continued to quarrel, throwing flames and stones at each other. In some places, the stones they threw almost blocked the river between them. That is why the Columbia River[5] is so narrow in the place called the Dalles today.

Loo-Wit was heartbroken over the pain caused by her beauty. She no longer wanted to be a beautiful young 90 woman. She could no longer find peace as a human being. The Creator took pity on her and changed her into a mountain also, the most beautiful of the mountains. She was placed so that she stood between Mount Adams and Mount Hood, and she was allowed to keep the fire within herself which she had once shared on the Great Stone Bridge. Eventually, she became known as Mount St. Helens[6] and she slept peacefully.

Though she was asleep, Loo-Wit was still aware, the people said. The Creator had placed her between the 100 two quarreling mountains to keep the peace, and it was intended that humans, too, should look at her beauty and remember to keep their hearts good, to share the land and treat it well. If we human beings do not treat the land with respect, the people said, Loo-Wit will wake up and let us know how unhappy she and the Creator have become again. So they said long before the day in the 1980s when Mount St. Helens woke again. **PAUSE & REFLECT**

---

4. **Mount Adams:** the second highest mountain in the state of Washington; Mount Hood: the highest mountain in Oregon. Both mountains are volcanoes and part of the Cascade Volcanic Arc.

5. **Columbia River:** the largest river in the Pacific Northwest. It forms much of the border between Washington and Oregon.

6. **Mount St. Helens:** an active volcano in Washington that erupted in 1980, killing 57 people and destroying hundreds of homes, bridges, highways, and railways.

After Reading

Text Analysis: Theme

What message or theme do these myths reveal about life or human nature?
Review your reading notes as you respond to the questions in the chart
below. Then state a theme that can apply to both myths.

"Pandora's Box"	Details:
How is the main conflict resolved?	
What lessons do the characters learn?	
What symbols help convey the theme?	
"Loo-Wit, the Fire-Keeper"	Details:
How is the main conflict resolved?	
What lessons do the characters learn?	
What symbols help convey the theme?	

State a theme that can apply to *both* myths.

_____

_____

Reading Strategy: Reading a Myth

Review your chart on page 223 and your reading notes as you compare and contrast aspects of the two myths. Then, complete the chart below.

	Pandora's Box	Loo-Wit, the Fire-Keeper
How do humans anger the supreme god and what consequences do they face?		
What does each myth explain?		

Why do we WANT what we don't have?

In "Loo-Wit, the Fire-Keeper," the Creator gives each chief plenty. Why do you think each man wanted what the other had?

_____

_____

_____

Vocabulary Practice

Write the word from the box that belongs in each sentence.

WORD LIST

adorn

ensnare

restrain

subtle

1. Zeus had a _____ plan for Epithemeus.

2. The goddesses want to _____ Pandora with gold garlands.

3. Aphrodite predicts that Pandora will _____ Epimetheus.

4. Epimetheus warns Pandora to _____ her interest in the casket.

Academic Vocabulary in Writing

comment	community	criteria	perspective	technique

In a paragraph, make a **comment** on the punishments made by Zeus in "Pandora's Box" and the Creator in "Loo-Wit, the Fire-Keeper." Which was more just? Use at least one Academic Vocabulary word in your response. Definitions of these words are on page 221.

_____

_____

_____

Assessment Practice

DIRECTIONS Use "Pandora's Box" and "Loo-Wit, the Fire-Keeper" to answer questions 1–6.

1 How can you tell that "Pandora's Box" and "Loo-Wit, the Fire-Keeper" are both myths?

  A Both are ancient stories.
  B Both are about human struggles between opposing desires.
  C Both have supernatural events involving one or more gods.
  D Both have themes and symbols.

2 The winged creatures that escape from Pandora's box are symbols of —

  A too much curiosity
  B pain and suffering in the world
  C ancient Greek gods
  D the connection between gods and humans

3 A symbol of peace in "Loo-Wit, the Fire-Keeper" is —

  A the Great Stone Bridge
  B the river valley
  C a single arrow for a bow
  D fire

4 To the Native Americans of the region, Mount St. Helens was a symbol of —

  A a beautiful mountain
  B the need for fire
  C their past warfare
  D peace and respect

5 The myth about Pandora explains the value of —

  A hope
  B love
  C wisdom
  D beauty

6 What is a theme in both "Pandora's Box" and "Loo-Wit, the Fire-Keeper"?

  A It is important to strive for new goals.
  B The gods punish humans for disobedience.
  C It is better to be plain than beautiful.
  D People must work together for peace.

The Old Grandfather and His Little Grandson

Russian Folk Tale Retold by **Leo Tolstoy**

The Wise Old Woman

Japanese Folk Tale Retold by **Yoshiko Uchida**

How well do we treat our ELDERS?

The senior citizens you know have probably cared for families, contributed on a job and in the community, witnessed important events, and learned from varied experiences. How well are they respected by younger people? The folk tales you will read show why our elders have earned special treatment.

LIST IT List three to five small things that you can do to show respect to a member of an older generation.

Text Analysis: Universal Theme

Almost every culture has its folk tales, simple stories passed down through generations by word of mouth. Folk tales typically express a **universal theme,** a message about life or human nature that is so fundamental to human existence that it is true for all people of all time periods and cultures.

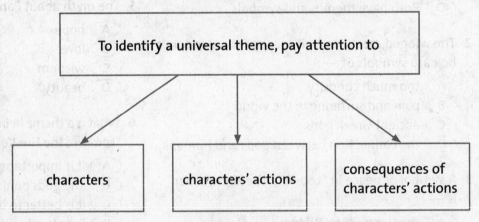

To identify a universal theme, pay attention to

characters → characters' actions → consequences of characters' actions

As you read the two folk tales that follow, look for a universal theme that they both share.

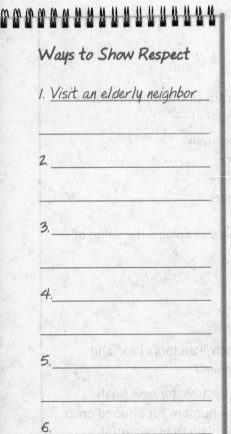

Ways to Show Respect

1. *Visit an elderly neighbor*
_____

2. _____
_____

3. _____
_____

4. _____
_____

5. _____
_____

6. _____
_____

Reading Strategy: Set a Purpose for Reading

In this lesson, your **purpose for reading** is to compare two folk tales and to identify the universal theme they share. As you read, take notes on the main characters in the chart below.

	"The Old Grandfather and His Little Grandson"	"The Wise Old Woman"
What are the qualities or characteristics of the important characters?	Grandfather:	Lord Higa:
	Son:	Young farmer:
	Daughter-in-law:	His mother:

Vocabulary in Context

Note: Words are listed in the order in which they appear in "The Wise Old Woman."

arrogant (ăr′ə-gənt) *adj.* displaying a sense of self-importance
  *The **arrogant** lord snapped his fingers to call a servant.*

haughtily (hô′tə-lē) *adv.* proudly; scornfully
  *He smiled **haughtily** as he gave one order after another.*

deceive (dĭ-sēv′) *v.* to cause to believe what is not true; to mislead
  *Nobody could act in secret to **deceive** the lord.*

bewilderment (bĭ-wĭl′dər-mənt) *n.* the state of being confused or astonished
  *The lord's impossible demand caused great **bewilderment**.*

SET A PURPOSE
FOR READING

Read this folk tale to find
out how a family treats an
elderly grandfather.

Ⓐ SET A PURPOSE FOR READING
Reread lines 1–12. Underline
the details that show the
grandfather was mistreated. Add
characteristics of the characters
to the chart on page 237.

Ⓑ UNIVERSAL THEME
Reread the last paragraph.
What have the son and his wife
realized about themselves?

The Old Grandfather and His Little Grandson

Russian Folk Tale retold by
LEO TOLSTOY

The grandfather had become very old. His legs would
not carry him, his eyes could not see, his ears could
not hear, and he was toothless. When he ate, bits of food
sometimes dropped out of his mouth. His son and his son's
wife no longer allowed him to eat with them at the table.
He had to eat his meals in the corner near the stove.

One day they gave him his food in a bowl. He tried to
move the bowl closer; it fell to the floor and broke. His
daughter-in-law scolded him. She told him that he spoiled
10 everything in the house and broke their dishes, and she
said that from now on he would get his food in a wooden
dish. The old man sighed and said nothing. Ⓐ

A few days later, the old man's son and his wife were
sitting in their hut, resting and watching their little boy
playing on the floor. They saw him putting together
something out of small pieces of wood. His father asked
him, "What are you making, Misha?"

The little grandson said, "I'm making a wooden bucket.
When you and Mamma get old, I'll feed you out of this
20 wooden dish."

The young peasant and his wife looked at each other
and tears filled their eyes. They were ashamed because they
had treated the old grandfather so meanly, and from that
day they again let the old man eat with them at the table
and took better care of him. Ⓑ

THE WISE OLD WOMAN

Japanese Folk Tale retold by

YOSHIKO UCHIDA

BACKGROUND "The Wise Old Woman" is set in feudal Japan. In that society a warlord ruled a village or group of villages. The lord had absolute power over his subjects: he could have them exiled or killed on a whim.

Many long years ago, there lived an **arrogant** and cruel young lord who ruled over a small village in the western hills of Japan.

"I have no use for old people in my village," he said **haughtily**. "They are neither useful nor able to work for a living. I therefore decree[1] that anyone over seventy-one must be banished[2] from the village and left in the mountains to die."

"What a dreadful decree! What a cruel and unreasonable
10 lord we have," the people of the village murmured. But the lord fearfully punished anyone who disobeyed him, and so villagers who turned seventy-one were tearfully carried into the mountains, never to return.

Gradually there were fewer and fewer old people in the village and soon they disappeared altogether. Then the young lord was pleased.

"What a fine village of young, healthy and hard-working people I have," he bragged. "Soon it will be the finest village in all of Japan." **C**

arrogant (ăr′ə-gənt) *adj.* displaying a sense of self-importance

haughtily (hô′tə-lē) *adv.* proudly; scornfully

C UNIVERSAL THEME
Reread lines 1–19. Why does the young lord decide that old people must be banished?

_____

_____

_____

_____

_____

_____

---

1. **decree** (dĭ-krē′): to make an order; an order that has the force of law.
2. **banished:** forced to leave a country or a place.

deceive (dĭ-sēv′) *v.* to cause to believe what is not true; to mislead

20   Now there lived in this village a kind young farmer and his aged mother. They were poor, but the farmer was good to his mother, and the two of them lived happily together. However, as the years went by, the mother grew older, and before long she reached the terrible age of seventy-one.

"If only I could somehow <u>deceive</u> the cruel lord," the farmer thought. But there were records in the village books and every one knew that his mother had turned seventy-one.

Each day the son put off telling his mother that he must take her into the mountains to die, but the people of the
30 village began to talk. The farmer knew that if he did not take his mother away soon, the lord would send his soldiers and throw them both into a dark dungeon to die a terrible death.

"Mother—" he would begin, as he tried to tell her what he must do, but he could not go on.

Then one day the mother herself spoke of the lord's dread decree. "Well, my son," she said, "the time has come for you to take me to the mountains. We must hurry before the lord sends his soldiers for you." And she did not seem worried at all that she must go to the mountains to die.

40   "Forgive me, dear mother, for what I must do," the farmer said sadly, and the next morning he lifted his mother to his shoulders and set off on the steep path toward the mountains. Up and up he climbed, until the trees clustered close and the path was gone. There was no longer even the sound of birds, and they heard only the soft wail of the wind in the trees. The son walked slowly, for he could not bear to think of leaving his old mother in the mountains. On and on he climbed, not wanting to stop and leave her behind. Soon, he heard his mother breaking
50 off small twigs from the trees that they passed.

"Mother, what are you doing?" he asked.

"Do not worry, my son," she answered gently. "I am just marking the way so you will not get lost returning to the village." **D**

The son stopped. "Even now you are thinking of me?" he asked, wonderingly.

D SET A PURPOSE FOR READING
Reread lines 20–54. Think about what this passage reveals about the farmer and his mother. Add descriptions of both characters' qualities to the chart on page 237.

The mother nodded. "Of course, my son," she replied. "You will always be in my thoughts. How could it be otherwise?"

60   At that, the young farmer could bear it no longer. "Mother, I cannot leave you in the mountains to die all alone," he said. "We are going home and no matter what the lord does to punish me, I will never desert you again." **E**

So they waited until the sun had set and a lone star crept into the silent sky. Then in the dark shadows of night, the farmer carried his mother down the hill and they returned quietly to their little house. The farmer dug a deep hole in the floor of his kitchen and made a small room where he could hide his mother. From that day, she spent all her
70 time in the secret room and the farmer carried meals to her there. The rest of the time, he was careful to work in the fields and act as though he lived alone. In this way, for almost two years, he kept his mother safely hidden and no one in the village knew that she was there.

Then one day there was a terrible commotion among the villagers for Lord Higa of the town beyond the hills threatened to conquer their village and make it his own.

"Only one thing can spare you," Lord Higa announced. "Bring me a box containing one thousand ropes of ash and
80 I will spare your village."

The cruel young lord quickly gathered together all the wise men of his village. "You are men of wisdom," he said. "Surely you can tell me how to meet Lord Higa's demands so our village can be spared."

But the wise men shook their heads. "It is impossible to make even one rope of ash, sire," they answered. "How can we ever make one thousand?"

"Fools!" the lord cried angrily. "What good is your wisdom if you cannot help me now?" PAUSE & REFLECT

90   And he posted a notice in the village square offering a great reward of gold to any villager who could help him save their village.

E UNIVERSAL THEME
Reread lines 60–63. Why does the son decide to disobey the decree even though he might be punished?

_____

_____

_____

_____

_____

_____

PAUSE & REFLECT
Why are the wise men of the village unable to solve the puzzle posed by Lord Higa?

_____

_____

_____

_____

_____

_____

But all the people in the village whispered, "Surely, it is an impossible thing, for ash crumbles at the touch of the finger. How could anyone ever make a rope of ash?" They shook their heads and sighed, "Alas, alas, we must be conquered by yet another cruel lord."

The young farmer, too, supposed that this must be, and he wondered what would happen to his mother if a new lord 100 even more terrible than their own came to rule over them.

When his mother saw the troubled look on his face, she asked, "Why are you so worried, my son?"

So the farmer told her of the impossible demand made by Lord Higa if the village was to be spared, but his mother did not seem troubled at all. Instead she laughed softly and said, "Why, that is not such an impossible task. All one has to do is soak ordinary rope in salt water and dry it well. When it is burned, it will hold its shape and there is your rope of ash! Tell the villagers to hurry and find one 110 thousand pieces of rope."

The farmer shook his head in amazement. "Mother, you are wonderfully wise," he said, and he rushed to tell the young lord what he must do. **F**

"You are wiser than all the wise men of the village," the lord said when he heard the farmer's solution, and he rewarded him with many pieces of gold. The thousand ropes of ash were quickly made and the village was spared.

In a few days, however, there was another great commotion in the village as Lord Higa sent another threat. 120 This time he sent a log with a small hole that curved and bent seven times through its length, and he demanded that a single piece of silk thread be threaded through the hole. "If you cannot perform this task," the lord threatened, "I shall come to conquer your village."

The young lord hurried once more to his wise men, but they all shook their heads in **bewilderment**. "A needle cannot bend its way through such curves," they moaned. "Again we are faced with an impossible demand."

bewilderment (bĭ-wĭl'dər-mənt) *n.* the state of being confused or astonished

How might the wise men show their bewilderment?

"And again you are stupid fools!'" the lord said, stamping
130 his foot impatiently. He then posted a second notice in the
village square asking the villagers for their help.

Once more the young farmer hurried with the problem
to his mother in her secret room.

"Why, that is not so difficult," his mother said with a
quick smile. "Put some sugar at one end of the hole. Then,
tie an ant to a piece of silk thread and put it in at the other
end. He will weave his way in and out of the curves to get
to the sugar and he will take the silk thread with him."

"Mother, you are remarkable!" the son cried, and he
140 hurried off to the lord with the solution to the second
problem.

Once more the lord commended the young farmer and
rewarded him with many pieces of gold. "You are a brilliant
man and you have saved our village again," he said gratefully.

But the lord's troubles were not over even then, for a
few days later Lord Higa sent still another demand. "This
time you will undoubtedly fail and then I shall conquer
your village," he threatened. "Bring me a drum that sounds
without being beaten."

150   "But that is not possible," sighed the people of the village.
"How can anyone make a drum sound without beating it?"

This time the wise men held their heads in their hands
and moaned, "It is hopeless. It is hopeless. This time Lord
Higa will conquer us all."

The young farmer hurried home breathlessly. "Mother,
Mother, we must solve another terrible problem or Lord
Higa will conquer our village!" And he quickly told his
mother about the impossible drum.

His mother, however, smiled and answered, "Why, this
160 is the easiest of them all. Make a drum with sides of paper
and put a bumblebee inside. As it tries to escape, it will
buzz and beat itself against the paper and you will have a
drum that sounds without being beaten." **G**

The young farmer was amazed at his mother's wisdom.
"You are far wiser than any of the wise men of the village,"

G UNIVERSAL THEME
By this point in the story, the
mother has solved three puzzles.
Why was she able to solve them
when nobody else in the village
could?

_____

_____

_____

_____

_____

_____

_____

_____

_____

_____

_____

_____

he said, and he hurried to tell the young lord how to meet Lord Higa's third demand.

When the lord heard the answer, he was greatly impressed. "Surely a young man like you cannot be wiser
170 than all my wise men," he said. "Tell me honestly, who has helped you solve all these difficult problems?"

The young farmer could not lie. "My lord," he began slowly, "for the past two years I have broken the law of the land. I have kept my aged mother hidden beneath the floor of my house, and it is she who solved each of your problems and saved the village from Lord Higa."

He trembled as he spoke, for he feared the lord's displeasure and rage. Surely now the soldiers would be summoned to throw him into the dark dungeon. But when
180 he glanced fearfully at the lord, he saw that the young ruler was not angry at all. Instead, he was silent and thoughtful, for at last he realized how much wisdom and knowledge old people possess.

"I have been very wrong," he said finally. "And I must ask the forgiveness of your mother and of all my people. Never again will I demand that the old people of our village be sent to the mountains to die. Rather, they will be treated with the respect and honor they deserve and share with us the wisdom of their years."

190   And so it was. From that day, the villagers were no longer forced to abandon their parents in the mountains, and the village became once more a happy, cheerful place in which to live. The terrible Lord Higa stopped sending his impossible demands and no longer threatened to conquer them, for he too was impressed. "Even in such a small village there is much wisdom," he declared, "and its people should be allowed to live in peace."

And that is exactly what the farmer and his mother and all the people of the village did for all the years thereafter.

Ⓗ UNIVERSAL THEME
Reread lines 184–189. What lesson does the young lord learn?

_____

_____

_____

_____

_____

_____

_____

_____

_____

_____

_____

_____

_____

_____

Text Analysis: Universal Theme

In folk tales, events often happen in threes. There may be three wishes, or three tasks, for example. These repeated events are called parallel episodes. Analyze the following parallel episodes from "The Wise Old Woman" to help you figure out its universal theme.

Parallel Episodes	Who Solves the Problem?
Lord Higa demands one thousand ropes of ash (lines 75–80).	☐ village wise men ☐ the old woman
Lord Higa demands that a piece of silk be threaded through a curved hole (lines 118–124).	☐ village wise men ☐ the old woman
Lord Higa demands a drum that sounds without being beaten (lines 145–149).	☐ village wise men ☐ the old woman

What universal theme do these parallel episodes suggest?

_____

_____

_____

Why do you think folk tales from many cultures might share that universal theme?

_____

_____

_____

_____

Reading Strategy: Set a Purpose for Reading

One purpose for reading these folk tales was to identify the universal theme they both share. Complete the chart below with details about characters' actions and their consequences. Then state the universal theme of both folk tales.

	"The Old Grandfather . . ."	"The Wise Old Woman"
Characters' behavior toward an elderly character		
What are the consequences of this behavior		

↓ ↓

What is the universal theme?	

How well do we treat our ELDERS?

What could these folk tales teach our culture about how to treat elderly people? Explain your answer.

_____

_____

_____

Vocabulary Practice

Circle the word that is most nearly the opposite the boldfaced word.

1. **haughtily:** (a) snobbishly, (b) modestly, (c) indifferently

2. **bewilderment:** (a) understanding, (b) confusion, (c) shock

3. **arrogant:** (a) smug, (b) humble, (c) aloof

4. **deceive:** (a) outsmart, (b) scam, (c) guide

Academic Vocabulary in Speaking

comment	community	criteria	perspective	technique

TURN AND TALK The young lord owes the villagers an apology and an explanation. Give a speech from his **perspective.** Use at least one Academic Vocabulary word in your response. Definitions of these words are on page 221.

Assessment Practice

DIRECTIONS Use "The Old Grandfather and His Little Grandson" and "The Wise Old Woman" to answer questions 1–6.

1 How does the son's wife change by the end of "The Old Grandfather and His Little Grandson?"

  (A) She becomes more understanding.
  (B) She feels greater pride in her son.
  (C) She develops feelings of love for the old grandfather.
  (D) She becomes more cruel.

2 What universal theme is found in "The Old Grandfather and His Little Grandson"?

  (A) The elderly have much to contribute.
  (B) Family members are responsible for one another.
  (C) A grandfather and grandson have a special connection.
  (D) Patience is rewarded.

3 What is most similar about both folk tales?

  (A) the relationship between the elderly parent and grown son
  (B) the lesson that characters learn
  (C) the qualities of the main characters
  (D) the conflict among family members

4 What is a theme in "The Wise Old Woman"?

  (A) Power over others does not bring happiness.
  (B) It is wrong to break a law.
  (C) A mother's love is selfless.
  (D) Villages in Japan were ruled by lords.

5 Which piece of dialogue conveys a theme in "The Wise Old Woman"?

  (A) *We must hurry before the lord sends his soldiers for you.*
  (B) *Surely you can tell me how to meet Lord Higa's demands so our village can be spared.*
  (C) *Why are you so worried, my son?*
  (D) *Even in such a small village there is much wisdom.*

6 What is a universal theme in *both* folk tales?

  (A) Even the weak may do heroic things.
  (B) People rarely learn from their mistakes.
  (C) Love conquers all.
  (D) Older people deserve respect.

from The Diary of Anne Frank
Drama by Frances Goodrich and Albert Hackett

What IMPACT will you have on the world?

Everyone makes an impact on the world. National leaders or sports heroes may inspire millions, while the rest of us influence friends and family through our actions and beliefs. In the play you're about to read, a young girl confides in her diary, not knowing that her thoughts will later influence readers all over the world.

QUICKWRITE What impact do you now have on others? What impact do you hope to have later in your life? List some ideas in the notebook.

Text Analysis: Theme

The play you are about to read is based on a diary written by Anne Frank, a teenager who spent more than two years hiding from the Nazis. When Anne's diary was published, readers worldwide were touched that, despite all she had been through, she still believed people were good at heart.

This **theme,** or message about life, is carried into the play that was adapted from her diary. As you read, use questions like the ones shown in the chart below to explore how Anne's thoughts and feelings, as well as the characters' relationships with each other, work together to express this theme.

My Impact on Others

In the present

_____

_____

_____

_____

In the future

_____

_____

_____

_____

_____

What **conflicts** do the characters face? How do they handle conflicts?

How do the **characters** reveal their qualities? What do they learn?

THEME

How does the **setting** affect events?

Is there a **symbol** that stands for something beyond itself? What might it represent?

Reading Strategy: Reading a Drama

In a drama, a playwright must tell the story through **dialogue**, the words that are spoken, and **stage directions**, which describe the action and setting. The conflict in a drama pits a **protagonist**, or main character, against an **antagonist**, or opposing force. As you read, notes in the side margin will ask you to collect the information the playwrights reveal about Anne (the protagonist) and the enemies (the antagonists) who have forced her into hiding.

Information About Anne	Information About Nazi Occupation
13 years old	Father lost business
German-born Jewish girl	Jews wore yellow stars

Vocabulary in Context

Note: Words are listed in the order in which they appear in the play.

unabashed (ŭn'ə-bǎsht') *adj.* obvious; bold
Unabashed, she repeated the embarrassing question.

indignantly (ĭn-dĭg'nənt-lē) *adv.* angrily
"Please show some manners," the woman said indignantly.

fortify (fôr'tə-fī') *v.* to make strong
Hopeful thoughts will fortify us for the troubles ahead.

Vocabulary Practice

Review the vocabulary words and think about their meanings. Then use at least two of the words to write about a lively and outspoken teenager.

_____

_____

_____

_____

_____

SET A PURPOSE FOR READING

Read these scenes from Act I of the play *The Diary of Anne Frank* to discover how the characters adjust to life in hiding.

Ⓐ THEME
Reread the Background information. What do you learn about the conflict the Frank family faces in the play?

_____

_____

_____

_____

_____

_____

_____

_____

_____

_____

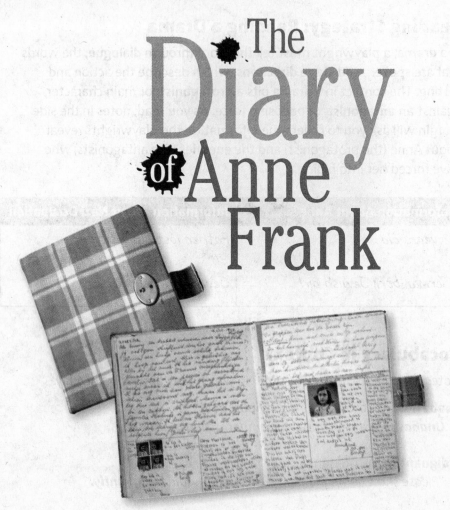

The Diary of Anne Frank

Drama by

FRANCES GOODRICH AND ALBERT HACKETT

BACKGROUND Anne Frank and her family were Jewish citizens of Germany. When the Nazi party, led by Adolf Hitler, came to power in 1933, the Nazis blamed the country's problems on the Jews. Jews were stripped of their rights. Many were eventually sent to concentration camps, where more than 6 million died in what became known as the Holocaust. The Franks moved to the Netherlands to avoid persecution, but the Nazis invaded that country in 1940. In order to survive, Anne's family went into hiding when she was 13 years old. They hid in attic rooms behind Mr. Frank's office, and several other Jews joined them. In this "Secret Annex," Anne kept a diary about her life in hiding. More than two years later, the group's worst fears came true when the Nazis found them. Everyone who had been living there was sent to concentration camps. Anne's diary was discovered later. Ⓐ

CHARACTERS

SECRET ANNEX RESIDENTS

Anne Frank

Margot Frank

Mr. Frank

Mrs. Frank

Peter Van Daan

Mr. Van Daan

Mrs. Van Daan

Mr. Dussel

WORKERS IN MR. FRANK'S BUSINESS Ⓑ

Miep Gies (mēp gēs)

Mr. Kraler (krä′lər)

TIME

July 1942–August 1944, November 1945

PLACE

Amsterdam, the Netherlands

Ⓑ THEME

Circle the names of the two characters listed as workers in Mr. Frank's business. Do you think they will create additional conflicts for the Frank family, or will they help the family cope with hiding from the Nazis? Explain your thinking.

_____

_____

_____

_____

_____

The scene remains the same throughout the play. It is the top floor of a warehouse and office building in Amsterdam, Holland. The sharply peaked roof of the building is outlined against a sea of other rooftops, stretching away into the distance. Nearby is the belfry of a church tower, the Westertoren, whose carillon rings out the hours. Occasionally faint sounds float up from below: the voices of children playing in the street, the tramp of marching feet, a boat whistle from the canal.

10 *The three rooms of the top floor and a small attic space above are exposed to our view. The largest of the rooms is in the center, with two small rooms, slightly raised, on either side. On the right is a bathroom, out of sight. A narrow steep flight of stairs at the back leads up to the attic. The rooms are sparsely furnished with a few chairs, cots, a table or two. The windows are painted over, or covered with makeshift blackout curtains. In the main room there is a sink, a gas ring for cooking and a wood-burning stove for warmth.*

The room on the left is hardly more than a closet. There is a skylight in the sloping ceiling. Directly under this room is a
20 *small steep stairwell, with steps leading down to a door. This is the only entrance from the building below. When the door is opened we see that it has been concealed on the outer side by a bookcase attached to it.* Ⓒ

Ⓒ THEME

The description of the set in lines 1–23 will help you picture the action on the stage. Underline the details that describe the three rooms and attic space. How might this setting affect the conflict in the play?

_____

_____

_____

_____

_____

Act 1

SCENE 1

The curtain rises on an empty stage. It is late afternoon November, 1945.

The rooms are dusty, the curtains in rags. Chairs and tables are overturned.

The door at the foot of the small stairwell swings open. Mr. Frank comes up the steps into view. He is a gentle,
30 *cultured European in his middle years. There is still a trace of a German accent in his speech.*

He stands looking slowly around, making a supreme effort at self-control. He is weak, ill. His clothes are threadbare.

After a second he drops his rucksack on the couch and moves slowly about. He opens the door to one of the smaller rooms, and then abruptly closes it again, turning away. He goes to the window at the back, looking off at the Westertoren as its carillon strikes the hour of six, then he moves restlessly on.

From the street below we hear the sound of a barrel organ
40 *and children's voices at play. There is a many-colored scarf hanging from a nail. Mr. Frank takes it, putting it around his neck. As he starts back for his rucksack, his eye is caught by something lying on the floor. It is a woman's white glove. He holds it in his hand and suddenly all of his self-control is gone. He breaks down, crying.* ⓓ

We hear footsteps on the stairs. Miep Gies comes up, looking for Mr. Frank. Miep is a Dutch girl of about twenty-two. She wears a coat and hat, ready to go home. She is pregnant. Her attitude toward Mr. Frank is protective, compassionate.

50 **Miep.** Are you all right, Mr. Frank?

Mr. Frank (*quickly controlling himself*). Yes, Miep, yes.

Miep. Everyone in the office has gone home . . . It's after six. (*then pleading*) Don't stay up here, Mr. Frank. What's the use of torturing yourself like this?

ⓓ **THEME**
Reread lines 28–45. Underline the words that help you know that Mr. Frank has been through a very hard time. Why do you think he starts to cry?

_____

_____

_____

_____

_____

_____

_____

_____

_____

_____

_____

_____

Mr. Frank. I've come to say good-bye . . . I'm leaving here, Miep.

Miep. What do you mean? Where are you going? Where?

Mr. Frank. I don't know yet. I haven't decided.

Miep. Mr. Frank, you can't leave here! This is your home!
60 Amsterdam is your home. Your business is here, waiting for you . . . You're needed here . . . Now that the war is over, there are things that . . .

Mr. Frank. I can't stay in Amsterdam, Miep. It has too many memories for me. Everywhere there's something . . . the house we lived in . . . the school . . . that street organ playing out there . . . I'm not the person you used to know, Miep. I'm a bitter old man. (*breaking off*) Forgive me. I shouldn't speak to you like this . . . after all that you did for us . . . the suffering . . . **E**

70 **Miep.** No. No. It wasn't suffering. You can't say we suffered. (*As she speaks, she straightens a chair which is overturned.*)

Mr. Frank. I know what you went through, you and Mr. Kraler. I'll remember it as long as I live. (*He gives one last look around.*) Come, Miep.

(*He starts for the steps, then remembers his rucksack, going back to get it.*)

Miep (*hurrying up to a cupboard*). Mr. Frank, did you see? There are some of your papers here. (*She brings a bundle of papers to him.*) We found them in a heap of rubbish on the
80 floor after . . . after you left.

Mr. Frank. Burn them.

(*He opens his rucksack to put the glove in it.*)

Miep. But, Mr. Frank, there are letters, notes . . .

Mr. Frank. Burn them. All of them.

Miep. Burn *this*?

(*She hands him a paperbound notebook.*)

E THEME
Reread lines 59–69. Underline the words that Mr. Frank uses to describe himself. Why is he planning to leave Amsterdam?

F READING A DRAMA

The playwrights use the diary to introduce the protagonist, Anne, and take audiences back to a date three years earlier. Reread lines 90–105, and fill out the chart below with information about Anne and about the Nazi occupation of Holland.

Information About Anne
13 years old
German-born Jewish girl

Information About Nazi Occupation

Mr. Frank (*quietly*). Anne's diary. (*He opens the diary and begins to read.*) "Monday, the sixth of July, nineteen forty-two." (*to* Miep) Nineteen forty-two. Is it possible, Miep? . . . Only three years ago. (*As he continues his reading, he sits down on the couch.*) "Dear Diary, since you and I are going to be great friends, I will start by telling you about myself. My name is Anne Frank. I am thirteen years old. I was born in Germany the twelfth of June, nineteen twenty-nine. As my family is Jewish, we emigrated to Holland when Hitler came to power."

(*As Mr. Frank reads on, another voice joins his, as if coming from the air. It is Anne's Voice.*)

Mr. Frank and Anne. "My father started a business, importing spice and herbs. Things went well for us until nineteen forty. Then the war came, and the Dutch capitulation, followed by the arrival of the Germans. Then things got very bad for the Jews."

(*Mr. Frank's Voice dies out. Anne's Voice continues alone. The lights dim slowly to darkness. The curtain falls on the scene.*) F

Anne's Voice. You could not do this and you could not do that. They forced Father out of his business. We had to wear yellow stars.[1] I had to turn in my bike. I couldn't go to a Dutch school any more. I couldn't go to the movies, or ride in an automobile, or even on a streetcar, and a million other things. But somehow we children still managed to have fun. Yesterday Father told me we were going into hiding. Where, he wouldn't say. At five o'clock this morning Mother woke me and told me to hurry and get dressed. I was to put on as many clothes as I could. It would look too suspicious if we walked along carrying suitcases. It wasn't until we were on our way that I learned where we were going. Our hiding place was to be upstairs

---

1. **yellow stars:** the six-pointed Stars of David that the Nazis ordered all Jews to wear for identification.

in the building where Father used to have his business.
120 Three other people were coming in with us . . . the Van
Daans and their son Peter . . . Father knew the Van Daans
but we had never met them . . .

(*During the last lines the curtain rises on the scene. The lights
dim on. Anne's Voice fades out.*)

SCENE 2

*It is early morning, July, 1942. The rooms are bare, as
before, but they are now clean and orderly.* **PAUSE & REFLECT**

Mr. Van Daan, *a tall, portly man in his late forties, is in
the main room, pacing up and down, nervously smoking a
cigarette. His clothes and overcoat are expensive and well cut.*
130 Mrs. Van Daan *sits on the couch, clutching her possessions,
a hatbox, bags, etc. She is a pretty woman in her early forties.
She wears a fur coat over her other clothes.*

Peter Van Daan *is standing at the window of the room
on the right, looking down at the street below. He is a shy,
awkward boy of sixteen. He wears a cap, a raincoat, and long
Dutch trousers, like "plus fours." At his feet is a black case, a
carrier for his cat.*

The yellow Star of David is conspicuous on all of their clothes.

Mrs. Van Daan (*rising, nervous, excited*). Something's
140 happened to them! I know it!

Mr. Van Daan. Now, Kerli!

Mrs. Van Daan. Mr. Frank said they'd be here at seven
o'clock. He said . . .

Mr. Van Daan. They have two miles to walk. You can't
expect . . .

Mrs. Van Daan. They've been picked up. That's what's
happened. They've been taken . . .

PAUSE & REFLECT
Reread lines 125–126. The same
set as in Scene 1 is shown, but
now everything is "clean and
orderly." What does the audience
understand as the curtain rises
for this scene?

A THEME

Reread lines 127–149. What do the stage directions and the dialogue reveal about the three characters introduced at the start of Scene 2?

Mr. Van Daan:

_____

_____

_____

_____

Mrs. Van Daan:

_____

_____

_____

_____

_____

Peter Van Daan:

_____

_____

_____

_____

_____

(Mr. Van Daan *indicates that he hears someone coming.*)

Mr. Van Daan. You see? **A**

150 (Peter *takes up his carrier and his schoolbag, etc., and goes into the main room as* Mr. Frank *comes up the stairwell from below.* Mr. Frank *looks much younger now. His movements are brisk, his manner confident. He wears an overcoat and carries his hat and a small cardboard box. He crosses to the Van Daans, shaking hands with each of them.*)

Mr. Frank. Mrs. Van Daan, Mr. Van Daan, Peter. (*then, in explanation of their lateness*) There were too many of the Green Police[2] on the streets . . . we had to take the long way around.

160 (*Up the steps come* Margot Frank, Mrs. Frank, Miep [*not pregnant now*] *and* Mr. Kraler. *All of them carry bags, packages, and so forth. The Star of David is conspicuous on all of the* Franks' *clothing.* Margot *is eighteen, beautiful, quiet, shy.* Mrs. Frank *is a young mother, gently bred, reserved. She, like* Mr. Frank, *has a slight German accent.* Mr. Kraler *is a Dutchman, dependable, kindly.*

As Mr. Kraler *and* Miep *go upstage to put down their parcels,* Mrs. Frank *turns back to call* Anne.)

Mrs. Frank. Anne?

170 (Anne *comes running up the stairs. She is thirteen, quick in her movements, interested in everything, mercurial in her emotions. She wears a cape, long wool socks and carries a schoolbag.*)

Mr. Frank (*introducing them*). My wife, Edith. Mr. and Mrs. Van Daan (Mrs. Frank *hurries over, shaking hands with them.*) . . . their son, Peter . . . my daughters, Margot and Anne.

(Anne *gives a polite little curtsy as she shakes* Mr. Van Daan's *hand. Then she immediately starts off on a tour of investigation of her new home, going upstairs to the attic*

---

2. **Green Police:** the Nazi police who wore green uniforms.

180 *room.* Miep *and* Mr. Kraler *are putting the various things they have brought on the shelves.*) **B**

Mr. Kraler. I'm sorry there is still so much confusion.

Mr. Frank. Please. Don't think of it. After all, we'll have plenty of leisure to arrange everything ourselves.

Miep (*to* Mrs. Frank). We put the stores of food you sent in here. Your drugs are here . . . soap, linen here.

Mrs. Frank. Thank you, Miep.

Miep. I made up the beds . . . the way Mr. Frank and Mr. Kraler said. (*She starts out.*) Forgive me. I have to

190 hurry. I've got to go to the other side of town to get some ration books[3] for you. **C**

Mrs. Van Daan. Ration books? If they see our names on ration books, they'll know we're here.

Mr. Kraler. There isn't anything . . .

Miep. Don't worry. Your names won't be on them. (*as she hurries out*) I'll be up later. ⎫ *Together*

Mr. Frank. Thank you, Miep.

Mrs. Frank (*to* Mr. Kraler). It's illegal, then, the ration
200 books? We've never done anything illegal.

Mr. Frank. We won't be living here exactly according to regulations. (*As* Mr. Kraler *reassures* Mrs. Frank, *he takes various small things, such as matches, soap, etc., from his pockets, handing them to her.*)

Mr. Kraler. This isn't the black market,[4] Mrs. Frank. This is what we call the white market . . . helping all of the hundreds and hundreds who are hiding out in Amsterdam. **D**

---

3. **ration books:** books of stamps or coupons issued by the government in wartime. With these coupons, people could purchase scarce items, such as food, clothing, and gasoline.

4. **black market:** a system for selling goods illegally, in violation of rationing and other restrictions.

B READING A DRAMA
Anne appears for the first time. Underline the stage directions in lines 170–181 that describe her. What kind of character does Anne seem to be?

_____

_____

_____

_____

C THEME
Reread lines 167–191 to circle the descriptions, words, and actions of Miep and Mr. Kraler. What do these descriptions tell you about how they will affect the play's conflict?

_____

_____

_____

_____

_____

D THEME
Why do you think Miep and Mr. Kraler are helping the Franks and the Van Daans? What risks are they taking?

_____

_____

_____

_____

_____

(*The carillon is heard playing the quarter-hour before eight.* Mr. Kraler *looks at his watch.* Anne *stops at the window as* 210 *she comes down the stairs.*)

Anne. It's the Westertoren!

Mr. Kraler. I must go. I must be out of here and downstairs in the office before the workmen get here. (*He starts for the stairs leading out.*) Miep or I, or both of us, will be up each day to bring you food and news and find out what your needs are. Tomorrow I'll get you a better bolt for the door at the foot of the stairs. It needs a bolt that you can throw yourself and open only at our signal. (*to* Mr. Frank) Oh . . . You'll tell them about the noise?

220 **Mr. Frank.** I'll tell them.

Mr. Kraler. Good-bye then for the moment. I'll come up again, after the workmen leave.

Mr. Frank. Good-bye, Mr. Kraler.

Mrs. Frank (*shaking his hand*). How can we thank you? (*The others murmur their good-byes.*)

Mr. Kraler. I never thought I'd live to see the day when a man like Mr. Frank would have to go into hiding. When you think—(*He breaks off, going out.* Mr. Frank *follows him down the steps, bolting the door after him. In the interval* 230 *before he returns,* Peter *goes over to* Margot, *shaking hands with her. As* Mr. Frank *comes back up the steps,* Mrs. Frank *questions him anxiously.*)

Mrs. Frank. What did he mean, about the noise?

Mr. Frank. First let us take off some of these clothes. (*They all start to take off garment after garment. On each of their coats, sweaters, blouses, suits, dresses, is another yellow Star of David.* Mr. *and* Mrs. Frank *are underdressed quite simply. The others wear several things, sweaters, extra dresses, bathrobes, aprons, nightgowns, etc.*)

PAUSE & REFLECT
Reread lines 234–239. Why do you think each character is wearing several layers of clothing?

PAUSE & REFLECT

Mr. Van Daan. It's a wonder we weren't arrested, walking along the streets . . . Petronella with a fur coat in July . . . and that cat of Peter's crying all the way.

Anne. (*as she is removing a pair of panties*). A cat?

Mrs. Frank (*shocked*). Anne, please!

Anne. It's all right. I've got on three more. (*She pulls off two more. Finally, as they have all removed their surplus clothes, they look to Mr. Frank, waiting for him to speak.*)

Mr. Frank. Now. About the noise. While the men are in the building below, we must have complete quiet. Every sound can be heard down there, not only in the workrooms, but in the offices too. The men come at about eight-thirty, and leave at about five-thirty. So, to be perfectly safe, from eight in the morning until six in the evening we must move only when it is necessary, and then in stockinged feet. We must not speak above a whisper. We must not run any water. We cannot use the sink, or even, forgive me, the w.c.[5] The pipes go down through the workrooms. It would be heard. No trash . . . (Mr. Frank *stops abruptly as he hears the sound of marching feet from the street below. Everyone is motionless, paralyzed with fear.* Mr. Frank *goes quietly into the room on the right to look down out of the window.* Anne *runs after him, peering out with him. The tramping feet pass without stopping. The tension is relieved.* Mr. Frank, *followed by* Anne, *returns to the main room and resumes his instructions to the group.*) . . . No trash must ever be thrown out which might reveal that someone is living up here . . . not even a potato paring. We must burn everything in the stove at night. This is the way we must live until it is over, if we are to survive. **E**

(*There is silence for a second.*)

Mrs. Frank. Until it is over.

E **THEME**
Reread lines 248–269. Underline what Mr. Frank says everyone must do for ten hours every day. What conflicts is this likely to cause?

---

5. **w.c.:** water closet; toilet.

Mr. Frank (*reassuringly*). After six we can move about . . . we can talk and laugh and have our supper and read and play games . . . just as we would at home. (*He looks at his watch.*) And now I think it would be wise if we all went to our rooms, and were settled before eight o'clock. Mrs. Van Daan, you and your husband will be upstairs. I regret that there's no place up there for Peter. But he will be here, near us. This will be our common room, where we'll meet to
280 talk and eat and read, like one family.

Mr. Van Daan. And where do you and Mrs. Frank sleep?

Mr. Frank. This room is also our bedroom.

Mrs. Van Daan. That isn't right. We'll sleep here and you take the room upstairs. ⎫
⎬ *Together*
Mr. Van Daan. It's your place. ⎭

Mr. Frank. Please. I've thought this out for weeks. It's the best arrangement. The only arrangement.

Mrs. Van Daan (*to* Mr. Frank). Never, never can we thank you. (*then to* Mrs. Frank) I don't know what would have
290 happened to us, if it hadn't been for Mr. Frank. **F**

Mr. Frank. You don't know how your husband helped me when I came to this country . . . knowing no one . . . not able to speak the language. I can never repay him for that. (*going to* Van Daan) May I help you with your things?

Mr. Van Daan. No. No. (*to* Mrs. Van Daan) Come along, *liefje.*[6]

Mrs. Van Daan. You'll be all right, Peter? You're not afraid?

Peter. (*embarrassed*). Please, Mother.

(*They start up the stairs to the attic room above.* Mr. Frank
300 *turns to* Mrs. Frank.)

---

6. *liefje* (lēf'yə) *Dutch:* little darling.

Mr. Frank. You too must have some rest, Edith. You didn't close your eyes last night. Nor you, Margot.

Anne. I slept, Father. Wasn't that funny? I knew it was the last night in my own bed, and yet I slept soundly.

PAUSE & REFLECT

Mr. Frank. I'm glad, Anne. Now you'll be able to help me straighten things in here. (*to* Mrs. Frank *and* Margot) Come with me . . . You and Margot rest in this room for the time being. (*He picks up their clothes, starting for the room on the right.*)

310 **Mrs. Frank.** You're sure . . . ? I could help . . . And Anne hasn't had her milk . . .

Mr. Frank. I'll give it to her. (*to* Anne *and* Peter) Anne, Peter . . . it's best that you take off your shoes now, before you forget. (*He leads the way to the room, followed by* Margot.)

Mrs. Frank. You're sure you're not tired, Anne?

Anne. I feel fine. I'm going to help Father.

Mrs. Frank. Peter, I'm glad you are to be with us.

Peter. Yes, Mrs. Frank.

(Mrs. Frank *goes to join* Mr. Frank *and* Margot.)

320 (*During the following scene* Mr. Frank *helps* Margot *and* Mrs. Frank *to hang up their clothes. Then he persuades them both to lie down and rest. The* Van Daans *in their room above settle themselves. In the main room* Anne *and* Peter *remove their shoes.* Peter *takes his cat out of the carrier.*)

Anne. What's your cat's name?

Peter. Mouschi.[7]

Anne. Mouschi! Mouschi! Mouschi! (*She picks up the cat, walking away with it. To* Peter.) I love cats. I have one . . . a darling little cat. But they made me leave her behind. I left

---

7. **Mouschi** (mōō′shē)

unabashed (ŭn′ə-băsht′) *adj.*
obvious; bold

G THEME
Reread lines 327–347. What do
you learn about Anne from her
conversation with Peter? What
do Anne's **unabashed** responses
to Peter show about her?

_____

_____

_____

_____

_____

_____

_____

_____

_____

_____

_____

_____

_____

_____

330 some food and a note for the neighbors to take care of her . . .
I'm going to miss her terribly. What is yours? A him or a her?

Peter. He's a tom. He doesn't like strangers.

(*He takes the cat from her, putting it back in its carrier.*)

Anne (<u>unabashed</u>). Then I'll have to stop being a stranger,
won't I? Is he fixed?

Peter (*startled*). Huh?

Anne. Did you have him fixed?

Peter. No.

Anne. Oh, you ought to have him fixed—to keep him
340 from—you know, fighting. Where did you go to school?

Peter. Jewish Secondary.

Anne. But that's where Margot and I go! I never saw you
around.

Peter. I used to see you . . . sometimes . . .

Anne. You did?

Peter. . . . in the school yard. You were always in the middle
of a bunch of kids. (*He takes a penknife from his pocket.*) **G**

Anne. Why didn't you ever come over?

Peter. I'm sort of a lone wolf. (*He starts to rip off his Star
350 of David.*)

Anne. What are you doing?

Peter. Taking it off.

Anne. But you can't do that. They'll arrest you if you go
out without your star.

(*He tosses his knife on the table.*)

Peter. Who's going out?

Anne. Why, of course! You're right! Of course we don't
need them any more. (*She picks up his knife and starts to*

take her star off.) I wonder what our friends will think
360 when we don't show up today?

Peter. I didn't have any dates with anyone.

Anne. Oh, I did. I had a date with Jopie to go and play
ping-pong at her house. Do you know Jopie de Waal?[8]

Peter. No.

Anne. Jopie's my best friend. I wonder what she'll think when
she telephones and there's no answer? . . . Probably she'll go
over to the house . . . I wonder what she'll think . . . we left
everything as if we'd suddenly been called away . . . breakfast
dishes in the sink . . . beds not made . . . (*As she pulls off her
370 star, the cloth underneath shows clearly the color and form of
the star.*) Look! It's still there! (Peter *goes over to the stove with
his star.*) What're you going to do with yours?

Peter. Burn it.

Anne. (*She starts to throw hers in, and cannot.*) It's funny,
I can't throw mine away. I don't know why.

Peter. You can't throw . . . ? Something they branded you
with . . . ? That they made you wear so they could spit on
you? ◐

Anne. I know. I know. But after all, it *is* the Star of David,
380 isn't it?

(*In the bedroom, right,* Margot *and* Mrs. Frank *are lying
down.* Mr. Frank *starts quietly out.*)

Peter. Maybe it's different for a girl.

(Mr. Frank *comes into the main room.*)

Mr. Frank. Forgive me, Peter. Now let me see. We must
find a bed for your cat. (*He goes to a cupboard.*) I'm glad
you brought your cat. Anne was feeling so badly about
hers. (*getting a used small washtub*) Here we are. Will it be
comfortable in that?

❶ THEME
Reread lines 371–378. Underline
Peter's opinion of the yellow star.
Now reread Anne's response
to Peter in lines 379–380. The
yellow star is a symbol. What
opposing ideas does it represent
to Peter and Anne?

_____

_____

_____

_____

_____

_____

_____

_____

_____

_____

_____

_____

_____

_____

_____

_____

_____

_____

---

8. **Jopie de Waal** (yō′pē də väl′)

PAUSE & REFLECT

Pause at line 407. What do you think Anne and Peter's relationship will be like?

390 **Peter** (*gathering up his things*). Thanks.

Mr. Frank (*opening the door of the room on the left*). And here is your room. But I warn you, Peter, you can't grow any more. Not an inch, or you'll have to sleep with your feet out of the skylight. Are you hungry?

Peter. No.

Mr. Frank. We have some bread and butter.

Peter. No, thank you.

Mr. Frank. You can have it for luncheon then. And tonight we will have a real supper . . . our first supper together.

400 **Peter.** Thanks. Thanks.

(*He goes into his room. During the following scene he arranges his possessions in his new room.*)

Mr. Frank. That's a nice boy, Peter.

Anne. He's awfully shy, isn't he?

Mr. Frank. You'll like him, I know.

Anne. I certainly hope so, since he's the only boy I'm likely to see for months and months. **PAUSE & REFLECT**

(Mr. Frank *sits down, taking off his shoes.*)

Mr. Frank. Annele,[9] there's a box there. Will you open it?

410 (*He indicates a carton on the couch. Anne brings it to the center table. In the street below there is the sound of children playing.*)

Anne (*as she opens the carton*). You know the way I'm going to think of it here? I'm going to think of it as a boarding house. A very peculiar summer boarding house, like the one that we—(*She breaks off as she pulls out some photographs.*) Father! My movie stars! I was wondering

---

9. **Annele/Anneke:** a nickname for Anne.

where they were! I was looking for them this morning . . . and Queen Wilhelmina! How wonderful! ❶

420 **Mr. Frank.** There's something more. Go on. Look further. (*He goes over to the sink, pouring a glass of milk from a thermos bottle.*)

Anne (*pulling out a pasteboard-bound book*). A diary! (*She throws her arms around her father.*) I've never had a diary. And I've always longed for one. (*She looks around the room.*) Pencil, pencil, pencil, pencil. (*She starts down the stairs.*) I'm going down to the office to get a pencil.

Mr. Frank. Anne! No! (*He goes after her, catching her by the arm and pulling her back.*)

430 **Anne** (*startled*). But there's no one in the building now.

Mr. Frank. It doesn't matter. I don't want you ever to go beyond that door.

Anne (*sobered*). Never . . . ? Not even at nighttime, when everyone is gone? Or on Sundays? Can't I go down to listen to the radio?

Mr. Frank. Never. I am sorry, Anneke. It isn't safe. No, you must never go beyond that door.

(*For the first time* Anne *realizes what "going into hiding" means.*)

440 **Anne.** I see. PAUSE & REFLECT

Mr. Frank. It'll be hard, I know. But always remember this, Anneke. There are no walls, there are no bolts, no locks that anyone can put on your mind. Miep will bring us books. We will read history, poetry, mythology. (*He gives her the glass of milk.*) Here's your milk. (*With his arm about her, they go over to the couch, sitting down side by side.*) As a matter of fact, between us, Anne, being here has certain advantages for you. For instance, you remember the battle

❶ **THEME**
Reread lines 413–416. Circle the words that tell how Anne plans to view her experience in hiding. What does this reveal about her outlook on life and a possible theme of the play?

_____
_____
_____
_____
_____
_____
_____

PAUSE & REFLECT
Pause at line 440. What does Anne realize about "going into hiding" that she had not realized before?

_____
_____
_____
_____
_____
_____
_____
_____
_____
_____

❶ THEME

Reread lines 441–456. Circle the words that suggest a theme of this play. Restate that theme in your own words.

_____

_____

_____

_____

_____

PAUSE & REFLECT

What reason might Mr. Frank have had for giving Anne the diary?

_____

_____

_____

_____

_____

_____

_____

_____

_____

_____

you had with your mother the other day on the subject of overshoes? You said you'd rather die than wear overshoes. But in the end you had to wear them? Well now, you see, for as long as we are here you will never have to wear overshoes! Isn't that good? And the coat that you inherited from Margot, you won't have to wear that any more. And the piano! You won't have to practice on the piano. I tell you, this is going to be a fine life for you! **❶**

(Anne's *panic is gone.* Peter *appears in the doorway of his room, with a saucer in his hand. He is carrying his cat.*)

Peter. I . . . I . . . I thought I'd better get some water for Mouschi before . . .

Mr. Frank. Of course.

(*As he starts toward the sink the carillon begins to chime the hour of eight. He tiptoes to the window at the back and looks down at the street below. He turns to* Peter, *indicating in pantomime that it is too late.* Peter *starts back for his room. He steps on a creaking board. The three of them are frozen for a minute in fear. As* Peter *starts away again,* Anne *tiptoes over to him and pours some of the milk from her glass into the saucer for the cat.* Peter *squats on the floor, putting the milk before the cat.* Mr. Frank *gives* Anne *his fountain pen, and then goes into the room at the right. For a second* Anne *watches the cat, then she goes over to the center table, and opens her diary.*) **PAUSE & REFLECT**

In the room at the right, Mrs. Frank *has sat up quickly at the sound of the carillon.* Mr. Frank *comes in and sits down beside her on the settee, his arm comfortingly around her.*

Upstairs, in the attic room, Mr. and Mrs. Van Daan *have hung their clothes in the closet and are now seated on the iron bed.* Mrs. Van Daan *leans back exhausted.* Mr. Van Daan *fans her with a newspaper.*

Anne *starts to write in her diary. The lights dim out, the curtain falls.*

In the darkness Anne's *Voice comes to us again, faintly at first, and then with growing strength.*)

Anne's Voice. I expect I should be describing what it feels like to go into hiding. But I really don't know yet myself. I only know it's funny never to be able to go outdoors . . . never to breathe fresh air . . . never to run and shout and jump. It's the silence in the nights that frightens me most.
490 Every time I hear a creak in the house, or a step on the street outside, I'm sure they're coming for us. The days aren't so bad. At least we know that Miep and Mr. Kraler are down there below us in the office. Our protectors, we call them. I asked Father what would happen to them if the Nazis found out they were hiding us. Pim said that they would suffer the same fate that we would . . . Imagine! They know this, and yet when they come up here, they're always cheerful and gay as if there were nothing in the world to bother them . . . Friday, the twenty-first of
500 August, nineteen forty-two. Today I'm going to tell you our general news. Mother is unbearable. She insists on treating me like a baby, which I loathe. Otherwise things are going better. The weather is . . . ⓚ

(*As* Anne's Voice *is fading out, the curtain rises on the scene.*)

SCENE 3

It is a little after six o'clock in the evening, two months later.
Margot is in the bedroom at the right, studying. Mr. Van Daan *is lying down in the attic room above.*

The rest of the "family" is in the main room. Anne *and* Peter *sit opposite each other at the center table, where they*
510 *have been doing their lessons.* Mrs. Frank *is on the couch.* Mrs. Van Daan *is seated with her fur coat, on which she has been sewing, in her lap. None of them are wearing their shoes.*

ⓚ READING A DRAMA
Reread lines 485–503. As Anne reads her diary entry aloud, what does she reveal about how the Nazi occupation affects her, Miep, and Mr. Kraler?

Anne:

_____

_____

_____

_____

_____

Miep:

_____

_____

_____

_____

_____

Mr. Kraler:

_____

_____

_____

_____

_____

A READING A DRAMA

Reread lines 513–522. Underline Anne's reaction to hearing that the last workman has left. What does that show about the effects of being in hiding?

_____

_____

_____

_____

_____

_____

_____

_____

_____

_____

_____

_____

_____

_____

Their eyes are on Mr. Frank, waiting for him to give them the signal which will release them from their day-long quiet. Mr. Frank, his shoes in his hand, stands looking down out of the window at the back, watching to be sure that all of the workmen have left the building below.

After a few seconds of motionless silence, Mr. Frank turns from the window.

520 **Mr. Frank** (*quietly, to the group*). It's safe now. The last workman has left. (*There is an immediate stir of relief.*)

Anne (*Her pent-up energy explodes.*) WHEE! **A**

Mrs. Frank (*startled, amused*). Anne!

Mrs. Van Daan. I'm first for the w.c. (*She hurries off to the bathroom. Mrs. Frank puts on her shoes and starts up to the sink to prepare supper. Anne sneaks Peter's shoes from under the table and hides them behind her back. Mr. Frank goes in to Margot's room.*)

Mr. Frank (*to Margot*). Six o'clock. School's over.

530 (*Margot gets up, stretching. Mr. Frank sits down to put on his shoes. In the main room Peter tries to find his.*)

Peter (*to Anne*). Have you seen my shoes?

Anne (*innocently*). Your shoes?

Peter. You've taken them, haven't you?

Anne. I don't know what you're talking about.

Peter. You're going to be sorry!

Anne. Am I? (*Peter goes after her. Anne, with his shoes in her hand, runs from him, dodging behind her mother.*)

Mrs. Frank (*protesting*). Anne, dear!

540 **Peter.** Wait till I get you!

Anne. I'm waiting! (*Peter makes a lunge for her. They both fall to the floor. Peter pins her down, wrestling with her to get the shoes.*) Don't! Don't! Peter, stop it. Ouch!

Mrs. Frank. Anne! . . . Peter!

(*Suddenly* Peter *becomes self-conscious. He grabs his shoes roughly and starts for his room.*)

Anne (*following him*). Peter, where are you going? Come dance with me.

Peter. I tell you I don't know how.

550 **Anne.** I'll teach you.

Peter. I'm going to give Mouschi his dinner.

Anne. Can I watch?

Peter. He doesn't like people around while he eats.

Anne. Peter, please.

Peter. No! (*He goes into his room.* Anne *slams his door after him.*)

Mrs. Frank. Anne, dear, I think you shouldn't play like that with Peter. It's not dignified.

Anne. Who cares if it's dignified? I don't want to be
560 dignified.

(Mr. Frank *and* Margot *come from the room on the right.* Margot *goes to help her mother.* Mr. Frank *starts for the center table to correct* Margot's *school papers.*)

Mrs. Frank (*to* Anne). You complain that I don't treat you like a grownup. But when I do, you resent it. **B**

Anne. I only want some fun . . . someone to laugh and clown with . . . After you've sat still all day and hardly moved, you've got to have some fun. I don't know what's the matter with that boy.

570 **Mr. Frank.** He isn't used to girls. Give him a little time.

Anne. Time? Isn't two months time? I could cry. (*catching hold of* Margot) Come on, Margot . . . dance with me. Come on, please.

B THEME

Two conflicts are shown in lines 532–565. Anne is in conflict with Peter. Anne is also in conflict with her mother. Briefly describe each conflict and tell why it might exist.

Against Peter:

_____

_____

_____

_____

_____

_____

_____

Against Mrs. Frank:

_____

_____

_____

_____

_____

_____

_____

_____

_____

_____

❻ THEME
Reread lines 571–579. Anne is
very eager to dance. What might
dancing represent to her?

_____

_____

_____

_____

_____

_____

_____

_____

_____

_____

_____

_____

_____

_____

_____

_____

_____

_____

_____

_____

Margot. I have to help with supper.

Anne. You know we're going to forget how to dance . . .
When we get out we won't remember a thing.

(*She starts to sing and dance by herself.* Mr. Frank *takes her in
his arms, waltzing with her.* Mrs. Van Daan *comes in from
the bathroom.*) ❻

580 **Mrs. Van Daan.** Next? (*She looks around as she starts putting
on her shoes.*) Where's Peter?

Anne (*as they are dancing*). Where would he be!

Mrs. Van Daan. He hasn't finished his lessons, has he? His
father'll kill him if he catches him in there with that cat
and his work not done. (Mr. Frank *and* Anne *finish their
dance. They bow to each other with extravagant formality.*)
Anne, get him out of there, will you?

Anne (*at Peter's door*). Peter? Peter?

Peter (*opening the door a crack*). What is it?

590 **Anne.** Your mother says to come out.

Peter. I'm giving Mouschi his dinner.

Mrs. Van Daan. You know what your father says. (*She sits on
the couch, sewing on the lining of her fur coat.*)

Peter. For heaven's sake, I haven't even looked at him since
lunch.

Mrs. Van Daan. I'm just telling you, that's all.

Anne. I'll feed him.

Peter. I don't want you in there.

Mrs. Van Daan. Peter!

600 **Peter** (*to Anne*). Then give him his dinner and come right
out, you hear? (*He comes back to the table.* Anne *shuts the
door of Peter's room after her and disappears behind the
curtain covering his closet.*)

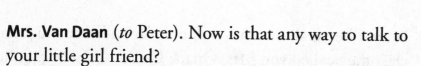

Mrs. Van Daan (*to* Peter). Now is that any way to talk to your little girl friend?

Peter. Mother . . . for heaven's sake . . . will you please stop saying that?

Mrs. Van Daan. Look at him blush! Look at him!

Peter. Please! I'm not . . . anyway . . . let me alone, will you?

610 **Mrs. Van Daan.** He acts like it was something to be ashamed of. It's nothing to be ashamed of, to have a little girl friend.

Peter. You're crazy. She's only thirteen.

Mrs. Van Daan. So what? And you're sixteen. Just perfect. Your father's ten years older than I am. (*to* Mr. Frank) I warn you, Mr. Frank, if this war lasts much longer, we're going to be related and then . . . **D**

Mr. Frank. *Mazeltov!*[10]

Mrs. Frank (*deliberately changing the conversation*). I wonder where Miep is. She's usually so prompt.

620 (*Suddenly everything else is forgotten as they hear the sound of an automobile coming to a screeching stop in the street below. They are tense, motionless in their terror. The car starts away. A wave of relief sweeps over them. They pick up their occupations again. Anne flings open the door of Peter's room, making a dramatic entrance. She is dressed in Peter's clothes. Peter looks at her in fury. The others are amused.*) **E**

Anne. Good evening, everyone. Forgive me if I don't stay. (*She jumps up on a chair.*) I have a friend waiting for me in there. My friend Tom. Tom Cat. Some people say that we 630 look alike. But Tom has the most beautiful whiskers, and I have only a little fuzz. I am hoping . . . in time . . .

Peter. All right, Mrs. Quack Quack!

Anne (*outraged—jumping down*). Peter!

---

10. **Mazeltov!** (mä′zəl tôf′) *Hebrew:* Congratulations!

D THEME
Reread lines 604–616. Underline the words that Mrs. Van Daan says to make her son feel very uncomfortable. What words would you use to describe Mrs. Van Daan?

_____

_____

_____

_____

_____

E READING A DRAMA
Reread lines 618–626. Circle the words in the stage directions that help you picture the abrupt change in action. What does the audience realize about what life in the Secret Annex is like? Explain your ideas about the Nazi occupation.

_____

_____

_____

_____

_____

_____

_____

_____

Peter. I heard about you . . . How you talked so much in class they called you Mrs. Quack Quack. How Mr. Smitter made you write a composition . . . "'Quack, quack,' said Mrs. Quack Quack."

Anne. Well, go on. Tell them the rest. How it was so good he read it out loud to the class and then read it to all his
640 other classes!

Peter. Quack! Quack! Quack . . . Quack . . . Quack . . .

(Anne *pulls off the coat and trousers.*)

Anne. You are the most intolerable, insufferable boy I've ever met!

(*She throws the clothes down the stairwell. Peter goes down after them.*)

Peter. Quack, quack, quack!

Mrs. Van Daan (*to* Anne). That's right, Anneke! Give it to him!

650 **Anne.** With all the boys in the world . . . Why I had to get locked up with one like you! . . .

Peter. Quack, quack, quack, and from now on stay out of my room!

(*As* Peter *passes her,* Anne *puts out her foot, tripping him. He picks himself up, and goes on into his room.*) **F**

Mrs. Frank (*quietly*). Anne, dear . . . your hair. (*She feels* Anne's *forehead.*) You're warm. Are you feeling all right?

Anne. Please, Mother. (*She goes over to the center table, slipping into her shoes.*)

660 **Mrs. Frank** (*following her*). You haven't a fever, have you?

Anne (*pulling away*). No. No.

Mrs. Frank. You know we can't call a doctor here, ever. There's only one thing to do . . . watch carefully. Prevent an illness before it comes. Let me see your tongue.

F THEME
Reread lines 624–655. Sum up the interaction between Anne and Peter. Why are they in conflict?

Anne. Mother, this is perfectly absurd.

Mrs. Frank. Anne, dear, don't be such a baby. Let me see your tongue. (*As* Anne *refuses,* Mrs. Frank *appeals to* Mr. Frank.) Otto . . . ?

Mr. Frank. You hear your mother, Anne. (Anne *flicks out her* 670 *tongue for a second, then turns away.*)

Mrs. Frank. Come on—open up! (*as* Anne *opens her mouth very wide*) You seem all right . . . but perhaps an aspirin . . .

Mrs. Van Daan. For heaven's sake, don't give that child any pills. I waited for fifteen minutes this morning for her to come out of the w.c.

Anne. I was washing my hair!

Mr. Frank. I think there's nothing the matter with our Anne that a ride on her bike, or a visit with her friend Jopie de Waal wouldn't cure. Isn't that so, Anne? **G**

680 (Mr. Van Daan *comes down into the room. From outside we hear faint sounds of bombers going over and a burst of ack-ack.*)

Mr. Van Daan. Miep not come yet?

Mrs. Van Daan. The workmen just left, a little while ago.

Mr. Van Daan. What's for dinner tonight?

Mrs. Van Daan. Beans.

Mr. Van Daan. Not again!

Mrs. Van Daan. Poor Putti! I know. But what can we do? That's all that Miep brought us.

(Mr. Van Daan *starts to pace, his hands behind his back.* 690 Anne *follows behind him, imitating him.*)

Anne. We are now in what is known as the "bean cycle." Beans boiled, beans en casserole, beans with strings, beans without strings . . .

G THEME
Reread lines 677–679. Explain why Mr. Frank says these words. What do his words show about him?

_____

_____

_____

_____

_____

_____

_____

_____

_____

_____

_____

_____

_____

(Peter *has come out of his room. He slides into his place at the table, becoming immediately absorbed in his studies.*)

Mr. Van Daan (*to* Peter). I saw you . . . in there, playing with your cat.

Mrs. Van Daan. He just went in for a second, putting his coat away. He's been out here all the time, doing his lessons.

700 **Mr. Frank** (*looking up from the papers*). Anne, you got an excellent in your history paper today . . . and very good in Latin.

Anne (*sitting beside him*). How about algebra?

Mr. Frank. I'll have to make a confession. Up until now I've managed to stay ahead of you in algebra. Today you caught up with me. We'll leave it to Margot to correct.

Anne. Isn't algebra *vile*, Pim!

Mr. Frank. Vile!  ⓗ

Margot (*to* Mr. Frank). How did I do?

710 **Anne** (*getting up*). Excellent, excellent, excellent, excellent!

Mr. Frank (*to* Margot). You should have used the subjunctive here . . .

Margot. Should I? . . . I thought . . . look here . . . I didn't use it here . . . (*The two become absorbed in the papers.*)

Anne. Mrs. Van Daan, may I try on your coat?

Mrs. Frank. No, Anne.

Mrs. Van Daan (*giving it to* Anne). It's all right . . . but careful with it. (Anne *puts it on and struts with it.*) My father gave me that the year before he died. He always 720 bought the best that money could buy.

Anne. Mrs. Van Daan, did you have a lot of boy friends before you were married?

ⓗ **READING A DRAMA**
Reread lines 700–708. Mr. Frank, Anne, and Margot are reviewing the day's lessons. How is daily life for Anne normal? How is it unusual?

_____

_____

_____

_____

_____

_____

_____

_____

Mrs. Frank. Anne, that's a personal question. It's not courteous to ask personal questions.

Mrs. Van Daan. Oh I don't mind. (*to* Anne) Our house was always swarming with boys. When I was a girl we had . . .

Mr. Van Daan. Oh, God. Not again!

Mrs. Van Daan (*good-humored*). Shut up! (*Without a pause, to* Anne. Mr. Van Daan *mimics* Mrs. Van Daan, *speaking the* 730 *first few words in unison with her.*) One summer we had a big house in Hilversum. The boys came buzzing round like bees around a jam pot. And when I was sixteen! . . . We were wearing our skirts very short those days and I had good-looking legs. (*She pulls up her skirt, going to* Mr. Frank.) I still have 'em. I may not be as pretty as I used to be, but I still have my legs. How about it, Mr. Frank?

Mr. Van Daan. All right. All right. We see them.

Mrs. Van Daan. I'm not asking you. I'm asking Mr. Frank.

Peter. Mother, for heaven's sake. ❶

740 **Mrs. Van Daan.** Oh, I embarrass you, do I? Well, I just hope the girl you marry has as good. (*then to* Anne) My father used to worry about me, with so many boys hanging round. He told me, if any of them gets fresh, you say to him . . . "Remember, Mr. So-and-So, remember I'm a lady."

Anne. "Remember, Mr. So-and-So, remember I'm a lady." (*She gives* Mrs. Van Daan *her coat.*)

Mr. Van Daan. Look at you, talking that way in front of her! Don't you know she puts it all down in that diary?

Mrs. Van Daan. So, if she does? I'm only telling the truth!

750 (Anne *stretches out, putting her ear to the floor, listening to what is going on below. The sound of the bombers fades away.*)

❶ **THEME**
Reread lines 725–739. Underline the words that show how Mr. Van Daan and Peter react to what Mrs. Van Daan is saying. How would you describe the relationship among the three Van Daans?

_____

_____

_____

_____

_____

_____

_____

_____

_____

_____

Mrs. Frank (*setting the table*). Would you mind, Peter, if I moved you over to the couch?

Anne (*listening*). Miep must have the radio on.

(Peter *picks up his papers, going over to the couch beside* Mrs. Van Daan.)

Mr. Van Daan (*accusingly, to* Peter). Haven't you finished yet?

Peter. No.

Mr. Van Daan. You ought to be ashamed of yourself.

760 **Peter.** All right. All right. I'm a dunce. I'm a hopeless case. Why do I go on?

Mrs. Van Daan. You're not hopeless. Don't talk that way. It's just that you haven't anyone to help you, like the girls have. (*to* Mr. Frank) Maybe you could help him, Mr. Frank?

Mr. Frank. I'm sure that his father . . . ?

Mr. Van Daan. Not me. I can't do anything with him. He won't listen to me. You go ahead . . . if you want.

Mr. Frank (*going to* Peter). What about it, Peter? Shall we make our school coeducational? ●

770 **Mrs. Van Daan** (*kissing* Mr. Frank). You're an angel, Mr. Frank. An angel. I don't know why I didn't meet you before I met that one there. Here, sit down, Mr. Frank . . . (*She forces him down on the couch beside* Peter.) Now, Peter, you listen to Mr. Frank.

Mr. Frank. It might be better for us to go into Peter's room. (Peter *jumps up eagerly, leading the way.*)

Mrs. Van Daan. That's right. You go in there, Peter. You listen to Mr. Frank. Mr. Frank is a highly educated man. (*As* Mr. Frank *is about to follow* Peter *into his room,*
780 Mrs. Frank *stops him and wipes the lipstick from his lips. Then she closes the door after them.*)

● THEME
Reread lines 759–769. What is Mr. Frank offering to do, and what does it show about him?

_____

_____

_____

_____

_____

_____

_____

_____

_____

_____

Anne (*on the floor, listening*). Shh! I can hear a man's voice talking.

Mr. Van Daan (*to* Anne). Isn't it bad enough here without your sprawling all over the place? (Anne *sits up.*)

Mrs. Van Daan (*to* Mr. Van Daan). If you didn't smoke so much, you wouldn't be so bad-tempered.

Mr. Van Daan. Am I smoking? Do you see me smoking?

Mrs. Van Daan. Don't tell me you've used up all those
790 cigarettes.

Mr. Van Daan. One package. Miep only brought me one package.

Mrs. Van Daan. It's a filthy habit anyway. It's a good time to break yourself.

Mr. Van Daan. Oh, stop it, please.

Mrs. Van Daan. You're smoking up all our money. You know that, don't you?

Mr. Van Daan. Will you shut up? (*During this,* Mrs. Frank *and* Margot *have studiously kept their eyes down. But*
800 Anne, *seated on the floor, has been following the discussion interestedly.* Mr. Van Daan *turns to see her staring up at him.*) And what are you staring at?

Anne. I never heard grownups quarrel before. I thought only children quarreled.

Mr. Van Daan. This isn't a quarrel! It's a discussion. And I never heard children so rude before.

Anne (*rising, indignantly*). *I,* rude!

Mr. Van Daan. Yes!

Mrs. Frank (*quickly*). Anne, will you get me my knitting?
810 (Anne *goes to get it.*) I must remember, when Miep comes, to ask her to bring me some more wool.

K THEME
Tell about the conflict shown by each of the following:

Mrs. Frank's action in line 780:

_____

_____

_____

_____

Mr. Van Daan's comment in lines 784–785:

_____

_____

_____

_____

_____

_____

Mr. and Mrs. Van Daan's dialogue in lines 786–797:

_____

_____

_____

_____

_____

Mr. Van Daan and Anne's dialogue in lines 803–807:

_____

_____

_____

_____

indignantly (ĭn-dĭg′nənt-lē) *adv.* angrily

● READING A DRAMA
Reread lines 816–824. How does Anne feel about Miep? What does the audience learn about the Nazi occupation? Add information to both sections of the chart below.

Information About Anne

Information About Nazi Occupation

Margot (*going to her room*). I need some hairpins and some soap. I made a list. (*She goes into her bedroom to get the list.*)

Mrs. Frank (*to* Anne). Have you some library books for Miep when she comes?

Anne. It's a wonder that Miep has a life of her own, the way we make her run errands for us. Please, Miep, get me some starch. Please take my hair out and have it cut. Tell me all the latest news, Miep. (*She goes over, kneeling on*
820 *the couch beside* Mrs. Van Daan.) Did you know she was engaged? His name is Dirk, and Miep's afraid the Nazis will ship him off to Germany to work in one of their war plants. That's what they're doing with some of the young Dutchmen . . . they pick them up off the streets— **●**

Mr. Van Daan (*interrupting*). Don't you ever get tired of talking? Suppose you try keeping still for five minutes. Just five minutes. (*He starts to pace again. Again* Anne *follows him, mimicking him.* Mrs. Frank *jumps up and takes her by the arm up to the sink, and gives her a glass of milk.*)

830 **Mrs. Frank.** Come here, Anne. It's time for your glass of milk.

Mr. Van Daan. Talk, talk, talk. I never heard such a child. Where is my . . . ? Every evening it's the same, talk, talk, talk. (*He looks around.*) Where is my . . . ?

Mrs. Van Daan. What're you looking for?

Mr. Van Daan. My pipe. Have you seen my pipe?

Mrs. Van Daan. What good's a pipe? You haven't got any tobacco.

Mr. Van Daan. At least I'll have something to hold in my mouth! (*opening* Margot's *bedroom door*) Margot, have you
840 seen my pipe?

Margot. It was on the table last night. (Anne *puts her glass of milk on the table and picks up his pipe, hiding it behind her back.*)

Mr. Van Daan. I know. I know. Anne, did you see my pipe? . . . Anne!

Mrs. Frank. Anne, Mr. Van Daan is speaking to you.

Anne. Am I allowed to talk now?

Mr. Van Daan. You're the most aggravating . . . The trouble with you is, you've been spoiled. What you need is a good old-fashioned spanking.

Anne (*mimicking* Mrs. Van Daan). "Remember, Mr. So-and-So, remember I'm a lady." (*She thrusts the pipe into his mouth, then picks up her glass of milk.*)

Mr. Van Daan (*restraining himself with difficulty*). Why aren't you nice and quiet like your sister Margot? Why do you have to show off all the time? Let me give you a little advice, young lady. Men don't like that kind of thing in a girl. You know that? A man likes a girl who'll listen to him once in a while . . . a domestic girl, who'll keep her house shining for her husband . . . who loves to cook and sew and . . .

Anne. I'd cut my throat first! I'd open my veins! I'm going to be remarkable! I'm going to Paris . . .

Mr. Van Daan (*scoffingly*). Paris!

Anne. . . . to study music and art.

Mr. Van Daan. Yeah! Yeah!

Anne. I'm going to be a famous dancer or singer . . . or something wonderful. (*She makes a wide gesture, spilling the glass of milk on the fur coat in* Mrs. Van Daan's *lap. Margot rushes quickly over with a towel. Anne tries to brush the milk off with her skirt.*)

Mrs. Van Daan. Now look what you've done . . . you clumsy little fool! My beautiful fur coat my father gave me . . .

Anne. I'm so sorry.

Ⓜ THEME
What is the conflict between Anne and Mr. Van Daan?

_____

_____

_____

_____

_____

_____

_____

_____

_____

_____

_____

PAUSE & REFLECT
Reread lines 854–880. Are the
Van Daans' responses to Anne
justified? Explain your reasoning.

_____

_____

_____

_____

_____

Ⓝ READING A DRAMA
Reread lines 883–896. Underline
Anne's words showing why she
refuses to be courteous and keep
her distance, like Margot. What
do her words reveal about her
attitude towards being in hiding?

_____

_____

_____

_____

_____

_____

_____

_____

_____

Mrs. Van Daan. What do you care? It isn't yours . . . So go on, ruin it! Do you know what that coat cost? Do you? And now look at it! Look at it!

Anne. I'm very, very sorry.

Mrs. Van Daan. I could kill you for this. I could just kill you! (Mrs. Van Daan *goes up the stairs, clutching the coat.* 880 Mr. Van Daan *starts after her.*) **PAUSE & REFLECT**

Mr. Van Daan. Petronella . . . *liefje! Liefje!* . . . Come back . . . the supper . . . come back!

Mrs. Frank. Anne, you must not behave in that way.

Anne. It was an accident. Anyone can have an accident.

Mrs. Frank. I don't mean that. I mean the answering back. You must not answer back. They are our guests. We must always show the greatest courtesy to them. We're all living under terrible tension. (*She stops as* Margot *indicates that* Van Daan *can hear. When he is gone, she continues.*) That's 890 why we must control ourselves . . . You don't hear Margot getting into arguments with them, do you? Watch Margot. She's always courteous with them. Never familiar. She keeps her distance. And they respect her for it. Try to be like Margot.

Anne. And have them walk all over me, the way they do her? No, thanks! Ⓝ

Mrs. Frank. I'm not afraid that anyone is going to walk all over you, Anne. I'm afraid for other people, that you'll walk on them. I don't know what happens to you, Anne. You are 900 wild, self-willed. If I had ever talked to my mother as you talk to me . . .

Anne. Things have changed. People aren't like that any more. "Yes, Mother." "No, Mother." "Anything you say, Mother." I've got to fight things out for myself! Make something of myself!

Mrs. Frank. It isn't necessary to fight to do it. Margot doesn't fight, and isn't she . . . ?

Anne (*violently rebellious*). Margot! Margot! Margot! That's all I hear from everyone . . . how wonderful Margot is . . .
910 "Why aren't you like Margot?"

Margot (*protesting*). Oh, come on, Anne, don't be so . . .

Anne (*paying no attention*). Everything she does is right, and everything I do is wrong! I'm the goat around here! . . . You're all against me! . . . And you worst of all!

(*She rushes off into her room and throws herself down on the settee, stifling her sobs. Mrs. Frank sighs and starts toward the stove.*)

Mrs. Frank (*to Margot*). Let's put the soup on the stove . . . if there's anyone who cares to eat. Margot, will you take the
920 bread out? (*Margot gets the bread from the cupboard.*) I don't know how we can go on living this way . . . I can't say a word to Anne . . . she flies at me . . .

Margot. You know Anne. In half an hour she'll be out here, laughing and joking.

Mrs. Frank. And . . . (*She makes a motion upwards, indicating the Van Daans.*) . . . I told your father it wouldn't work . . . but no . . . no . . . he had to ask them, he said . . . he owed it to him, he said. Well, he knows now that I was right! These quarrels! . . . This bickering! ⊙

930 **Margot** (*with a warning look*). Shush. Shush.

(*The buzzer for the door sounds. Mrs. Frank gasps, startled.*)

Mrs. Frank. Every time I hear that sound, my heart stops!

Margot (*starting for Peter's door*). It's Miep. (*She knocks at the door.*) Father?

(*Mr. Frank comes quickly from Peter's room.*)

Mr. Frank. Thank you, Margot. (*as he goes down the steps to open the outer door*) Has everyone his list?

⊙ **THEME**
Reread lines 925–929.
Mrs. Frank's words reveal a conflict. What might that conflict have to do with a major idea in this play?

_____

_____

_____

_____

_____

_____

_____

_____

_____

Margot. I'll get my books. (*giving her mother a list*) Here's your list. (Margot *goes into her and* Anne's *bedroom on the* 940 *right.* Anne *sits up, hiding her tears, as* Margot *comes in.*) Miep's here.

(Margot *picks up her books and goes back.* Anne *hurries over to the mirror, smoothing her hair.*)

Mr. Van Daan (*coming down the stairs*). Is it Miep?

Margot. Yes. Father's gone down to let her in.

Mr. Van Daan. At last I'll have some cigarettes!

PAUSE & REFLECT

Mrs. Frank (*to* Mr. Van Daan). I can't tell you how unhappy I am about Mrs. Van Daan's coat. Anne should never have touched it.

950 **Mr. Van Daan.** She'll be all right.

Mrs. Frank. Is there anything I can do?

Mr. Van Daan. Don't worry.

(*He turns to meet* Miep. *But it is not* Miep *who comes up the steps. It is* Mr. Kraler, *followed by* Mr. Frank. *Their faces are grave.* Anne *comes from the bedroom.* Peter *comes from his room.*)

Mrs. Frank. Mr. Kraler!

Mr. Van Daan. How are you, Mr. Kraler?

Margot. This is a surprise.

960 **Mrs. Frank.** When Mr. Kraler comes, the sun begins to shine.

Mr. Van Daan. Miep is coming?

Mr. Kraler. Not tonight.

(Kraler *goes to* Margot *and* Mrs. Frank *and* Anne, *shaking hands with them.*)

Mrs. Frank. Wouldn't you like a cup of coffee? . . . Or, better still, will you have supper with us?

PAUSE & REFLECT

Why do you think the characters' attitudes change when they believe Miep is arriving?

_____

_____

_____

_____

_____

_____

_____

_____

_____

_____

_____

_____

_____

Mr. Frank. Mr. Kraler has something to talk over with us. Something has happened, he says, which demands an immediate decision.

970 **Mrs. Frank** (*fearful*). What is it? **P**

(Mr. Kraler *sits down on the couch. As he talks he takes bread, cabbages, milk, etc., from his briefcase, giving them to* Margot *and* Anne *to put away.*)

Mr. Kraler. Usually, when I come up here, I try to bring you some bit of good news. What's the use of telling you the bad news when there's nothing that you can do about it? But today something has happened . . . Dirk . . . Miep's Dirk, you know, came to me just now. He tells me that he has a Jewish friend living near him. A dentist. He says 980 he's in trouble. He begged me, could I do anything for this man? Could I find him a hiding place? . . . So I've come to you . . . I know it's a terrible thing to ask of you, living as you are, but would you take him in with you?

Mr. Frank. Of course we will. **Q**

Mr. Kraler (*rising*). It'll be just for a night or two . . . until I find some other place. This happened so suddenly that I didn't know where to turn.

Mr. Frank. Where is he?

Mr. Kraler. Downstairs in the office.

990 **Mr. Frank.** Good. Bring him up.

Mr. Kraler. His name is Dussel . . . Jan Dussel.

Mr. Frank. Dussel . . . I think I know him.

Mr. Kraler. I'll get him. (*He goes quickly down the steps and out.* Mr. Frank *suddenly becomes conscious of the others.*)

Mr. Frank. Forgive me. I spoke without consulting you. But I knew you'd feel as I do.

Mr. Van Daan. There's no reason for you to consult anyone. This is your place. You have a right to do exactly as you

P THEME
The stage direction says that Mrs. Frank sounds fearful as she asks, "What is it?" in line 970. Why is she fearful?

_____

_____

_____

_____

_____

_____

Q READING A DRAMA
Reread lines 974–984. Underline the request that Mr. Kraler makes. What does the request show about conditions outside the Secret Annex?

_____

_____

_____

_____

_____

_____

_____

_____

_____

R THEME

Reread lines 984–1013. How do the different characters listed below react to the news of Mr. Dussel's arrival?

Mr. Frank:

_____

_____

_____

Mr. Van Daan:

_____

_____

_____

Mrs. Frank:

_____

_____

_____

Peter:

_____

_____

_____

_____

Anne:

_____

_____

_____

_____

please. The only thing I feel . . . there's so little food as it
1000 is . . . and to take in another person . . .

(Peter *turns away, ashamed of his father.*)

Mr. Frank. We can stretch the food a little. It's only for a few days.

Mr. Van Daan. You want to make a bet?

Mrs. Frank. I think it's fine to have him. But, Otto, where are you going to put him? Where?

Peter. He can have my bed. I can sleep on the floor. I wouldn't mind.

Mr. Frank. That's good of you, Peter. But your room's too
1010 small . . . even for you.

Anne. I have a much better idea. I'll come in here with you and Mother, and Margot can take Peter's room and Peter can go in our room with Mr. Dussel. **R**

Margot. That's right. We could do that.

Mr. Frank. No, Margot. You mustn't sleep in that room . . . neither you nor Anne. Mouschi has caught some rats in there. Peter's brave. He doesn't mind.

Anne. Then how about *this?* I'll come in here with you and Mother, and Mr. Dussel can have my bed.

1020 **Mrs. Frank.** No. No. *No!* Margot will come in here with us and he can have her bed. It's the only way. Margot, bring your things in here. Help her, Anne.

(*Margot hurries into her room to get her things.*)

Anne (*to her mother*). Why Margot? Why can't I come in here?

Mrs. Frank. Because it wouldn't be proper for Margot to sleep with a . . . Please, Anne. Don't argue. Please. (Anne *starts slowly away.*)

Mr. Frank. (*to* Anne). You don't mind sharing your room
1030 with Mr. Dussel, do you, Anne?

Anne. No. No, of course not.

Mr. Frank. Good. (Anne *goes off into her bedroom, helping*
Margot. Mr. Frank *starts to search in the cupboards.*) Where's
the cognac?

Mrs. Frank. It's there. But, Otto, I was saving it in case of
illness.

Mr. Frank. I think we couldn't find a better time to use it.
Peter, will you get five glasses for me? PAUSE & REFLECT

(Peter *goes for the glasses.* Margot *comes out of her bedroom,*
1040 *carrying her possessions, which she hangs behind a curtain in*
the main room. Mr. Frank *finds the cognac and pours it into*
the five glasses that Peter *brings him.* Mr. Van Daan *stands*
looking on sourly. Mrs. Van Daan *comes downstairs and looks*
around at all the bustle.)

Mrs. Van Daan. What's happening? What's going on?

Mr. Van Daan. Someone's moving in with us.

Mrs. Van Daan. In here? You're joking.

Margot. It's only for a night or two . . . until Mr. Kraler
finds him another place.

1050 **Mr. Van Daan.** Yeah! Yeah!

(Mr. Frank *hurries over as* Mr. Kraler *and* Dussel *come up.*
Dussel *is a man in his late fifties, meticulous, finicky . . .*
bewildered now. He wears a raincoat. He carries a briefcase,
stuffed full, and a small medicine case.)

Mr. Frank. Come in, Mr. Dussel.

Mr. Kraler. This is Mr. Frank.

Dussel. Mr. Otto Frank?

PAUSE & REFLECT

Reread lines 1034–1038. Cognac
is a kind of liquor that has been
used as a medicine and is also
used to celebrate a happy event.
Why does Mr. Frank insist that
they have cognac now?

_____

_____

_____

_____

_____

_____

_____

_____

_____

_____

Mr. Frank. Yes. Let me take your things. (*He takes the hat and briefcase, but* Dussel *clings to his medicine case.*) This is my wife Edith . . . Mr. and Mrs. Van Daan . . . their son, Peter . . . and my daughters, Margot and Anne.

(Dussel *shakes hands with everyone.*)

Mr. Kraler. Thank you, Mr. Frank. Thank you all. Mr. Dussel, I leave you in good hands. Oh . . . Dirk's coat.

(Dussel *hurriedly takes off the raincoat, giving it to* Mr. Kraler. *Underneath is his white dentist's jacket, with a yellow Star of David on it.*)

Dussel (*to* Mr. Kraler). What can I say to thank you . . . ?

Mrs. Frank (*to* Dussel). Mr. Kraler and Miep . . . They're our life line. Without them we couldn't live.

Mr. Kraler. Please. Please. You make us seem very heroic. It isn't that at all. We simply don't like the Nazis. (*to* Mr. Frank, *who offers him a drink*) No, thanks. (*then going on*) We don't like their methods. We don't like . . .

Mr. Frank (*smiling*). I know. I know. "No one's going to tell us Dutchmen what to do with our damn Jews!" **S**

Mr. Kraler (*to* Dussel). Pay no attention to Mr. Frank. I'll be up tomorrow to see that they're treating you right. (*to* Mr. Frank) Don't trouble to come down again. Peter will bolt the door after me, won't you, Peter?

Peter. Yes, sir.

Mr. Frank. Thank you, Peter. I'll do it.

Mr. Kraler. Good night. Good night.

Group. Good night, Mr. Kraler. We'll see you tomorrow, (*etc., etc.*)

(Mr. Kraler *goes out with* Mr. Frank. Mrs. Frank *gives each one of the "grownups" a glass of cognac.*)

S THEME
Reread lines 1068–1076. Underline Mr. Kraler's explanation for why he is helping Dutch Jews. What idea about heroism does this play suggest?

_____

_____

_____

_____

_____

_____

_____

_____

_____

_____

_____

_____

_____

_____

Mrs. Frank. Please, Mr. Dussel, sit down.

(Mr. Dussel *sinks into a chair.* Mrs. Frank *gives him a glass* 1090 *of cognac.*)

Dussel. I'm dreaming. I know it. I can't believe my eyes. Mr. Otto Frank here! (*to* Mrs. Frank) You're not in Switzerland then? A woman told me . . . She said she'd gone to your house . . . the door was open, everything was in disorder, dishes in the sink. She said she found a piece of paper in the wastebasket with an address scribbled on it . . . an address in Zurich. She said you must have escaped to Zurich.

Anne. Father put that there purposely . . . just so people 1100 would think that very thing!

Dussel. And you've been here all the time?

Mrs. Frank. All the time . . . ever since July.

(Anne *speaks to her father as he comes back.*)

Anne. It worked, Pim . . . the address you left! Mr. Dussel says that people believe we escaped to Switzerland. **T**

Mr. Frank. I'm glad . . . And now let's have a little drink to welcome Mr. Dussel. (*Before they can drink,* Mr. Dussel *bolts his drink.* Mr. Frank *smiles and raises his glass.*) To Mr. Dussel. Welcome. We're very honored to have you with us.

1110 **Mrs. Frank.** To Mr. Dussel, welcome.

(*The* Van Daans *murmur a welcome. The "grown-ups" drink.*)

Mrs. Van Daan. Um. That was good.

Mr. Van Daan. Did Mr. Kraler warn you that you won't get much to eat here? You can imagine . . . three ration books among the seven of us . . . and now you make eight.

(Peter *walks away, humiliated. Outside a street organ is heard dimly.*)

T **READING A DRAMA**
Reread lines 1091–1105. The dialogue explains how the Franks tried to leave the impression that they had left Holland for safety in Switzerland. What did Anne and her family do to keep their real destination a secret?

_____

_____

_____

_____

_____

_____

_____

_____

_____

_____

_____

_____

_____

_____

_____

_____

_____

_____

_____

_____

Ⓤ **READING A DRAMA**
Reread lines 1118–1139. Mr. Dussel
brings terrible news about the
Nazi occupation. How does that
news affect Anne? Add this
information to the chart.

Information About Anne

Information About Nazi Occupation

Dussel (*rising*). Mr. Van Daan, you don't realize what is
happening outside that you should warn me of a thing like
1120 that. You don't realize what's going on . . . (*As* Mr. Van
Daan *starts his characteristic pacing,* Dussel *turns to speak to
the others.*) Right here in Amsterdam every day hundreds of
Jews disappear . . . They surround a block and search house
by house. Children come home from school to find their
parents gone. Hundreds are being deported . . . people that
you and I know . . . the Hallensteins . . . the Wessels . . .

Mrs. Frank (*in tears*). Oh, no. No!

Dussel. They get their call-up notice . . . come to the Jewish
theatre on such and such a day and hour . . . bring only
1130 what you can carry in a rucksack. And if you refuse the
call-up notice, then they come and drag you from your
home and ship you off to Mauthausen.[11] The death camp!

Mrs. Frank. We didn't know that things had got so much
worse.

Dussel. Forgive me for speaking so.

Anne (*coming to Dussel*). Do you know the de Waals? . . .
What's become of them? Their daughter Jopie and I are in
the same class. Jopie's my best friend.

Dussel. They are gone. Ⓤ

1140 **Anne.** Gone?

Dussel. With all the others.

Anne. Oh, no. Not Jopie!

(*She turns away, in tears.* Mrs. Frank *motions to* Margot
to comfort her. Margot *goes to* Anne, *putting her arms
comfortingly around her.*)

Mrs. Van Daan. There were some people called Wagner.
They lived near us . . . ?

Mr. Frank (*interrupting, with a glance at* Anne). I think we should put this off until later. We all have many questions 1150 we want to ask . . . But I'm sure that Mr. Dussel would like to get settled before supper.

Dussel. Thank you. I would. I brought very little with me.

Mr. Frank (*giving him his hat and briefcase*). I'm sorry we can't give you a room alone. But I hope you won't be too uncomfortable. We've had to make strict rules here . . . a schedule of hours . . . We'll tell you after supper. Anne, would you like to take Mr. Dussel to his room?

Anne (*controlling her tears*). If you'll come with me, Mr. Dussel? (*She starts for her room.*)

1160 **Dussel** (*shaking hands with each in turn*). Forgive me if I haven't really expressed my gratitude to all of you. This has been such a shock to me. I'd always thought of myself as Dutch. I was born in Holland. My father was born in Holland, and my grandfather. And now . . . after all these years . . . (*He breaks off.*) If you'll excuse me. **ⓥ**

(Dussel *gives a little bow and hurries off after* Anne. Mr. Frank *and the others are subdued.*)

Anne (*turning on the light*). Well, here we are.

(Dussel *looks around the room. In the main room* Margot 1170 *speaks to her mother.*)

Margot. The news sounds pretty bad, doesn't it? It's so different from what Mr. Kraler tells us. Mr. Kraler says things are improving.

Mr. Van Daan. I like it better the way Kraler tells it.

(*They resume their occupations, quietly.* Peter *goes off into his room. In* Anne's *room,* Anne *turns to* Dussel.)

Anne. You're going to share the room with me.

ⓥ THEME
Reread lines 1160–1165. Describe Mr. Dussel's emotional state, and explain the reason for it.

_____

_____

_____

_____

_____

_____

_____

_____

_____

_____

_____

_____

_____

Ⓦ THEME
Reread lines 1177–1196. What conflicts might Dussel have with Anne or the other characters?

_____

_____

_____

_____

_____

_____

fortify (fôr'tə-fī') *v.* to make strong

Ⓧ READING A DRAMA
Reread lines 1197–1205. Underline Anne's description of what she sees from the window. What does that description reveal about how she is coping with being in hiding?

_____

_____

_____

_____

_____

_____

Dussel. I'm a man who's always lived alone. I haven't had to adjust myself to others. I hope you'll bear with me until I
1180 learn.

Anne. Let me help you. (*She takes his briefcase.*) Do you always live all alone? Have you no family at all?

Dussel. No one. (*He opens his medicine case and spreads his bottles on the dressing table.*)

Anne. How dreadful. You must be terribly lonely.

Dussel. I'm used to it.

Anne. I don't think I could ever get used to it. Didn't you even have a pet? A cat, or a dog?

Dussel. I have an allergy for fur-bearing animals. They give
1190 me asthma.

Anne. Oh, dear. Peter has a cat.

Dussel. Here? He has it here?

Anne. Yes. But we hardly ever see it. He keeps it in his room all the time. I'm sure it will be all right.

Dussel. Let us hope so.

(*He takes some pills to* <u>fortify</u> *himself.*) Ⓦ

Anne. That's Margot's bed, where you're going to sleep. I sleep on the sofa there. (*indicating the clothes hooks on the wall*) We cleared these off for your things. (*She goes over*
1200 *to the window.*) The best part about this room . . . you can look down and see a bit of the street and the canal. There's a houseboat . . . you can see the end of it . . . a bargeman lives there with his family . . . They have a baby and he's just beginning to walk and I'm so afraid he's going to fall into the canal some day. I watch him . . . Ⓧ

Dussel (*interrupting*). Your father spoke of a schedule.

Anne (*coming away from the window*). Oh, yes. It's mostly about the times we have to be quiet. And times for the w.c. You can use it now if you like.

1210 **Dussel** (*stiffly*). No, thank you.

Anne. I suppose you think it's awful, my talking about a thing like that. But you don't know how important it can get to be, especially when you're frightened . . . About this room, the way Margot and I did . . . she had it to herself in the afternoons for studying, reading . . . lessons, you know . . . and I took the mornings. Would that be all right with you?

Dussel. I'm not at my best in the morning.

Anne. You stay here in the mornings then. I'll take the
1220 room in the afternoons.

Dussel. Tell me, when you're in here, what happens to me? Where am I spending my time? In there, with all the people?

Anne. Yes.

Dussel. I see. I see.

Anne. We have supper at half past six.

Dussel (*going over to the sofa*). Then, if you don't mind . . . I like to lie down quietly for ten minutes before eating. I find it helps the digestion.

1230 **Anne.** Of course. I hope I'm not going to be too much of a bother to you. I seem to be able to get everyone's back up.

(Dussel *lies down on the sofa, curled up, his back to her.*) ❶

Dussel. I always get along very well with children. My patients all bring their children to me, because they know I get on well with them. So don't you worry about that.

(Anne *leans over him, taking his hand and shaking it gratefully.*)

❶ **THEME**
Reread lines 1218–1232. Underline details that reveal Mr. Dussel's qualities. Explain why those qualities might cause conflicts in the Secret Annex.

PAUSE & REFLECT

Reread lines 1238–1257. Tell how the audience knows that Anne is reading from her diary. Why might the playwrights have decided to use this technique?

_____

_____

_____

_____

_____

_____

_____

_____

_____

_____

_____

_____

_____

_____

_____

_____

_____

_____

Anne. Thank you. Thank you, Mr. Dussel.

(*The lights dim to darkness. The curtain falls on the scene. Anne's Voice comes to us faintly at first, and then with* 1240 *increasing power.*)

Anne's Voice. . . . And yesterday I finished Cissy Van Marxvelt's latest book. I think she is a first-class writer. I shall definitely let my children read her. Monday the twenty-first of September, nineteen forty-two. Mr. Dussel and I had another battle yesterday. Yes, Mr. Dussel! According to him, nothing, I repeat . . . nothing, is right about me . . . my appearance, my character, my manners. While he was going on at me I thought . . . sometime I'll give you such a smack that you'll fly right up to the ceiling! 1250 Why is it that every grownup thinks he knows the way to bring up children? Particularly the grownups that never had any. I keep wishing that Peter was a girl instead of a boy. Then I would have someone to talk to. Margot's a darling, but she takes everything too seriously. To pause for a moment on the subject of Mrs. Van Daan. I must tell you that her attempts to flirt with Father are getting her nowhere. Pim, thank goodness, won't play. **PAUSE & REFLECT**

(*As she is saying the last lines, the curtain rises on the darkened scene.* Anne's Voice *fades out.*)

Text Analysis: Theme

Readers can find a number of different themes in the excerpt from
The Diary of Anne Frank. Look back at your reading notes and fill out the
chart. Use the details you record to state a possible theme of the play, such
as "people are basically good at heart."

What **conflicts** do the characters face?	
What is the main **character** like?	
Why is the **setting** important?	
What **symbols** did you find, and what do they stand for?	

Possible Theme: _____ _____ _____ _____

Reading Strategy: Reading a Drama

Dialogue and stage directions provide information about Anne and the Nazi occupation. Reread the lines below, and sum up what you learn about the conflict.

Lines	Information About the Conflict
106–122	
248–280	
816–824	

What IMPACT will you have on the world?

Review your notes on page 248. What effect has reading these scenes had on your thinking about your possible impact on the world?

_____

_____

_____

Vocabulary Practice

Circle the word in each sentence that answers the question.

1. If people fortify themselves, do they become stronger or weaker?

2. If someone spoke indignantly, would they sound friendly or annoyed?

3. Would an unabashed action show shyness or boldness?

Academic Vocabulary in Speaking

| comment | community | criteria | perspective | technique |

TURN AND TALK A play is meant to be performed for an audience. Readers of a play must visualize the action and imagine how the characters sound. Discuss the **techniques** the playwrights use to make these scenes from *The Diary of Anne Frank* come alive for you. Use at least one Academic Vocabulary word in your response. Definitions of these words are on page 221.

Assessment Practice

DIRECTIONS Use *The Diary of Anne Frank* to answer questions 1–6.

1 What do the stage directions in lines 620–623 help you understand?
   - (A) the patience it requires to live together
   - (B) the conflicts among family members
   - (C) the tight living quarters
   - (D) the fear that is always ready to rise

2 Which of these is NOT a conflict in the play?
   - (A) the desire for a normal life vs. the strangeness of a life in hiding
   - (B) Jews in Holland vs. Nazi occupiers
   - (C) Anne vs. her father
   - (D) Anne vs. her mother

3 Which detail from the play supports the theme, "People are good at heart"?
   - (A) the actions of Mr. Kraler
   - (B) the actions of Mr. Dussel
   - (C) the relationship between Anne and Mrs. Van Daan
   - (D) Peter's responses to Anne's teasing

4 What can you tell about Anne from the dialogue in lines 902–914?
   - (A) She wants to be courteous but can't.
   - (B) She feels frightened.
   - (C) She wants to share things.
   - (D) She wants to be her own person.

5 Which of the following from the play is a symbol of the pleasures of a past life that is no more?
   - (A) the secret annex
   - (B) Peter's cat
   - (C) Anne's diary
   - (D) Mrs. Van Daan's fur coat

6 What is a theme in the play?
   - (A) Some Dutch citizens risked their lives to rescue Jews.
   - (B) The Nazis were occupiers in Holland.
   - (C) People must help one another when times are hard.
   - (D) It is better to forget the past than remember painful times.

UNIT 5 Painting with Words

POETRY

Be sure to read the Text Analysis Workshop on pp. 604–609 in *Holt McDougal Literature*.

Academic Vocabulary for Unit 5

Academic Vocabulary is the language you use to discuss literary and informational texts. Preview the following Academic Vocabulary words. You will use these words as you write and talk about the selections in this unit.

attitude (ăt′ĭ-tōōd′) *n.* a state of mind or feeling
*Describe the speaker's **attitude** toward freedom.*

create (krē-āt′) *v.* to cause to exist; to make, form, or bring into being
*Which phrases help to **create** an image of the flower in your mind?*

emphasis (ĕm′fə-sĭs) *n.* special attention or effort directed toward something to make it stand out
*How does its **emphasis** on the weather develop the poem's mood?*

mental (mĕn′tl) *adj.* of or related to the mind
*What words help listeners develop a **mental** image of the scene?*

style (stīl) *n.* the unique way in which something is said, done, expressed, or performed
*Is the author's **style** formal or conversational?*

Think of a story or poem you've read recently. Describe your **attitude** toward the text before and after the experience, using at least two Academic Vocabulary words in your response. How did your attitude change?

_____

_____

_____

_____

_____

Simile: Willow and Ginkgo
Poem by Eve Merriam

Introduction to Poetry
Poem by Billy Collins

How can WORDS create pictures?

Have you ever seen the movie version of a book you've already read? Then you probably have had the experience of being surprised when a character didn't look the way you had pictured him or her. Words can create such distinct and powerful images that what you imagine while reading can seem as "real" as what you see. The poems you are about to read might help you see words themselves in a fresh, new way.

QUICKWRITE Choose a photograph from a magazine. Try to think of how the pictured item might feel, sound, smell, or taste, in addition to how it appears. Then write words or phrases that appeal to the senses to describe the item.

Poetic Form: Stanza

Many poems are divided into **stanzas,** or groupings of two or more lines that form a unit. In poetry a stanza serves a similar purpose to a paragraph in prose. Stanzas may be used for several purposes:

- to separate ideas

- to add emphasis

- to create a certain appearance on the page

Stanzas work together to convey the overall message of a poem.

Description

Sight: _____

_____

_____

Sound: _____

_____

_____

Smell: _____

_____

_____

Taste: _____

_____

_____

Touch: _____

_____

_____

My item is _____.

Text Analysis: Metaphor and Simile

Figurative language consists of words used in an imaginative way to communicate meaning beyond their literal definitions. Here are three types of figurative language:

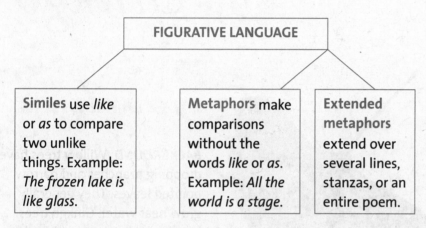

As you read the following poems, look for examples of metaphors and similes and note how the poets use them to create an emotional response, present vibrant images, or express complex ideas with just a few words.

Reading Strategy: Visualize

One way to help yourself enjoy the richness of a poem is to take the time to **visualize** the words, or form pictures in your mind. To visualize, pay attention to details that help you imagine how something looks, sounds, smells, feels, or even tastes. Combine these details with your own knowledge and experiences. As you read these poems, notes in the side column will ask you to keep track of what you visualize in a chart like the one below.

What I Visualize	Words and Phrases That Helped
dark, jerky lines	"crude sketch"

**SET A PURPOSE
FOR READING**

Read this poem to explore new ways of looking at common things.

Ⓐ METAPHOR AND SIMILE
Underline the similes used to describe the willow and the ginkgo in lines 9–12.

Ⓑ VISUALIZE
Reread lines 9–12. How do you visualize the willow and the ginkgo? Write your thoughts in the chart.

What I Visualize

↓

Words and Phrases That Helped

Simile: *Willow and Ginkgo*

Poem by
EVE MERRIAM

BACKGROUND Willow trees have drooping branches and narrow, pointed leaves. They generally grow near water. Ginkgo trees have stubby stems and fan-shaped leaves and have a very different appearance than willow trees.

The willow is like an etching,
Fine-lined against the sky.
The ginkgo is like a crude sketch,
Hardly worthy to be signed.

5 The willow's music is like a soprano,
Delicate and thin.
The ginkgo's tune is like a chorus
With everyone joining in.

The willow is sleek as a velvet-nosed calf;
10 The ginkgo is leathery as an old bull.
The willow's branches are like silken thread;
The ginkgo's like stubby rough wool. Ⓐ Ⓑ

The willow is like a nymph with streaming hair;
Wherever it grows, there is green and gold and fair.
15 The willow dips to the water,
Protected and precious, like the king's favorite daughter.

The ginkgo forces its way through gray concrete;
Like a city child, it grows up in the street.
Thrust against the metal sky,
20 Somehow it survives and even thrives. **G**

My eyes feast upon the willow,
But my heart goes to the ginkgo.

G STANZA
Why do you think the poet
started a new stanza at line 17?

_____

_____

_____

_____

_____

_____

_____

_____

Introduction *to* Poetry

Poem by
BILLY COLLINS

SET A PURPOSE FOR READING

Read this poem to learn what "they" want to do to a poem.

D VISUALIZE
Reread lines 1–4. Circle the words that help you visualize what the poet describes. To which senses do the details appeal?

_____

_____

_____

E STANZA
Mark the number of lines next to each stanza on this page. Why does the poet break each stanza where he does?

_____

_____

_____

_____

_____

_____

_____

BACKGROUND Billy Collins has been called America's most popular poet. He served as the Poet Laureate of the United States from 2001 to 2003. During this time he created the 180 Project, which provided high schools across the country with poems to be read along with daily announcements. He hoped to make poetry part of everyday life for young people.

I ask them to take a poem
and hold it up to the light
like a color slide

or press an ear against its hive. **D**

5 I say drop a mouse into a poem
and watch him probe his way out,

or walk inside the poem's room
and feel the walls for a light switch. **E**

I want them to waterski
10 across the surface of a poem
waving at the author's name on the shore.

But all they want to do
is tie the poem to a chair with rope
and torture a confession out of it. **F**

15 They begin beating it with a hose
to find out what it really means. PAUSE & REFLECT

F METAPHOR AND SIMILE
In lines 12–14, what extended metaphor is used to describe the poem?

_____

_____

_____

_____

_____

_____

PAUSE & REFLECT
What advice might the speaker give to teachers and students who are studying poetry?

_____

_____

_____

_____

_____

_____

_____

_____

_____

Text Analysis: Metaphor and Simile

For each poem, identify as many figurative comparisons as you can. In the chart, list what is being described and what it is compared to. Then identify whether the comparison is a simile or a metaphor.

"Simile: Willow and Gingko"			
Line(s)	What Is Being Described	What It Is Compared To	Simile or Metaphor

"Introduction to Poetry"			

How can WORDS create pictures?

Which words in the two poems created the most vivid images for you?
What did you visualize?

_____

_____

_____

_____

Academic Vocabulary in Speaking

attitude	create	emphasis	mental	style

TURN AND TALK Collins uses an extended metaphor to describe how many
readers respond to a poem. Restate his messages in lines 1–11 and in the last
two stanzas. How do you relate to poetry? Discuss your ideas with a partner.
Use at least one Academic Vocabulary word in your response. Definitions of
these words are on page 297.

Assessment Practice

DIRECTIONS Use "Simile: Willow and Ginkgo" and "Introduction to
Poetry" to answer questions 1–4.

1 In "Simile: Willow and Ginkgo," line 5 is —
- **A** a simile
- **B** hyperbole
- **C** internal rhyme
- **D** an extended metaphor

2 Why might Merriam have made the last two
lines a separate stanza?
- **A** to change the subject from the ginkgo to
  the willow
- **B** to emphasize the speaker's conclusion
- **C** to complete the rhythm of the poem
- **D** to match the other stanzas

3 The speaker of "Introduction to Poetry" compares
a poem to all of the following except a —
- **A** beehive
- **B** maze
- **C** room
- **D** tree

4 Which of the following lines from "Introduction
to Poetry" includes a metaphor?
- **A** *and hold it up to the light*
- **B** *or walk inside the poem's room*
- **C** *I want them to waterski*
- **D** *to find out what it really means*

Speech to the Young
Speech to the Progress-Toward
Poem by Gwendolyn Brooks

Mother to Son
Poem by Langston Hughes

What is good ADVICE?

Suggestions about how to improve your grades or how to approach the new guy at school can be welcome, but how do you know if it is good advice? Sometimes it depends on who gives it. Is it someone who has been there and learned from his or her own experience? Is it someone who cares about you or has a stake in the outcome? In the two poems you are about to read, the speakers share what they have learned with a younger generation.

DISCUSS Imagine you need to bring up your grade in science class. In a small group, brainstorm a list of three people you would ask for advice on how to improve your study habits and grade, and tell why you consider these people a good source for advice.

For good advice, I would ask . . .

1. _____ because
_____
_____

2. _____ because
_____
_____

3. _____ because
_____
_____

Poetic Form: Lyric Poetry

If you're a poet and you want to share your deepest feelings on a topic such as love, death, or the power of nature, what kind of poem will you write? A good choice would be a **lyric poem.** The purpose of a lyric poem is to express personal thoughts and feelings. To achieve this purpose, lyric poems have the following characteristics. They

- are short

- have a single speaker who expresses personal thoughts and feelings

- focus on a single, strong idea

Look for these characteristics in the two poems you are about to read.

Text Analysis: Sound Devices

Writers use sound devices to create a musical quality and to call attention to certain words. The sound devices described in the chart below use repetition to create a musical quality.

Sound Device	Uses Repetition of ...	Example
Alliteration	consonant sounds	*When the <u>w</u>ind <u>w</u>hispers*
Assonance	vowel sounds	*P<u>o</u>etry is <u>o</u>ld, ancient, g<u>o</u>es back far.*

As you read the following poems, notice the alliteration and assonance, and think about the effect of these sound devices.

Reading Skill: Make Inferences

As you try to understand the speakers and the advice they give in these two poems, look for clues that hint at their experiences, attitudes, and personality. Combine these clues with your own knowledge or experience to **make inferences,** logical guesses about what the poet doesn't state directly. Use inference equations like the one shown to record your inferences about the speakers.

Clues from the Text		My Experience		My Inference
The title of the poem is "Speech to the Young."	**+**	Older people like to give advice.	**=**	Speaker is an older person.

Speech to
the Young
Speech to the
Progress-Toward
(Among them Nora and Henry III)

SET A PURPOSE FOR READING

Read this poem to discover what advice the speaker gives.

A SOUND DEVICES
Reread the first stanza and underline the alliteration. What consonant sounds does the poet repeat?

_____

_____

B MAKE INFERENCES
What attitude does the speaker express in lines 10–12? Make an inference equation to explain your thoughts.

Clue from the Text

+

My Experience

=

My Inference

Speech to
the Young
Speech to the
Progress-Toward
(Among them Nora and Henry III)

Poem by
GWENDOLYN BROOKS

BACKGROUND When Gwendolyn Brooks was sixteen, she went to hear Langston Hughes speak at her church. Brooks's mother insisted that she show her work to Hughes. He read her poems on the spot and told her she had talent. In the poem you are about to read, Brooks has words of advice for young people.

Say to them,
say to the down-keepers,
the sun-slappers,
the self-soilers,
5 the harmony-hushers,
"Even if you are not ready for day
it cannot always be night."
You will be right.
For that is the hard home-run. **A**

10 Live not for battles won.
Live not for the-end-of-the-song.
Live in the along. **B**

Mother *to* Son

Poem by
LANGSTON HUGHES

SET A PURPOSE FOR READING

Read this poem to discover the mother's advice to her son.

BACKGROUND An **extended metaphor** is a metaphor that develops its comparison over several lines of a poem or even throughout a whole poem. Notice the extended metaphor Langston Hughes uses in "Mother to Son."

Well, son, I'll tell you:
Life for me ain't been no crystal stair.
It's had tacks in it,
And splinters,
5 And boards torn up,
And places with no carpet on the floor—
Bare.
But all the time
I'se been a-climbin' on,
10 And reachin' landin's,
And turnin' corners,
And sometimes goin' in the dark
Where there ain't been no light.
So boy, don't you turn back. **C**
15 Don't you set down on the steps
'Cause you finds it's kinder hard.
Don't you fall now—
For I'se still goin', honey,
I'se still climbin',
20 And life for me ain't been no crystal stair. **D**

C SOUND DEVICES
Notice the assonance created by the use of the long *o* sound in lines 12–14. Underline the words that contain this sound.

D LYRIC POETRY
What message about her life is the speaker expressing?

_____

_____

_____

_____

_____

_____

Text Analysis: Sound Devices

In the chart below, record the instances of alliteration and assonance in each poem.

"Speech to the Young"	
Alliteration	Assonance

"Mother to Son"	
Alliteration	Assonance

Which poem makes greater use of these sound devices? Cite examples from your chart.

_____

_____

_____

What is good ADVICE?

Which speaker's advice do you think is best? Why?

_____

_____

_____

Academic Vocabulary in Writing

attitude	create	emphasis	mental	style

What **mental** image do you have of the speakers? Explain why you picture them as you do. Use at least one Academic vocabulary word in your response. Definitions of these words appear on page 297.

_____

_____

Assessment Practice

DIRECTIONS Use "Speech to the Young . . ." and "Mother to Son" to answer questions 1–4.

1 What is the speaker's message in "Speech to the Young"?

- **A** Life is a challenge.
- **B** Live in the present.
- **C** Love is the answer.
- **D** Stay true to yourself.

2 Which of the following lines from "Speech to the Young" includes alliteration?

- **A** *say to the down-keepers,*
- **B** *You will be right.*
- **C** *For that is the hard home-run.*
- **D** *Live not for battles won.*

3 In "Mother to Son," the line "Life for me ain't been no crystal stair" is an example of —

- **A** a metaphor
- **B** assonance
- **C** hyperbole
- **D** alliteration

4 What can you infer about the speaker in "Mother to Son"?

- **A** She has had an easy life.
- **B** She is quick to anger.
- **C** She loves her son.
- **D** She is sad.

On the Grasshopper and Cricket

Poem by John Keats

Ode on Solitude

Poem by Alexander Pope

When does FORM matter?

"Bend from the waist." "Lift your chin." "Hold your arms like this." Learning almost any new skill—swinging a bat or a tennis racket, swimming and diving, cartwheeling or dancing—involves learning form. In the poems you are about to read, two of the most well-respected poets in the English language use traditional forms to create meaning.

LIST IT Make a list of activities that involve form. Rank them in order to show which requires the most attention to form.

Poetic Form: Traditional Forms

The poems that follow are examples of two traditional **forms,** or types. Poems that follow traditional forms usually have a specific number of lines and stanzas or an regular pattern of rhythm and rhyme.

Both are **lyric poems,** or short poems in which a speaker expresses personal thoughts and feelings.

- "On the Grasshopper and Cricket" is a **sonnet**—a lyric poem with 14 lines and regular patterns of **rhyme** and **rhythm**.

- "Ode on Solitude" is an **ode,** a type of lyric poem that characteristically deals with an important topic.

Activities Involving Form

1. *baseball* _____

2. _____

3. _____

4. _____

5. _____

Text Analysis: Rhyme Scheme

Rhyme scheme is the pattern of rhyming words at the ends of a poem's lines. You can use letters to identify rhyme scheme. Write the letter *a* next to the first rhyming word and all words that rhyme with it. Then write the letter *b* next to the second rhyming word and the words that rhyme with it, and so on.

Happy the man, whose wish and <u>care</u>	*a*
A few paternal acres <u>bound</u>,	*b*
Content to breathe his native <u>air</u>	*a*
In his own <u>ground</u>	*b*

The letter *a* identifies all the words at the ends of lines that rhyme with *care*. The letter *b* indicates all the words that rhyme with *bound*. As you read each of these poems, you will mark the rhyme scheme as shown above.

Reading Strategy: Paraphrase

Since these poems use language in a way that is seldom heard today, they can be challenging to read. One good way to make sure you understand a poem is to **paraphrase** it, or restate it in your own words.

As you read the poems, look for punctuation marks that show where a thought begins and ends. Then check your understanding by paraphrasing the idea, using a chart like this one. If you still find a thought difficult to "translate," reread the lines slowly and use the context and a dictionary to decode important words you don't know.

Original line(s):
"The poetry of earth is ceasing never:"

↓

Context or definitions that help me:
ceasing means stopping

↓

My paraphrase:
Earth's poetry never stops.

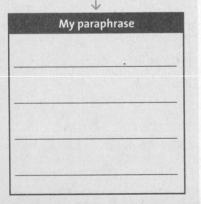

SET A PURPOSE FOR READING

Read this poem to discover what the poet has to say about the earth's poetry.

A RHYME SCHEME

Mark the rhyme scheme of lines 1–4 using letters to indicate rhyming lines. Note that *mead* is a shortened form of *meadow,* so it is pronounced mĕd.

B PARAPHRASE

Use the chart to paraphrase lines 10–12.

Context or definitions that help me

↓

My paraphrase

ON THE
Grasshopper
AND Cricket

Poem by

JOHN KEATS

BACKGROUND "On the Grasshopper and the Cricket" was written as the result of a sonnet-writing contest that John Keats had with another poet, his friend Leigh Hunt. On a winter's night in 1816, the two poets heard the chirping of a cricket. Hunt challenged Keats to see which of them could write the better sonnet on the subject of the grasshopper and the cricket—within 15 minutes.

The poetry of earth is never dead:
   When all the birds are faint with the hot sun,
   And hide in cooling trees, a voice will run
From hedge to hedge about the new-mown mead; **A**
5 That is the Grasshopper's—he takes the lead
   In summer luxury,—he has never done
   With his delights; for when tired out with fun
He rests at ease beneath some pleasant weed.
The poetry of earth is ceasing never:
10   On a lone winter evening, when the frost
   Has wrought[1] a silence, from the stove there shrills
The Cricket's song, in warmth increasing ever, **B**
   And seems to one in drowsiness half lost,
   The Grasshopper's among some grassy hills.

1. **wrought** (rôt): made; produced.

Ode on Solitude

Poem by
ALEXANDER POPE

BACKGROUND Alexander Pope was famous for his poetry, essays, and satires. Lines from his essays—such as "To err is human, to forgive, divine"—have been frequently quoted over time.

SET A PURPOSE FOR READING

Read this poem to learn how the speaker feels about being alone.

Happy the man whose wish and care
    A few paternal[1] acres bound,
Content to breathe his native[2] air,
    In his own ground.

5 Whose herds with milk, whose fields with bread,
    Whose flocks supply him with attire,
Whose trees in summer yield him shade,
    In winter fire. **C**

Blest, who can unconcern'dly find
10   Hours, days, and years slide soft away,
In health of body, peace of mind,
    Quiet by day, **D**

---

1. **paternal** (pə-tûr′nəl): received from a father.
2. **native:** being one's own because of one's birthplace.

C PARAPHRASE
Use the chart to paraphrase the second stanza.

Context or definitions that help me

↓

My paraphrase

D RHYME SCHEME
In the third stanza, circle the words at ends of lines that rhyme with *find* and underline the words at ends of lines that rhyme with *away*.

E TRADITIONAL FORMS
Odes are usually written with a serious **tone,** or attitude toward a subject. The poet may praise nature or an abstract quality, or pay tribute to a person or event. Which words and phrases in lines 17–20 reflect Pope's serious attitude towards his subject? Underline them.

PAUSE & REFLECT
State the speaker's message about self-reliance in your own words.

_____

_____

_____

_____

_____

_____

_____

_____

_____

_____

_____

_____

_____

_____

_____

_____

Sound sleep by night; study and ease,
    Together mixt; sweet recreation;
15 And Innocence, which most does please
    With meditation.

Thus let me live, unseen, unknown,
    Thus unlamented[3] let me die,
Steal from the world, and not a stone
20   Tell where I lie. **E** **PAUSE & REFLECT**

---

3. **unlamented** (ŭn-lə-mĕnt′ĕd): not missed; not mourned for.

Text Analysis: Rhyme Scheme

Mark the rhyme scheme of lines 1–8 of "On the Grasshopper and Cricket" by writing letters next to each line. Then circle the words that are emphasized by the rhyme.

> The poetry of earth is never dead:
>> When all the birds are faint with the hot sun,
>> And hide in cooling trees, a voice will run
> From hedge to hedge about the new-mown mead;
> That is the Grasshopper's—he takes the lead
>> In summer luxury,—he has never done
>> With his delights; for when tired out with fun
> He rests at ease beneath some pleasant weed.

What idea or image does Keats develop in this stanza?

_____

_____

_____

_____

_____

Now mark the rhyme scheme of this stanza from "Ode on Solitude" and circle the words that are emphasized by the rhyme.

> Happy the man whose wish and care
>> A few paternal acres bound,
> Content to breathe his native air,
>> In his own ground.

What idea or image does Pope develop in this stanza?

_____

_____

_____

_____

Reading Strategy: Paraphrase

Choose two especially challenging lines from each poem and "translate" them into your own words. What does each paraphrase help you understand about the poem?

"On the Grasshopper and Cricket"
Original line(s):

↓

Context or definitions that help me:

↓

My paraphrase:

↓

What the paraphrase helps me understand:

"Ode on Solitude"
Original line(s):

↓

Context or definitions that help me:

↓

My paraphrase:

↓

What the paraphrase helps me understand:

When does FORM matter?

Which of these poems seems most influenced by its form? Explain your choice.

_____

_____

_____

Academic Vocabulary in Speaking

attitude	create	emphasis	mental	style

TURN AND TALK The speaker in "Ode on Solitude" has an opinion about self-reliance and happiness. Do you agree with his **attitude** towards living "unseen" and "unknown," but blessed with "peace of mind"? Use at least one Academic Vocabulary word in your discussion. Definitions of these words are on page 297.

Assessment Practice

DIRECTIONS Use "On the Grasshopper and Cricket" and "Ode on Solitude" to answer questions 1–4.

1 What idea is repeated in "On the Grasshopper and Cricket"?

- (A) winter is a time of endings
- (B) the poetry of the earth never ceases
- (C) the cricket's song increases in warmth
- (D) the grasshopper takes the lead in summer luxury

2 "On the Grasshopper and Cricket" is a sonnet, meaning it includes

- (A) a serious tone
- (B) 3-line stanzas
- (C) a short, musical narrative
- (D) regular patterns of rhythm and rhyme

3 According to the speaker of "Ode on Solitude," which of the following makes a man happy?

- (A) living on his own land
- (B) friends and family
- (C) having children
- (D) fame

4 In lines 17–20 of "Ode on Solitude," what does the speaker say he wants besides solitude in life?

- (A) purpose and meaning
- (B) solitude in death
- (C) immortality
- (D) peace

Boots of Spanish Leather
Poem by **Bob Dylan**

from The Song of Hiawatha
Poem by Henry Wadsworth Longfellow

When do poems tell a STORY?

When you hear the word *story*, you might think of plots that unfold in short stories, novels, or movies. But some of the first stories that people told took the form of poetry. Ever since, some writers have used the stanzas, rhythm, and rhyme of poetry to tell about characters, setting, and conflict. The following two works are examples of stories told in poetic form.

DISCUSS Think of a poem or song you know that tells a story. List some key ideas on the lines to the left. Then summarize the story in your own words to your group. How many of your classmates can guess the original work?

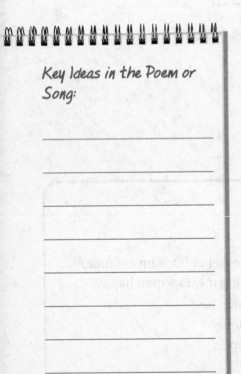

Key Ideas in the Poem or Song:

_____

_____

_____

_____

_____

_____

_____

Poetic Form: Narrative Poetry

The two poems that follow are examples of specific types of **narrative poetry,** or poetry whose purpose is to tell a story.

- "Boots of Spanish Leather is a **ballad,** a narrative poem that is meant to be sung and focuses on a single tragic event.

- *The Song of Hiawatha* is an **epic,** a long narrative poem about the life of a hero whose actions reflect the values of the group he or she belongs to.

Like all narrative poems, ballads and epics contain characters, plot, and setting.

Text Analysis: Rhythm and Meter

Rhythm is the pattern of stressed (´) and unstressed (˘) syllables in a line of poetry. Narrative poetry often has a regular, repeated pattern of rhythm, which is called **meter.**

Rhythm and meter create the overall tempo or pace of a poem. They give poems their musical sound and help poets to emphasize certain words or phrases. For example, look at the following lines from *The Song of Hiawatha:*

Lines from Poem	Rhythm and Meter
Bý thĕ shóres ŏf Gítchĕ Gúmĕe, Bý thĕ shíniŋ Bíg-Sĕa-Wátĕr,	← regular pattern of stressed and unstressed syllables creates a soothing rhythm.

As you read the poems, listen for the way rhythm and meter create emphasis and add a musical effect.

Reading Strategy: Summarize

When you **summarize,** you briefly retell the main ideas and most important details of a piece of writing in your own words. Summarizing narrative poetry can help you make sure you understand the characters' feelings, thoughts, and actions. As you read each poem, a chart like the one shown will help you summarize each stanza or section.

Stanza/Section	Main Idea	Detail(s)
Section 1 of *The Song of Hiawatha.*	A woman lives in the forest by the water.	Her name is Nokomis.

Boots of Spanish Leather

Poem by
BOB DYLAN

SET A PURPOSE FOR READING

Read this ballad to discover how the loved one feels when the speaker sails away.

BACKGROUND Bob Dylan burst onto the folk music scene in New York City in the 1960s and has been making groundbreaking recordings for nearly 50 years. He draws on classic literature and traditional American music as sources for his songs. His lyrics are widely regarded as important poems.

Ⓐ NARRATIVE POETRY
Reread the first two stanzas. What do you know about the speaker in the first stanza? Who is the speaker in the second?

_____

_____

_____

_____

_____

_____

_____

_____

_____

_____

Oh, I'm sailin' away my own true love,
I'm sailin' away in the morning.
Is there something I can send you from across the sea,
From the place that I'll be landing?

5 No, there's nothin' you can send me, my own true love,
There's nothin' I wish to be ownin'.
Just carry yourself back to me unspoiled,
From across that lonesome ocean. Ⓐ

Oh, but I just thought you might want something fine
10 *Made of silver or of golden,*
Either from the mountains of Madrid[1]
Or from the coast of Barcelona.[2]

---

1. **Madrid** (mə-drĭd): the capital of Spain, located in the central part of the country.
2. **Barcelona** (bär'-sə-lōnə): a northeastern Spanish city, located on the Mediterranean Sea coast.

Oh, but if I had the stars from the darkest night
And the diamonds from the deepest ocean,
15 I'd forsake³ them all for your sweet kiss,
For that's all I'm wishin' to be ownin'. **B**

That I might be gone a long time
And it's only that I'm askin',
Is there something I can send you to remember me by,
20 *To make your time more easy passin'.*

Oh, how can, how can you ask me again,
It only brings me sorrow.
The same thing I want from you today,
I would want again tomorrow. **C**

25 I got a letter on a lonesome day,
It was from her ship a-sailin',
Saying I don't know when I'll be comin' back again,
It depends on how I'm a-feelin'.

Well, if you, my love, must think that-a-way,
30 I'm sure your mind is roamin'.
I'm sure your heart is not with me,
But with the country to where you're goin'.

So take heed, take heed of the western wind,
Take heed of the stormy weather.
35 And yes, there's something you can send back to me,
Spanish boots of Spanish leather. **D**

---

3. **forsake** (fôr-sāk'): to give up (something that was formerly precious).

B SUMMARIZE
Underline the details that convey this speaker's attitude toward the offered gift in lines 13–16. Then summarize it in your chart.

Main Idea

↓

Summary

C NARRATIVE POETRY
State the **conflict** between the two speakers.

_____
_____
_____
_____

D RHYTHM AND METER
Reread lines 33–36. Which words are emphasized by the repetition and rhythm? Underline them. Why do you think these words are emphasized?

_____
_____
_____
_____

**SET A PURPOSE
FOR READING**
Read this poem to discover
what Hiawatha learns from
his grandmother.

THE
Song
OF Hiawatha

Poem by

HENRY WADSWORTH
LONGFELLOW

BACKGROUND During his lifetime, Henry
Wadsworth Longfellow was America's most
popular poet. Many of his poems, including
"The Song of Hiawatha," were inspired by
actual events in American history.

E NARRATIVE POETRY
What is the **setting** of this poem?
Underline words that help you
identify the setting.

_____

_____

_____

_____

_____

_____

_____

_____

_____

By the shores of Gitche Gumee,
By the shining Big-Sea-Water,
Stood the wigwam of Nokomis,
Daughter of the Moon, Nokomis.
5 Dark behind it rose the forest,
Rose the black and gloomy pine trees,
Rose the firs with cones upon them;
Bright before it beat the water,
Beat the clear and sunny water,
10 Beat the shining Big-Sea-Water. **E**
    There the wrinkled old Nokomis
Nursed the little Hiawatha,
Rocked him in his linden[1] cradle,
Bedded soft in moss and rushes,
15 Safely bound with reindeer sinews;
Stilled his fretful wail by saying,

---

1. **linden** (lĭn′dən): made of wood from a linden tree.

"Hush! the Naked Bear will hear thee!"
Lulled him into slumber, singing,
"Ewa-yea! my little owlet!
20 Who is this, that lights the wigwam?
With his great eyes lights the wigwam?
Ewa-yea! my little owlet!"

    Many things Nokomis taught him
Of the stars that shine in heaven;
25 Showed him Ishkoodah, the comet,
Ishkoodah, with fiery tresses;[2]
Showed the Death-Dance of the spirits,
Warriors with their plumes and war-clubs,
Flaring far away to northward
30 In the frosty nights of Winter;
Showed the broad white road in heaven,
Pathway of the ghosts, the shadows,
Running straight across the heavens,
Crowded with the ghosts, the shadows. **F**

35   At the door on summer evenings
Sat the little Hiawatha;
Heard the whispering of the pine-trees,
Heard the lapping of the waters,
Sounds of music, words of wonder;
40 "Minne-wawa!" said the pine-trees,
"Mudway-aushka!" said the water.

    Saw the firefly, Wah-wah-taysee,
Flitting through the dusk of evening,
With the twinkle of its candle
45 Lighting up the brakes[3] and bushes,
And he sang the song of children,
Sang the song Nokomis taught him:
"Wah-wah-taysee, little firefly,
Little, flitting, white-fire insect,

F SUMMARIZE
Each new section in this poem begins with an indented line. Reread lines 23–34. Underline what Nokomis taught Hiawatha. How would you summarize this section?

Summary

---

2. **tresses:** long locks or ringlets of hair.

3. **brakes:** areas overgrown with dense bushes; thickets.

G RHYTHM AND METER
Read lines 42–53 aloud, tapping your pencil to the rhythm. Mark the stressed and unstressed syllables. Is the rhythm regular?

_____

_____

H NARRATIVE POETRY
Nokomis, Hiawatha's grandmother, raises him as her own. What kind of relationship do the woman and boy seem to have?

_____

_____

_____

_____

_____

_____

_____

_____

50 Little, dancing, white-fire creature,
   Light me with your little candle,
   Ere upon my bed I lay me,
   Ere in sleep I close my eyelids!" **G**
      Saw the moon rise from the water
55 Rippling, rounding from the water,
   Saw the flecks and shadows on it,
   Whispered, "What is that, Nokomis?"
   And the good Nokomis answered:
   "Once a warrior, very angry,
60 Seized his grandmother, and threw her
   Up into the sky at midnight;
   Right against the moon he threw her;
   'Tis her body that you see there."
      Saw the rainbow in the heaven,
65 In the eastern sky, the rainbow,
   Whispered, "What is that, Nokomis?"
   And the good Nokomis answered:
   "'Tis the heaven of flowers you see there
   All the wildflowers of the forest,
70 All the lilies of the prairie,
   When on earth they fade and perish,
   Blossom in that heaven above us."
      When he heard the owls at midnight,
   Hooting, laughing in the forest,
75 "What is that?" he cried in terror,
   "What is that," he said, "Nokomis?"
   And the good Nokomis answered:
   "That is but the owl and owlet,
   Talking in their native language,
80 Talking, scolding at each other." **H**

Then the little Hiawatha
Learned of every bird its language,
Learned their names and all their secrets:
How they built their nests in Summer,
85 Where they hid themselves in Winter;
Talked with them whene'er he met them,
Called them "Hiawatha's Chickens."

Of all beasts he learned the language,
Learned their names and all their secrets:
90 How the beavers built their lodges,
Where the squirrels hid their acorns,
How the reindeer ran so swiftly,
Why the rabbit was so timid,
Talked with them whene'er he met them,
95 Called them "Hiawatha's Brothers." ❶

Then Iagoo, the great boaster,
He the marvelous storyteller,
He the traveler and the talker,
He the friend of old Nokomis,
100 Made a bow for Hiawatha;
From a branch of ash he made it,
From an oak bough made the arrows,
Tipped with flint,⁴ and winged with feathers
And the cord he made of deerskin.
105 Then he said to Hiawatha:
"Go, my son, into the forest,
Where the red deer herd together.
Kill for us a famous roebuck,
Kill for us a deer with antlers!"
110 Forth into the forest straightway
All alone walked Hiawatha
Proudly, with his bow and arrows;
And the birds sang round him, o'er him,

Monitor Your Comprehension

❶ **SUMMARIZE**
Reread lines 81–95. Summarize what Hiawatha learns in this section in your chart.

Summary

---

4. **flint:** a hard, gray or black quartz.

"Do not shoot us, Hiawatha!"
115 Sang the robin, the Opechee,
Sang the bluebird, the Owaissa,
"Do not shoot us, Hiawatha!"
    Up the oak tree, close beside him,
Sprang the squirrel, Adjidaumo,
120 In and out among the branches,
Coughed and chattered from the oak tree,
Laughed, and said between his laughing,
"Do not shoot me, Hiawatha!"
    And the rabbit from his pathway
125 Leaped aside, and at a distance
Sat erect upon his haunches,
Half in fear and half in frolic,
Saying to the little hunter,
"Do not shoot me, Hiawatha!"
130   But he heeded[5] not, nor heard them,
For his thoughts were with the red deer;
On their tracks his eyes were fastened,
Leading downward to the river,
To the ford across the river,
135 And as one in slumber walked he.   **PAUSE & REFLECT**
    Hidden in the alder bushes,
There he waited till the deer came,
Till he saw two antlers lifted,
Saw two eyes look from the thicket,
140 Saw two nostrils point to the windward,
And a deer came down the pathway,
Flecked with leafy light and shadow.
And his heart within him fluttered,
Trembled like the leaves above him,

PAUSE & REFLECT
Recall what Hiawatha learned
in lines 81–95. How would you
describe Hiawatha as a hunter?

_____

_____

_____

_____

_____

_____

_____

_____

_____

_____

_____

5. **heeded:** listened to and considered; paid attention to.

145 Like the birch leaf palpitated,
    As the deer came down the pathway. **J**
        Then, upon one knee uprising,
    Hiawatha aimed an arrow;
    Scarce a twig moved with his motion,
150 Scarce a leaf was stirred or rustled,
    But the wary roebuck started,
    Stamped with all his hooves together,
    Listened with one foot uplifted,
    Leaped as if to meet the arrow;
155 Ah! the singing, fatal arrow,
    Like a wasp it buzzed and stung him!
        Dead he lay there in the forest,
    By the ford across the river,
    Beat his timid heart no longer;
160 But the heart of Hiawatha
    Throbbed and shouted and exulted,[6]
    As he bore the red deer homeward,
    And Iagoo and Nokomis
    Hailed his coming with applauses.
165   From the red deer's hide Nokomis
    Made a cloak for Hiawatha,
    From the red deer's flesh Nokomis
    Made a banquet to his honor.
    All the village came and feasted,
170 All the guests praised Hiawatha,
    Called him Strong-Heart, Soan-ge-taha!
    Called him Loon-Heart, Mahn-go-taysee! **K**

---

6. **exulted** (ĭg-zŭltd′): rejoiced; felt jubilant and triumphant.

J RHYTHM AND METER
The meter Longfellow uses in this poem is called **trochaic tetrameter**. In a trochaic meter, a stressed syllable is followed by an unstressed syllable. The term *tetrameter* means that this pattern is repeated four times in each line of poetry. Reread lines 136–146 and mark the meter of the last two lines. How does the powerful beat of the trochaic tetrameter help convey the suspense of a hunt?

_____

_____

_____

_____

_____

_____

K NARRATIVE POETRY
What **conflict** does Hiawatha face? How is it resolved?

_____

_____

_____

_____

_____

_____

_____

_____

Text Analysis: Rhythm and Meter

Mark the meter of this stanza from "Boots of Spanish Leather" by writing ˘ above each unstressed syllable and ´ above each stressed syllable.

> Well, if you, my love, must think that-a-way,
>
> I'm sure your mind is roamin'.
>
> I'm sure your heart is not with me,
>
> But with the country to where you're goin'.

What words or ideas are emphasized in this stanza?

_____

_____

_____

Now mark the meter of this section from *The Song of Hiawatha*.

> When he heard the owls at midnight,
>
> Hooting, laughing in the forest,
>
> "What is that?" he cried in terror,
>
> "What is that," he said, "Nokomis?"
>
> And the good Nokomis answered:
>
> "That is but the owl and owlet,
>
> Talking in their native language,
>
> Talking, scolding at each other."

What effect does the regular rhythm create?

_____

_____

_____

When do poems tell a STORY?

Did the stories told in these poems satisfy you in the same way a good short story does? (Review your reading notes and summaries before you answer.) Explain your response, making sure to evaluate elements such as character development, plot development, and conflict resolution.

_____

_____

_____

_____

_____

Academic Vocabulary in Writing

attitude	create	emphasis	mental	style

TURN AND TALK Why is Hiawatha an epic hero? Discuss your ideas with a partner, using at least one Academic Vocabulary word in your response. Definitions of these words are on page 297.

Assessment Practice

DIRECTIONS Use "Boots of Spanish Leather" and *The Song of Hiawatha* to answer questions 1–4.

1 "Boots of Spanish Leather" is a narrative poem because —

   (A) two speakers are in conflict
   (B) the setting is in the past
   (C) it is meant to be sung
   (D) it tells a story

2 What is the conflict in "Boots of Spanish Leather"?

   (A) A man misses his lover.
   (B) The speaker's ship might not return.
   (C) A traveler cares more about her travels than her beloved.
   (D) The speaker cannot find his boots of Spanish leather.

3 Which of the following is a summary of *The Song of Hiawatha*?

   (A) Hiawatha learns to respect nature and becomes a skilled hunter.
   (B) Hiawatha is raised by Nokomis.
   (C) The forest animals speak to Hiawatha.
   (D) Hiawatha must learn to hunt dear.

4 The meter of *The Song of Hiawatha* is

   (A) irregular
   (B) regular
   (C) rhyming
   (D) epic

UNIT

6

A Unique Imprint

STYLE, VOICE, AND TONE

Be sure to read the Text Analysis Workshop on pp. 688–693 in *Holt McDougal Literature*.

Academic Vocabulary for Unit 6

Academic Vocabulary is the language you use to discuss literary and informational texts. Preview the following Academic Vocabulary words. You will use these words as you write and talk about the selections in this unit.

achieve (ə-chēv´) *v.* to accomplish or to succeed

*Which of the author's works helped her **achieve** success as a writer?*

•

income (ĭn´kŭm) *n.* money one receives as wages, salary, or by other means of profit

*How does the need to earn an **income** affect the author's choice of subjects?*

•

individual (ĭn´də-vĭj´ōō-əl) *adj.* single; relating to one human being or thing

*Which of the subject's **individual** accomplishments is most inspiring?*

•

strategy (străt´ə-jē) *n.* a plan of action intended to accomplish a goal

*How does the main character's **strategy** help her to reach her goal?*

•

trend (trĕnd) *n.* the general direction in which something tends to move; current style

*Which scientific **trend** does the author suggest will lead to advances?*

Think of a story or a book in which a character **achieves** a great success. Describe how that success comes about, using at least two Academic Vocabulary words in your response. What **strategies** does the character use?

_____

_____

_____

_____

The Lady, or the Tiger?
Short Story by **Frank R. Stockton**

How do you make DECISIONS?

How we make decisions depends on the situation. A simple coin toss can help you decide who goes first when playing a video game. But would you choose to flip a coin if you faced a more serious decision? In the story you are about to read, a decision has life-or-death consequences.

QUICKWRITE Would you flip a coin to decide which movie to go to? To decide which high school to attend? Record your thoughts about how you would make each decision.

Text Analysis: Tone

Writers often express an attitude, or **tone,** toward the subject, setting, or characters they're writing about. A tone can often be described with one word, such as *angry, proud,* or *playful.* Just as knowing a friend's attitude can help you decide whether she's joking or serious, knowing a writer's tone can help you grasp his or her message. As you read the selection that follows, look for words and details that help you understand how the writer feels about his topic. Ask yourself questions like these:

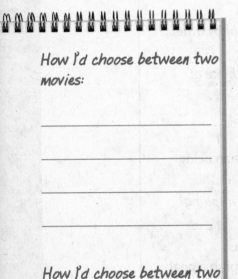

How I'd choose between two movies:

How I'd choose between two high schools:

Questions to ask about tone

Do his descriptions of the **characters** suggest whether he thinks they're smart, foolish, kind, or cruel?	Does the description of the **setting** show that he admires the society's customs?	Does his language show that he takes the **plot events** seriously, or not?

Reading Strategy: Paraphrase

One way to understand what you read is to **paraphrase** it, or restate the writer's language in your own words. To paraphrase, first identify the main ideas and determine the meaning of any unfamiliar words. Then restate the ideas and details in your own words. As you read, notes in the side column will ask you to paraphrase ideas.

Line numbers	Paraphrase
1–4	Long ago, there lived a rough cruel king. He had been influenced by forward-thinking cultures, but he was still uncivilized.

Vocabulary in Context

Note: Words are listed in the order in which they appear in the story.

progressiveness (prə-grĕs′ĭv-nĭs) *n.* the state of advancing toward better conditions or new policies, ideas, or methods
  *The **progressiveness** of the mayor's agenda will benefit us all.*

assert (ə-sûrt′) *v.* to act forcefully; to take charge
  *Once elected, she was quick to **assert** her authority.*

impartial (ĭm-pär′shəl) *adj.* not partial or biased; unprejudiced
  *The ballots were counted fairly by an **impartial** staff.*

subordinate (sə-bôr′dn-ĭt) *adj.* secondary; belonging to a lower rank
  *The mayor assigned the task to a **subordinate** staff member.*

conventional (kən-vĕn′shə-nəl) *adj.* conforming to established practice or accepted standards; traditional
  *Being independent, she does not follow **conventional** party lines.*

waver (wā′vər) *v.* to exhibit indecision; to hesitate
  *He urged the mayor not to **waver** from her original decision.*

aspire (ə-spīr′) *v.* to have a great ambition or an ultimate goal; to desire strongly
  *Together, we **aspire** to improve the lives of everyone.*

devious (dē′vē-əs) *adj.* departing from the straight or direct course
  *Following a **devious** path will distract us from our goal.*

anguished (ăng′gwĭsht) *adj.* tormented; distressed
  *Harsh budget cuts were made by a clearly **anguished** council.*

The Lady, or the Tiger?

Short Story by
FRANK R. STOCKTON

BACKGROUND Much of the action in "The Lady, or the Tiger?" takes place in an amphitheater. One of the most famous amphitheaters in history is the Colosseum. The Colosseum was built in ancient Rome in the year A. D. 72, and could seat 50,000 people. It was the scene of gruesome "games" involving slaves, prisoners, or animals fighting gladiators (professionally trained swordsmen) to the death.

progressiveness
(prə-grĕs′ĭv-nĭs) *n.* the state of advancing toward better conditions or new policies, ideas, or methods

In the very olden time, there lived a semi-barbaric king, whose ideas, though somewhat polished and sharpened by the **progressiveness** of distant Latin neighbors, were still large, florid,[1] and untrammeled,[2] as became the half of him which was barbaric.[3] He was a man of exuberant fancy, and, withal, of an authority so irresistible that, at his will, he turned his varied fancies into facts. He was greatly given to self-communing;[4] and, when he and himself agreed upon anything, the thing was done. When

---

1. **florid** (flôr′ĭd): very ornate; flowery.
2. **untrammeled** (ŭn-trăm′əld): not limited or restricted.
3. **barbaric** (bär-bär′ĭk): marked by crudeness or lack of restraint in taste, style, or manner.
4. **self-communing:** the act of "talking" things over with oneself only.

10 every member of his domestic and political systems moved smoothly in its appointed course, his nature was bland and genial; but whenever there was a little hitch, and some of his orbs got out of their orbits, he was blander and more genial still, for nothing pleased him so much as to make the crooked straight, and crush down uneven places. **Ⓐ**

Among the borrowed notions by which his barbarism had become semifixed was that of the public arena, in which, by exhibitions of manly and beastly valor, the minds of his subjects were refined and cultured.

20 But even here the exuberant and barbaric fancy <u>asserted</u> itself. The arena of the king was built, not to give the people an opportunity of hearing the rhapsodies of dying gladiators, nor to enable them to view the inevitable conclusion of a conflict between religious opinions and hungry jaws, but for purposes far better adapted to widen and develop the mental energies of the people. This vast amphitheater, with its encircling galleries, its mysterious vaults, and its unseen passages, was an agent of poetic justice, in which crime was punished, or virtue rewarded,

30 by the decrees of an impartial and incorruptible chance.

When a subject was accused of a crime of sufficient importance to interest the king, public notice was given that on an appointed day the fate of the accused person would be decided in the king's arena—a structure which well deserved its name; for, although its form and plan were borrowed from afar, its purpose emanated solely from the brain of this man, who, every barleycorn a king,[5] knew no tradition to which he owed more allegiance than pleased his fancy, and who ingrafted on every adopted form of human thought and

40 action the rich growth of his barbaric idealism. **Ⓑ**

When all the people had assembled in the galleries and the king, surrounded by his court, sat high up on his throne

---

5. **every barleycorn a king:** a playful exaggeration of the expression "every ounce a king," meaning "thoroughly kingly." (Grains of barley were formerly used as units of measurement.)

Ⓐ TONE
Based on the words he uses to describe the king, how do you think the narrator feels about this character? Underline words and phrases in lines 1–15 that support your ideas.

_____

_____

_____

_____

_____

_____

_____

assert (ə-sûrt′) *v.* to act forcefully; to take charge

Ⓑ PARAPHRASE
Reread lines 31–40. Paraphrase this passage. Was the amphitheater used in the same way in this kingdom as it was elsewhere?

Line Numbers

31–40

Paraphrase

_____

_____

_____

_____

of royal state on one side of the arena, he gave a signal, a door beneath him opened, and the accused subject stepped out into the amphitheater. Directly opposite him, on the other side of the enclosed space, were two doors, exactly alike and side by side. It was the duty and the privilege of the person on trial to walk directly to these doors and open one of them. He could open either door he pleased; 50 he was subject to no guidance or influence but that of the aforementioned **impartial** and incorruptible chance. If he opened the one, there came out of it a hungry tiger, the fiercest and most cruel that could be procured, which immediately sprang upon him and tore him to pieces, as a punishment for his guilt. The moment that the case of the criminal was thus decided, doleful iron bells were clanged, great wails went up from the hired mourners posted on the outer rim of the arena, and the vast audience, with bowed heads and downcast hearts, wended slowly their homeward 60 way, mourning greatly that one so young and fair, or so old and respected, should have merited so dire a fate.

But if the accused person opened the other door, there came forth from it a lady, the most suitable to his years and station that his majesty could select among his fair subjects; and to this lady he was immediately married, as a reward for his innocence. It mattered not that he might already possess a wife and family, or that his affections might be engaged upon an object of his own selection: the king allowed no such **subordinate** arrangements to interfere 70 with his great scheme of retribution and reward. The exercises, as in the other instance, took place immediately and in the arena. Another door opened beneath the king, and a priest, followed by a band of choristers and dancing maidens blowing joyous airs on golden horns and treading an epithalamic measure,[6] advanced to where the pair

impartial (ĭm-pär′shəl) *adj.* not partial or biased; unprejudiced

subordinate (sə-bôr′dn-ĭt) *adj.* secondary; belonging to a lower rank

---

6. **treading an epithalamic** (ĕp′ə-thə-lā′mĭk) **measure**: dancing to wedding music.

stood, side by side; and the wedding was promptly and cheerily solemnized.[7] Then the gay brass bells rang forth their merry peals, the people shouted glad hurrahs, and the innocent man, preceded by children strewing flowers on 80 his path, led his bride to his home. **PAUSE & REFLECT**

This was the king's semi-barbaric method of administering justice. Its perfect fairness is obvious. The criminal could not know out of which door would come the lady: he opened either he pleased, without having the slightest idea whether, in the next instant, he was to be devoured or married. On some occasions the tiger came out of one door and on some out of the other. The decisions of this tribunal[8] were not only fair, they were positively determinate: the accused person was instantly punished if 90 he found himself guilty; and, if innocent, he was rewarded on the spot, whether he liked it or not. There was no escape from the judgments of the king's arena. **C**

The institution was a very popular one. When the people gathered together on one of the great trial days, they never knew whether they were to witness a bloody slaughter or a hilarious wedding. This element of uncertainty lent an interest to the occasion which it could not otherwise have attained. Thus, the masses were entertained and pleased, and the thinking part of the community could bring no 100 charge of unfairness against this plan; for did not the accused person have the whole matter in his own hands?

This semi-barbaric king had a daughter as blooming as his most florid fancies, and with a soul as fervent[9] and imperious[10] as his own. As is usual in such cases, she

---

7. **solemnized** (sŏl′əm-nīzd′): celebrated or observed with dignity.
8. **tribunal** (trī-byōō′nəl): something that has the power to determine guilt or innocence.
9. **fervent** (fûr′vənt): having or showing great emotion or zeal.
10. **imperious** (ĭm-pîr′ē-əs): arrogantly domineering or overbearing.

PAUSE & REFLECT
Pause at line 80. The narrator has described the purpose of the king's arena and emphasizes that the accused person's fate will be decided by "impartial and incorruptible chance." Do you think this system of justice sounds fair? Why or why not?

C PARAPHRASE
Reread lines 81–92. How would you explain the king's "perfect" system of justice?

Line Numbers

81–92

Paraphrase

conventional (kən-vĕn'shə-nəl)
adj. conforming to established
practice or accepted standards;
traditional

Underline the characteristics of
conventional heroes that the
writer describes.

waver (wā'vər) *v.* to exhibit
indecision; to hesitate

D TONE
Reread lines 118–124. Stockton
describes citizens as being
"greatly interested" in the "novel
and startling" events that are
unfolding. In what way might
this description be **ironic,** stating
the opposite of what Stockton
believes?

_____

_____

_____

_____

_____

_____

_____

_____

_____

was the apple of his eye and was loved by him above all
humanity. Among his courtiers was a young man of that
fineness of blood and lowness of station common to the
<u>conventional</u> heroes of romance who love royal maidens.
This royal maiden was well satisfied with her lover, for he
110 was handsome and brave to a degree unsurpassed in all
this kingdom; and she loved him with an ardor that had
enough of barbarism in it to make it exceedingly warm
and strong. This love affair moved on happily for many
months, until one day the king happened to discover its
existence. He did not hesitate nor <u>waver</u> in regard to his
duty in the premises. The youth was immediately cast
into prison, and a day was appointed for his trial in the
king's arena. This, of course, was an especially important
occasion; and his majesty, as well as all the people, was
120 greatly interested in the workings and development of this
trial. Never before had such a case occurred; never before
had a subject dared to love the daughter of a king. In after-
years such things became commonplace enough, but then
they were, in no slight degree, novel and startling. **D**

The tiger-cages of the kingdom were searched for the
most savage and relentless beasts, from which the fiercest
monster might be selected for the arena; and the ranks
of maiden youth and beauty throughout the land were
carefully surveyed by competent judges, in order that the
130 young man might have a fitting bride in case fate did not
determine for him a different destiny. Of course, everybody
knew that the deed with which the accused was charged
had been done. He had loved the princess, and neither he,
she, nor any one else thought of denying the fact; but the
king would not think of allowing any fact of this kind to
interfere with the workings of the tribunal, in which he
took such great delight and satisfaction. No matter how
the affair turned out, the youth would be disposed of; and

the king would take an aesthetic[11] pleasure in watching the
140 course of events, which would determine whether or not
the young man had done wrong in allowing himself to love
the princess. **E**

The appointed day arrived. From far and near the people
gathered, and thronged the great galleries of the arena,
and crowds, unable to gain admittance, massed themselves
against its outside walls. The king and his court were
in their places, opposite the twin doors,—those fateful
portals, so terrible in their similarity.

All was ready. The signal was given. A door beneath the
150 royal party opened, and the lover of the princess walked
into the arena. Tall, beautiful, fair, his appearance was
greeted with a low hum of admiration and anxiety. Half
the audience had not known so grand a youth had lived
among them. No wonder the princess loved him! What a
terrible thing for him to be there!

As the youth advanced into the arena, he turned, as
the custom was, to bow to the king: but he did not think
at all of that royal personage; his eyes were fixed upon
the princess, who sat to the right of her father. Had it
160 not been for the moiety[12] of barbarism in her nature, it
is probable that lady would not have been there; but her
intense and fervid[13] soul would not allow her to be absent
on an occasion in which she was so terribly interested.
From the moment that the decree had gone forth, that her
lover should decide his fate in the king's arena, she had
thought of nothing, night or day, but this great event and
the various subjects connected with it. Possessed of more
power, influence, and force of character than any one who
had ever before been interested in such a case, she had done
170 what no other person had done—she had possessed herself
of the secret of the doors. She knew in which of the two

---

11. **aesthetic** (ĕs-thĕt′ĭk): concerning the artistic appreciation of beauty.
12. **moiety** (moi′ĭ-tē): a portion.
13. **fervid** (fûr′vĭd): passionate.

E PARAPHRASE
Paraphrase lines 131–142. What
is the young man's fate? Rewrite
this passage in your own words.

Line Numbers

131–142

Paraphrase

_____

_____

_____

_____

_____

_____

_____

_____

_____

_____

_____

_____

_____

_____

_____

_____

_____

_____

F TONE
Reread lines 156–179. What is Stockton's attitude toward the princess? Underline words and details in the passage that reveal this attitude.

_____

_____

_____

_____

aspire (ə-spīr′) *v.* to have a great ambition or an ultimate goal; to desire strongly

G TONE
Stockton frequently refers to barbarism in this story. What does this reveal about his attitude toward the characters?

_____

_____

_____

_____

_____

_____

_____

_____

_____

rooms, that lay behind those doors, stood the cage of the tiger, with its open front, and in which waited the lady. Through these thick doors, heavily curtained with skins on the inside, it was impossible that any noise or suggestion should come from within to the person who should approach to raise the latch of one of them; but gold, and the power of a woman's will, had brought the secret to the princess. **F**

180   And not only did she know in which room stood the lady ready to emerge, all blushing and radiant, should her door be opened, but she knew who the lady was. It was one of the fairest and loveliest of the damsels of the court who had been selected as the reward of the accused youth, should he be proved innocent of the crime of **aspiring** to one so far above him; and the princess hated her. Often had she seen, or imagined that she had seen, this fair creature throwing glances of admiration upon the person of her lover, and sometimes she thought these glances were

190 perceived and even returned. Now and then she had seen them talking together; it was but for a moment or two, but much can be said in a brief space; it may have been on most unimportant topics, but how could she know that? The girl was lovely, but she had dared to raise her eyes to the loved one of the princess; and, with all the intensity of the savage blood transmitted to her through long lines of wholly barbaric ancestors, she hated the woman who blushed and trembled behind that silent door. **G**

    When her lover turned and looked at her, and his eyes

200 met hers as she sat there paler and whiter than anyone in the vast ocean of anxious faces about her, he saw, by that power of quick perception which is given to those whose souls are one, that she knew behind which door crouched the tiger, and behind which stood the lady.

He had expected her to know it. He understood her nature, and his soul was assured that she would never rest until she had made plain to herself this thing, hidden to all other lookers-on, even to the king. The only hope for the youth in which there was any element of certainty was
210 based upon the success of the princess in discovering this mystery; and the moment he looked upon her, he saw she had succeeded, as in his soul he knew she would succeed.

Then it was that his quick and anxious glance asked the question: "Which?" It was as plain to her as if he shouted it from where he stood. There was not an instant to be lost. The question was asked in a flash; it must be answered in another.

Her right arm lay on the cushioned parapet[14] before her. She raised her hand and made a slight, quick movement
220 toward the right. No one but her lover saw her. Every eye but his was fixed on the man in the arena.

He turned, and with a firm and rapid step he walked across the empty space. Every heart stopped beating, every breath was held, every eye was fixed immovably upon that man. Without the slightest hesitation, he went to the door on the right and opened it.

Now, the point of the story is this: Did the tiger come out of that door, or did the lady?

The more we reflect upon this question, the harder it
230 is to answer. It involves a study of the human heart which leads us through **devious** mazes of passion, out of which it is difficult to find our way. Think of it, fair reader, not as if the decision of the question depended upon yourself, but upon that hot-blooded, semi-barbaric princess, her soul at a white heat beneath the combined fires of despair and jealousy. She had lost him, but who should have him? Ⓗ

devious (dē′vē-əs) *adj.* departing from the straight or direct course

Ⓗ **PARAPHRASE**
Use the chart below to paraphrase what Stockton is saying in lines 229–236. Your paraphrase should be about as long as the original text.

Line Numbers
229–236
Paraphrase

14. **parapet** (păr′ə-pĭt): a low railing at the edge of a balcony.

anguished (ăng′gwĭsht) *adj.*
tormented; distressed

PAUSE & REFLECT
Based on what you know of the princess, which door do you think she chooses? Use details from the story to support your response.

_____

_____

_____

_____

_____

_____

_____

_____

_____

_____

_____

_____

_____

_____

240 How often, in her waking hours and in her dreams, had she started in wild horror, and covered her face with her hands as she thought of her lover opening the door on the other side of which waited the cruel fangs of the tiger!

But how much oftener had she seen him at the other door! How in her grievous reveries[15] had she gnashed her teeth, and torn her hair, when she saw his start of rapturous[16] delight as he opened the door of the lady! How her soul had burned in agony when she had seen him rush to meet that woman, with her flushing cheek and sparkling eye of triumph; when she had seen him lead her forth, his whole frame kindled with the joy of recovered life; when 250 she had heard the glad shouts from the multitude, and the wild ringing of the happy bells; when she had seen the priest, with his joyous followers, advance to the couple, and make them man and wife before her very eyes; and when she had seen them walk away together upon their path of flowers, followed by the tremendous shouts of the hilarious multitude, in which her one despairing shriek was lost and drowned!

Would it not be better for him to die at once, and go to wait for her in the blessed regions of semi-barbaric futurity?

And yet, that awful tiger, those shrieks, that blood!

260 Her decision had been indicated in an instant, but it had been made after days and nights of **anguished** deliberation. She had known she would be asked, she had decided what she would answer, and, without the slightest hesitation, she had moved her hand to the right.

The question of her decision is one not to be lightly considered, and it is not for me to presume to set myself up as the one person able to answer it. And so I leave it with all of you: Which came out of the opened door—the lady, or the tiger? **PAUSE & REFLECT**

---

15. **reveries** (rĕv′ə-rēz): daydreams.
16. **rapturous** (răp′chər-əs): filled with great joy; ecstatic.

Text Analysis: Tone

Consider the way Frank R. Stockton describes the place, time, characters, events, and customs in the story's kingdom. Then describe his tone with one of these words: *sarcastic, sad, serious, playful, bitter, anxious, sentimental,* or *curious*. Write the word at the top of the chart. Support your choice with words and details about the characters, setting, and situation.

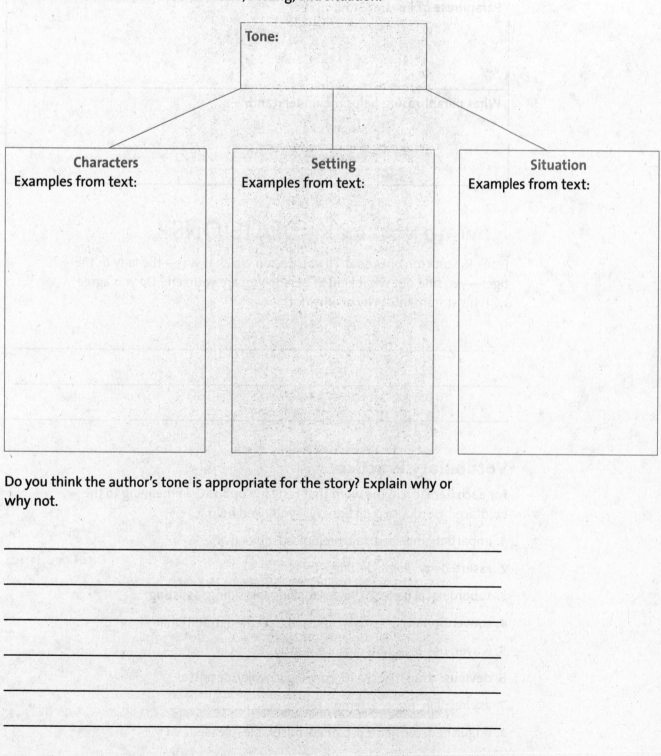

Tone:

Characters	Setting	Situation
Examples from text:	Examples from text:	Examples from text:

Do you think the author's tone is appropriate for the story? Explain why or why not.

_____

_____

_____

_____

_____

_____

Reading Strategy: Paraphrase

In the chart below, paraphrase the narrator's statements in lines 93–101. Then explain what paraphrasing these lines helps you understand about the trial.

Paraphrase of lines 93–101:
What paraphrasing helps me understand:

How do you make DECISIONS?

Frank R. Stockton once said. "If you decide which it was—the lady or the tiger—you find out what kind of person you are yourself." Do you agree with his statement? Why or why not?

_____

_____

_____

Vocabulary Practice

For each item, circle the word that is nearly opposite in meaning to the boldfaced word. Use a dictionary if you need help.

1. **impartial**: unbiased, fair, prejudiced, objective

2. **assert**: deny, claim, declare, stress

3. **subordinate**: beneath, lower-ranking, presiding, assisting

4. **conventional**: customary, unusual, accepted, traditional

5. **waver**: hesitate, falter, pause, continue

6. **devious**: straightforward, cunning, sneaky, deceitful

7. **aspire**: plan, hope, attempt, fail

8. **anguished**: tormented, pained, miserable, pleased

9. **progressiveness**: close-minded, acceptance, open, tolerance.

Academic Vocabulary in Writing

achieve	income	individual	strategy	trend

The young man standing before the door has a plan of action in mind. In a paragraph, explain whether you agree with his **strategy,** using at least one Academic Vocabulary word. Definitions of these words are on page 333.

_____

_____

_____

_____

Assessment Practice

DIRECTIONS Use "The Lady, or the Tiger?" to answer questions 1–6.

1 Which best describes the author's tone?
- (A) conversational and breezy
- (B) angry but playful
- (C) forceful and argumentative
- (D) formal but mocking

2 When the narrator says of the king, "at his will, he turned his varied fancies into facts," he means that the king —
- (A) was evil and cunning
- (B) made his own decisions and didn't bother with facts
- (C) made his decisions in a light-hearted way
- (D) often changed his mind

3 How do the citizens of the kingdom feel about the king's system of justice?
- (A) They are entertained by it and enjoy it.
- (B) They find it outrageous and unfair.
- (C) They dislike it but are forced to attend.
- (D) They appreciate its logic and seriousness.

4 What crime has the young man committed?
- (A) He has publicly humiliated the king.
- (B) He has fallen in love with the king's daughter.
- (C) He has refused to attend a trial.
- (D) He has lied about his background.

5 The narrator informs the reader that the princess —
- (A) does not really love the young man
- (B) intends to save her suitor
- (C) knows what is behind each door
- (D) disagrees with her father's system

6 How does the story end?
- (A) The young man faces a tiger.
- (B) The narrator explains the young man's choice.
- (C) The young man faces a lady.
- (D) The narrator asks the reader to decide what happens.

The Monty Hall Debate
Newspaper Article

Background

In "The Lady, or the Tiger?" choosing one of two doors was a life-or-death decision. The following article is about a similar (although far less serious) decision faced by contestants of "Let's Make a Deal," a television game show popular in the 1960s and 1970s.

Standards Focus: Use a Graphic Aid

The host of "Let's Make a Deal," Monty Hall, asked contestants to guess which of three doors hid a big prize. After a contestant picked a door, Hall would open one of the other two doors to show that the prize wasn't behind it. Then he'd offer a choice: Do you want to change your guess to the other door or stick with the door you originally picked?

The article you're about to read explains why one choice is better than the other. The explanation is somewhat complicated, but the diagram here can help you understand it. Like other **graphic aids,** this diagram provides a visual representation of ideas. You'll need to refer to the diagram as you read the article. Use the following tips to help you interpret it:

- Use the arrow symbols to help you follow the diagram.

- Note labels and relate them to what you read in the article.

- Look for patterns in the use of shading. For example, does one type of information always get shaded a certain way?

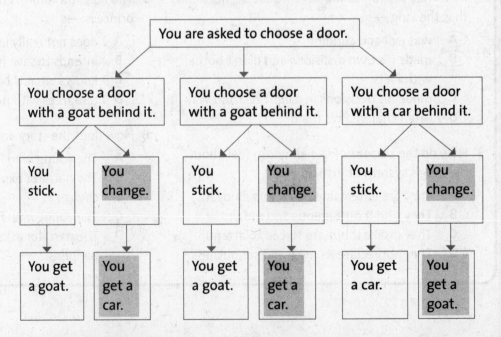

The Monty Hall Debate

By John Tierney

Reprinted from *The New York Times*

Marilyn vos Savant, a magazine columnist who is listed in the *Guinness Book of World Records* for highest IQ, was once asked this question:

Suppose you're on a game show, and you're given the choice of three doors: Behind one door is a car; behind the others, goats. You pick a door, say No. 1, and the host, who knows what's behind the other doors, opens another door, say No. 3, which has a goat. He then says to you, "Do you want to stick with your original
10 choice or pick door No. 2?" Is it to your advantage to take the switch? Ⓐ

SET A PURPOSE FOR READING

Read "The Monty Hall Debate" to find out how choices on a game show set off a controversy.

Ⓕ**OCUS ON FORM**

"The Monty Hall Debate" is an excerpt from a longer **newspaper article,** which means that not all of the original article is included.

Ⓐ **GRAPHIC AID**

Note that the description in lines 1–11 is represented in the diagram on page 348. The first row shows the choice you are given. The second row shows each of your possible choices. Tell what the third and fourth rows show.
The third row shows

_____

_____

_____

The fourth row shows

_____

_____

_____

Ms. vos Savant's answer was that you should always change and pick the other door, because the chances are two in three that there will be a car behind that door. Since she gave her answer, Ms. vos Savant estimates she has received 10,000 letters, the great majority disagreeing with her. . . . Of the critical letters she received, close to 1,000 carried signatures with Ph.D.'s, and many were on
20 letterheads of mathematics and science departments. . . .

PAUSE & REFLECT

PAUSE & REFLECT
Are you surprised that most people who wrote to Ms. vos Savant disagreed with her? Explain.

Robert Sachs, a professor of mathematics at George Mason University in Fairfax, Va., expressed the prevailing view that there was no reason to switch doors.

"You blew it!" he wrote. "Let me explain: If one door is shown to be a loser, that information changes the probability of either remaining choice—*neither of which has any reason to be more likely*—to ½. As a professional mathematician, I'm very concerned with the general public's lack of mathematical skills. Please
30 help by confessing your error and, in the future, being more careful." . . .

Monty Hall, the game show host who actually gave contestants this choice on "Let's Make a Deal," said he was not surprised at the experts' insistence that the probability was one out of two. "That's the same assumption contestants would make on the show after I showed them there was nothing behind one door," he said. "They'd think the odds on their door had now gone up to one in two, so they hated to give up the door
40 no matter how much money I offered.[1] By opening one

1. **how much money I offered:** Monty Hall would sometimes increase the drama of the show by offering contestants money to change their minds about whether to switch doors.

of the other doors we were applying pressure." . . .

Mr. Hall said he realized the contestants were wrong, because the odds on Door 1 were still only one in three even after he opened another door. Since the only other place the car could be was behind Door 2, the odds on that door must now be two in three. **B**

Sitting at his dining room table, Mr. Hall quickly conducted ten rounds of the game as this contestant tried the non-switching strategy. The result was four
50 cars and six goats. Then for the next ten rounds the contestant tried switching doors, and there was a dramatic improvement: eight cars and two goats. A pattern was emerging.

"So her answer's right: you should switch," Mr. Hall said, reaching the same conclusion as the tens of thousands of students who conducted similar experiments at Ms. vos Savant's suggestion. That conclusion was also reached eventually by many of her critics in academia, although most did not bother to
60 write letters of retraction. Dr. Sachs, whose letter was published in her column, was one of the few with the grace to concede his mistake.

"I wrote her another letter," Dr. Sachs said, "telling her that after removing my foot from my mouth I'm now eating humble pie.² I vowed as penance to answer all the people who wrote to castigate³ me. It's been an intense professional embarrassment." . . .

B GRAPHIC AID
Reread lines 42–46. Then review the diagram on page 348. What does the shading in the chart indicate?

_____

_____

_____

_____

_____

_____

_____

_____

_____

_____

_____

_____

_____

_____

_____

_____

_____

_____

2. **after removing my foot . . . eating humble pie:** after making a careless comment I'm now forced to make an embarrassing apology.

3. **castigate** (kăs'tĭ-gāt'): severely criticize.

Practicing Your Skills

Review the diagram that shows the choices involved in "The Monty Hall Debate." Circle the paths that show choices that result in winning a car.

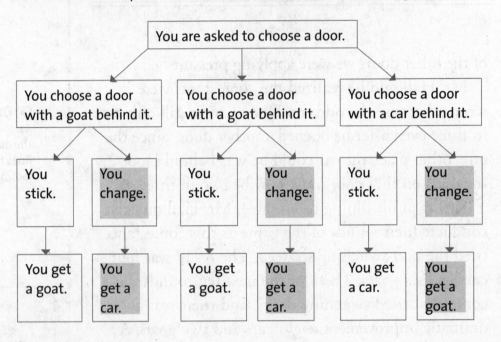

Use a Graphic Aid

How does the shading on the diagram help you understand that a contestant has a two-in-three chance of getting a car if he or she changes doors? Also explain how the shading reveals what the chance of getting the car is if the contestant sticks with his or her original choice.

_____

_____

_____

_____

_____

_____

_____

_____

Academic Vocabulary in Writing

achieve	income	individual	strategy	trend

Imagine that you were chosen to be a contestant on a game show. Based on what you've read, what are some **strategies** you could employ to **achieve** success? Include at least one Academic Vocabulary word in your response. Definitions of these words are on page 333.

_____

_____

_____

_____

Assessment Practice

DIRECTIONS Use "The Monty Hall Debate" to answer questions 1–4.

1 Which of the following puts Marilyn vos Savant in a unique category?

- **A** She has the highest IQ of any woman alive.
- **B** She is a math professor at George Mason University.
- **C** She is listed in the Guinness Book of World Records for having the highest IQ.
- **D** She is a magazine columnist.

2 The majority of people who responded to vos Savant's column —

- **A** were former contestants on "Let's Make a Deal"
- **B** agreed with her strategy
- **C** were professors of math and science
- **D** disagreed with her strategy

3 According to vos Savant, switching doors will —

- **A** increase your chances of winning
- **B** change the odds from 1 in 3 to 1 in 2
- **C** decrease your chances of winning
- **D** not change your odds of winning

4 The third row of the diagram on page 348 indicates —

- **A** the initial choice you are given
- **B** the two options you have after viewing the goat behind another door
- **C** each of your possible choices
- **D** the outcome of each possible choice

from Roughing It
Memoir by Mark Twain

Why do we EXAGGERATE?

"I have about a million hours of homework to do!" "This backpack weighs two hundred pounds!" We all exaggerate sometimes, even though we know it's not accurate. In the memoir you are about to read, Mark Twain uses exaggeration not only to make us laugh, but also to make us think.

DISCUSS How good are you at exaggerating? Choose a simple event—catching the bus, or yesterday's band practice. First describe the story in its most basic form. Then write some ideas for a version in which you exaggerate the events and descriptive details. Be creative as you stretch the truth! When you are done, share your story with a small group.

Text Analysis: Voice and Style

In literature, **voice** refers to a writer's unique use of language. The way an author chooses words, constructs sentences, and expresses ideas makes his or her personality come through on the page. Note the elements of the author's voice and style in the passage below.

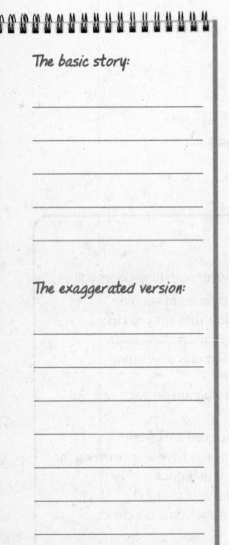

The basic story:

_____

_____

_____

_____

The exaggerated version:

_____

_____

_____

_____

_____

_____

_____

The other day at the drugstore, I remembered that I needed toothpaste. In the dental hygiene aisle, I was faced with hundreds of choices: toothpaste in a menu of screaming flavors; toothpaste to bleach your teeth to a blinding whiteness, to ensure enduring popularity, to improve not only your smile but your IQ. . . . The next thing I knew, a clerk was standing over me, peering closely. "You all right, sir?" she asked. "Just need something to clean my teeth. . . ." I muttered.	Note how the author uses: • complex sentences containing amusing descriptions • hyperbole, or exaggeration • understatement, or downplaying something's importance

As you read "Roughing It," look for ways Mark Twain achieves his humorous voice through these distinctive elements of style.

Reading Strategy: Monitor

To help you understand Twain's long sentences and old-fashioned vocabulary, **monitor** yourself, pausing to check your understanding. Use strategies such as these:

- **Adjust your reading rate.** Slow down at complicated passages.

- **Use context clues** or a dictionary for unfamiliar words.

- **Note descriptive details** to help you picture story elements.

- **Reread difficult passages** to clarify information.

As you read, notes in the side column will ask you to record strategies that help you clarify difficult passages.

Vocabulary in Context

Note: Words are listed in the order in which they appear in the story.

livelihood (lĭv′lē-hŏŏd′) *n.* a means of support; a way of making a living
*I want a **livelihood** that will allow for time off in summer.*

tolerable (tŏl′ər-ə-bəl) *adj.* fairly good; passable
*Jan makes a **tolerable** salary in her part-time job.*

yield (yēld) *v.* to give in to another
*The flashing light means you have to **yield** to pedestrians.*

contrive (kən-trĭv′) *v.* to invent or fabricate, especially by improvisation
*Nick **contrived** a crazy story to explain why he was late.*

array (ə-rā′) *n.* a large number of items
*That closet is stocked with an **array** of computer supplies.*

conspicuous (kən-spĭk′yōō-əs) *adj.* easy to notice; obvious
*Juan's ringing cell phone made him **conspicuous** at the meeting.*

sensational (sĕn-sā′shə-nəl) *adj.* intended to arouse strong curiosity or interest, especially through exaggerated details
*Are **sensational** stories the way to get the public's attention?*

rigid (rĭj′ĭd) *adj.* inflexible; strict
*Karl's company has **rigid** policies about arriving late to work.*

legitimate (lə-jĭt′ə-mĭt) *adj.* genuine; authentic
*Judy did not have a **legitimate** reason to miss work yesterday.*

SET A PURPOSE
FOR READING

Read this excerpt from "Roughing It" to discover how Mark Twain came to choose a profession.

ROUGHING IT

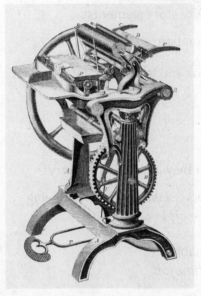

Memoir by
MARK TWAIN

BACKGROUND Mark Twain got his first job as a reporter in the mid-1800s. At this time, newspapers were increasing in popularity. Advances in technology made newspapers readily available and reduced the price of a single copy. Twain made a name for himself traveling around the world and writing newspaper accounts about his adventures.

Ⓐ MONITOR
Twain's statement in lines 2–8 is complex. Underline the text within the parentheses in these lines. Use your own words to complete a sentence that summarizes what Twain means.

Twain needed to support himself because _____

_____

_____

_____

_____

_____

livelihood (lĭv'lē-hŏod') *n.* a means of support; a way of making a living

What to do next?

It was a momentous question. I had gone out into the world to shift for myself,[1] at the age of thirteen (for my father had indorsed[2] for friends, and although he left us a sumptuous legacy of pride in his fine Virginian stock and its national distinction, I presently found that I could not live on that alone without occasional bread to wash it down with). I had gained a <u>livelihood</u> in various vocations, but Ⓐ had not dazzled anybody with my successes; still the list

10 was before me, and the amplest liberty in the matter of choosing, provided I wanted to work—which I did not, after being so wealthy. I had once been a grocery clerk, for one day, but had consumed so much sugar in that time that

---

1. **shift for myself:** take care of myself.
2. **indorsed** (ĭn-dôrsd'): endorsed; signed financial documents; perhaps this means that Twain's father backed up friends' unwise financial schemes, and lost all of his own money as a result.

I was relieved from further duty by the proprietor;[3] said he wanted me outside, so that he could have my custom. I had studied law an entire week, and then given it up because it was so prosy and tiresome. I had engaged briefly in the study of blacksmithing, but wasted so much time trying to fix the bellows so that it would blow itself, that the master turned me adrift in disgrace, and told me I would come to no good. I had been a bookseller's clerk for a while, but the customers bothered me so much I could not read with any comfort, and so the proprietor gave me a furlough and forgot to put a limit to it. I had clerked in a drug store part of a summer, but my prescriptions were unlucky, and we appeared to sell more stomach-pumps than soda-water. **B** So I had to go. I had made of myself a **tolerable** printer, under the impression that I would be another Franklin some day, but somehow had missed the connection thus far. There was no berth[4] open in the Esmeralda *Union*, and besides I had always been such a slow compositor[5] that I looked with envy upon the achievements of apprentices of two years' standing; and when I took a "take," foremen were in the habit of suggesting that it would be wanted "some time during the year." I was a good average St. Louis and New Orleans pilot and by no means ashamed of my abilities in that line; wages were two hundred and fifty dollars a month and no board[6] to pay, and I did long to stand behind a wheel again and never roam any more—but I had been making such a fool of myself lately in grandiloquent letters home about my blind lead and my European excursion that I did what many and many a poor disappointed miner had done before; said, "It is all over with me now, and I will never go back home to be pitied— and snubbed." I had been a private secretary, a silver-miner

B VOICE AND STYLE
Recall that **understatement** means downplaying something's importance. Underline an example of understatement Twain uses in lines 24–26. What is Twain downplaying in a humorous way?

_____

_____

_____

_____

_____

_____

_____

tolerable (tŏl′ər-ə-bəl) *adj.* fairly good; passable

---

3. **proprietor** (prə-prī′ĭ-tər): one who owns and manages a business.
4. **berth:** job.
5. **compositor** (kəm-pŏz′ĭ-tər): a worker who sets type for a printing business.
6. **board:** meals.

yield (yēld) *v.* to give in to another

contrive (kən-trīv′) *v.* to invent or fabricate, especially by improvisation

C MONITOR
Pause at line 76. How did Twain get a job offer from the *Enterprise*? Use the monitoring tips on page 355 if you have trouble answering the question.

_____

_____

_____

_____

_____

_____

_____

_____

_____

_____

and a silver-mill operative, and amounted to less than nothing in each, and now—

What to do next?

I <u>yielded</u> to Higbie's appeals and consented to try the
50 mining once more. We climbed far up on the mountainside and went to work on a little rubbishy claim of ours that had a shaft on it eight feet deep. Higbie descended into it and worked bravely with his pick till he had loosened up a deal of rock and dirt, and then I went down with a long-handled shovel (the most awkward invention yet <u>contrived</u> by man) to throw it out. You must brace the shovel forward with the side of your knee till it is full, and then, with a skillful toss, throw it backward over your left shoulder. I made the toss, and landed the mess just
60 on the edge of the shaft and it all came back on my head and down the back of my neck. I never said a word, but climbed out and walked home. I inwardly resolved that I would starve before I would make a target of myself and shoot rubbish at it with a long-handled shovel. I sat down, in the cabin, and gave myself up to solid misery—so to speak. Now in pleasanter days I had amused myself with writing letters to the chief paper of the territory, the Virginia *Daily Territorial Enterprise*, and had always been surprised when they appeared in print. My good opinion of
70 the editors had steadily declined; for it seemed to me that they might have found something better to fill up with than my literature. I had found a letter in the post-office as I came home from the hillside, and finally I opened it. Eureka! [I never did know what Eureka meant, but it seems to be as proper a word to heave in as any when no other that sounds pretty offers.] It was a deliberate offer to me of **C**

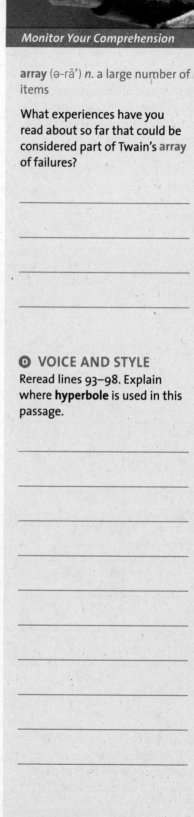

Twenty-five Dollars a week to come up to Virginia and be city editor of the *Enterprise*.

I would have challenged the publisher in the "blind
80 lead" days—I wanted to fall down and worship him,
now. Twenty-five Dollars a week—it looked like bloated luxury—a fortune, a sinful and lavish waste of money. But my transports[7] cooled when I thought of my inexperience and consequent unfitness for the position—and straightway, on top of this, my long **array** of failures rose up before me. Yet if I refused this place I must presently become dependent upon somebody for my bread, a thing necessarily distasteful to a man who had never experienced such a humiliation since he was
90 thirteen years old. Not much to be proud of, since it is so common—but then it was all I had to be proud of. So I was scared into being a city editor. I would have declined, otherwise. Necessity is the mother of "taking chances." I do not doubt that if, at that time, I had been offered a salary to translate the Talmud[8] from the original Hebrew, I would have accepted—albeit with diffidence and some misgivings— and thrown as much variety into it as I could for the money.

I went up to Virginia and entered upon my new
100 vocation. I was a rusty-looking city editor, I am free to confess—coatless, slouch hat, blue woolen shirt, pantaloons stuffed into boot-tops, whiskered half down to the waist, and the universal navy revolver slung to my belt. But I secured a more conservative costume and discarded the revolver. I had never had occasion to kill anybody, nor ever felt a desire to do so, but had worn the thing in deference to popular sentiment, and in order that I might not, by its absence, be offensively **conspicuous**, and a subject of remark. But the other editors, and all the printers,

---

7. **transports:** joyful excitement.
8. **Talmud** (täl'mood): a collection of ancient writings by rabbis; this is the basis of Orthodox Jewish law.

array (ə-rā') *n.* a large number of items

What experiences have you read about so far that could be considered part of Twain's **array** of failures?

_____

_____

_____

_____

D VOICE AND STYLE
Reread lines 93–98. Explain where **hyperbole** is used in this passage.

_____

_____

_____

_____

_____

_____

_____

_____

_____

conspicuous (kən-spĭk'yōo-əs) *adj.* easy to notice; obvious

E MONITOR
Which part of lines 99–116
do you find confusing? Use a
strategy from page 355 to clarify
your understanding.

_____

_____

_____

_____

_____

_____

_____

_____

_____

_____

_____

_____

sensational (sĕn-sā'shə-nəl)
adj. intended to arouse strong
curiosity or interest, especially
through exaggerated details

110 carried revolvers. I asked the chief editor and proprietor
(Mr. Goodman, I will call him, since it describes him as
well as any name could do) for some instructions with
regard to my duties, and he told me to go all over town and
ask all sorts of people all sorts of questions, make notes of
the information gained, and write them out for publication.
And he added: **E**

"Never say 'We learn' so-and-so, or 'It is reported,' or
'It is rumored,' or 'We understand' so-and-so, but go to
headquarters and get the absolute facts, and then speak
120 out and say 'It is so-and-so.' Otherwise, people will not
put confidence in your news. Unassailable[9] certainty is the
thing that gives a newspaper the firmest and most valuable
reputation."

It was the whole thing in a nutshell; and to this day,
when I find a reporter commencing his article with "We
understand," I gather a suspicion that he has not taken as
much pains to inform himself as he ought to have done.
I moralize well, but I did not always practise well when
I was a city editor; I let fancy get the upper hand of fact
130 too often when there was a dearth[10] of news. I can never
forget my first day's experience as a reporter. I wandered
about town questioning everybody, boring everybody,
and finding out that nobody knew anything. At the end
of five hours my note-book was still barren. I spoke to
Mr. Goodman. He said:

"Dan used to make a good thing out of the hay-wagons
in a dry time when there were no fires or inquests. Are
there no hay-wagons in from the Truckee? If there are, you
might speak of the renewed activity and all that sort of
140 thing, in the hay business, you know. It isn't **sensational** or
exciting, but it fills up and looks business-like."

---

9. **unassailable** (ŭn'ə-sā'lə-bəl): impossible to dispute or disprove; undeniable.
10. **dearth** (dûrth): a scarce supply; a lack.

I canvassed the city again and found one wretched old hay-truck dragging in from the country. But I made affluent use of it. I multiplied it by sixteen, brought it into town from sixteen different directions, made sixteen separate items of it, and got up such another sweat about hay as Virginia City had never seen in the world before. **ⓕ**

This was encouraging. Two nonpareil[11] columns had to be filled, and I was getting along. Presently, when things
150 began to look dismal again, a desperado killed a man in a saloon and joy returned once more. I never was so glad over any mere trifle before in my life. I said to the murderer:

"Sir, you are a stranger to me, but you have done me a kindness this day which I can never forget. If whole years of gratitude can be to you any slight compensation, they shall be yours. I was in trouble and you have relieved me nobly and at a time when all seemed dark and drear. Count me your friend from this time forth, for I am not a man to forget a favor." **ⓖ**

160 If I did not really say that to him I at least felt a sort of itching desire to do it. I wrote up the murder with a hungry attention to details, and when it was finished experienced but one regret—namely, that they had not hanged my benefactor on the spot, so that I could work him up too.

Next I discovered some emigrant-wagons[12] going into camp on the plaza and found that they had lately come through the hostile Indian country and had fared rather roughly. I made the best of the item that the circumstances permitted, and felt that if I were not confined within **rigid**
170 limits by the presence of the reporters of the other papers I could add particulars that would make the article much more interesting. However, I found one wagon that was going on to California, and made some judicious inquiries of the proprietor. When I learned, through his short

---

11. **nonpareil** (nŏn′pə-rě′): unequalled; peerless.
12. **emigrant-wagons** (ĕm′ĭ-grənt): wagons in which pioneers rode on their way to settle in the West.

ⓕ MONITOR
Note Twain's use of the word *affluent* in line 144. What context clues help you understand the meaning of this word? Refer to a dictionary to confirm its meaning.

ⓖ VOICE AND STYLE
Reread lines 153–159. Do you think Twain really responded to the murder in this way? Explain your answer.

rigid (rĭj′ĭd) *adj.* inflexible; strict

and surly answers to my cross-questioning, that he was certainly going on and would not be in the city next day to make trouble, I got ahead of the other papers, for I took down his list of names and added his party to the killed and wounded. Having more scope here, I put this wagon through an Indian fight that to this day has no parallel in history.

My two columns were filled. When I read them over in the morning I felt that I had found my **legitimate** occupation at last. I reasoned within myself that news, and stirring news, too, was what a paper needed, and I felt that I was peculiarly endowed[13] with the ability to furnish it. Mr. Goodman said that I was as good a reporter as Dan. I desired no higher commendation. With encouragement like that, I felt that I could take my pen and murder all the immigrants on the plains if need be, and the interests of the paper demanded it. **PAUSE & REFLECT**

legitimate (lə-jĭt′ə-mĭt) *adj.* genuine; authentic

PAUSE & REFLECT

Having read this selection, what inferences can you make about how Twain approached his life and times?

_____

_____

_____

_____

_____

_____

_____

_____

_____

_____

_____

_____

13. **peculiarly endowed** (pĭ-kyool′yər-lē ĕn-doud′): specifically supplied with a talent or quality.

Text Analysis: Voice and Style

The use of exaggeration is a key element of Mark Twain's style in "Roughing It." Although an exaggeration may be misleading, it often contains a grain of truth, as you can see in the example provided below. Identify two more examples of exaggeration Twain uses in the selection and tell what you can infer from each one.

> **Exaggeration:** "I inwardly resolved that I would starve before I would make a target of myself" (lines 62–63)

↓

> **Inference:** The author is desperate to find a line of work that suits him.

> **Exaggeration:**

↓

> **Inference:**

> **Exaggeration:**

↓

> **Inference:**

Identify another element of style that Twain uses. How does it help his voice come through on the page?

_____

_____

_____

Reading Strategy: Monitor

Review the strategies listed in the chart below. Write *yes* or *no* to show which strategies you used while reading "Roughing It."

Strategy	Did you use it? (yes/no)
Adjust your reading rate	
Use context clues	
Note descriptive details	
Reread difficult passages	

Explain which strategy you found most helpful, and why.

_____

_____

Why do we EXAGGERATE?

Review your retelling of a simple event from page 354. What might you change to make it more amusing after reading the selection?

_____

_____

Vocabulary Practice

Synonyms have a similar meaning; **antonyms** are words that have nearly opposite meanings. Write *synonyms* or *antonyms* next to each word pair.

1. rigid/permission _____

2. tolerable/acceptable _____

3. conspicuous/noticeable _____

4. livelihood/occupation _____

5. legitimate/wrong _____

6. yield/resist _____

7. array/variety _____

8. sensational/understated _____

9. contrive/invent _____

Academic Vocabulary in Writing

achieve	income	individual	strategy	trend

Think about Twain's explanations for his dismissals from various jobs. In a paragraph, explain why you think he fails to **achieve** success in most of them. Include at least one Academic Vocabulary word in your paragraph. Definitions of these words are on page 333.

_____

_____

_____

_____

Assessment Practice

DIRECTIONS Use "Roughing It" to answer questions 1–4.

1 The excerpt from "Roughing It" is primarily about —
  - (A) Twain's search for a suitable livelihood
  - (B) what Twain learned from being a newspaper reporter
  - (C) Twain's travels in his youth
  - (D) the difficulties Twain faced as a writer

2 Which of the following is an example of Twain's use of hyperbole?
  - (A) *I let fancy get the upper hand of fact too often. . . .*
  - (B) *I had never had occasion to kill anybody, nor ever felt a desire to do so. . . .*
  - (C) *I put this wagon through an Indian fight that to this day has no parallel in history.*
  - (D) *I had studied law an entire week. . . .*

3 Which of the following best describes the strategy Twain employed most often in his early days as a newspaper reporter?
  - (A) He never interviewed anyone in connection with any of the stories he was writing.
  - (B) He felt strongly that a reporter had a moral responsibility to report events as they occurred.
  - (C) He studied reports in other newspapers and wrote his articles based on the others he had read.
  - (D) He elaborated on details and stretched the truth about what actually happened.

4 Twain's style in "Roughing It" can best be described as —
  - (A) forceful and persuasive
  - (B) amusing and complicated
  - (C) experimental and informal
  - (D) authoritative and dry

O Captain! My Captain!
I Saw Old General at Bay

Poems by Walt Whitman

What is the COST of victory?

Triumph often comes with consequences. For example, the Union victory in the Civil War preserved the United States and ended slavery, but more than 700,000 lives were lost and countless others suffered. In the two poems you are about to read, Walt Whitman reflects on the great cost of victory in the Civil War.

QUICKWRITE Nearly every victory has a cost. For example, suppose you and your best friend argue over an issue that is important to both of you. You might win the argument but lose a friend in the process. Write a brief explanation about a time in your life when victory had a price. Was winning worth the cost?

Text Analysis: Style in Poetry

Walt Whitman is known for his uniquely American **style,** or way of using language to express ideas. The following elements are part of Whitman's style:

- strong **imagery,** or words and phrases that appeal to the reader's five senses

- **repetition** of a sound, word, phrase, or line for emphasis

- **irony,** or a contrast between what is expected and what actually happens

As you read Whitman's poems, use the chart to identify elements of the legendary poet's style.

	"O Captain! My Captain!"	"I Saw Old General at Bay"
Imagery		
Repetition		
Irony		

A Victory I Won:

_____

_____

_____

The Price of Victory:

_____

_____

_____

Reading Skill: Understand Historical Context

As with other works of literature, Whitman's poems are easier to understand once you know their **historical context,** the real events and people that influenced them. For example, in "O Captain! My Captain!" Whitman uses an extended metaphor that you can only understand if you are aware of the poem's historical context. An **extended metaphor** is a comparison that extends through several lines or stanzas of a poem. Read the Background information provided with "O Captain! My Captain!" Then, use the side notes within the selection and the chart below to identify the extended metaphor in "O Captain! My Captain!"

Element	What It Represents
captain	*President Lincoln*
fearful trip	
ship	
prize	
storm	
arrival at port	

SET A PURPOSE FOR READING

As you read this poem, think about the historical context in which Abraham Lincoln lived.

O Captain! My Captain!

Poem by
WALT WHITMAN

BACKGROUND On April 14, 1865, only five days after the end of the Civil War, President Abraham Lincoln was assassinated because of his anti-slavery beliefs. Walt Whitman was a great admirer of Lincoln's. He wrote "O Captain! My Captain!" to capture the sense of tragedy that overwhelmed the nation upon Lincoln's death.

Ⓐ HISTORICAL CONTEXT
Given what the **Background** tells you about why Whitman wrote this poem, who do you think is the captain, and what is his ship? Add this information to your chart on page 367.

Ⓑ STYLE IN POETRY
Reread lines 1–8. In what way does the description of the rejoicing crowds help emphasize the tragedy and **irony** of the captain's death?

O Captain! my Captain! our fearful trip is done,
The ship has weather'd every rack,[1] the prize we sought[2]
   is won, Ⓐ
The port is near, the bells I hear, the people all exulting,
While follow eyes the steady keel,[3] the vessel grim and
   daring:
5   But O heart! heart! heart!
         O the bleeding drops of red,
            Where on the deck my Captain lies,
             Fallen cold and dead. Ⓑ

---

1. **rack:** a mass of wind-driven clouds.
2. **sought** (sôt): searched for; tried to gain.
3. **keel:** the main part of a ship's structure.

O Captain! my Captain! rise up and hear the bells;

10 Rise up—for you the flag is flung[4]—for you the bugle
    trills,

For you bouquets and ribbon'd wreaths—for you the
    shores a-crowding,

For you they call, the swaying mass, their eager faces
    turning;

      Here Captain! dear father!

        This arm beneath your head!

15   It is some dream that on the deck,

            You've fallen cold and dead. **C**

My Captain does not answer, his lips are pale and still,

My father does not feel my arm, he has no pulse nor will,

The ship is anchor'd safe and sound, its voyage closed and
    done,

20 From fearful trip the victor ship comes in with object won;

      Exult O shores, and ring O bells!

        But I with mournful tread,[5]

          Walk the deck my Captain lies,

            Fallen cold and dead.

PAUSE & REFLECT

4. **flung:** suddenly put out.
5. **tread** (trĕd): footsteps.

Monitor Your Comprehension

C **STYLE IN POETRY**
Reread lines 9–16. Circle the **imagery** Whitman uses to convey the people's adoration of their leader. Add the imagery to your chart on page 366.

Note that Whitman repeats the words "fallen cold and dead" in the last line of each stanza. Reread lines 9–14. Underline two additional examples of **repetition** in these lines.

PAUSE & REFLECT
Why do you think Whitman refers to Lincoln as "father" (line 18)?

_____

_____

_____

_____

_____

_____

_____

_____

_____

SET A PURPOSE FOR READING

Read this poem to learn what "desperate emergency" the general faces.

I Saw Old General at Bay

Poem by
WALT WHITMAN

BACKGROUND When his brother George, a Union soldier, was injured in battle in 1862, Walt Whitman went to Virginia to care for him. Whitman was moved by the sight of the injured soldiers and decided to stay in Washington D.C., volunteering in army hospitals. The poem "I Saw Old General at Bay" was published in a collection called *Drum Taps*, which included many poems expressing Whitman's feelings about the war.

D STYLE IN POETRY
Reread line 2. Underline descriptive words and details that help you understand what the general looks like. Then add them to your chart on page 366.

PAUSE & REFLECT
Reread the last line. Which of Whitman's observances best helps you interpret its meaning?

_____

_____

_____

_____

_____

I saw old General at bay,
(Old as he was, his gray eyes yet shone out in battle like
    stars,) **D**
His small force was now completely hemm'd[1] in, in his
    works,
He call'd for volunteers to run the enemy's lines, a
    desperate emergency,
5 I saw a hundred and more step forth from the ranks, but
    two or three were selected,
I saw them receive their orders aside, they listen'd with
    care, the adjutant[2] was very grave,
I saw them depart with cheerfulness, freely risking their
    lives. **PAUSE & REFLECT**

---

1. **hemm'd:** hemmed; surrounded or enclosed.
2. **adjutant** (ăj'ə-tənt): a staff officer who helps a commanding officer with administrative affairs.

Text Analysis: Analyze Style in Poetry

Complete the charts to identify and describe the effects of imagery in selected lines from Whitman's two poems.

from "O Captain! My Captain!"
My father does not feel my arm, he has no pulse or will, (line 18)
Sense(s) imagery appeals to:
Effect on the reader:

But I with mournful tread,
   Walk the deck my Captain lies,
     Fallen cold and dead. (lines 22–24)

Sense(s) imagery appeals to:
Effect on the reader:

from "I Saw Old General at Bay"
He call'd for volunteers to run the enemy's lines, a desperate emergency, I saw a hundred and more step forth from the ranks, but two or three were selected (lines 4–6)
Sense(s) imagery appeals to:
Effect on the reader:

Which of these do you find most powerful? Why?

_____

_____

_____

Reading Skill: Understand Historical Context

How does knowing about Whitman's life and times help you understand the extended metaphor in "O Captain! My Captain!"? Complete the chart to tell how historical context helped you understand the poem.

Lines from Poem	How Historical Context Helped
1–8	
9–16	
17–24	

What is the COST of victory?

Look back at the explanation you wrote on page 366. Think about how you might write a poem about a victory. What are some examples of imagery you might include?

_____

_____

_____

Academic Vocabulary in Writing

achieve	income	individual	strategy	trend

Whitman strove to make his voice **individual** and, at the same time,
represent many voices. Do you think he **achieves** that goal in these poems?
Explain, using at least one Academic Vocabulary word in your response.
Definitions of these words are on page 333.

_____

_____

_____

_____

Assessment Practice

DIRECTIONS Use the two poems to answer questions 1–4.

1 In "O Captain! My Captain!" the line "Rise up—for
you the flag is flung" is an example of —

- (A) imagery
- (B) repetition
- (C) irony
- (D) extended metaphor

2 How does Whitman most likely feel about the
scene he describes in "I Saw Old General at Bay"?

- (A) He feels happy that the young soldiers will
  experience an exciting battle.
- (B) He admires the general and his soldiers for
  their bravery.
- (C) He believes the general is too old to be
  leading troops into battle.
- (D) He is angered by the destructiveness of war.

3 Whitman uses irony in "O Captain! My Captain!"
to point out that —

- (A) Lincoln's assassination was a heinous crime
- (B) the nation did not appreciate all that Lincoln
  had accomplished
- (C) slavery and the war were finished, but
  Lincoln lost his life and the nation its leader
- (D) our nation depends too much on its leaders

4 Reread the last line of "I Saw Old General at Bay."
What do the volunteers' attitudes say about the
general?

- (A) The general is too old to fight.
- (B) The volunteers are afraid of him.
- (C) The general is unaware of the danger he
  places them in.
- (D) The volunteers respect and trust him.

UNIT 7

Our Place in the World

HISTORY, CULTURE, AND THE AUTHOR

Be sure to read the Text Analysis Workshop on pp. 782–787 in *Holt McDougal Literature*.

Academic Vocabulary for Unit 7

Academic Vocabulary is the language you use to discuss literary and informational texts. Preview the following Academic Vocabulary words. You will use these words as you write and talk about the selections in this unit.

contribute (kən-trĭb′yo͞ot) *v.* to give something for a common purpose; to give to an organization

*Which elements of the setting **contribute** to the story's festive mood?*

culture (kŭl′chər) *n.* a society's way of life, including behavior, arts, beliefs, and all other products of work and thought

*What do you learn about this **culture's** view of nature from the tale?*

interpret (ĭn-tûr′prĭt) *v.* to explain the meaning of

*How do you **interpret** the character's actions? What does he want to happen?*

perceive (pər-sēv′) *v.* to become aware of something through one of the senses; to understand

*What connection do you **perceive** between the two stories?*

similar (sĭm′ə-lər) *adj.* the same, but not identical

*In what ways are the characters' reactions **similar**?*

Think of a book or a movie that reflects a specific **culture** through a character's behavior or beliefs. Explain what aspect of the culture the book or movie addresses, using at least two Academic Vocabulary words in your response.

_____

_____

_____

_____

The Snapping Turtle
Short Story by Joseph Bruchac

Where do we get our VALUES?

Do you remember when you learned that honesty is the best policy? Or that hard work pays off? Our values come from varied sources, including important people in our lives, communities around us, and mass media. The boy in "The Snapping Turtle" gets his values from his grandparents.

LIST IT Take a few minutes to list several values that are important to you. Circle one that especially influences how you live your life. Then, make a class list, and discuss how you learned these values.

Text Analysis: Cultural Context

Authors write within a **cultural context,** which includes the events, social problems, traditions, and values in the world around them. This cultural context is often reflected in the **themes,** or messages about life, that authors share with readers. The chart below shows some examples of themes that grow out of cultural contexts.

Cultural Context	Possible Theme
Events: wartime experiences	Extreme conditions bring out the best and the worst in people.
Social problem: racial discrimination	It takes courage to stand up for one's rights and the rights of others.
Tradition: family meals	Particular foods have special meaning if connected to memories.
Values: respect for nature	Humans and other living things are connected and need one another.

Use the Background information about author Joseph Bruchac on page 378 and the notes in the side margin to think about cultural context and possible themes of "The Snapping Turtle."

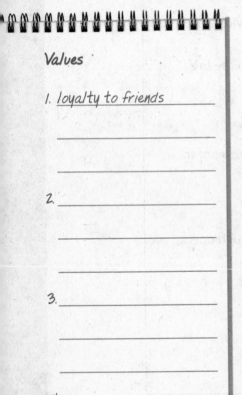

Values

1. *loyalty to friends*

2.

3.

4.

Reading Skill: Compare and Contrast

To **compare** two or more things, identify ways in which they are alike. To **contrast** them, find differences. As you read, notice how the narrator is like and unlike other boys.

Vocabulary in Context

Note: Words are listed in the order in which they appear in the story.

philosophy (fĭ-lŏs′ə-fē) *n.* a system of values or beliefs
*My **philosophy** about hiking is "Leave nothing but footprints."*

immortality (ĭm′ôr-tăl′ĭ-tē) *n.* the condition of having an endless life
*They created the memorial garden to give the hero **immortality.***

traipse (trāps) *v.* to walk or tramp around
*Every weekend nature-lovers like to **traipse** around this meadow.*

inclination (ĭn-klə-nā′shən) *n.* a tendency to prefer one thing over another
*On warm, sunny days, we have an **inclination** to go outdoors.*

craftiness (krăf′tē-nĕs) *n.* deviousness or deception
*It takes **craftiness** to outwit a raccoon.*

cache (kăsh) *v.* to store in a hiding place
*Campers need to **cache** their food so that animals don't find it.*

migration (mī-grā′shən) *n.* the act of changing location seasonally
(used here as an adjective)
*The geese flew north along their **migration** route.*

impregnable (ĭm-prĕg′ nə-bəl) *adj.* impossible to enter by force
*The thick undergrowth made the forest **impregnable.***

basking (băsk′ĭng) *adj.* warming oneself pleasantly, as in sunlight
*The **basking** snake was motionless as a statue on the rock.*

undaunted (ŭn-dôn′tĭd) *adj.* not discouraged; courageous
***Undaunted** by its failure to catch the rabbit, the fox trotted on.*

The SNAPPING TURTLE

Short Story by

JOSEPH BRUCHAC

BACKGROUND Joseph Bruchac was
descended from the Abenaki (ä′bə-nä′kē), a
Native American group that originally lived
in New England and southern Canada. The
Abenaki believe in honoring their elders,
treating the earth with respect by not
wasting its resources, and sharing food and
possessions with others.

Ⓐ CULTURAL CONTEXT
Underline the Abenaki beliefs
noted in the Background
paragraph. Then reread lines 1–11.
Which Abenaki values are
reflected in these lines?

_____

_____

_____

_____

_____

_____

My grandmother was working in the flower garden
near the road that morning when I came out with
my fishing pole. She was separating out the roots of iris.
As far as flowers go, she and I were agreed that iris had the
sweetest scent. Iris would grow about anywhere, shooting
up green sword shaped leaves like the mythical soldiers that
sprang from the planted teeth of a dragon. But iris needed
some amount of care. Their roots would multiply so thick
and fast that they could crowd themselves right up out
10 of the soil. Spring separating and replanting were, as my
grandmother put it, just the ticket.[1] Ⓐ

Later that day, I knew, she would climb into our
blue 1951 Plymouth to drive around the back roads of

---

1. **just the ticket:** the perfect solution.

Greenfield, a box of iris in the back seat. She would stop at farms where she had noticed a certain color of iris that she didn't have yet. Up to the door she would go to ask for a root so that she could add another splash of color to our garden. And, in exchange, she would give that person, most often a flowered-aproned and somewhat elderly woman like
20 herself, some of her own iris.

It wasn't just that she wanted more flowers herself. She had a **philosophy**. If only one person keeps a plant, something might happen to it. Early frost, insects, animals, Lord knows what. But if many have that kind of plant, then it may survive. Sharing meant a kind of **immortality**. I didn't quite understand it then, but I enjoyed taking those rides with her, carrying boxes and cans and flowerpots with new kinds of iris back to the car. **B**

"Going fishing, Sonny?" she said now.

30 Of course, she knew where I was going. Not only the evidence of the pole in my hand, but also the simple facts that it was a Saturday morning in late May and I was a boy of ten, would have led her to that natural conclusion. But she had to ask. It was part of our routine.

"Un hun," I answered, as I always did. "Unless you and Grampa need some help." Then I held my breath, for though my offer of aid had been sincere enough, I really wanted to go fishing.

Grama thrust her foot down on the spading² fork,
40 carefully levering out a heavy clump of iris marked last fall with a purple ribbon to indicate the color. She did such things with half my effort and twice the skill, despite the fact I was growing, as she put it, like a weed. "No, you go on along. This afternoon Grampa and I could use some help, though."

"I'll be back by then," I said, but I didn't turn and walk away. I waited for the next thing I knew she would say.

"You stay off of the state road, now."

---

2. **spading:** digging.

philosophy (fĭ-lŏs′ə-fē) *n.* a system of values or beliefs

immortality (ĭm′ôr-tăl′ĭ-tē) *n.* the condition of having an endless life

B CULTURAL CONTEXT
Reread lines 12–28. Underline the words that help you understand the grandmother's attitude or beliefs. Explain whether you think this belief reflects the cultural context in which the work was written.

_____

_____

_____

_____

_____

_____

_____

_____

In my grandmother's mind, Route 9N, which came
50 down the hill past my grandparents' little gas station
and general store on the corner, was nothing less than a
Road of Death. If I ever set foot on it, I would surely be
as doomed as our four cats and two dogs that met their
fates there.

"Runned over and kilt," as Grampa Jesse put it.

Grampa Jesse, who had been the hired man for my
grandmother's parents before he and Grama eloped, was
not a person with book learning like my college-educated
grandmother. His family was Abenaki Indian, poor
60 but honest hill people who could read the signs in the
forest, but who had never **traipsed** far along the trails of
schoolhouse ways. Between Grama's books and Grampa's
practical knowledge, some of which I was about to apply to
bring home a mess of[3] trout, I figured I was getting about
the best education a ten year old boy could have. I was
lucky that my grandparents were raising me. **C**

"I'll stay off the state road," I promised. "I'll just follow
Bell Brook."

Truth be told, the state road made me a little nervous,
70 too. It was all too easy to imagine myself in the place of
one of my defunct pets, stunned by the elephant bellow of
a tractor trailer's horn, looking wild eyed up to the shiny
metal grill; the thud, the lightning-bolt flash of light,
and then the eternal dark. I imagined my grandfather
shoveling the dirt over me in a backyard grave next to that
of Lady, the collie, and Kitty kitty, the gray cat, while my
grandmother dried her eyes with her apron and said, "I told
him to stay off that road!"

I was big on knowledge but very short on courage in
80 those years. I mostly played by myself because the other

traipse (trăps) *v.* to walk or tramp around

C COMPARE AND CONTRAST
Reread lines 56–66. Underline the words that point out a contrast between Grama and Grampa. Record their differences and a similarity in this chart.

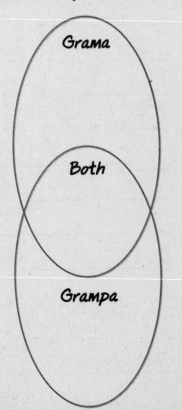

Grama

Both

Grampa

---

3. **a mess of:** an amount of (food).

kids my age from the houses and farms scattered around our rural township regarded me as a Grama's boy who would tell if they were to tie me up and threaten to burn my toes with matches, a ritual required to join the local society of pre teenage boys. A squealer. And they were right.

I didn't much miss the company of other kids. I had discovered that most of them had little interest in the living things around them. They were noisier than Grampa and 90 I were, scaring away the rabbits that we could creep right up on. Instead of watching the frogs catching flies with their long, gummy tongues, those boys wanted to shoot them with their BB guns. I couldn't imagine any of them having the patience or **inclination** to hold out a hand filled with sunflower seeds, as Grampa had showed me I could, long enough for a chickadee to come and light on an index finger. **D**

Even fishing was done differently when I did it Grampa's way. I knew for a fact that most of those boys would go 100 out and come home with an empty creel. They hadn't been watching for fish from the banks as I had in the weeks before the trout season began, so they didn't know where the fish lived. They didn't know how to keep low, float your line in, wait for that first tap, and then, after the strike that bent your pole, set the hook. And they never said thank you to every fish they caught, the way I remembered to do. **E**

Walking the creek edge, I set off downstream. By mid morning, my bait can of moss and red earthworms that 110 Grampa and I had dug from the edge of our manure pile was near empty. I'd gone half a mile and had already caught seven trout. All of them were squaretails, native

D COMPARE AND CONTRAST
Reread lines 79–97. The narrator contrasts himself with other boys. Underline the words that illustrate these differences.

VISUAL VOCABULARY
creel: a basket used to carry caught fish

E CULTURAL CONTEXT
Reread lines 87–107. What Abenaki customs and attitudes are reflected in this passage?

_____

_____

_____

_____

_____

_____

_____

_____

brook trout whose sides were patterned with a speckled rainbow of bright circles—red, green, gold. I'd only kept the ones more than seven inches long, and I'd remembered to wet my hand before taking the little ones off the hook. Grasping a trout with a dry hand would abrade the slick coat of natural oil from the skin and leave it open for infection and disease.

120　　As always, I'd had to keep the eyes in the back of my head open just as Grampa had told me to do whenever I was in the woods.

"Things is always hunting one another," he'd said.

And he was right. Twice, at places where Bell Brook swung near Mill Road I'd had to leave the stream banks to take shelter when I heard the ominous crunch of bicycle tires on the gravel. Back then, when I was ten, I was smaller than the other boys my age. I made up for it by being harder to catch. Equal parts of **craftiness** and plain old

130 panic at being collared by bullies I viewed as close kin to Attila the Hun[4] kept me slipperier than an eel.

From grapevine tangles up the bank, I'd watched as Pauly Roffmeier, Ricky Holstead, and Will Backus rolled up to the creek, making more noise than a herd of hippos, to plunk their own lines in. Both times, they caught nothing. It wasn't surprising, since they were talking like jaybirds, scaring away whatever fish might have been within half a mile. And Will kept lighting matches and throwing them down to watch them hiss out when they

140 struck the water. Not to mention the fact that I had pulled a ten inch brook trout out of the first hole and an eleven incher out of the second before they even reached the stream. **F**

craftiness (krăf′tē-nĕs) *n.* deviousness or deception

F COMPARE AND CONTRAST

Reread lines 132–143. How is the boys' approach to fishing different from that of the narrator?

_____

_____

_____

_____

_____

_____

_____

_____

_____

_____

_____

_____

_____

_____

4. **Attila the Hun:** a barbarian leader who successfully invaded the Roman Empire in the A.D. 400s.

I looked up at the sky. I didn't wear a watch then. No watch made by man seemed able to work more than a few days when strapped to my wrist. It was a common thing on my Grampa's side of the family. "We jest got too much 'lectricity in us," he explained.

150 Without a watch, I could measure time by the sun. I could see it was about ten. I had reached the place where Bell Brook crossed under the state road. Usually I went no further than this. It had been my boundary for years. But somewhere along the way I had decided that today would be different. I think perhaps a part of me was ashamed of hiding from the other boys, ashamed of always being afraid. I wanted to do something that I'd always been afraid to do. I wanted to be brave. **PAUSE & REFLECT**

I had no need to fish further. I had plenty of trout for our supper. I'd cleaned them all out with my Swiss Army
160 knife, leaving the entrails[5] where the crows and jays could get them. If you did that, the crows and jays would know you for a friend and not sound the alarm when they saw you walking in the woods. I sank the creel under water, wedged it beneath a stone. The water of the brook was deep and cold and I knew it would keep the flesh of the trout fresh and firm. Then I <u>cached</u> my pole and bait can under the spice bushes. As I looked up at the highway, Grama's words came back to me:

"Stay off the state road, Sonny."
170 "*Under*," I said aloud, "is not *on*."

Then, taking a deep breath, bent over at the waist, I waded into the culvert[6] that dove under the Road of Death. I had gone no more than half a dozen steps before I

---

5. **entrails** (ĕn'trālz'): the internal organs.
6. **culvert** (kŭl'vərt): a drain that passes under a road.

PAUSE & REFLECT
The narrator describes an internal conflict in lines 149–157. What opposing forces is the narrator struggling with? What choice will he probably make?

_____

_____

_____

_____

_____

_____

_____

_____

cache (kăsh) *v.* to store in a hiding place

G **CULTURAL CONTEXT**
Reread the description of the narrator's encounter with the spider in lines 171–195. The hourglass shape on the spider's body means that it is a Black Widow spider, with a bite that can cause excruciating abdominal pain in people. What does the narrator's interaction with the spider reveal about him and what he has learned from his grandparents?

walked into a spider web so strong that it actually bounced me back. I splashed a little water from the creek up onto it and watched the beads shape a pattern of concentric circles. The orb weaver sat unmoving in a corner, one leg resting on a strand of the web. She'd been waiting for the vibration of some flying creature caught in the sticky strands of her net. Clearly, I was much more than she had hoped for. She sat there without moving. Her wide back was patterned with a shape like that of a red and gold hourglass. Her compound eyes, jet black on her head, took in my giant shape. Spiders gave some people the willies.[7] I knew their bite would hurt like blue blazes, but I still thought them graced with great beauty.

"Excuse me," I said. "Didn't mean to bother you."

The spider raised one front leg. A nervous reaction, most likely, but I raised one hand back. Then I ducked carefully beneath the web, entering an area where the light was different. It was like passing from one world into another. I sloshed through the dark culvert, my fingertips brushing the rushing surface of the stream, the current pushing at my calves. My sneakered feet barely held their purchase[8] on the ridged metal, slick with moss. **G**

When I came out the other side, the sunlight was blinding. Just ahead of me the creek was overarched with willows. They were so thick and low that there was no way I could pass without either going underwater or breaking a way through the brush. I wasn't ready to do either. So I made my way up the bank, thinking to circle back and pick up the creek farther down. For what purpose, I wasn't sure, aside from just wanting to do it. I was nervous as a hen yard when a chicken hawk is circling overhead. But

7. **the willies:** a feeling of fear and/or disgust.
8. **held their purchase:** gripped; refrained from slipping.

I was excited, too. This was new ground to me, almost a mile from home. I'd gone farther from home in the familiar directions of north and west, into the safety of the woods, but this was different: Across the state road, in the direction of town; someone else's hunting territory. I stayed low to the ground and hugged the edges of the brush as I moved. Then I saw something that drew me away from the creek: The glint of a wider expanse of water. The Rez, the old Greenfield Reservoir. **PAUSE & REFLECT**

I'd never been to the Rez, though I knew the other boys went there. As I'd sat alone on the bus, my bookbag clasped tightly to my chest, I'd heard them talk about swimming there, fishing for bass, spearing bullfrogs five times as big as the little frogs in Bell Brook.

I knew I shouldn't be there, yet I was. Slowly I moved to the side of the wide trail that led to the edge of the deep water, and it was just as well that I did: Their bikes had been stashed in the brush down the other side of the path. They'd been more quiet than usual. I might have walked up on them if I hadn't heard a voice. . . .

I picked up some of the dark mud with my fingertips and drew lines across my cheeks. Grampa had explained it would make me harder to see. Then I slid to a place where an old tree leaned over the bank, cloaked by the cattails that grew from the edge of the Rez. I made my way out on the trunk and looked. . . .

"It's not gonna come up," Ricky said. He picked up something that looked like a makeshift spear. "You lied."

"I did not. It was over there. The biggest snapper I ever saw." Will shaded his eyes with one hand and looked right in my direction without seeing me. "If we catch it, we

PAUSE & REFLECT
Reread lines 196–213. Underline the sentence with the words *hunting territory*. Why does the narrator use that term?

_____

_____

_____

_____

_____

_____

_____

_____

_____

_____

_____

_____

_____

_____

_____

migration (mī-grā'shən) *n.*
the act of changing location
seasonally (used here as an
adjective)

impregnable (ĭm-prĕg'nə-bəl)
adj. impossible to enter by force

H CULTURAL CONTEXT
Reread lines 245–262. Describe
the spring tradition the narrator
shares with his grandparents.
What is the narrator learning,
and what does the author want
readers to learn?

_____

_____

_____

_____

_____

_____

_____

_____

_____

_____

_____

_____

could sell it for ten dollars to that man on Congress Street.
They say snapping turtles have seven different kinds of
meat in them."

"Hmph," Pauly said, throwing his own spear aside.
240 "Let's go find something else to do."

One by one, they picked up their fishing poles and went
back down the path. I waited without moving, hearing
their heavy feet on the trail and then the rattle of their bike
chains. . . . All I could think of was that snapping turtle.

I knew a lot about turtles. There were mud turtles and
map turtles. There was the smart orange legged wood
turtle and the red eared slider with its cheeks painted
crimson as if it was going to war. Every spring Grama and
Grampa and I would drive around, picking up those whose
250 old **migration** routes had been cut by the recent and lethal
ribbons of road. Spooked by a car, a turtle falls into that
old defense of pulling head and legs and tail into its once
impregnable fortress. But a shell does little good against
the wheels of a Nash or a DeSoto.[9]

Some days we'd rescue as many as a dozen turtles,
taking them home for a few days before releasing them
back into the wild. Painted turtles, several as big as two
hands held together, might nip at you some, but they
weren't really dangerous. And the wood turtles would learn
260 in a day or so to reach out for a strawberry or a piece of
juicy tomato and then leave their heads out for a scratch
while you stroked them with a finger. **H**

Snappers though, they were different. Long tailed, heavy
bodied and short tempered, their jaws would gape wide
and they'd hiss when you came up on them ashore. Their
heads and legs were too big to pull into their shells and

---

9. **Nash . . . DeSoto:** car brands that were popular during the 1950s.

they would heave up on their legs and lunge forward as they snapped at you. They might weigh as much as fifty pounds, and it was said they could take off a handful of fingers in one bite. There wasn't much to recommend a snapping turtle as a friend. **❶**

Most people seemed to hate snappers. Snappers ate the fish and the ducks; they scared swimmers away. Or I should say that people hated them alive. Dead, they were supposed to be the best eating turtle of all. *Ten dollars,* I thought. *Enough for me to send away to the mail-order pet place and get a pair of real flying squirrels.* I'd kept that clipping from *Field and Stream* magazine thumbtacked over my bed for four months now. A sort of plan was coming into my mind. **❶**

People were afraid of getting bit by snappers when they were swimming. But from what I'd read, and from what Grampa told me, they really didn't have much to worry about.

"Snapper won't bother you none in the water," Grampa said. If you were even to step on a snapping turtle resting on the bottom of a pond, all it would do would be to move away. On land, all the danger from a snapper was to the front or the side. From behind, a snapper couldn't get you. Get it by the tail, you were safe. That was the way.

And as I thought, I kept watch. And as I kept watch, I kept up a silent chant inside my mind.

Come here, I'm waiting for you.
Come here, I'm waiting for you.

Before long, a smallish log that had been sticking up farther out in the pond began to drift my way. It was, as

❶ CULTURAL CONTEXT

Reread lines 263–271. Do you think Bruchac has had experiences similar to those the narrator describes here? Explain your answer.

❶ COMPARE AND CONTRAST

Reread lines 272–280. What does the narrator have in common with Will, the boy who speaks in lines 233–238?

basking (băsk'ĭng) *adj.* warming oneself pleasantly, as in sunlight

PAUSE & REFLECT
Based on what you know about the values of the narrator's grandparents, what might they think about the narrator's decision to capture and sell a turtle?

_____

_____

_____

_____

_____

_____

_____

_____

_____

_____

_____

_____

_____

_____

I had expected, no log at all. It was a turtle's head. I stayed still. The sun's heat beat on my back, but I lay there like a **basking** lizard. Closer and closer the turtle came, heading 300 right into water less than waist deep. It was going right for shore, for the sandy bank bathed in sun. I didn't think about why then, just wondered at the way my wanting seemed to have called it to me.

When it was almost to shore, I slid into the water on the other side of the log I'd been waiting on. The turtle surely sensed me, for it started to swing around as I moved slowly toward it, swimming as much as walking. But I lunged and grabbed it by the tail. Its tail was rough and ridged, as easy to hold as if coated with sandpaper. I pulled hard and 310 the turtle came toward me. I stepped back, trying not to fall and pull it on top of me. My feet found the bank, and I leaned hard to drag the turtle out, its clawed feet digging into the dirt as it tried to get away. A roaring hiss like the rush of air from a punctured tire came out of its mouth, and I stumbled, almost losing my grasp. Then I took another step, heaved again, and it was mine.

Or at least it was until I let go. I knew I could not let go. I looked around, holding its tail, moving my feet to keep it from walking its front legs around to where it would snap 320 at me. It felt as if it weighed a thousand pounds. I could only lift up the back half of its body. I started dragging it toward the creek, fifty yards away. It seemed to take hours, a kind of dance between me and the great turtle, but I did it. I pulled it back through the roaring culvert, water gushing over its shell, under the spider web, and past my hidden pole and creel. I could come back later for the fish. Now there was only room in the world for Bell Brook, the turtle, and me. PAUSE & REFLECT

The long passage upstream is a blur in my memory. I
330 thought of salmon leaping over falls and learned a little that
day how hard such a journey must be. When I rounded
the last bend and reached the place where the brook edged
our property, I breathed a great sigh. But I could not rest.
There was still a field and the back yard to cross.

My grandparents saw me coming. From the height
of the sun it was now mid afternoon, and I knew I was
dreadful late.

"Sonny, where have you . . . ?" began Grama.

Then she saw the turtle.

340 "I'm sorry. It took so long because of . . ." I didn't finish
the sentence because the snapping turtle, **undaunted** by his
backward passage, took that opportunity to try once more
to swing around and get me. I had to make three quick
steps in a circle, heaving at its tail as I did so.

"Nice size turtle," Grampa Jesse said.

My grandmother looked at me. I realized then I must
have been a sight. Wet, muddy, face and hands scratched
from the brush that overhung the creek.

"I caught it at the reservoir," I said. I didn't think
350 to lie to them about where I'd been. I waited for my
grandmother to scold me. But she didn't.

"Jesse," she said, "Get the big washtub."

My grandfather did as she said. He brought it back and
then stepped next to me.

"Leave go," he said.

My hands had a life of their own, grimly determined
never to let loose of that all too familiar tail, but I forced
them to open. The turtle flopped down Before it could
move, my grandfather dropped the big washtub over it. All
360 was silent for a minute as I stood there, my arms aching as

undaunted (ûn-dôn′tĭd) *adj.* not
discouraged; courageous

How does the narrator know
that the snapper is **undaunted**
by its ordeal?

_____

_____

_____

_____

_____

K COMPARE AND CONTRAST

Reread lines 345–365. What similar qualities do Grama and Grampa display?

_____

_____

_____

_____

_____

_____

_____

_____

_____

_____

_____

_____

_____

_____

_____

_____

_____

_____

_____

_____

they hung by my side. Then the washtub began to move. My grandmother sat down on it and it stopped.

She looked at me. So did Grampa. It was wonderful how they could focus their attention on me in a way that made me feel they were ready to do whatever they could to help. **K**

"What now?" Grama said.

"I heard that somebody down on Congress Street would pay ten dollars for a snapping turtle."

"Jack's," Grampa said.

370 My grandmother nodded. "Well," she said, "if you go now you can be back in time for supper. I thought we were having trout." She raised an eyebrow at me.

"I left them this side of the culvert by 9N," I said. "Along with my pole."

"You clean up and put on dry clothes. Your grandfather will get the fish."

"But I hid them."

My grandmother smiled. "Your grandfather will find them." And he did.

380 An hour later, we were on the way to Congress Street. . . . In the 1950s, Congress Street was like a piece of Harlem[10] dropped into an upstate town. We pulled up in front of Jack's, and a man who looked to be my grandfather's age got up and walked over to us. His skin was only a little darker than my grandfather's, and the two nodded to each other.

My grandfather put his hand on the trunk of the Plymouth.

"What you got there?" Jack said.

390 "Show him, Sonny."

I opened the trunk. My snapping turtle lifted up its head as I did so.

---

10. **Harlem:** a New York City neighborhood that was and is largely African American.

"I heard you might want to buy a turtle like this for ten dollars," I said.

Jack shook his head. "Ten dollars for a little one like that? I'd give you two dollars."

I looked at my turtle. Had it shrunk since Grampa wrestled it into the trunk?

"That's not enough," I said.

400   "Three dollars. My last offer."

I looked at Grampa. He shrugged his shoulders.

"I guess I don't want to sell it," I said.

"All right," Jack said. "You change your mind, come on back." He touched his hat with two fingers and walked back over to his chair in the sun.

As we drove back toward home, neither of us said anything for a while. Then my grandfather spoke.

"Would five dollars've been enough?"

"No," I said.

410   "How about ten?"

I thought about that. "I guess not."

"Why you suppose that turtle was heading for that sandbank?" Grampa said.

I thought about that, too. Then I realized the truth of it.

"It was coming out to lay its eggs."

"Might be."

I thought hard then. I'd learned it was never right for a hunter to shoot a mother animal, because it hurt the next generation to come. Was a turtle any different? **L**

420   "Can we take her back?" I asked.

"Up to you, Sonny."

And so we did. Gramp drove the Plymouth right up the trail to the edge of the Rez. He held a stick so the turtle would grab onto it as I hauled her out of the trunk. I put

L CULTURAL CONTEXT
Reread lines 411–419. What lesson does the narrator learn? Tell how this lesson reflects Bruchac's values.

_____

_____

_____

_____

_____

_____

_____

_____

_____

_____

_____

_____

_____

_____

_____

_____

_____

_____

PAUSE & REFLECT

Why does Sonny let the turtle go? How do his actions reflect his beliefs?

_____

_____

_____

_____

_____

_____

_____

_____

_____

_____

_____

_____

_____

_____

_____

_____

_____

_____

_____

her down and she just stayed there, her nose a foot from the water but not moving.

"We'll leave her," Grampa said. We turned to get into the car. When I looked back over my shoulder, she was gone. Only ripples on the water, widening circles rolling on

430 toward other shores like generations following each other, like my grandmother's flowers still growing in a hundred gardens in Greenfield, like the turtles still seeking out that sandbank, like this story that is no longer just my own but belongs now to your memory, too. **PAUSE & REFLECT**

Text Analysis: Cultural Context

Reread the biographical information about Joseph Bruchac in the Background on page 378, and think about the Abenaki culture that influenced his upbringing. In what ways does "The Snapping Turtle" reflect the values of this culture? In the chart below, give examples from the story.

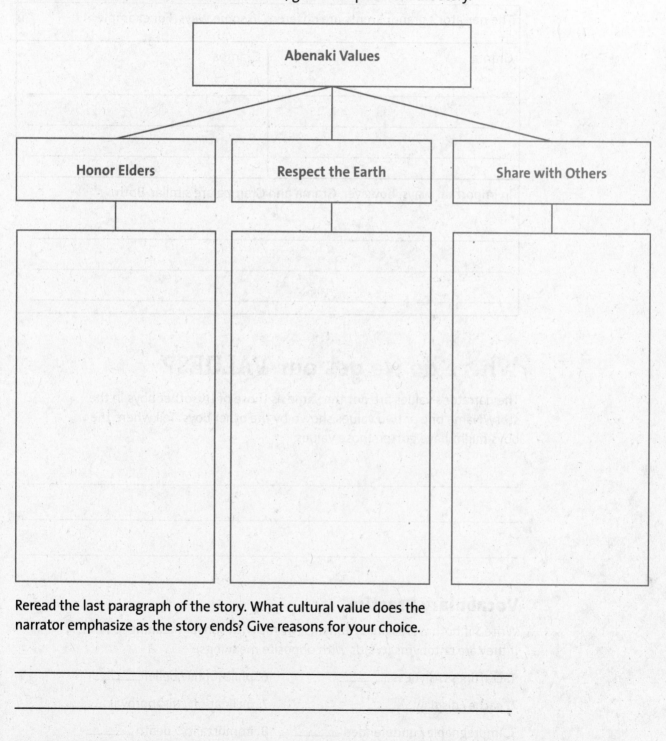

```
          ┌─────────────────────┐
          │   Abenaki Values    │
          └─────────────────────┘

┌──────────────┐  ┌──────────────────┐  ┌──────────────────┐
│ Honor Elders │  │ Respect the Earth│  │ Share with Others│
└──────────────┘  └──────────────────┘  └──────────────────┘

┌──────────────┐  ┌──────────────────┐  ┌──────────────────┐
│              │  │                  │  │                  │
│              │  │                  │  │                  │
│              │  │                  │  │                  │
│              │  │                  │  │                  │
│              │  │                  │  │                  │
│              │  │                  │  │                  │
└──────────────┘  └──────────────────┘  └──────────────────┘
```

Reread the last paragraph of the story. What cultural value does the narrator emphasize as the story ends? Give reasons for your choice.

_____

_____

_____

Reading Skill: Compare and Contrast

How are Grama and Grampa alike? How are they different? Consider their backgrounds, values, and traits. Complete the compare-and-contrast frame below by citing evidence from the story.

The narrator's grandparents are different in some ways. For example:	
Grama: _____ _____ _____	Grampa: _____ _____ _____

In important ways, however, Grama and Grampa are similar. Both

_____

_____

_____

Where do we get our VALUES?

The narrator's values are not the same as those of the other boys in the story. Name one or two values shown by the other boys. Tell where the boys might have gotten those values.

_____

_____

_____

Vocabulary Practice

Write **S** if both words are synonyms (words with similar meanings). Write **A** if they are antonyms (words with opposite meanings).

1. craftiness / slyness _____

2. cache / display _____

3. impregnable / undefended _____

4. migration / relocation _____

5. traipse / stroll _____

6. philosophy / belief _____

7. inclination / disapproval _____

8. immortality / death _____

9. undaunted / fearful _____

10. basking / sunbathing _____

Academic Vocabulary in Speaking

contribute	culture	interpret	perceive	similar

TURN AND TALK Imagine that the narrator has been asked to tell his class how the Abenaki **culture** views nature. What might he say? Give a speech from his point of view, using at least one of the Academic Vocabulary words. Definitions of these words are on page 375.

Assessment Practice

DIRECTIONS Use "The Snapping Turtle" to answer questions 1–6.

1 What is an example of a cultural value in the story?

- **A** succeeding in school
- **B** using cleverness to make money
- **C** behaving with shyness around others
- **D** living in harmony with nature

2 What is one similarity between the narrator and the other boys in the story?

- **A** their interest in the living things around them
- **B** their urge to be part of a group
- **C** their desire to show bravery
- **D** their methods of catching fish

3 Which detail from the story supports the theme, "Sharing what you have is better than keeping it"?

- **A** what Grama does with her iris
- **B** what happens to the narrator's four cats and two dogs
- **C** what the narrator does when he sees the spider
- **D** what Jack says about the snapping turtle

4 What is a difference between snapping turtles and other turtles?

- **A** Snapping turtles cannot be released back into the wild.
- **B** Snapping turtles come out of the water to lay eggs.
- **C** Snapping turtles do not have shells.
- **D** Snapping turtles are more dangerous.

5 How does the narrator's attitude about snappers change at the end of the story?

- **A** He realizes that snappers should be allowed to grow large before being caught.
- **B** He realizes that a snapper that is about to lay eggs should be allowed to live.
- **C** He decides that it is wrong to hunt a snapper for food.
- **D** He recognizes the importance of friendship with turtles.

6 What is a theme in the story?

- **A** The natural world is a safe place.
- **B** People must protect wildlife.
- **C** The Abenaki people are Native Americans.
- **D** Money is less valuable than family love.

Out of Bounds
Short Story by **Beverley Naidoo**

How do you Know what's RIGHT?

Can you think of a situation when you weren't sure what to do? If so, you know that it's not always easy to tell right from wrong. Sometimes you must rely on your internal compass to guide your behavior. In this story, a boy decides to disobey a rule in order to help someone in need.

DISCUSS What purpose do rules serve in families and society? When might rules have to be changed? Jot down answers to these questions. Discuss your answers with a partner.

Text Analysis: Cultural Conflict

When you read a story set in another country, knowledge of the area's history and culture provide important background information. It can help you to understand characters' behavior and the cultural conflicts that unfold. A **cultural conflict** is a struggle that arises because of differing values, customs, or circumstances between groups of people. A story's plot may focus on any of the causes of cultural conflict shown in the graphic below.

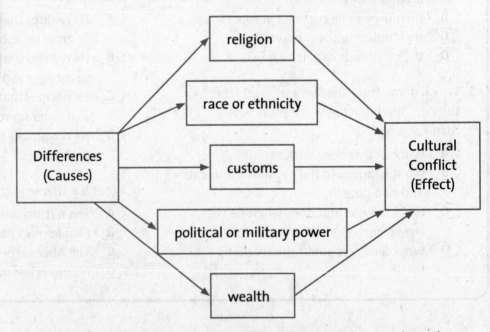

Rules

Their Purpose

_____

_____

_____

Reasons to Change Them

_____

_____

_____

"Out of Bounds" takes place in South Africa. As you read, notice how the conflicts reflect the history and culture of South Africa. The Background on page 398 will provide you with some of the information you need.

Reading Skill: Make Inferences

When you figure out something that the author has not stated directly, you are making an inference. To **make inferences,** you combine clues from the story with your own knowledge. Notes in the side column of "Out of Bounds" will ask you to make inferences as shown in the chart below.

Evidence from Story	My Knowledge	Inference
Rohan goes to private school.	Private schools are expensive.	Rohan's family is well-off.

Vocabulary in Context

Note: Words are listed in the order in which they appear in the story.

straggle (străg'əl) *v.* to spread out in a scattered group
*On the way home, the boy **straggled** behind his older brother.*

maroon (mə-rōon') *v.* to leave behind in a place from which there is little hope of escape
*The flood could **maroon** people on rooftops.*

sect (sĕkt) *n.* a religious group
*Members of the church broke off to form a new **sect.***

vigorously (vĭg'ər-əs-lē) *adv.* energetically
*South Africans fought **vigorously** for equality.*

glimmer (glĭm'ər) *n.* a faint sign
*The peace talks gave people a **glimmer** of hope.*

engross (ĕn-grōs') *v.* to completely occupy
*A fascinating story can **engross** readers for hours.*

bound (bound) *v.* to leap forward
*We watched the boy **bound** up the steep hill with ease.*

hamper (hăm'pər) *v.* to prevent the free movement of
*Continuing rain will **hamper** our flood-control efforts.*

OUT OF BOUNDS

Short Story by

BEVERLEY NAIDOO

**SET A PURPOSE
FOR READING**

Read "Out of Bounds" to find out what Rohan learns about the people who live in shacks down the hill.

BACKGROUND Until 1994, whites ruled South Africa under a system called Apartheid (apartness). Under this system, Africans received the fewest rights even though they were a large majority. The government could determine where one lived, conducted business, or owned land. The effects of apartheid continue to influence South African society. "Out of Bounds" is set in 2000. That year, severe storms devastated southern Africa. Floods swept away schools, roads, crops, and livestock. **Ⓐ**

Ⓐ CULTURAL CONFLICT
Why would stories set in South Africa be likely to deal with cultural conflicts?

_____

_____

_____

_____

_____

_____

_____

O *ut of bounds.*

That's what his parents said as soon as the squatters[1] took over the land below their house. Rohan's dad added another meter of thick concrete bricks to their garden wall and topped it with curling barbed wire. He certainly wasn't going to wait for the first break in and be sorry later. They lived on the ridge of a steep hill with the garden sloping down. Despite the high wall, from his bedroom upstairs, Rohan could see over the spiked wire circles down to the
10 place where he and his friends used to play. The wild fig trees under which they had made their hideouts were still there. They had spent hours dragging planks, pipes, sheets of metal and plastic—whatever might be useful—up

_____

1. **squatters:** people who occupy public land in order to gain ownership of it.

the hill from rubbish tipped in a ditch below. The first
squatters pulled their hideouts apart and used the same old
scraps again for their own constructions. Rohan could still
see the "ski slope"—the red earth down which he and his
friends had bumped and flown on a couple of old garbage
can lids. The squatters used it as their road up the hill.
20 Now it looked like a crimson scar cut between the shacks
littering the hillside.

   "There's only one good thing about this business,"
Ma said after the back wall was completed. "We won't
have to wash that disgusting red dust out of your clothes
any more!" **B**

   Rohan said nothing. How could he explain what he
had lost?

   At first, some of the squatter women and children came
up to the houses with buckets asking for water. For a couple
30 of weeks his mother opened the gate after checking that no
men were hanging around in the background. She allowed
the women to fill their buckets at the outside tap. Most of
her neighbors found themselves doing the same. Torrential
rains and floods had ushered in the new millennium by
sweeping away homes, animals and people in the north
of the country. The television was awash with pictures of
homeless families and efforts to help them. No one knew
from where exactly the squatters had come. But as Ma said,
how could you refuse a woman or child some water?

40   It wasn't long before all that changed. The first
complaint of clothes disappearing off the washing line
came from their new neighbors. The first African family,
in fact, to move in among the Indians on Mount View.
No one had actually seen anyone but everyone was
suspicious including the neighbor, Mrs. Zuma.

   "You can't really trust these people, you know," Mrs.
Zuma tutted[2] when she came to ask if Ma had seen anyone
hanging around. However, it was when thieves broke

---

2. **tutted:** made a "tut tut" sound with the tongue to express annoyance.

B CULTURAL CONFLICT
Reread lines 1–25. Underline the
words that show how Rohan's
parents feel about the squatters.
Why might they have those
feelings?

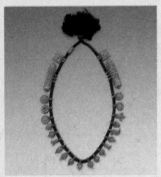

VISUAL VOCABULARY

thali *n.* neckless given by a groom to his bride at a Hindu wedding ceremony.

Why was Mrs. Pillay's thali stolen?

_____

_____

_____

C **MAKE INFERENCES**
Reread lines 40–56. Underline the details that help you infer the ethnicity of Rohan and his family.

straggle (străg'əl) *v.* to spread out in a scattered group

into old Mrs. Pillay's house, grabbed the gold **thali** from around her neck, and left her with a heart attack that views hardened. Young men could be seen hanging around the shacks. Were some of them not part of the same gang? Mrs. Pillay's son demanded the police search through the settlement immediately. But the police argued they would need more evidence and that the thieves could have come from anywhere. **C**

A new nervousness now gripped the house owners on top of the hill. Every report of theft, break in, or car hijacking, anywhere in the country, led to another conversation about the squatters on the other side of their garden walls.

At night Rohan peered through the bars of his window before going to sleep. Flickering lights from candles and lamps were the only sign that people were living out there in the thick darkness. In the daytime, when Ma heard the bell and saw that it was a woman or child with a bucket, she no longer answered the call.

All the neighbors were agreed. Why should private house owners be expected to provide water for these people? That was the Council's job. If the squatters were refused water, then perhaps they would find somewhere else to put up their shacks. A more suitable place. Or even, go back to where they came from.

The squatters did not go away. No one knew from where they managed to get their water or how far they had to walk. On the way to school, Rohan and his dad drove past women walking with buckets on their heads.

"These people are tough as ticks! You let them settle and it's impossible to get them out," complained Dad. "Next thing they'll be wanting our electricity."

But Rohan wasn't really listening. He was scanning the line of African children who **straggled** behind the women and who wore the black and white uniform of Mount View Primary, his old school. He had been a pupil there until his parents had moved him to his private school in Durban[3] with its smaller classes, cricket pitch, and its own rugby ground.[4] Most of the African children at Mount View had mothers who cleaned, washed, and ironed for the families on top of the hill. But since the New Year they had been joined by the squatter children and each week the line grew longer.

The queue[5] of traffic at the crossroads slowed them down, giving Rohan more time to find the "wire car" boy. He was looking for a boy who always steered a wire car in front of him with a long handle. He was about his own age—twelve or thirteen perhaps—and very thin and wiry himself. What interested Rohan was that the boy never had the same car for more than two or three days. Nor had he ever seen so many elaborate designs simply made out of wire, each suggesting a different make of car. They were much more complicated than the little wire toys in the African Crafts shop at the mall. **D**

"Hey, cool!" Rohan whistled. "See that, Dad?" The boy must have heard because he glanced toward them. His gaze slid across the silver hood of their car toward the trunk but didn't rise up to look at Rohan directly.

"It's a Merc[6]—like ours, Dad! What a beaut! Do you think—"

"*Don't* think about it, son! You want us to stop and ask how much he wants, don't you?"

Rohan half frowned, half smiled. How easily his father knew him!

"No way! If we start buying from these people, we'll be encouraging them! That's not the message we want them to get now, is it?"

---

3. **Durban** (dûr′bən): a city in South Africa.
4. **cricket pitch and rugby ground:** playing fields for ballgames that originated in England.
5. **queue** (kyoō): a waiting line.
6. **Merc:** short for Mercedes, a brand of car.

D **CULTURAL CONFLICT**
Reread lines 80–101. What differences between Rohan's life and the life of the "wire car" boy are illustrated in these lines?

_____
_____
_____
_____
_____
_____
_____
_____
_____
_____
_____
_____
_____
_____
_____
_____
_____
_____
_____
_____
_____
_____
_____

Ⓔ CULTURAL CONFLICT
Reread lines 106–117. Circle Rohan's reason for agreeing with his father's view of the squatters. How is Rohan's reason different from his father's reason?

_____

_____

_____

_____

_____

_____

_____

maroon (mə-rōōn′) v. to leave behind in a place from which there is little hope of escape

Rohan was quiet. He couldn't argue with his dad's logic. If the squatters moved away, he and his friends could get their territory back again. Ⓔ

Rohan returned home early from school. A precious half day. In the past he would have spent it in his hideout.
120 Instead he flicked on the television. News. As his finger hovered over the button to switch channels, the whirr of a helicopter invaded the living room.

"Hey, Ma! Look at this!"

Ma appeared from the kitchen, her hands cupped, white and dusty with flour. On the screen, a tight human knot swung at the end of a rope above a valley swirling with muddy water.

"A South African Air Force rescue team today saved a baby from certain death just an hour after she was born in
130 a tree. Her mother was perched in the tree over floodwaters that have devastated Mozambique. The mother and her baby daughter were among the lucky few. Many thousands of Mozambicans are still waiting to be lifted to safety from branches and rooftops. They have now been **marooned** for days by the rising water that has swallowed whole towns and villages."

"Those poor people! What a place to give birth!" Ma's floury hands almost looked ready to cradle a baby.

Rohan was watching how the gale from the rotors[7]
140 forced the leaves and branches of the tree to open like a giant flower until the helicopter began to lift. Members of the mother's family still clung desperately to the main trunk. Rohan saw both fear and determination in their eyes.

He and Ma listened to the weather report that followed. Although Cyclone Eline was over, Cyclone Gloria[8] was now

---

7. **rotors** (rō′tərz): helicopter blades.
8. **Cyclone Eline, Cyclone Gloria:** tropical storms that struck in 2000.

whipping up storms across the Indian Ocean and heading toward Mozambique. Where would it go next? Durban was only down the coast. Rohan had seen a program about a 150 **sect** who believed the new millennium would mark the end of the world. They were convinced that the floods were a sign that The End was beginning.

"What if the cyclone comes here, Ma?"

"No, we'll be all right son. But that lot out there will get it. The government really should do something." Ma nodded in the direction of the squatters. **F**

"Now, let me finish these *rotis*[9] for your sister!"

Ma returned to her bread making. When she had finished, she wanted Rohan to come with her to his 160 married sister's house. He pleaded to stay behind.

"I've got homework to do, Ma! I'll be fine."

"You won't answer the door unless it's someone we know, will you?"

"No, Ma!" he chanted. Ma said the same thing every time.

Alone in the house, Rohan daydreamed at his desk. He was close enough to the window to see down the hill. What if there was so much rain that a river formed along the road below! As the water rose, people would have to 170 abandon their shacks to climb higher up. They would be trapped between the flood below and the torrents above. In assembly they had heard the story of Noah building the ark. Perhaps it wasn't just a story after all. Perhaps the people had tried to cling on to the tops of trees as tightly as those they had seen on television.

Tough as ticks.

The phrase popped into his mind. Wasn't that what his dad had said about the squatters? Yet the one sure way

sect (sĕkt) *n.* a religious group

G MAKE INFERENCES
Reread lines 145–156. Underline Ma's response to Rohan's question about the cyclone coming to their city. What does her response reveal about her attitude toward the squatters?

_____

_____

_____

_____

_____

_____

_____

_____

_____

_____

_____

_____

_____

_____

9. *rotis* (rō′tēs): Indian flatbreads that are cooked on a griddle.

G MAKE INFERENCES
Reread lines 176–181. Note the change in Rohan's attitude toward squatters. What has caused this change? Complete this chart with your ideas.

Evidence from Story
Rohan sees how the Mozambicans are affected by the floods.

↓

My Knowledge
_____
_____
_____
_____
_____
_____
_____

↓

Inference
_____
_____
_____
_____
_____
_____
_____

to get rid of ticks was to cover them in liquid paraffin.[10]
180 Drown them. A terrible thought. He should push it
right away. **G**

Rohan was about to stretch out for his math book when
a figure caught his eye on the old ski slope. It was the thin
wiry boy, but he wasn't pushing a car this time. He was
carrying two large buckets, one on his head, the other by
his side. He descended briskly down the slope and turned
along the road in the opposite direction to that taken by
the women who carried buckets on their heads. Rohan
followed the figure until he went out of sight, then forced
190 himself to open his book.

The bell rang just as he was getting interested in the first
question. Nuisance! He hurried to the landing. If someone
was standing right in front of the gate, it was possible
to see who it was from the window above the stairs. He
stood back, careful not to be seen himself. It was the same
boy, an empty container on the ground each side of him!
Didn't he know not to come to the house up here? But he
was only a child, and it looked as if he just wanted some
water. It would be different if it were an adult or a complete
200 stranger. Rohan's daydream also made him feel a little
guilty. He could see the boy look anxiously through the
bars, his hand raised as if wondering whether to ring the
bell again. Usually when the boy was pushing his wire car
on the way to school, he appeared relaxed and calm.

By the time the bell rang a second time, Rohan had
decided. He hurried downstairs but slowed himself as he
walked outside toward the gate.

"What do you want?" Rohan tried not to show that he
recognized the boy.

210 "I need water for my mother. Please." The boy held
his palms out in front of him as if asking for a favor.

---

10. **paraffin** (păr′ə-fĭn): wax.

"My mother—she's having a baby—it's bad—there's no more water. Please."

This was an emergency. Not on television but right in front of him. Still Rohan hesitated. His parents would be extremely cross that he had put himself in this situation by coming to talk to the boy. Weren't there stories of adults who used children as decoys to get people to open their gates so they could storm in? He should have stayed inside.
220 Should he tell the boy to go next door where there would at least be an adult? But the boy had chosen to come here. Perhaps he had seen Rohan watching him from the car and knew this was his house. **PAUSE & REFLECT**

"We stay there." The boy pointed in the direction of the squatter camp. "I go to school there." He pointed in the direction of Mount View Primary. He was trying to reassure Rohan that it would be OK to open the gate. He was still in his school uniform but wore a pair of dirty blue rubber sandals. His legs were as thin as sticks.
230 "Isn't there a doctor with your mother?" It was such a silly question that as soon as it was out, Rohan wished he could take it back. If they could afford a doctor, they wouldn't be squatters on a bare hillside. The boy shook his head **vigorously**. If he thought it was stupid, he didn't let it show on his troubled face.

"Wait there!" Rohan returned to the house. The button for the electric gate was inside the front door. The boy waited while the wrought iron bars slowly rolled back.

"OK. Bring your buckets over here." Rohan pointed to
240 the outside tap. The buckets clanked against each other as the boy jogged toward him.

"Thank you," he said quietly.

The unexpected softness in his voice had a strange effect on Rohan. It sounded so different from his own

PAUSE & REFLECT
Reread lines 205–223. Why is Rohan nervous about opening the gate?

_____

_____

_____

_____

_____

_____

_____

_____

_____

_____

_____

_____

vigorously (vĭgʹər-əs-lē) adv. energetically

H MAKE INFERENCES

Paying attention to a character's thoughts can help you make inferences about his or her qualities. What qualities does Rohan reveal in lines 243–259?

_____

_____

_____

_____

_____

I CULTURAL CONFLICT

Reread lines 260–269. Underline the reason that Rohan doesn't want to be seen. What is Rohan afraid of, and why?

_____

_____

_____

_____

_____

_____

_____

glimmer (glĭm′ər) *n.* a faint sign

bossy tone. Suddenly he felt a little ashamed. This was the same boy whose wire cars he admired! If he were still at Mount View Primary they would probably be in the same class. They might even have been friends, and he would be learning how to make wire cars himself. Why had he spoken so arrogantly? It was really only a small favor that was being asked for. The water in the bucket gurgling and churning reminded Rohan of the water swirling beneath the Mozambican woman with her baby. *Her* rescuer had been taking a really big risk but hadn't looked big headed.[11] He had just got on with the job.

When both buckets were full, the boy stooped to lift one on to his head. Rohan saw his face and neck muscles strain under the weight. How would he manage to keep it balanced and carry the other bucket too? **H**

"Wait! I'll give you a hand." Rohan's offer was out before he had time to think it through properly. If the boy was surprised, he didn't show it. All his energy seemed to be focused on his task. Rohan dashed into the kitchen to grab the spare set of keys. Ma would be away for another hour at least. He would be back soon, and she need never know. It was only after the gate clicked behind them that Rohan remembered the neighbors. If anyone saw him, they were bound to ask Ma what he was doing with a boy from the squatter camp. He crossed the fingers of one hand. **I**

At first Rohan said nothing. Sharing the weight of the bucket, he could feel the strain all the way up from his fingers to his left shoulder. When they reached the corner and set off down the hill, the bucket seemed to propel them forward. It was an effort to keep a steady pace. Rohan glanced at the container on the boy's head, marveling at how he kept it balanced. He caught the boy's eye.

"How do you do that? You haven't spilled a drop!"

The boy gave a **glimmer** of a smile.

---

11. **big headed:** conceited.

"You learn."

280 Rohan liked the simple reply. He should ask the boy about the cars. This was his chance, before they turned into the noisy main road and reached the squatter camp.

"I've seen you with wire cars. Do you make them yourself?"

"Yes—and my brother."

"You make them together? Do you keep them all?"

"My brother—he sells them at the beach." The boy waved his free hand in the direction of the sea. "The tourists—they like them." **J**

290 "Your cars are better than any I've seen in the shops! Do you get lots of money for them?"

"Mmhh!" The boy made a sound something between a laugh and a snort. Rohan realized that he had asked another brainless question. Would they be staying in a shack if they got lots of money? Rohan had often seen his own father bargaining to get something cheaper from a street hawker.[12] He tried to cover his mistake.

"There's a shop in the mall where they sell wire cars. They charge a lot and yours are a hundred times better!"

300 "We can't go there. The guards—they don't let us in."

Rohan knew the security guards at the entrance to the mall. Some of them even greeted his parents with a little salute. Rohan had seen poor children hanging around outside. They offered to push your trolley,[13] to clean your car—anything for a few cents. Sometimes Ma gave an orange or an apple from her shopping bag to a child. Other times she would just say "No thank you" and wave a child away. Ma never gave money. . . . Rohan had never thought what it would be like to be chased away. How did the

310 guards decide who could enter? How could the boy and his brother go and show the lady in the African Crafts shop his cars if they weren't allowed in? **K**

---

12. **hawker:** seller.
13. **trolley:** shopping cart.

J MAKE INFERENCES
Reread lines 270–289. Use details in the passage, along with your own knowledge, to make an inference about the boy's qualities. Show your ideas in the chart below.

Evidence from Story

↓

My Knowledge

↓

Inference

K CULTURAL CONFLICT
Reread lines 300–312. Underline the question that Rohan asks himself. How does society's treatment of Rohan differ from the treatment of the boy?

_____

_____

_____

_____

_____

ⓛ MAKE INFERENCES
Reread lines 327–339. Underline
what Rohan says when the boy
asks him if he wants to go home.
What gives Rohan renewed
determination to help? Fill out
the chart below.

Evidence from Story

↓

My Knowledge

↓

Inference

Rohan was quiet as they reached the main road and turned toward the squatter camp. The noise of vehicles roaring past was deafening. He never normally walked down here. Not by himself nor with anyone else. His family went everywhere by car. With all the locks down, of course. The only people who walked were poor people. His eyes were drawn to a group of young men walking toward 320 them. They were still some distance away, but already Rohan began to feel uneasy. They were coming from the crossroads that his dad always approached on full alert. Rohan knew how his father jumped the red lights when the road was clear, especially at night. Everyone had heard stories of gangs who hijacked cars waiting for the lights to change.

The handle had begun to feel like it was cutting into his fingers. The boy must have sensed something because he signaled to Rohan to lower the bucket. For a few seconds 330 they each stretched their fingers.

"It's too far? You want to go?" The boy was giving him a chance to change his mind. To leave and go back home. He had already helped carry the water more than half the way. He could make an excuse about the time. But the thought of running back to the house along the road on his own now worried him.

"No, it's fine. Let's go." Rohan heard a strange brightness in his own voice. He curled his fingers around the handle again. ⓛ

340 As they drew nearer the men, Rohan felt their gaze on him and suddenly his head was spinning with questions. Why on earth had he offered to help carry the water? What did he think he was doing coming down here? And he hadn't even yet entered the squatter camp itself!

"We go here." The boy's voice steadied him a little.

Rohan turned and stared up at his old ski slope. He felt the force of the young men's eyes on his back as he and the boy began to ascend the rough track. Someone behind called out something in Zulu[14] and, without turning, the
350 boy shouted back.

The words flew so quickly into one another that Rohan didn't pick up any even though he was learning Zulu in school. They must be talking about him, but he was too embarrassed—and frightened—to ask. He could feel his heart pumping faster and told himself it was because of the stiff climb. He needed to concentrate where he put each foot. The track was full of holes and small stones. A quick glance over his shoulder revealed that the young men had also entered the squatter camp but seemed to be heading
360 for a shack with a roof covered in old tires on the lower slope. A couple of them were still watching. He must just look ahead and control his fear. As long as he was with the boy, he was safe, surely? Ⓜ

A bunch of small children appeared from nowhere, giggling and staring. He couldn't follow their chatter but heard the word *"iNdiya!"* The boy ignored them until a couple of children started darting back and forth in front of them, sweeping up the red dust with their feet.

"Hambani!" Rohan could hear the boy's irritation as he
370 waved them away. But the darting and dancing continued just out of reach.

"Hambani bo!" This time the boy's voice deepened to a threat, and the cluster of children pulled aside with one or two mischievous grins. Beads of sweat had begun trickling down the boy's face. With his own skin prickling with sticky heat, Rohan wondered at the wiry strength of

14. **Zulu** (zo͞o′lo͞o): the language of the Zulu, a Bantu people of South Africa.

engross (ĕn-grōs´) *v.* to completely occupy

PAUSE & REFLECT
What do you learn about the boy's life as Rohan follows him to his home in the squatters' camp?

_____

_____

_____

_____

_____

_____

_____

_____

_____

_____

_____

_____

_____

_____

the boy whose back, head, and bucket were still perfectly upright as they mounted the hill.

"It's that one—we stay there." The boy, at last, pointed to a structure of corrugated iron,[15] wood, and black plastic a little further up. It was not far from the old fig trees. For a moment Rohan thought he would say something about his hideout which the first squatters had pulled down. But he stopped himself. Maybe the boy had even been one of them!

As they drew nearer, they heard a woman moaning and a couple of other women's voices that sounded as if they were comforting her. The boy lowered the bucket swiftly from his head and pushed aside a plywood sheet, the door to his home.

Rohan wasn't sure what to do. He knew he couldn't follow. The sounds from within scared him. The moans were rapid and painful. . . .

Rohan folded his arms tightly, trying not to show how awkward he felt. The little children were still watching but keeping their distance. They could probably also hear the cries. It would be hard to keep anything private here. The only other people nearby were two gray haired men sitting on boxes a little lower down the hill. One of them was bent over an old fashioned sewing machine placed on a metal drum, a makeshift table. Normally Rohan would have been very curious to see what he was stitching, but now he was just grateful that both men were **engrossed** in talking and didn't seem interested in him. **PAUSE & REFLECT**

He turned to look up the hill—toward his house and the others at the top protected by their walls with wires, spikes, and broken bottles. When he had hidden in his hideout down here, he had always loved the feeling of being safe yet almost in his own separate little country. But that had been

_____

15. **corrugated** (kôr´ə-gā´tĭd) **iron:** sheet iron with parallel ridges.

410 a game and he could just hop over the wall to return to the other side. Surrounded now by homes made out of scraps and other people's leftovers, this place seemed a complete world away from the houses on the hill. In fact, how was he going to get home? If he didn't leave soon, Ma would be back before him. Would the boy at least take him part of the way through the squatter camp? He needed him to come outside so that he could ask him.

"What do you want here?"

Rohan spun around. A man with half closed eyes and
420 his head tilted to one side stood with his hands on his hips, surveying Rohan from head to foot. His gaze lingered for a moment on Rohan's watch.

"I . . . I brought water with . . . with . . ." Rohan stammered. He hadn't asked the boy his name! Panic stricken, he pointed to the door of the shack. The man stepped forward, and Rohan stumbled back against the wall of corrugated iron. The clattering brought the boy to the door. The man immediately switched into loud, fast Zulu. The boy spoke quietly at first, but when the man's
430 voice didn't calm down, the boy's began to rise too. Even when he pointed to the bucket and Rohan, the man's face remained scornful. Rohan was fully expecting to be grabbed when a sharp baby's cry interrupted the argument. The boy's face lit up, and the man suddenly fell silent. Rohan's heart thumped wildly as the man's eyes mocked him before he turned and walked away. **N**

Rohan folded his arms tightly, trying not to shake. Before he could say anything, a lady appeared behind the boy, placing a hand on his shoulder.
440 "You have a little sister!" She smiled at the boy and then at Rohan. She looked friendly but tired. Her cheeks shone

N CULTURAL CONFLICT
Reread lines 418–436. Why do you think the man is scornful and mocks Rohan with his eyes?

_____

_____

_____

_____

_____

_____

_____

_____

_____

_____

_____

_____

_____

◎ **CULTURAL CONFLICT**
Reread lines 459–471. What
do Rohan's neighborhood and
the squatters' camp have in
common?

_____

_____

_____

_____

_____

_____

_____

_____

_____

_____

_____

_____

_____

_____

_____

as if she too had been perspiring. It was obviously hard work helping to deliver a baby.

"Tell your mother thank you for the water. You really helped us today."

Rohan managed to smile back.

"It's OK." His voice came out strangely small.

"Solani will take you back now—before it gets dark."

Rohan felt a weight lifting. He did not need to ask.

450 The sun was getting lower and made long rodlike shadows leap beside them as they scrambled down the slope. Knowing the boy's name made Rohan feel a little easier, and he wondered why he hadn't asked him earlier. He told Solani his own, and the next thing he was telling him about riding on garbage can lids down the ski slope. Solani grinned.

"It's good! But this place—it's a road now. We can't do it. The people will be angry if we knock someone down."

Rohan understood that. But what he didn't understand 460 was why the man with scornful eyes had been so angry with him. And why had those other young men looked at him so suspiciously? He decided to ask Solani.

"They don't know you. Sometimes people come and attack us. So if a stranger comes, they must always check first."

When they reached the road, neither spoke. The hometime traffic would have drowned their voices anyway. Rohan thought about what Solani had said about him being a stranger. Surely they knew that he was from one of 470 the houses on top of the hill. The houses that also did not welcome strangers. Like the squatters. ◎

They parted at the top of the hill. Rohan was anxious to reach the house before his mother returned, and Solani was eager to see his baby sister. Opening the electronic gates, Rohan was relieved that his mother's car was neither in the yard nor the garage. He dashed upstairs to his room and peered out of the window over to the squatter camp. The evening was falling very rapidly. His mother would be home any minute—and his dad. Neither liked to drive in 480 the dark if they could help it.

Rohan fixed his eyes on the deep crimson scar, hoping to see Solani climbing the slope. How strange to think that he had been there himself less than half an hour ago. In that other world. Yes! There was Solani! A tiny, wiry figure **bounding** up the hill. Not **hampered** this time with a container of water on his head. Rohan watched Solani weave through other figures traveling more slowly until three quarters of the way up the hill, he darted off and disappeared into the darkening shadow that was his home.

490 Rohan surprised his parents by joining them for the eight o'clock news. The story about the rescue of mother and baby from the floods in Mozambique was repeated.

"Sophia Pedro and her baby daughter Rositha were among the lucky few. Many thousands of Mozambicans are still waiting to be lifted to safety. . . ."

This time the reporter added their names. Rohan observed the mother more closely. Had she also cried and moaned like Solani's mother? With the roaring waters underneath, how many people had heard her? **P**

500 "It's nice to see these South African soldiers doing some good," said Ma when the news was finished.

Rohan wished he could say what he too had done that afternoon. But he feared the storm that it would let loose and went upstairs to his bedroom. Before slipping between his sheets, he peered out once again through the bars at

bound (bound) v. to leap forward

How does Solani look as he **bounds** up the hill? How is this different from the way he looked when he and Rohan were carrying the water?

_____

_____

_____

_____

hamper (hăm′pər) v. to prevent the free movement of

P MAKE INFERENCES
Reread lines 490–499. Why has Rohan become more interested in the news? Fill out the chart below.

Evidence from Story
_____
_____

↓

My Knowledge
_____
_____

↓

Inference
_____
_____

ⓠ MAKE INFERENCES
Reread lines 502–522. What
qualities does Rohan show?
Explain why those qualities are
important to the story's theme,
or message about life.

_____

_____

_____

_____

_____

_____

_____

_____

_____

_____

_____

_____

_____

_____

_____

_____

_____

_____

the hill swallowed up by the night. He thought he saw a
light still flickering in Solani's home and wondered how
many people were tucked inside the sheets of iron, plastic,
and wood. He prayed that Cyclone Gloria would keep
510 well away.

Next morning, the glint of metal beside the gate caught
his eye from the front door. His dad was reversing the car out
of the garage. Rohan ran across the drive. There, just inside
the gate, was a wire car. A small, perfect Merc! Who could it
be from, except Solani? He must have slipped it through the
bars of the gate in the early morning. Quickly Rohan pushed
it behind a cluster of scarlet gladioli. If his parents saw it, they
would want to know from where it had come. They would
discover he had gone out of bounds. . . . Well, so had Solani!
520 Each of them had taken a risk. He needed time to think.
In the meantime, the car would have to be his secret. Their
secret. His and Solani's. **ⓠ**

Text Analysis: Cultural Conflict

What causes the residents of Mount View to discriminate against the squatters? Consider what you know about the history and culture of South Africa, as well as events in the story's plot. Record your response in this diagram.

Cause:

Cause:

Effect:

discrimination against squatters

Cause:

The story is told from the viewpoint of Rohan, who lives in Mount View. How would the conflict differ if it were told from the viewpoint of Solani, who lives in the squatters' camp?

_____

_____

_____

_____

_____

Reading Skill: Make Inferences

Rohan and Solani have many cultural differences, but you can infer that they are also alike in some ways. Name two qualities that they share, and give supporting evidence from the story.

Shared Qualities	Evidence from Story

How do you know what's RIGHT?

Reread lines 214–238. Why does Rohan decide to disregard his mother's instructions and open the gate to Solani?

_____

_____

_____

Vocabulary Practice

For each item, circle the letter of the word that differs most in meaning from the other words. Refer to a dictionary if necessary.

1. **(a)** bound, **(b)** leap, **(c)** spring, **(d)** stroll

2. **(a)** engross, **(b)** distract, **(c)** involve, **(d)** interest

3. **(a)** glimmer, **(b)** trace, **(c)** fraction, **(d)** excess

4. **(a)** hamper, **(b)** free, **(c)** prevent, **(d)** hinder

5. **(a)** maroon, **(b)** rescue, **(c)** save, **(d)** retrieve

6. **(a)** sect, **(b)** denomination, **(c)** group, **(d)** everyone

7. **(a)** straggle, **(b)** lead, **(c)** scatter, **(d)** dawdle

8. **(a)** vigorously, **(b)** energetically, **(c)** enthusiastically, **(d)** weakly

Academic Vocabulary in Writing

contribute	culture	interpret	perceive	similar

Rohan feels a connection to the South African soldiers helping the Mozambicans. In a paragraph, explain whether you think his actions are **similar** to the soldiers'. Use at least one of the Academic Vocabulary words. Definitions of these words are on page 375.

_____

_____

_____

_____

Assessment Practice

DIRECTIONS Use "Out of Bounds" to answer questions 1–6.

1 What can you infer about Rohan's father from his remarks in lines 112–114?

- Ⓐ He doesn't like to spend money.
- Ⓑ He appreciates cleverly made things.
- Ⓒ He has no sympathy for the squatters.
- Ⓓ He believes that the squatters can't understand messages.

2 Cultural conflict in this story arises from different —

- Ⓐ religious beliefs
- Ⓑ racial or ethnic origins
- Ⓒ views of family life
- Ⓓ feelings and emotions

3 The conflict in this story is between —

- Ⓐ people who have many things and people who have almost nothing
- Ⓑ victims of a flood and victims of poverty
- Ⓒ an Indian boy and an African boy
- Ⓓ people who want to protect their families and people who want to cause harm

4 Rohan has an internal conflict caused by —

- Ⓐ his promise to his mother and his desire to help someone
- Ⓑ his admiration for the wire car and his fear of its owner
- Ⓒ his hatred of the squatters and his respect for his parents
- Ⓓ the change from his public school to his private school

5 How does Rohan feel when he is in the squatter camp?

- Ⓐ angry about the poor conditions
- Ⓑ proud that he has helped
- Ⓒ grateful that he has a fine home
- Ⓓ frightened and out of place

6 Why is the wire car important to the story?

- Ⓐ It is a symbol of creativity.
- Ⓑ It is a connection between two worlds.
- Ⓒ It is extremely well made.
- Ⓓ It shows how different the two boys are.

UNIT 8

Believe It or Not

FACTS AND INFORMATION

Be sure to read the Text Analysis Workshop on pp. 884–889 in *Holt McDougal Literature*.

Academic Vocabulary for Unit 8

Academic Vocabulary is the language you use to discuss literary and informational texts. Preview the following Academic Vocabulary words. You will use these words as you write and talk about the selections in this unit.

challenge (chăl′ənj) *n.* a test of one's abilities or resources in a demanding but stimulating undertaking

*What **challenge** does the author face as she tries to reach her goal?*

communicate (kə-myōō′nĭ-kāt) *v.* to convey information about; make known; impart

*In what ways does the editorial **communicate** the writer's frustration?*

design (dē-zīn′) *v.* to conceive or fashion in the mind; invent

*What events prompted the doctor to **design** her new nutrition program?*

job (jŏb) *n.* a task that must be done

*Which of the **jobs** described in the article seems most demanding?*

method (mĕth′əd) *n.* means or manner of procedure, especially a regular and systematic way of accomplishing something

*What **method** does the author use record ideas during the interview?*

Think of a book or a movie in which a character fails to meet a great **challenge**. How does that failure affect your reaction to the character? Use at least two Academic Vocabulary words in your response.

_____

_____

_____

_____

_____

The Spider Man Behind *Spider-Man*
Feature Article by Bijal P. Trivedi

What is your DREAM JOB?

Ever since you were little, people have probably asked you what you want to be when you grow up. Now that you're older and know yourself better, your dream job might be coming into focus. Is it a job that would take you outdoors? Onto a movie set? Into a sports arena? Your ideal career probably reflects your individual talents, interests, and personality. In the article that follows, you'll read about a man who turned his passion into a dream job.

SURVEY Interview several classmates to find out what their dream jobs would be. Ask why they chose the jobs they did. Include your own responses, too.

Text Analysis: Text Features

Nonfiction articles often utilize **text features,** design elements that highlight the structural patterns of the text and help you identify key ideas. Common text features include:

- **headings**—the title of the article
- **subheadings**—headings that signal the beginning of a new topic or section within a written piece
- **sidebars**—additional information set in a box alongside, below, or within an article
- **bulleted lists**—lists of items of equal value or importance. This list of text features is an example of a bulleted list.

Before you read "The Spider Man Behind *Spider-Man*," scan the article to get an idea of the text features it includes and the information that is highlighted. As you read the article, notice how the text features help you locate information on particular topics.

Name: *Kayla*

Dream Job: *Veterinarian*

Why? *Likes caring for*

animals; good grades in

science

Name: _____

_____

Dream Job: _____

_____

Why? _____

_____

Name: _____

_____

Dream Job: _____

_____

Why? _____

_____

Reading Strategy: Summarize

When you **summarize** a piece of writing, you briefly retell the main idea or key points in the order in which they appear in the original text. Summarizing is a way to check your understanding and remember information. As you read "The Spider Man Behind *Spider-Man*," questions in the side margin will ask you to take notes on key points in a chart similar to the one below.

What Steven Kutcher Does	His Training and Background	His *Spider-Man* Experience

Vocabulary in Context

Note: Words are listed in the order in which they appear in the article.

potential (pə-tĕn'shəl) *n.* the ability to grow or develop
*Maria has the **potential** to become a first-rate scientist.*

engaging (ĕn-gāj'ĭng) *adj.* charming; likeable
*Bill is an **engaging** person whom everyone likes.*

perseverance (pûr'sə-vîr'əns) *n.* steady persistence in sticking to a course of action
*Kiera has the **perseverance** necessary to finish the job.*

rendition (rĕn-dĭsh'ən) *n.* a pictorial representation; an interpretation
*Anton's watercolor **rendition** of his dream earned praise from his art teacher.*

Vocabulary Practice

Review the vocabulary words and think about their meanings. Then write a brief introduction to a story about someone who wants to make movies. Include at least two of the words in your writing.

_____

_____

_____

SET A PURPOSE FOR READING

Read "The Spider Man Behind *Spider-Man*" to discover what Steven Kutcher wants to teach people about insects.

THE SPIDER MAN BEHIND SPIDER-MAN

Feature Article by **BIJAL P. TRIVEDI**

BACKGROUND In 1962, writer Stan Lee and artist Steve Ditko created the character of Peter Parker, a teenager who gains spider-like powers through the bite of a radioactive spider and becomes Spider-Man. Spider-Man has been a popular comic book character ever since. In the movies about the superhero, CGI, or computer-generated imagery, made it appear that the character could swing from one tall building to another, stick to walls, and do other incredible feats that only a Spider-Man could do.

Entomologist Steven Kutcher is the spider man behind *Spider-Man*. "He's the guy to call in Hollywood when you need insects—he is the ultimate insect trainer," says Robin Miller, property master for the movie *Spider-Man*.

"I know how to get a cockroach to run across the floor and flip onto its back. I can get cockroaches, beetles, and spiders to crawl to a quarter four feet away on cue. I can make bees swarm indoors and I can repair
10 butterfly wings," says Kutcher. He has even made a live wasp fly into an actor's mouth. "I study insect behavior, and learn what they do and then adapt the behavior to what the director wants," says Kutcher. Ⓐ

Passion for Bugs Ⓑ

Kutcher's love of insects began as a toddler when he collected fireflies in New York. But he was also influenced by very "positive early childhood experiences in nature" when his family would spend summers in the Catskills.[1] "Something about seeing fish, catching butterflies, lit a fire within me," says
20 Kutcher.

Kutcher followed his passion for bugs and studied entomology in college, receiving his B.S. from the University of California, Davis, and later an M.A. in biology—with an emphasis on entomology,[2] insect behavior, and ecology[3] from the California State

---

1. **Catskills** (kăt′skĭlz′): the Catskill Mountain region in New York state. It is a popular vacation area.
2. **entomology** (ĕn′tə-mŏl′ə-jē): the study of insects.
3. **ecology** (ĭ-kŏl′ə-jē): the study of relationships among living things and their environment.

Ⓐ **SUMMARIZE**
Reread lines 1–13. What are some of Kutcher's unique skills? Record them in the chart that follows.

What Steven Kutcher Does

Ⓑ **TEXT FEATURES**
Based on this **subheading** and what you've read so far, what information do you expect to find in this section?

University in Long Beach. He had planned to pursue a Ph.D.,[4] but when he wasn't accepted at the graduate school of his choice he decided to reevaluate his career options.

30   One day he received a call from his former academic advisor asking him to baby-sit 3,000 locusts that were to be used for the movie *Exorcist 2*. Kutcher had to

C TEXT FEATURES
Note the **sidebar** that appears at this point in the article, and read its **heading**. Why do you think it might be included here?

_____

_____

_____

_____

_____

perseverance (pûr′sə-vîr′əns) *n.* steady persistence in sticking to a course of action

So You Want to Be an Entomologist? C

Do you get grossed out when you see a spider or earwig[5] crawling up your wall? Or does the spider's web and the inchworm's movement fascinate you? If the latter question describes you, then entomology could be the perfect career for you.

Entomologists study the classification, life cycle, and habits of insects and related life forms, and plan and implement insect surveys and pest management programs. They also investigate ways to control insect pests and manage beneficial insects such as plant pollinators,[6] insect parasites, and insect predators.

Interests and Skills
Entomologists need the intellect, curiosity, creativity, patience, and **perseverance** required to pursue answers to complex research questions about bugs. Because there are thousands and thousands of insect species, entomologists must also have a good memory. Entomologists must be able to work well both independently and as part of a team.

4. **B.S.; M.A.; Ph.D.:** Bachelor of Science, an undergraduate degree; Master of Arts, a graduate degree; Doctor of Philosophy, a graduate degree that is usually more time-consuming and difficult to earn than a master's degree.

5. **earwig** (îr′wĭg′): an insect that has two pincers protruding from the rear of its abdomen.

6. **pollinators** (pŏl′ə-nāt′tərs): animals that carry pollen from one plant to another, causing the plants to produce fruit.

place the locusts wherever they were needed, including on the stars Richard Burton and Linda Blair. That was his first job, and it has been Hollywood creepy crawlies ever since.

After doing a long survey of movies Kutcher found that about one third of all movies had an insect in it. "I saw immediate job <u>potential</u>," Kutcher says.

potential (pə-tĕn'shəl) *n.* the ability to grow or develop

Typical Tasks

- Study the evolution of insects

- Discover and describe new species of insects

- Conduct research into the impact and control of insect pest problems

- Conduct field and laboratory tests of pesticides to evaluate their effect on different species of insects under different conditions

- Curate museum insect collections

- Prepare publications that make it possible to identify insect, spider, mite, and tick species

- Coordinate public awareness and education programs **D**

AVERAGE EARNINGS

Maximum Salary: $71,270

Average Salary: $47,740

Entry Level Salary: $29,260

Educational Paths

Students interested in a career working with insects should prepare for college by taking a variety of science classes. Many students get a general undergraduate degree in biology or zoology[7] and then specialize in entomology at the post-graduate level. For those wishing to lead research teams or teach at the university level, a Ph.D. is a requirement.

D TEXT FEATURES
What does the **bulleted list** in the sidebar help you understand?

_____

_____

_____

_____

_____

_____

_____

_____

_____

_____

_____

_____

_____

_____

_____

7. **zoology** (zōō-ŏl'ə-jē): the study of animals.

engaging (ĕn-gāj'ĭng) *adj.*
charming; likeable

Why might it be important for his work that Kutcher has an engaging personality?

_____

_____

_____

E SUMMARIZE
Reread lines 30–58. What are two of the most important pieces of information in these paragraphs? Record them in the chart that follows.

What Steven Kutcher Does
_____
_____
_____
_____

rendition (rĕn-dĭsh'ən) *n.* a pictorial representation; an interpretation

F TEXT FEATURES
Reread the **subheading** and first sentence of this section. What "perfect match" does the subheading refer to?

_____

_____

_____

40   Almost 25 years after his first job Kutcher now holds an impressive list of movie, television, music video, and commercial credits that include his biggest movie, *Arachnophobia,* the comedy-thriller in which a California town is overrun with deadly spiders. He also supervised the bug and spider stunts in *Alien, Contact, Jurassic Park, Pacific Heights,* and *Wild Wild West.*

"He is a very observant and <u>engaging</u> guy," says Lucinda Strub, a special effects person who worked with Kutcher on *Arachnophobia.* "One of his main
50 goals is to educate the public about how fascinating and interesting insects are. He is really out to teach people about bugs," says Strub, who then . . . clarified that "of course spiders are not bugs, they are arachnids."

Even with his busy filmmaking schedule, Kutcher still finds time to teach once a week at a local community college. He also started the annual Insect Fair at the Los Angeles Arboretum. **E**

The Perfect Match

Kutcher's most recent challenge has been finding the
60 perfect spider for the movie *Spider-Man.* . . . The concept designer for the movie produced a computer <u>rendition</u> that combined traits of up to four arachnids to create an image of the mutant spider that bites Peter Parker (a.k.a. Spider-Man) and endows him with spider powers. **F**

"I was given this drawing of a spider that didn't exist and told to find a real spider that matched it," says Miller, whose responsibilities include assembling all the props in the entire film. The spider resembled a black 70 widow, which wasn't an option because its bite is too dangerous.

Miller contacted Steven Kutcher and showed him the picture. Kutcher then arranged a "spider Olympics" for *Spider-Man* director Sam Raimi. Kutcher brought in different types of spiders to showcase the talents of each, says Miller. "He literally had the spiders doing tricks." One spider could jump, another was able to spin webs very quickly, and yet another was able to produce a drag line and essentially swing out of the 80 way—all activities that Spider-Man can do.

The spider that Raimi selected was *Steatoda grossa,* a brown spider with a smooth, swollen body and thin twiggy legs. The problem was that the color was wrong, "we needed a spider that had metallic blue and a radioactive[8] red-orange color to it," says Miller.

The answer was spider make-up. Originally Kutcher wanted to make an entire costume for the spider, but the timing came down to the wire and he finally settled on body paint. "I had to find a non-toxic[9] paint, 90 design a little harness to hold the spider as he was painted, and supervise the artist painting *Steatoda.*"

"I need the spider to go from A to B to C and Steve can train it to do that," says Miller, who has worked with Kutcher on several movies. "He is very creative; Ⓖ

Ⓖ SUMMARIZE
What crucial jobs did Kutcher perform in the making of *Spider-Man*? Record them in the chart below.

His *Spider-Man* Experience

---

8. **radioactive** (rā′dē-ō-ăk′tĭv): exhibiting radiation emissions that possibly result from a nuclear explosion.

9. **non-toxic:** not poisonous or otherwise life-threatening.

PAUSE & REFLECT
What part of the article did you find most interesting?

_____

_____

_____

_____

_____

_____

_____

he can figure out how to get the creature to do what he wants while being very delicate," says Strub.

Why, in this age of computer-generated special effects, did the director simply not animate the spider? "The real thing always looks best, especially when it fills the whole movie screen," says Miller. And computer-generated graphics are very expensive, although the scene where the mutant spider bites Peter Parker is computer-generated.

"People find me, and I'm off on these adventures," says Kutcher, "problem solving, and exploring, and teaching, and educating people about insects." But Steven Kutcher's hat best describes his life, his love, and his philosophy: "Bugs are my business."

PAUSE & REFLECT

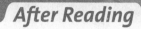

Text Analysis: Text Features

The feature article "The Spider Man Behind *Spider-Man*" uses a number of **text features.** Identify the text feature that helped you find each piece of information listed in the chart below. Include specific subheadings as needed.

Information	Text Feature That Helps You Find It
Broad focus of the article	
Kutcher's interest in bugs	
General information about entomologists	
Typical tasks performed by entomologists	
Which type of spider Kutcher chose for *Spider-Man*	
Characteristics needed for a career in entomology	

In what ways can the text features in this article help you before you read it?

_____

_____

_____

In what ways can the text features in this article help you after you read it?

_____

_____

_____

Reading Strategy: Summarize

Review the selection and your notes on the article about Steven Kutcher. Use the chart below to record the main ideas and supporting details that you would include in a summary of an article.

Title:
Main Ideas:
Important Details:

What is your DREAM JOB?

Steven Kutcher had to rethink his idea of a dream job when his original idea didn't work out. Review your response from page 420. What other careers might allow you to use the same talents and interests if your original dream job isn't possible?

_____

_____

Vocabulary Practice

Synonyms are words that have a similar meanings; antonyms have nearly opposite meanings. Write *synonyms* or *antonyms* next to each word pair.

1. perseverance/laziness   _____

2. rendition/interpretation   _____

3. engaging/disagreeable   _____

4. potential/promise   _____

Academic Vocabulary in Writing

challenge	communicate	design	job	method

Imagine that you are applying for a **job** as Steven Kutcher's assistant. What makes you a good candidate? Include at least one Academic Vocabulary word in your response. Definitions of these words are on page 419.

_____

_____

_____

_____

Assessment Practice

DIRECTIONS Use "The Spider Man Behind *Spider-Man*" to answer questions 1–6.

1 What makes Steven Kutcher "the guy to call in Hollywood when you need insects"?
  - (A) He is an entomologist.
  - (B) He enjoys sharing his knowledge of bugs.
  - (C) He can train insects.
  - (D) He presents workshops on insects.

2 Which text feature would help you find information on how much entomologists earn?
  - (A) the title
  - (B) the subheading *The Perfect Match*
  - (C) the sidebar
  - (D) the bulleted list

3 Which movie did Kutcher first work on?
  - (A) *Spider-Man*
  - (B) *Exorcist 2*
  - (C) *Alien*
  - (D) *Jurassic Park*

4 Information on how to become an entomologist can be found under the subheading —
  - (A) The Perfect Match
  - (B) Interests and Skills
  - (C) Typical Tasks
  - (D) Educational Paths

5 Kutcher solved a problem for *Spider-Man* by—
  - (A) using paint for the spider
  - (B) training a black widow spider
  - (C) teaching spiders to spin webs quickly
  - (D) using computer-generated special effects

6 What is the best summary of the sidebar subheading *Educational Paths*?
  - (A) Science studies in high school though a Ph.D. can lead to a career in entomology.
  - (B) Entomologists have a variety of duties.
  - (C) A career in entomology is difficult and challenging.
  - (D) Most entomologists need only a degree in biology or zoology.

Robo-Legs
Magazine Article by Michel Marriott

Eureka: Scientific Twists of Fate
Online Article

How has SCIENCE changed our lives?

Do you think about science when you answer a cell phone, turn on a light, or take your asthma medicine? Science has made it possible for doctors, engineers, and inventors to develop technologies and medicines that make our lives healthier and more convenient. In the articles that follow, you'll read about some amazing scientific breakthroughs that have helped us lead longer, better lives.

QUICKWRITE What one scientific development could you just not live without? Think beyond handy technological gadgets. Choose a development and then briefly explain what a day might be like if this discovery had never taken place.

Text Analysis: Organization of Ideas

Many nonfiction texts are organized in what might be called **part-by-part order.** One idea or group of ideas suggests another, which suggests another, and so on, as shown in the graphic.

idea
↓
idea
↓
idea

To understand part-by part order, pay attention to:

- topic sentences within paragraphs and new ideas they introduce and discuss

- subheadings that introduce new but related parts and topics

As you read each article, notice how each new idea is related to the ones that come before it.

Scientific development I could not live without:

_____

_____

_____

What my day might be like without it:

_____

_____

_____

_____

_____

_____

_____

_____

_____

Reading Strategy: Monitor

When you **monitor** your reading, you pause to check your comprehension of the text. To monitor effectively, pause when the text confuses you and use one of the following strategies to clarify the information:

- **Ask questions** about the information presented.
- **Visualize,** or picture, events and details being described.
- **Reread** passages that you find confusing.

Use a chart similar to the one shown to monitor your reading of the following articles.

Where I Paused	What Confused Me	How I Clarified the Information

Vocabulary in Context

Note: Words are listed in the order in which they appear in the articles.

mobility (mō-bĭl′ĭ-tē) *n.* the capability of moving from place to place
*Roberto gains **mobility** by using a wheelchair.*

rehabilitation (rē′hə-bĭl′ĭ-tā′shən) *n.* the process of restoring someone to physical capability, usually through exercise and physical therapy
*Mrs. Blake needed **rehabilitation** following knee surgery.*

keener (kēn′ər) *adj.* more acutely sensitive
*I need **keener** eyesight to thread the needle.*

appendage (ə-pĕn′dĭj) *n.* a body part, such as an arm or leg, that is attached to the main part of the body
*People who lose an **appendage** can still exercise.*

serendipitous (sĕr′ən-dĭp′ĭ-təs) *adj.* found by fortunate accident
*The scientist's **serendipitous** discovery led to a cure.*

pervasive (pər-vā′sĭv) *adj.* present throughout
*The **pervasive** infection spread throughout her body.*

infectious (ĭn-fĕk′shəs) *adj.* capable of being transmitted by infection
***Infectious** diseases can be transmitted quickly.*

contaminate (kən-tăm′ə-nāt) *v.* to make impure or unclean through contact
*The pollution could **contaminate** the water supply.*

SET A PURPOSE FOR READING

Read "Robo-Legs" to discover how modern technology is redefining life for people with artificial limbs.

Ⓐ MONITOR
Reread the Background information. Underline words that help you to **visualize** the types of prosthetic devices used throughout history.

mobility (mō-bĭl′ĭ-tē) *n.* the capability of moving from place to place

Ⓑ ORGANIZATION
Reread lines 1–9. Underline the name of the person the author introduces to begin the article. What does Marriott emphasize about him?

_____

_____

_____

_____

Robo-Legs

Magazine Article by Michel Marriott

BACKGROUND Throughout history, scientists and inventors have worked to improve the lives of those with physical disabilities. Prosthetics, used to replace missing arms and legs, were made of wood or metal as long ago as the days of ancient Rome. Today, scientists draw on robotics and a better understanding of the human body to create prosthetics that are very similar to real limbs. Ⓐ

*N*ew prosthetic limbs[1] *are providing increased* <u>mobility</u> *for many amputees—and blurring the line between humans and machines*

With his blond hair, buff torso, and megawatt smile, Cameron Clapp is in many ways the typical California teenager. There are, however, a few things that set him apart: For starters, this former skater boy is now making his way through life on a pair of shiny, state-of-the-art[2] robotic legs. Ⓑ

1. **prosthetic limbs** (prŏs-thĕt′ĭk lĭmz): artificial arms and legs.
2. **state-of-the-art:** made using the newest technology available.

10   "I make it look easy," he says.

Clapp, 19, lost both his legs above the knee and his right arm just short of his shoulder after getting hit by a train almost five years ago near his home in Grover Beach, California. Following years of <u>rehabilitation</u> and a series of prosthetics, each more technologically advanced than the last, he has become part of a new generation of people who are embracing breakthrough technologies as a means of overcoming their own bodies' limitations.

20   "I do have a lot of motivation and self-esteem," Clapp says, "but I might look at myself differently if technology was not on my side."

The technology he's referring to is the C-Leg. Introduced by Otto Bock HeathCare, a German company that makes advanced prosthetics, the C-Leg combines computer technology with hydraulics. Sensors monitor how the leg is being placed on the ground, and microprocessors[3] guide the limb's hydraulic system, enabling it to imitate a natural

30 step. It literally does the walking for the walker. The technology, however, is not cheap; a single C-Leg can cost more than $40,000.

The C-Leg is one of the examples of how blazing advancements, including tiny programmable microprocessors, lightweight materials, and <u>keener</u> sensors, are restoring remarkable degrees of mobility to amputees, says William Hanson, president of . . . a

rehabilitation (rē'hə-bĭl'ĭ-tā'shən) *n.* the process of restoring someone to physical capability, usually through exercise and physical therapy

How might technologically-advanced prosthetics have helped with Clapp's rehabilitation?

_____

_____

_____

_____

_____

keener *adj.* moe acutely sensitive

---

3. **microprocessors**: tiny computer parts that operators can program, or give new instructions to.

C MONITOR

To help you monitor your understanding as you read, **ask yourself questions** such as the following, and then answer them. **Lines 23–32:** What technologies are involved in creating modern prosthetics?

_____

_____

_____

_____

_____

_____

_____

Lines 40–50: How do limbs like the C-Leg improve life for people like Cameron Clapp?

_____

_____

_____

_____

_____

_____

_____

_____

Massachusetts company that specializes in developing and distributing advanced prosthetic arms and hands.

Three Sets of Legs

40 For example, Clapp, who remains very involved in athletics despite his condition, has three different sets of specialized prosthetic legs: one for walking, one for running, and one for swimming. He put all of them to use at the Endeavor Games in Edmond, Oklahoma—an annual sporting event for athletes with disabilities—where he competed in events like the 200-meter dash and the 50-yard freestyle 50 swim. **C**

Man or Machine?

But increased mobility is only part of the story. Something more subtle, and possibly far-reaching, is also occurring: The line that has long separated human beings from the machines that assist them is blurring, as complex technologies become a visible part of the people who depend upon them.

Increasingly, amputees, especially young men like Clapp, and soldiers who have lost limbs in Afghanistan 60 and Iraq, are choosing not to hide their prosthetics under clothing as previous generations did. Instead, some of the estimated 1.2 million amputees in the United States—more than two-thirds of whom are men—proudly polish and decorate their electronic limbs for all to see. . . . **D**

Many young people, especially those who have been using personal electronics since childhood, are comfortable recharging their limbs' batteries in public and plugging their prosthetics into their computers to
70 adjust the software, Hanson says.

Nick Springer, 20, a student at Eckerd College in St. Petersburg, Florida, who lost his arms and legs to meningitis when he was 14, recalls doing just that at a party when the lithium-ion batteries[4] for his legs went dead.

"I usually get 30 hours out of them before I have to charge them again," he says. "But I didn't charge them up the day before."

Terminator Legs

When his legs ran out of power, he spent most of his
80 time sitting on a couch talking to people while his legs were plugged into an electrical outlet nearby. According to Springer, no one at the party seemed to care, and his faith in his high-tech <u>appendages</u> appears unfazed. "I love my Terminator[5] legs," he says. **E**

Springer also remembers going to see *Star Wars: Episode III—Revenge of the Sith* with his father. While he liked the movie, he found the final scenes—in which Anakin Skywalker loses his arms and legs in a light-saber battle and is rebuilt with fully functional

---

4. **lithium-ion batteries** (lĭth′ē-əm-ī′ŏn′ băt′ə-rēz): very light, small batteries with a great deal of energy packed into a small space.
5. **Terminator:** a robotic character in a 1984 film, The Terminator.

D ORGANIZATION
Is the topic of the article still Clapp and his set of legs? If not, what new topic is introduced in lines 51–65? How is it related to the previous topic?

_____

_____

_____

_____

_____

_____

_____

_____

appendage (ə-pĕn′dĭj) *n.* a body part, such as an arm or leg, that is attached to the main part of the body

E ORGANIZATION
Does the subheading "Terminator Legs" introduce a new idea, or do lines 79–84 support the idea under the previous subheading? Explain your response.

_____

_____

_____

_____

_____

PAUSE & REFLECT

What do you think explains the differences between the way today's amputees feel about their prosthetics and the way those of past generations felt?

_____

_____

_____

_____

_____

_____

_____

_____

_____

_____

_____

_____

_____

_____

_____

90 prosthetics to become the infamous Darth Vader—a little far-fetched.

"We have a long way to go before we get anything like that," he says. "But look how far humanity has come in the past decade. Who knows? The hardest part is getting the ball rolling. We pretty much got it rolling." **PAUSE & REFLECT**

EUREKA:
Scientific *Twists of Fate*

PAUSE & REFLECT

BACKGROUND Scientists make many of their discoveries by coming up with a theory, testing and adjusting it, and then confirming their observations. However, there are occasions when scientists made critical findings by accident. The article you are about to read will tell you about a few of these important accidental discoveries.

SET A PURPOSE FOR READING

Read "Eureka: Scientific Twists of Fate" to learn about the sometimes unpredictable factors that lead to scientific discoveries.

PAUSE & REFLECT

Eureka comes from a Greek word that means "I have found (it)." Do you think the title is appropriate for an article about "accidental discoveries"? Explain your thinking.

_____

_____

_____

_____

_____

_____

_____

_____

_____

_____

_____

_____

_____

_____

. . . We are all familiar with the tale of Newton's apple. While sitting in his orchard one day in 1665, Isaac Newton's[1] curiosity was sparked by a falling apple, leading him to "discover" the law of gravity. As doubtful as the story sounds, writings by Newton and his contemporaries verify the incident. Though science often seems an orderly and methodical process, history is dotted with surprising discoveries such as these. Were they merely luck? Or the results of a gifted mind?
10 Actually, a bit of both. Sometimes scientific discoveries come from the most unexpected places, when talented

---

1. **Isaac Newton:** mathematician and scientist (1642–1727) who developed the theory of gravity.

serendipitous (sĕr'ən-dĭp'ĭ-təs)
adj. found by fortunate accident

F ORGANIZATION
Reread lines 1–13 and underline
a sentence that expresses the
main idea that is introduced.
Based on the last sentence of the
paragraph, how do you expect
the next part of this article to be
related to it?

_____

_____

_____

_____

pervasive (pər-vā'sĭv) *adj.*
present throughout

people are watching out for them. Here are two
examples of similarly **serendipitous** finds. **F**

The Smallpox Cure

In the late 1700s, Edward Jenner, a young English
doctor-in-training, was told by a local milkmaid that
she was safe from smallpox[2] because she had already
had cowpox. Like its deadly cousin, cowpox also
produced painful blisters, yet doctors had not made a
connection between the two diseases. After extensive
20 research, Jenner discovered that what she said was
true—milkmaids exposed to a common strain of
cowpox almost never contracted smallpox.

Jenner's supervising physicians took little interest in
his findings. Then, in 1796, he injected a young boy
named James Phipps with tissue taken from a cowpox
blister on a milkmaid's hand. He then exposed the
boy to the deadly smallpox virus. So **pervasive** and
devastating was this disease at the time that the boy's
family was willing to take this unimaginable risk.
30 But their gamble paid off. Young James remained
completely healthy, and the vaccination process
was born.

Jenner's idea opened the door not only to the
eradication of smallpox but to the subsequent
perfection of the immunization procedure by Louis
Pasteur.[3] The modern term "vaccine," from the Latin

2. **smallpox:** a highly infectious, often fatal disease characterized by high
fevers and blisters that leave pockmarks on the skin.
3. **Louis Pasteur** (lōō'ē păs-tûr'): French chemist (1822–1895) who founded
modern microbiology and developed several life-saving vaccines.

word for "cow," honors Jenner and his life-saving inspiration. . . . **G**

Penicillin

Arguably the most important medical discovery of
40 the 20th century came about purely by accident.
Throughout the 1920s, Scottish scientist Alexander
Fleming was searching for a cure for **infectious** disease,
the major cause of death throughout much of human
history. As part of his research, Fleming was cultivating
several species of bacteria in separate petri dishes.

One day, Fleming noticed that a mold had
contaminated the petri dish containing the bacteria
Staphylococcus, a common microbe responsible for a
variety of ailments ranging from the earaches to deadly
50 post-operative infections. But before tossing away the
moldy dish, Fleming realized that the intruder had
actually killed off much of the bacteria culture.

The tiny, wind-born mold spore must have landed
in the Staphylococcus colony during a brief moment
Fleming had uncovered the dish. Fleming isolated
the mold and identified it as a member of the genus
Penicillium. He called the antibiotic substance it
secreted penicillin.

Fleming's further investigation found that penicillin
60 killed off several, but not all, strains of the disease-
causing microbes he was growing in his lab. Had the
penicillium contaminated a different dish, Fleming
might never have discovered its medicinal benefits.

G MONITOR
Reread the subheading of this section on the previous page. Based on this subheading, what question about smallpox should you be able to answer? If you cannot answer the question, use a monitoring strategy and complete the chart below.

Where I Paused

↓

What Confused Me

↓

How I Clarified the Information

infectious (ĭn-fĕk′shəs) *adj.* capable of being transmitted by infection

contaminate (kən-tăm′ə-nāt′) *v.* to make impure or unclean through

ⓗ MONITOR
Why is penicillin important? What can you do if you don't know the answer?

_____

_____

_____

_____

_____

PAUSE & REFLECT
Do you agree with the article's idea that some scientific discoveries "are not quite as random as they seem"? Why or why not?

_____

_____

_____

_____

_____

_____

   Additionally, Fleming found penicillin was non-toxic to humans and animals. Realizing the strategic advantage in possessing the world's first antibiotic, the U.S. and Britain joined forces to mass-produce the drug, and treated thousands of Allied troops wounded in the D-Day invasion of Europe. It has saved

70 countless lives ever since. In 1945, Fleming shared the Nobel Prize in Medicine for his work on the "Wonder Drug" penicillin. . . . ⓗ

Serendipity or Smarts?

Each of these examples of serendipity helped advance the scope of human knowledge by great leaps and bounds. But these accidents and twists of fate are not quite as random as they seem. Each discovery occurred in the presence of a well-trained intellect. . . . As Louis Pasteur once said, "In the fields of observation, chance favors only the prepared mind." **PAUSE & REFLECT**

Text Analysis: Organization of Ideas

Complete the chart to analyze the organization of ideas in the two articles you have just read.

	"Robo-Legs"	"Eureka"
Method of organization:	*part-by-part*	*part-by-part*
How main idea is introduced:		
Examples used to support the main idea:		
How article concludes:		

Think about the subject matter, purpose, and organization of each article. What are some reasons these two articles are presented together in a single lesson?

_____

_____

_____

_____

Reading Strategy: Monitor

Review a section from each selection as noted below. Then identify which strategy would best help you monitor your comprehension, such as asking questions, visualizing, or rereading.

	"Robo-Legs," lines 51–65	"Eureka," lines 46–59
Strategy to check comprehension:		
Why?		

How has SCIENCE changed our lives?

In light of the two articles you've just read, what is another scientific development you couldn't live without? Why?

_____

_____

Vocabulary Practice

Circle the description that best matches each boldfaced word.

1. an **appendage:**   your back   your leg

2. something that **contaminates:**   bacteria   salt

3. something **infectious:**   a cold   an injury

4. **keener** eyesight: gets better   gets worse

5. provides **mobility:**   an armchair   a car

6. a **pervasive** attitude: shared by many   shared by a few

7. **rehabilitation** needed for: a cold   a broken leg

8. a **serendipitous** discovery: lucky   unlucky

Academic Vocabulary in Writing

challenge	communicate	design	job	method

Stretch your imagination to think of a technology you could **design** to improve people's lives. Describe your idea, including at least one Academic Vocabulary word in your response. Definitions of these words are on page 419.

_____

_____

_____

Assessment Practice

DIRECTIONS Use the two selections you have just read to answer questions 1–4.

1 The author of "Robo-Legs" suggests that —

- **A** technologies like the C-Leg are very similar to prosthetics used centuries ago
- **B** the current generation of amputees do not view their prosthetics as something to hide
- **C** people like Cameron Clapp still lead very limited lives because of their disabilities
- **D** many users of technologies like the C-Leg are better athletes than people without disabilities

2 In "Eureka," James Phipps's family supported his involvement in Jenner's work because —

- **A** Phipps was already sick with the smallpox virus
- **B** Jenner had already proven that he could stop the spread of smallpox
- **C** they had invested a great deal of money in Jenner's work
- **D** of the potential to prevent the smallpox virus from spreading further

3 The quotation from Louis Pasteur at the end of "Eureka" serves to —

- **A** show that scientists do not always share the same opinions
- **B** explain that he too made his discoveries by accident
- **C** reinforce the main idea of the article
- **D** present an opposing view

4 Which element of organization is not used by both of the selections?

- **A** introducing ideas related to previous ideas
- **B** subheadings
- **C** ideas about how the topic has changed over time
- **D** stories of actual people

Guide to Computers
Technical Directions

Background

In "Robo-Legs," you read about new designs for artificial limbs that are improving the lives of amputees. Now you will read a guide to computers, the invention that made such new designs possible.

Standards Focus: Analyze Technical Directions

You have probably spent a lot of time working on a computer, but would you be able to set one up? If not, you could learn how by following a set of **technical directions.** Technical directions are a type of procedural text, or text that explains how to do something. Specifically, technical directions explain how to assemble or operate a device. Some products, such as computers, game systems, or cameras, are accompanied by instruction manuals that include technical directions. These directions usually contain:

• a parts list or glossary of key terms that you will need to know

• illustrations, diagrams, and photos that show key steps

• clearly labeled instructions that appear in a logical sequence

Readers are expected to connect information from all of these elements.

As you read the following guide, use this checklist to make sure you analyze the technical directions carefully and avoid mistakes. Remember, if steps are missing, or if you skip steps or perform them out of order, the device may not work.

Checklist

☐ **Scan** the heading and any subheadings to learn what process is being explained. Look for numbers or letters that tell you the order in which the steps should be followed.

☐ **Read** the entire directions through once. Figure out what you need to accomplish.

☐ **Go back and reread** the instructions one step at a time. After reading each step, do it.

☐ **Examine** the diagrams or other graphics. They may help you visualize what the written directions are telling you to do, or they may offer other information.

GUIDE TO COMPUTERS

What is a Computer?

Did a computer help you wake up this morning? You might think of a computer as something you use to send e-mail or surf the Internet, but computers are around you all of the time. Computers are in alarm clocks, cars, phones, and even MP3 players. An MP3 player, like the one in **FIGURE 1**, allows you to build your own music lists and carry thousands 10 of songs with you wherever you go.

A **computer** is an electronic device that performs tasks by processing and storing information. A computer performs a task when it is given a command and has the instructions necessary 20 to carry out that command. Computers do not operate by themselves, or "think." **Ⓐ**

FIGURE 1 Believe it or not, this MP3 player contains a computer!

SET A PURPOSE FOR READING

Read "Guide to Computers" to learn about computers, their basic functions, and how to set up a desktop computer.

Ⓕ OCUS ON FORM

"Guide to Computers" is an **instruction manual,** a booklet or electronic file that provides information about a product. Instruction manuals identify basic parts, describe functions, and provide technical directions for assembling or operating a product.

Ⓐ INSTRUCTION MANUAL

Reread lines 12–23. What are the basic functions of a computer?

_____

_____

_____

_____

_____

_____

_____

Basic Functions

The basic functions a computer performs are shown in **FIGURE 2.** The information you give to a computer is called **input.** Downloading songs onto your MP3 player or setting your alarm clock is a type of input. To perform a task, a computer **processes** the input, changing it to the desired form. Processing can mean

30 adding a list of numbers, executing a drawing, or even moving a piece of equipment. Input doesn't have to be processed immediately; it can be stored until it is needed. Computers store information in their **memory.** For example, your MP3 player stores the songs you have chosen to input. It can then process this stored information by playing the songs you request. **Output** is the final result of the task performed by the computer. The output of an MP3 player is the music you hear when you put on your headphones! B

B INSTRUCTION MANUAL
How does the diagram labeled Figure 2 help you understand the functions of a computer described in lines 24–39?

_____

_____

_____

_____

_____

_____

_____

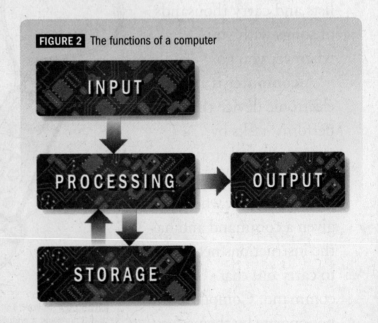

FIGURE 2 The functions of a computer

INPUT

PROCESSING → OUTPUT

STORAGE

The Internet—A Global Network

40 Thanks to high-speed connections and computer software, it is possible to connect many computers and allow them to communicate with one another. That's what the **Internet** is—a huge computer network consisting of millions of computers that can all share information with one another. **C**

How the Internet Works

Computers can connect to one another on the Internet by using a modem to dial into an Internet service provider, or ISP. A home computer connects to an ISP over a phone or cable line. A school, business, or other
50 group can connect all of its computers to form a local area network (LAN). Then, a single network connection can be used to connect the LAN to an ISP. As depicted in **FIGURE 3,** ISPs are connected globally by satellite. And that's how computers go global! **PAUSE & REFLECT**

G INSTRUCTION MANUAL
Reread lines 40–45. What is the purpose of the Internet?

_____

_____

_____

_____

_____

PAUSE & REFLECT
Acronyms, such as ISP and LAN, use the first letters of important words as a way to shorten a long term. Why do you think so many acronyms are associated with computer use?

_____

_____

_____

_____

_____

_____

FIGURE 3 Through a series of connections like these, every computer on the Internet can store information.

D INSTRUCTION MANUAL
How do the illustrations
in Figure 4 add to your
understanding of the
instructions?

_____

_____

_____

_____

_____

_____

_____

_____

_____

_____

_____

_____

_____

_____

_____

_____

_____

_____

Computer Hardware

For each function of a computer, there is a
corresponding part of the computer where that
function occurs. Hardware refers to the parts, or
equipment, that make up a computer. As you read
about each piece of hardware, refer to **FIGURE 4.**

Input Devices

60 An **input device** is a piece of hardware that
feeds information to the computer. You can enter
information into a computer by using a keyboard,
mouse, scanner, digitizing pad and pen, or digitizing
camera—or even your own voice!

Central Processing Unit

A computer performs tasks within an area called
the **central processing unit,** or CPU. In a personal
computer, the CPU is a microprocessor. Input goes
through the CPU for immediate processing or for

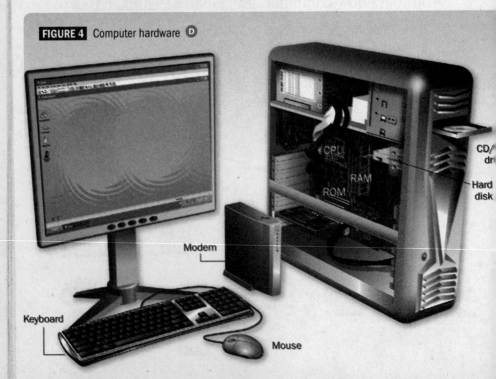

FIGURE 4 Computer hardware **D**

Keyboard

Mouse

Modem

CPU

RAM

ROM

CD/
dri

Hard
disk

storage in memory. The CPU is where the computer
70 does calculations, solves problems, and executes the
instructions it is given. Some computers now come
with two or more CPUs to process information more
effectively. **E**

Memory

Information can be stored in the computer's memory
until it is needed. CD-ROMs, DVDs, and flash
drives inserted into a computer and hard disks inside
a computer have memory to store information. Two
other types of memory are **ROM** (read-only memory)
and **RAM** (random-access memory).

80   ROM is permanent. It handles functions such
as computer start-up, maintenance, and hardware
management. ROM normally cannot be added to or
changed, and it cannot be lost when the computer is
turned off. On the other hand, RAM is temporary. It
stores information only while that information is being

E INSTRUCTION MANUAL
Reread lines 65–73. Underline
the sentence that explains what
the CPU does. Why might an
instruction manual explain what
input devices and the CPU do?

_____

_____

_____

_____

_____

_____

_____

_____

_____

_____

_____

_____

_____

_____

_____

_____

_____

_____

_____

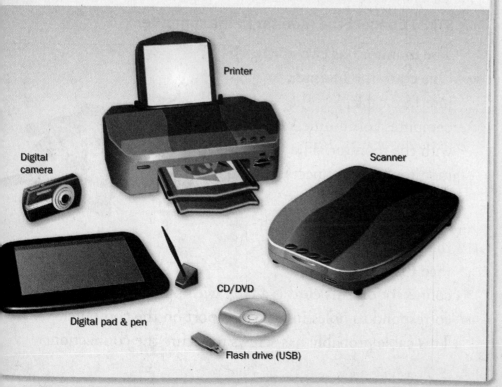

Printer

Digital
camera

Scanner

Digital pad & pen

CD/DVD

Flash drive (USB)

used. RAM is sometimes called working memory. The more RAM a computer has, the more information can be input and the more powerful the computer is. **G**

Output Devices

Once a computer performs a task, it shows the results of
90 the task on an **output device.** Monitors, printers, and speaker systems are all examples of output devices.

Modems

One piece of computer hardware that serves as an input device as well as an output device is a **modem**. Modems allow computers to communicate. One computer can input information into another computer over a telephone or cable line as long as each computer has its own network connection. In this way, modems permit computers to "talk" with each other. **G**

How to Set Up a Desktop Computer

STEP 1 Connect the monitor to the computer.

The monitor has two cords.
100 One cord, the monitor interface cable, lets the computer communicate with the monitor. The monitor cable connects to the video port (the port designated for monitors) at the back of the computer. (See **FIGURE 5.**) The connector on this cord is a plug with pins in it; the pins
110 correspond to holes in the video port on the computer. This cable probably has screws to secure the connection.

Monitor

The other cord is the monitor's power cord, which plugs into a wall outlet or surge protector, a plug-in device that protects electronic equipment from high-voltage electrical surges (see Step 5). **⊕**

STEP 2 Connect the printer to the computer.

The connector on the cable that is attached to your printer is most likely a USB cable.

120 USB ports (USB stands for Universal Serial Bus) can accept any device with a USB connector. Connect one end to the back of your printer. Then connect the other end to an available USB port on the back of your computer. (See **FIGURE 5.**) **⊙**

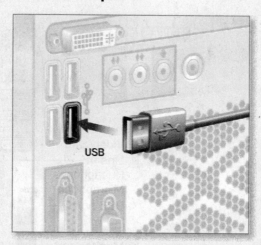

USB

STEP 3 Connect the keyboard and mouse.

Look at the connector on the cord that is attached to
130 the keyboard or mouse. If this connector is round, plug the cord into a matching port on the back of the computer. (See **FIGURE 5.**) If the connector on the cord is flat, plug it into any available USB port. (See Step 2 illustration.) If you are using a cordless keyboard or mouse, connect it to the computer using the manufacturer's technical directions.

Cordless mouse

⊕ TECHNICAL DIRECTIONS
Reread lines 99–115. Underline the names of the two types of cords discussed in Step 1. How can you tell the difference between the two cords?

_____

_____

_____

_____

_____

_____

⊙ TECHNICAL DIRECTIONS
Reread lines 116–128. Note that the directions say that the printer can be connected to any available USB port. Why do you think that there is more than one USB port?

_____

_____

_____

_____

_____

_____

J TECHNICAL DIRECTIONS
Study the graphic labeled
Figure 5. Why is this graphic
especially important for users?
Why do you think a number of
the graphic's parts are labeled?

_____

_____

_____

_____

_____

_____

_____

_____

_____

_____

_____

_____

_____

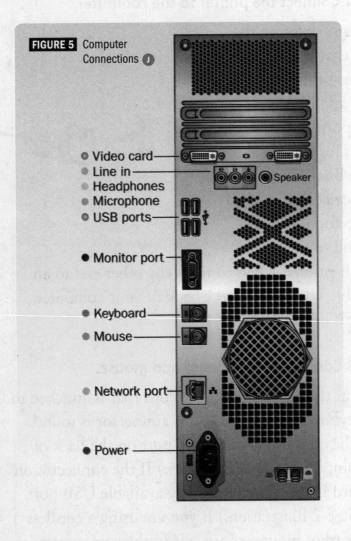

FIGURE 5 Computer Connections **J**

● Video card
● Line in
● Headphones
● Microphone
● USB ports
● Speaker
● Monitor port
● Keyboard
● Mouse
● Network port
● Power

Step 4 Connect the modem to the computer by using a network cable.

Connect the network cable to the network port on the back of
140 your computer. (See **FIGURE 5.**) Connect the other end of the network cable to your modem. As long as you have an active Internet connection,

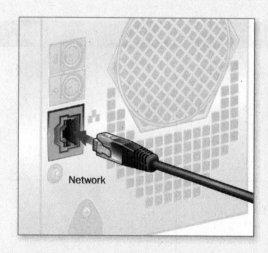

Network

the software should automatically detect that you are connected to the Internet when your computer starts. **Ⓚ**

Step 5 Connect the power cords.

The power cord is
150 a three-pronged, grounded cord that you attach to your computer. First, attach one end of the power cord to the computer; then plug the other end of the cord into a surge protector. (See

Power cord

FIGURE 5.) Plug the surge protector into a grounded
160 wall outlet. Turn on the monitor and then the computer, and you are ready to go! **Ⓛ**

Ⓚ TECHNICAL DIRECTIONS
Which step should you complete first—connecting to the printer or connecting to the modem? How do you know?

_____

_____

_____

_____

_____

_____

Ⓛ TECHNICAL DIRECTIONS
What would happen if you were to skip Step 5?

_____

_____

_____

_____

_____

_____

_____

Practicing Your Skills

Review the fourth item on the checklist on page 446. Think about whether the graphics in "Guide to Computers" fulfill their purpose, are easy to understand, and would be useful for someone setting up a computer. Then, use the chart below to assess the graphics' purpose, clarity, and usefulness.

Graphics	
Purpose	
Clarity	
Usefulness	

Analyze Technical Directions

What, if any, information seems to be missing from the directions in "Guide to Computers"? What information seems to be extraneous, or not really necessary? Is the information in the guide up to date? Explain your answer, citing examples from the text.

_____

_____

_____

_____

_____

Academic Vocabulary in Writing

challenge	communicate	design	job	method

Many consumers expect to be able to use new technology right "out of the box," meaning that they do not want to read a manual or a set of technical directions to get started. Why might this expectation present a **challenge** for manufacturers who **design** computers? Include at least one Academic Vocabulary word in your response. Definitions of these words are on page 419.

_____

_____

_____

_____

Assessment Practice

DIRECTIONS Use "Guide to Computers" to answer questions 1–4.

1 Both diagrams and text are used in this manual —
   - (A) because some users need only diagrams, while others cannot follow diagrams
   - (B) because not all computers look the same
   - (C) to accommodate users who do not speak English
   - (D) to explain reasons for the directions, and to make the instructions easier to follow

2 Which of the following is NOT an example of an output device?
   - (A) a printer
   - (B) a speaker system
   - (C) a mouse
   - (D) a monitor

3 What purpose do pages 447–449 of the guide serve?
   - (A) They show the steps to follow to set up a computer.
   - (B) They show different computer components.
   - (C) They give background on how a computer works and describe the Internet.
   - (D) They explain how the Internet works.

4 According to the guide, what step should you take after you connect the printer to the monitor?
   - (A) connect the power cords
   - (B) connect the modem to the computer
   - (C) connect the printer to the computer
   - (D) connect the monitor to the computer

UNIT 9

State Your Case

ARGUMENT AND PERSUASION

Be sure to read the Text Analysis Workshop on pp. 982–987 in *Holt McDougal Literature*.

Resolved: That the federal government should establish a policy to substantially increase renewable energy use in the United States

Academic Vocabulary for Unit 9

Academic Vocabulary is the language you use to discuss literary and informational texts. Preview the following Academic Vocabulary words. You will use these words as you write and talk about the selections in this unit.

accurate (ăkʹyər-ĭt) *adj.* without error, factual; correct and exact

How can you confirm that the writer's evidence is accurate?

bias (bīʹəs) *n.* a preference for something or someone that prevents fair decision-making

In what ways does the article reveal the writer's bias?

contrast (kən-trăstʹ) *v.* to show differences in one or more things when compared to each other

Contrast the two versions of the events. How are they different?

convince (kən-vĭnsʹ) *v.* to persuade; to cause one to feel sure about something

Give reasons that will convince others to agree with your opinion.

logic (lŏjʹĭk) *n.* correct reasoning; a system of reasoning

Explain the logic that supports your opinion.

Think of a book or a movie that you greatly enjoyed. How might you **convince** a friend of the quality of the work? What **logic** would you use? Use at least two Academic Vocabulary words in your response.

_____

_____

_____

_____

_____

Zoos: Myth and Reality
Online Article by Rob Laidlaw

Zoos Connect Us to the Natural World
Opinion Piece by Michael Hutchins

Should WILDLIFE stay wild?

Close your eyes and picture an elephant. Are you picturing it in the zoo or in the wild? As humans inhabit more and more of the earth's land, some species of wildlife are more likely to be found in captivity than in their natural habitat. But is this a good thing? The writers of the selections you're about to read have different views on whether or not zoos are good for humans and animals.

LIST IT With a group, make a list of the good things and bad things about zoos. Do the pros outnumber the cons, or vice versa? Discuss whether you think zoos are a good idea.

Text Analysis: Argument

Effective arguments include the elements shown in the graphic below.

> **Claim:** the writer's position on an issue or problem

> **Support:** reasons and evidence that back up the claim

> **Counterargument:** arguments made to disprove an opposing viewpoint

Look for the claim and support in both selections. Both selections also include a counterargument. In the first selection the author summarizes the zoo industry's argument for having and maintaining zoos, and then argues against it. Try to identify the counterargument in the second selection.

As you read each selection, look for the elements of the author's argument. Then ask yourself whether the writer's argument is strong enough and broad enough to adequately support the writer's conclusion.

Pros

1. *They keep animals safe.*

2. _____

3. _____

4. _____

5. _____

Cons

1. _____

2. _____

3. _____

4. _____

5. _____

Reading Skill: Set a Purpose for Reading

When you **set a purpose** for reading, you decide what you want to accomplish as you read. In this lesson, your purpose is to compare and contrast two persuasive texts that reach different conclusions about the same topic. As you read, complete the chart below by writing down the line numbers that tell where the elements of each argument are.

	Myth and Reality	**. . . Natural World**
Claim	*lines 5–7*	
Support		
Conclusion		

Vocabulary in Context

Note: Words are listed in the order in which they appear in the selections.

propaganda (prŏp′ə-găn′də) *n.* information that supports a certain cause
   Zoos' **propaganda** *claims that their purpose is conservation.*

deprivation (dĕp′rə-vā′shən) *n.* the condition of not having one's needs met; a lack of
   Some animals face lives of **deprivation** *in unsuitable habitats.*

futility (fyōō-tĭl′ĭ-tē) *n.* uselessness
   The **futility** *of releasing captive animals into the wild is proven.*

sterile (stĕr′əl) *adj.* barren; lacking vitality
   In the past, animals were housed in **sterile,** *barren cages.*

languish (lăng′gwĭsh) *v.* to lose strength and vitality
   These animals would **languish** *and die from improper care.*

counterpart (koun′tər-pärt′) *n.* one that has the same functions and traits as another
   Captive animals' lives differ from their wild **counterparts.**

exotic (ĭg-zŏt′ĭk) *adj.* foreign; unusual; exciting
   Few people go to **exotic** *lands to see animals in the wild.*

exploit (ĕk′sploit′) *v.* to use for selfish purposes
   Many disagree about whether zoos **exploit** *or protect animals.*

Vocabulary Practice

Review the vocabulary words and think about their meanings. Then use the words to discuss your opinion about zoos with a partner.

SET A PURPOSE FOR READING

Read this article about zoos to learn the author's feelings about the treatment of animals in captivity.

Ⓐ ARGUMENT

Based on the information in the Background paragraph, what do you expect the author's claim about zoos will be?

_____

_____

_____

_____

File   Edit   View   Favorites   Tools   Help

Back   Forward   Stop   Refresh   Home   Search   Mail   Print

Zoos:
Myth and Reality

Online Article by Rob Laidlaw

BACKGROUND Rob Laidlaw has dedicated himself to improving the conditions of animals in captivity. He has worked with Canada's government on establishing standards for zoos, developed a humane stray dog program, and investigated Canada's role in the pet reptile trade. His interest in the well-being of animals is clear in the article you are about to read. Ⓐ

🌐 Internet

In recent years, zoos have become the target of intense public scrutiny and criticism. In response, many have tried to repackage themselves as institutions devoted to wildlife conservation, public education, and animal welfare. But most zoos fail to live up to their own **propaganda** and vast numbers of zoo animals continue to endure lives of misery and **deprivation**. ⓑ

Nearly every zoo, from the smallest amateur operation to the largest professional facilities, claims to be making
10 important contributions to conservation, usually through participation in endangered species captive propagation initiatives and public education programming. The zoo world buzzword[1] of the moment is "conservation."

Yet, with an estimated 10,000 organized zoos worldwide, representing tens of thousands of human workers and billions of dollars in operating budgets, only a tiny percentage allocate the resources necessary to participate in captive propagation initiatives, and fewer still provide any real support for the *in situ*[2]
20 protection of wildlife and their natural habitat.

So far, the record on reintroductions to the wild is dismal. Only 16 species have established self-sustaining populations in the wild as a result of captive breeding efforts, and most of those programs were initiated by government wildlife agencies—not zoos. The contribution of zoos in this regard has been

---

1. **buzzword:** a word or phrase connected with a specialized field or group that sounds important or technical and is usually used to impress those outside the group.

2. **in situ** (ĭn sē'tōō): a Latin phrase; in zoology, it refers to studying an animal without removing it from its natural habitat.

---

propaganda (prŏp'ə-găn'də) *n.* information that supports a certain cause

deprivation (dĕp'rə-vā'shən) *n.* the condition of not having one's needs met; a lack of

ⓑ **ARGUMENT**
According to Laidlaw, what three benefits do many zoos say they offer? Underline them. What does Laidlaw claim instead?

C ARGUMENT
Reread lines 21–29. Underline the author's opinion stated in line 21. Circle the facts that support that opinion.

futility (fyōō-tĭl'ĭ-tē) *n.* uselessness

D ARGUMENT
Reread lines 30–46. What **counterargument** does the author present to disprove the zoos' claim that they are educating the public?

_____

_____

_____

_____

_____

_____

_____

_____

_____

_____

_____

_____

File   Edit   View   Favorites   Tools   Help

Back   Forward   Stop   Refresh   Home   Search   Mail   Print

minimal, and often involves supplementing existing wild populations with a small number of captive-born individuals who are ill-prepared for life in the wild. **C**

30   As the <u>futility</u> of captive breeding as a major conservation tool becomes evident to those in the industry, many zoos are now turning to education to justify themselves. Yet, zoos claim that they teach visitors about wildlife conservation and habitat protection, and their contention that they motivate members of the public to become directly involved in wildlife conservation work doesn't stand up to scrutiny. The truth is that scant empirical evidence exists to prove that the primary vehicle for education

40   in most zoos—the animal in the cage—actually teaches anyone anything. In fact, viewing animals in cages may be counterproductive educationally by conveying the wrong kinds of messages to the public. Also, the legions[3] of conservationists that zoos should have produced, if their claims were true, have never materialized. **D**

Humane Treatment

But there is one issue about which there appears to be widespread agreement—at least in principle. So long as wild animals are kept in captivity, they ought to be

50   treated humanely.

Internet

---

3. **legions** (lē'jənz): large numbers.

Studies have shown that animals can suffer physically, mentally, and emotionally. For this reason, captive environments must be complex enough to compensate for the lack of natural freedom and choice, and they must facilitate expression of natural movement and behavior patterns. This principle has been widely espoused by the modern zoo community in various articles, books, and television documentaries. **E**

Yet despite the best of intentions or claims, most
60 animals in zoos in North America are still consigned to lead miserable lives in undersized, impoverished enclosures, both old and new, that fail to meet their biological and behavioral needs. Many in the zoo industry will bristle[4] at this statement and point to numerous improvements in the zoo field. They'll claim they've shifted from menagerie-style[5] entertainment centers where animals were displayed in barred, <u>sterile</u>, biologically irrelevant cages, to kinder, gentler, more scientifically-based kinds of institutions.

70 But many of the "advances" in zoo animal housing and husbandry are superficial and provide little benefit to the animals. For example, the many new, heavily promoted, Arctic "art deco" polar bear exhibits that are springing up in zoos across the continent consistently ignore the natural biology and behavior of these animals. The artificial rockwork and hard floor surfaces typically resemble a Flintstones movie set more

E ARGUMENT
Reread lines 51–58. Underline the support the author provides here. Explain whether this support is convincing to you.

_____
_____
_____
_____
_____
_____
_____

sterile (stĕr′əl) *adj.* barren; lacking vitality

Why would living in sterile cages have been difficult for wild animals?

_____
_____
_____
_____
_____
_____

---

4. **bristle** (brĭs′əl): to show annoyance or anger.
5. **menagerie** (mə-năj′ə-rē): a collection of live wild animals on display.

F ARGUMENT
Reread lines 59–88. What part
of the zoo industry's argument
does Laidlaw oppose here?

_____

_____

_____

_____

_____

Underline the sentence in which
Laidlaw says that this part of the
industry's argument is false.

than the natural Arctic ice and tundra habitat of polar
bears. These exhibits are made for the public and dupe
them into believing things are getting better. What
they really achieve is more misery and deprivation.

In addition, many new exhibits are hardly larger
than the sterile, barred cages of days gone by. And one
look at the prison-like, off-display holding and service
areas in most zoos, where many animals spend a good
portion of their lives, is proof of the hypocrisy of zoo
claims that things are better for the animals than they
were in the past. **F**

Behind the Invisible Bars

If not all is well behind the invisible bars of North
America's more luxurious zoos, a more transparent
problem is found in the hundreds of substandard roadside
zoos that dot the continent. These amateurish operations
fall far below any professional standard and do nothing
but cause misery and death to thousands of animals.

My own investigations have revealed animals in
visible distress lying unprotected from the full glare of
the hot summer sun; primates in barren cages with no
opportunity to climb; groups of black bears begging for
marshmallows as they sit in stagnant moats of excrement-
filled water, scarred and wounded from fighting;
nocturnal[6] animals kept without shade or privacy;

Internet

---

6. **nocturnal** (nŏk-tûr′nəl): habitually active at night and asleep during the
daytime.

File   Edit   View   Favorites   Tools   Help

Back   Forward   Stop   Refresh   Home   Search   Mail   Print

animals without water; and the list goes on and on.

PAUSE & REFLECT

Many zoos, including those that meet industry
guidelines, also annually produce a predictable surplus
in animals that often end up in the hands of private
collectors, animal auctions, circuses and novelty acts,
substandard zoos, and even "canned hunt" operations
where they're shot as trophies.

A look at compliance with the zoo industry's
110 own standards (which in the author's view do not
necessarily constitute adequate standards) demonstrates
how bad the situation really is. Of the estimated 200
public display facilities in Canada, only 26—slightly
more than 10 percent—have been deemed to meet the
standards of the Canadian Association of Zoos and
Aquariums (CAZA).

In the U.S., out of the 1,800–2,000 licensed
exhibitors of wild animals (which includes biomedical
research institutions, breeding facilities, small exhibitors,
120 travelling shows, educational programs using live
animals, zoos and aquariums), about 175 are accredited
by the American Zoo and Aquarium Association (AZA),
equivalent to less than 10 percent of all facilities. **G**

Times are changing, and with them, public
attitudes. Increasingly, members of the public find the

Internet

PAUSE & REFLECT
Why are roadside zoos even
worse than accredited zoos,
according to Laidlaw?

_____

_____

_____

_____

_____

_____

_____

G ARGUMENT
Laidlaw states that accredited
zoos make up only 10 percent
of "licensed exhibitors of wild
animals." What part of his claim
does this fact help him support?
For help, refer to his original
claim in lines 5–7.

_____

_____

_____

_____

_____

H ARGUMENT
Reread lines 144–152. What is Laidlaw's conclusion? Write it in your chart.

Conclusion

Explain whether the evidence he has presented effectively supports his conclusion.

File   Edit   View   Favorites   Tools   Help

Back   Forward   Stop   Refresh   Home   Search   Mail   Print

confinement of animals in substandard conditions offensive. Zoos across the continent are feeling the pressure. They have to accept that if wild animals are to be kept in captivity, their needs must be met.

130   Are there good captive environments where the biological and behavioral needs of animals are being satisfied? The answer is yes. A recent Zoocheck Canada survey of black bear and gray wolf facilities in North America revealed a number of outstanding exhibits where the animals displayed an extensive range of natural movements and behaviors. But they are few and far between.

Can zoos make a useful contribution to conservation and education? Again, the answer is yes.
140 The Durrell Wildlife Conservation Trust (Jersey Zoo) in the U.K., for example, clearly shows that zoos can become leaders in conservation education and wildlife protection. But few actually do.

I can't understand why the more responsible segments of the zoo industry have not come to their senses and acknowledged the obvious—the present state of zoos is untenable. Either zoos can voluntarily adopt humane policies and practices, push for the closure of substandard facilities, and participate in
150 advocating for laws to help wildlife, or they can be dragged kicking and screaming into the new millennium. It's their choice. **H**

Internet

Zoos Connect Us to the Natural World ●

Opinion Piece by Michael Hutchins

BACKGROUND As the executive director of the Wildlife Society, Michael Hutchins has traveled to more than 33 countries. His efforts have involved trapping and tagging mountain goats in the Olympic Mountains, scuba diving with manta rays, and tracking jaguars.

The scene of Little Joe, the curious young gorilla out of his zoo exhibit wandering through Franklin Park,[1] certainly sold papers last month. But less well covered was the very real success that our nation's

---

1. **Franklin Park:** a Boston, Massachusetts, park that has a zoo in it.

SET A PURPOSE FOR READING

Read to discover this author's opinion of zoos.

● ARGUMENT
Based on the title, what is one reason Hutchins will probably give for having and maintaining good zoos?

_____

_____

_____

_____

_____

_____

J ARGUMENT
Reread lines 1–6. What point is Hutchins making here?

_____

_____

_____

_____

languish (lăng′gwĭsh) *v.* to lose strength and vitality

counterpart (koun′tər-pärt′) *n.* one that has the same functions and traits as another

K ARGUMENT
How does Hutchins support the statement that zoos have had some very real successes in nurturing animals?

_____

_____

_____

_____

_____

_____

_____

_____

best zoos have had in nurturing the animals who live within their walls. **J**

At the turn of the last century, gorillas—these strange, human-like creatures from "darkest Africa"—still flourished in the wild and thoroughly captivated 10 the American public. But once relocated from their jungle habitat, gorillas <u>languished</u>. Zoos found it impossible to keep the animals alive for more than a few weeks since little was known about the natural history of gorillas. Even as late as the 1960s and '70s, most zoo gorillas were kept singly or in pairs in small, sterile concrete and tile cages and fed inappropriate foods. But things began to change as information from field and zoo biologists brought more understanding of both the physiological and psychological needs of these 20 remarkable creatures.

Gorillas in today's zoos are typically kept in large, naturalistic exhibits, maintained in appropriate social groupings, fed nutritionally appropriate diets, and provided with excellent veterinary care. The result is that zoo gorillas exhibit behavior similar to their wild <u>counterparts</u>, reproduce consistently, and live longer on average than they do in nature. **K**

In fact, recent advances in exhibit design, animal nutrition, genetic management, and veterinary medicine 30 have revolutionized animal welfare and care in our zoos. Today, more than 90 percent of mammals housed in accredited[2] facilities were born in zoos and not taken from the wild. They are under the charge of animal curators and caretakers who are trained professionals, with both academic and practical experience. Furthermore, accredited zoos have become "learning organizations" that constantly strive to improve the lives and health of the animals in their care.

40 So why should we have gorillas or any other wild animals in zoos today? Before speculating about the role of these institutions in contemporary society, I must first draw a distinction between accredited zoos and other kinds of facilities that keep wild animals for public display. All of my statements are focused exclusively on the 213 facilities accredited by the American Zoo and Aquarium Association. AZA members undergo a detailed peer-review[3] process, which is more comprehensive than existing local, state, or federal regulations.

50 At a time when children learn more about the world around them from television and computers than from personal experience, modern zoos—and aquariums, for that matter—offer fun, safe opportunities to view living wild animals up close and personal. In 2002, over 140 million people visited AZA zoos and aquariums, more than attended all professional baseball, football, basketball, and ice hockey games combined. Modern zoological parks provide us a wonderful opportunity to build awareness and 60 appreciation of wildlife in an increasingly urbanized populace—a group that is becoming progressively disconnected from the natural world. **L**

Only a small percentage of our nation's citizens can afford to travel to <u>exotic</u> locations to view wild tigers,

L ARGUMENT
In the chart below, restate Hutchins's claim in your own words. Then record the evidence he cites to support his claim.

Claim

↓

Support

---

2. **accredited** (ə-krĕd′ĭtəd): meeting certain standards that have been set by a respected authority (in this case, the American Zoo and Aquarium Association).

3. **peer-review:** evaluation by equals (in this case, other zoo officials).

exotic (ĭg-zŏt′ĭk) *adj.* foreign; unusual; exciting

elephants, or giant pandas or to dive with sharks or moray eels. Zoos provide exhilarating experiences that can't be replicated on two-dimensional television or computer screens. Seeing, smelling, and in some cases even touching real, live animals is a powerful

70 experience. **PAUSE & REFLECT**

The best zoos include conservation, education, and science among their core missions,[4] and the animals in their collections can be viewed as ambassadors for their counterparts in the wild. Many species are endangered or threatened and would have little chance of survival without human intervention. Increasingly, zoos are playing an important role in those efforts. Last year alone, AZA member institutions supported 1,400 field conservation[5] and associated educational and scientific

80 projects in over 80 countries worldwide. These ranged from restoring habitat for endangered Karner blue butterflies[6] in Ohio to attempting to curb the illegal, commercial harvest of wildlife for meat in Africa to rehabilitating injured marine mammals and sea turtles and returning them to the sea.

Some critics have characterized zoos and aquariums as "<u>exploiting</u>" animals for personal financial gain, but that's not true of the professionals I know. As a curatorial intern at New York's Bronx Zoo/Wildlife

90 Conservation Society in the late 1980s, I went on rounds with the staff veterinarians as they cared for

PAUSE & REFLECT
Do you find Hutchins's argument convincing so far? Give reasons for your answer.

_____

_____

_____

_____

_____

_____

_____

exploit (ĕk'sploit') *v.* to use for selfish purposes

4. **core missions:** central goals and beliefs.
5. **field conservation:** conservation of wild organisms in their natural habitats (not in zoos).
6. **Karner blue butterflies:** endangered butterflies of the northern U.S. and Canada.

sick and injured animals. They worked long hours for comparatively little pay, and their dedication was inspiring. I also witnessed animal keepers weeping over the loss of their favorite animals and spending their own money to attend training programs to improve their knowledge and skills.

In my opinion, a society that values wildlife and nature should support our best zoos and aquariums. 100 Habitat conservation is the key to saving endangered species, and professionally managed zoos and aquariums and their expert, dedicated staffs play a vital role by supporting on-the-ground conservation efforts and by encouraging people to care for and learn about wildlife and nature.

ⓜ ARGUMENT
Reread lines 86–97. Underline the opposing viewpoint Hitchins presents. What is his **counterargument?**

_____

_____

_____

_____

_____

_____

_____

Zoos and aquariums are reinventing themselves, but while many are in the process of rebuilding their aging infrastructures, still others retain vestiges of the past or have been hit hard by recent state or local budget cuts.
110 Good zoos and aquariums are invaluable community assets, and they deserve our attention and enthusiastic support. **Ⓝ**

Ⓝ ARGUMENT

Reread lines 106–112 and underline Hutchins's conclusion. Then tell whether you think his argument is broad enough to support his conclusion.

_____

_____

_____

_____

Text Analysis: Argument

In the chart below, identify each author's claim and list three reasons or pieces of evidence used to support each claim.

"Zoos: Myth and Reality"
Claim:

↓

1.

2.

3.

"Zoos Connect Us to the Natural World"
Claim:

↓

1.

2.

3.

Reading Skill: Set a Purpose for Reading

Your purpose for reading was to compare and contrast these two persuasive texts that reach different conclusions about the same topic. In the Venn diagram below, tell how the persuasive texts were similar and different. Consider each writer's claims, support, and conclusion in your response.

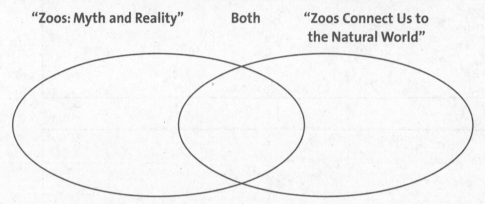

"Zoos: Myth and Reality"   Both   "Zoos Connect Us to the Natural World"

Should WILDLIFE stay wild?

Refer to the list you made of the good and bad things about zoos. What might you add to this list now that you have read these two articles?

_____

_____

_____

Vocabulary Practice

For each item, choose the word that differs most in meaning from the other words.

1. **(a)** suffer, **(b)** languish, **(c)** enjoy, **(d)** endure

2. **(a)** exploit, **(b)** aid, **(c)** help, **(d)** befriend

3. **(a)** hope **(b)** uselessness, **(c)** futility, **(d)** meaninglessness

4. **(a)** unadorned, **(b)** desolate, **(c)** lush, **(d)** sterile

5. **(a)** suffering, **(b)** deprivation, **(c)** lack, **(d)** wealth

6. **(a)** persuasion **(b)** truth **(c)** propaganda, **(d)** bias

7. **(a)** boss, **(b)** equal, **(c)** peer, **(d)** counterpart

8. **(a)** ordinary, **(b)** exotic, **(c)** foreign, **(d)** extraordinary

Academic Vocabulary in Writing

accurate	bias	contrast	convince	logic

What is your opinion of keeping animals in zoos? In a paragraph, state your opinion along with two reasons you might give to **convince** someone to adopt it. Use at least one Academic Vocabulary word in your paragraph. Definitions of these words are on page 459.

_____

_____

_____

Assessment Practice

DIRECTIONS Use "Zoos: Myth and Reality" and "Zoos Connect Us to the Natural World" to answer questions 1–6.

1 According to "Zoos: Myth and Reality," what can happen to surplus animals from zoos?

   (A) They can be left to die.
   (B) They can become pets.
   (C) They can be used in hunts.
   (D) They can be neglected by zookeepers.

2 According to Laidlaw, how are the new zoo exhibits similar to the older ones?

   (A) They help educate the public.
   (B) They are nearly as small and sterile.
   (C) They mimic the animals' natural habitats.
   (D) They have artificial rockwork and hard floors.

3 Which statement supports Laidlaw's claim that zoos are not as good as they say they are?

   (A) *So far, the record on reintroductions to the wild is dismal.*
   (B) *The zoo world buzzword of the moment is "conservation."*
   (C) *So long as wild animals are kept in captivity, they ought to be treated humanely.*
   (D) *Many zoos are now turning to education to justify themselves.*

4 According to "Zoos Connect Us to the Natural World," what is one way zoos benefit people?

   (A) They provide entertainment.
   (B) They keep animals safe and healthy.
   (C) They educate people about animals.
   (D) They are beautiful respites from urban life.

5 What led to changes in the treatment of zoo gorillas?

   (A) information from biologists
   (B) falling profits and attendance
   (C) protests by animal-rights groups
   (D) a massive letter-writing campaign

6 What do both writers agree about?

   (A) It is important to treat zoo animals well.
   (B) Zoos do a good job of educating the public.
   (C) Zoos conservation efforts have been significant.
   (D) Captive breeding helps preserve endangered species.

Position on Dodgeball in Physical Education
Position Statement by the National Association for Sport and Physical Education

The Weak Shall Inherit the Gym
Opinion Piece by Rick Reilly

Are all GAMES worth playing?

Have you ever watched a customer at a carnival game spend 20 or 30 dollars trying to win a cheap stuffed animal? Seeing this might make you question whether all games are worth playing. You're about to read two very different opinions on whether the game of dodgeball is fun or torture for those who play it.

LIST IT Make two lists. On the first, list five games you think are worth playing. On the second, list five games you think are not worth the time, money, or risk. Compare your lists with a partner's. Do any games appear on both the good and not-so-good lists?

Text Analysis: Persuasion

Writers rely on more than arguments to be convincing. They may use a tone that encourages readers to take their side or use **persuasive techniques** such as these:

	Emotional Appeals	**Ethical Appeals**
What Is It?	words, descriptions, or images that stir up strong feelings, such as pity, fear, or anger	attempts to gain moral support for a claim by linking the claim to a widely-accepted value
Example	"Innocent puppies are horribly mistreated in puppy mills."	"We need this law because animals deserve decent treatment."

As you read, notice the ways the authors use persuasive techniques in their arguments.

Games Worth Playing

1. board games
2. _____
3. _____
4. _____
5. _____

Games Not Worth Playing

1. _____
2. _____
3. _____
4. _____
5. _____

Reading Skill: Analyze Rhetoric and Reasoning

A **rhetorical fallacy** is writing that is false or misleading. A **logical fallacy** is an error in reasoning. Here are three common fallacies:

- **Loaded terms**—words or phrases with strongly positive or negative connotations: *immature* is more negative than *young*.

- **Leading questions**—questions that contain their own answer, such as, "You don't want all the forests to disappear, do you?"

- **Caricatures**—cartoon-like portrayals of opposing arguments, such as, "They want you to go around hugging trees."

As you read the selections, you'll record and analyze a variety of fallacies in a chart like the one below.

	Position on Dodgeball in Physical Education	The Weak Shall Inherit the Gym
Fallacies		Loaded terms: "Whiners"

Vocabulary in Context

Note: Words are listed in the order in which they appear in the selections.

impropriety (ĭm′prə-prī′ĭ-tē) *n.* an unsuitable or inappropriate act or quality
*If you witness someone cheating, report the **impropriety**.*

adequately (ăd′ĭ-kwĭt-lē) *adv.* enough to satisfy a requirement or meet a need
*Students are not **adequately** prepared for competition.*

eliminate (ĭ-lĭm′ə-nāt′) *v.* to remove from consideration by defeating
*We were able to **eliminate** the other players one by one.*

ban (băn) *v.* to prohibit
*Our school might **ban** the game of dodgeball.*

aggression (ə-grĕsh′ən) *n.* hostile or destructive behavior or action
*Is dodgeball a safe way to take out **aggression**?*

Vocabulary Practice

Review the vocabulary words and think about their meanings. Then discuss with a partner whether playing dodgeball in school is a good idea. Try to use some of the vocabulary words in your discussion.

SET A PURPOSE FOR READING

Read this selection to learn one group's opinion of whether or not dodgeball should be played at your school.

Position on Dodgeball in Physical Education

National Association for Sport and Physical Education

A **PERSUASION**
Reread the Background paragraph. Underline the types of professionals involved in NASPE. What opinion of dodgeball would you expect the group to have?

_____

_____

_____

BACKGROUND The National Association for Sport and Physical Education, or NASPE, is made up of gym teachers, coaches, athletic directors, athletic trainers, sports management professionals, researchers, and college faculty. By researching, developing standards, and spreading information, NASPE helps students learn about fitness and stay active all their lives. **A**

With the recent release of both a movie and television show about dodgeball, debate about the game's merits and <u>improprieties</u> has escalated in the media and on the NASPE listserv.[1] Thus, the National Association for Sport and Physical Education (NASPE) would like to reiterate its position about including dodgeball in school physical education programs.

NASPE believes that dodgeball is **not** an appropriate
10 activity for K–12 school physical education programs. The purpose of physical education is to provide students with:

- The knowledge, skills, and confidence needed to be physically active for a lifetime

- A daily dose of physical activity for health benefits

- Positive experiences so that kids want to be physically active outside of physical education class and throughout their lifetime

The goals of physical education can be obtained
20 through a wide variety of appropriate physical activities. **B**

Getting and keeping children and adolescents active is one of the biggest challenges facing parents and youth leaders.

- 61.5% of children aged 9–13 years do not participate in any organized physical activity during their non-school hours and 22.6% do not engage in any free-time physical activity.

impropriety (ĭm′prə-prī′ĭ-tē)
n. an unsuitable or inappropriate act or quality

B PERSUASION
Underline the NASPE's position on dodgeball in school physical education programs.

---

1. **listserv** (lĭst-sûrv): an e-mail list that allows a group of people to hold a discussion by writing to each other via the Internet.

adequately (ăd´ĭ-kwĭt-lē) *adv.*
enough to satisfy a requirement
or meet a need

⊙ PERSUASION
Reread lines 25–33. Based on
these lines, what word or phrase
would you use to describe the
tone of this document?

_____

_____

**⊙ ANALYZE RHETORIC
AND REASONING**
Reread lines 34–42, in which the
association describes a "quality"
physical education class. Which
type of **rhetorical fallacy** is
shown by the use of the word
quality? Write it in your chart.

Fallacies
_____
_____
_____
_____
_____
_____
_____

eliminate (ĭ-lĭm´ə-nāt´) *v.* to
remove from consideration by
defeating

- One-third of high school students are not
  adequately active and over 10% do not participate
  in any physical activity at all.

- 16% of U.S. youth aged 6–19 are overweight—triple
  the proportion of 25 years ago. **⊙**

According to NASPE's *Appropriate Practices for
Elementary School Physical Education* (2000), "in a
quality physical education class teachers involve ALL
children in activities that allow them to participate
actively, both physically and mentally. Activities
such as relay races, dodgeball, and elimination tag
provide limited opportunities for everyone in the class,
especially the slower, less agile students who need the
activity the most." **⊙**

The students who are **eliminated** first in dodgeball
are typically the ones who most need to be active and
practice their skills. Many times these students are also
the ones with the least amount of confidence in their
physical abilities. Being targeted because they are the
"weaker" players, and being hit by a hard-thrown ball,
does not help kids to develop confidence.

The arguments most often heard in favor of dodgeball
are that it allows for the practice of important physical
skills—and kids like it.

- Dodgeball does provide a means of practicing some important physical skills—running, dodging, throwing, and catching. However, there are many activities that allow practice of these skills without using human targets or eliminating students from play.

60 - Some kids may like it—the most skilled, the most confident. But many do not! Certainly not the student who gets hit hard in the stomach, head, or groin. And it is not appropriate to teach our children that you win by hurting others. **ⓔ**

In a recent article about the new GSN (games network) TV show called "Extreme Dodgeball," there is talk of "developing and executing extreme strategies to annihilate opponents" and the use of terms such as "throw-to-kill ratios," and "headshots." NASPE asks, "Is this the type of game that you want children to be
70 exposed to?" **ⓕ**

ⓔ PERSUASION
Reread lines 59–63. Underline the sentence in which an **emotional appeal** is being made. Then put a box around the sentence in which an **ethical appeal** is made. Are these persuasive techniques effective? Explain.

_____

_____

_____

_____

_____

_____

_____

ⓕ ANALYZE RHETORIC AND REASONING
A **leading question** is a question that contains its answer. A **rhetorical question** is one that has such an obvious answer that it does not require a reply. Reread lines 69–70. Which type of question is this? Explain.

_____

_____

_____

_____

**SET A PURPOSE
FOR READING**
Read this selection to
discover another opinion
on playing dodgeball.

The Weak Shall Inherit the Gym

Opinion Piece by Rick Reilly

**Ⓖ ANALYZE RHETORIC
AND REASONING**
What **loaded term** does Reilly
use in his introduction? Record it
on your chart.

Fallacies

BACKGROUND Rick Reilly has been called "one of the
funniest humans on the planet." A large part of his
reputation rests on his writing about sports. He has written
about such topics as facing fastballs from eight-time all-star
Nolan Ryan and playing 108 holes of golf in one day. He has
been voted National Sportswriter of the Year 10 times.

Not to alarm you, but America is going softer
than left-out butter. Exhibit 9,137: Schools
have started banning dodgeball. Ⓖ

I kid you not. Dodgeball has been outlawed by
some school districts in New York, Texas, Utah and
Virginia. Many more are thinking about it, like Cecil

County, Md., where the school board wants to **ban** any game with "human targets." **H**

Human targets? What's tag? What's a snowball fight?
10 What's a close play at second? Neil Williams, a physical education professor at Eastern Connecticut State, says dodgeball has to go because it "encourages the best to pick on the weak." Noooo! You mean there's weak in the world? There's strong? Of course there is, and dodgeball is one of the first opportunities in life to figure out which one you are and how you're going to deal with it. **I**

We had a bully, Big Joe, in our seventh grade. Must have weighed 225 pounds, . . . We also had a kid named Melvin, who was so thin we could've faxed
20 him from class to class. I'll never forget the dodgeball game in which Big Joe had a ball in each hand and one sandwiched between his knees, firing at our side like a human tennis-ball machine, when, all of a sudden, he got plunked. . . . Joe whirled around to see who'd done it and saw that it was none other than Melvin, all 83 pounds of him, most of it smile.

Some of these . . . whiners say dodgeball is inappropriate in these violent times. Are you kidding? Dodgeball is one of the few times in life when you get
30 to let out your **aggressions**, no questions asked. We don't need less dodgeball in schools, we need more!

I know what all these . . . parents want. They want their Ambers and their Alexanders to grow up in a cozy womb of noncompetition, where everybody shares tofu[1] and Little Red Riding Hood and the big, bad wolf set up

---

1. **tofu** (tō'fōō): a protein-rich soybean curd that many vegetarians eat in place of meat.

ban (băn) *v.* to prohibit

H PERSUASION
What word or phrase would you describe Reilly's **tone**?

_____

_____

_____

I PERSUASION
Why does Neil Williams object to dodgeball? Describe Reilly's response to this objection.

_____

_____

_____

_____

_____

_____

aggression (ə-grĕsh'ən) *n.* hostile or destructive behavior or action

Why does the author think that letting out **aggressions** in dodgeball would be useful?

_____

_____

_____

J ANALYZE RHETORIC AND REASONING

A **caricature** is a cartoon-like depiction of an opposing argument. Underline the caricature in lines 32–40.

K PERSUASION

What widely-accepted value does Reilly use to make an **ethical appeal?** Consider whether he seems to respect the job of filling chalupas.

_____

_____

_____

_____

PAUSE & REFLECT

How does Reilly use humor to make his point?

_____

_____

_____

_____

_____

_____

a commune.[2] Then their kids will stumble out into the bright light of the real world and find out that, yes, there's weak and there's strong and teams and sides and winning and losing. You'll recognize those kids. They'll be the
40 ones filling up chalupas.[3] Very noncompetitive. **J K**

But Williams and his fellow whiners aren't stopping at dodgeball. In their Physical Education Hall of Shame they've also included duck-duck-goose and musical chairs. Seriously. So, if we give them dodgeball, you can look for these games to be banned next:

Tag. Referring to any child as *it* is demeaning and hurtful. Instead of the child hollering, "You're it!" we recommend, "You're special!"

Baseball. Involves wrong-headed notions of *stealing,*
50 *errors* and gruesome *hit-and-run.* Players should always be safe, never out.

Capture the flag. Mimics war.

Kick the can. Unfair to the can.

If we let these PC twinkies[4] have their way, we'll be left with:

Duck-duck-duck. Teacher spends the entire hour patting each child softly on the head.

Upsy down. The entire class takes turns fluffing the gym teacher's pillow before her nap.
60 *Swedish baseball.* Players are allowed free passage to first, second or third, where they receive a relaxing two-minute massage from opposing players. **PAUSE & REFLECT**

---

2. **commune** (kŏm′yoon′): a cooperative community in which a group of people who are not necessarily related live and work together.

3. **chalupas** (chə-loo′päs): fried tortillas filled with meat, a Mexican dish similar to tacos that is served at several U.S. fast-food chains.

4. **PC twinkies:** Reilly's expression for people who are too concerned (politically correct) with offending others by words or actions.

Text Analysis: Persuasion

In the chart below, give two examples of persuasive techniques the authors use to convince their readers. Identify if each is an emotional appeal or an ethical appeal. Then give your opinion about how effective each technique is.

"Position on Dodgeball in Physical Education"		
Persuasive Technique	**Type of Appeal**	**Effectiveness**

"The Weak Shall Inherit the Gym"		
Persuasive Technique	**Type of Appeal**	**Effectiveness**

Reading Skill: Analyze Rhetoric and Reasoning

Each selection is written to convince you that the argument in the piece is correct. However, both selections contain fallacies such as loaded words and phrases, leading questions, and caricatures. Record an example of each fallacy in the chart below. Then, explain the effect the fallacy has on the argument. Consider whether the fallacy strengthens or weakens the argument.

Fallacy	Example	Effect on Argument
Loaded Word or Phrase		
Leading Question		
Caricature		

Are all GAMES worth playing?

Now that you have read the two selections, look back at the two lists of games you made on page 478. Would you move any of the games from one list to the other? Why or why not?

_____

_____

_____

Vocabulary Practice

Tell whether the words in each pair are synonyms or antonyms.

1. adequately / insufficiently _____

2. aggression / ferocity _____

3. ban / legalize _____

4. eliminate / banish _____

5. impropriety / rudeness _____

Academic Vocabulary in Writing

accurate	bias	contrast	convince	logic

What gym class activity would you like to see either added to or banned from your school? Why? Share your opinion and the **logic** behind it in a paragraph. Use at least one Academic Vocabulary word. Definitions of these words are on page 459.

_____

_____

_____

Assessment Practice

DIRECTIONS Use "Position on Dodgeball in Physical Education" and "The Weak Shall Inherit the Gym" to answer questions 1–6.

1 Which of the following is NOT a purpose of physical education, according to the NASPE?
- **A** to provide students with skills
- **B** to teach students how to compete
- **C** to give students a daily dose of activity
- **D** to give students positive experiences

2 The NASPE uses which of the following to support its argument?
- **A** facts about bullying
- **B** quotations from athletes
- **C** statistics about the need to keep children active
- **D** examples of students hurt while playing dodgeball

3 In "The Weak Shall Inherit the Gym," what is the author's tone towards opponents?
- **A** conciliatory
- **B** scornful
- **C** angry
- **D** formal

4 Reilly's description of parents who oppose dodgeball in schools is an example of —
- **A** a caricature
- **B** an ethical appeal
- **C** a rhetorical question
- **D** a claim

5 Reilly claims that dodgeball —
- **A** makes kids better athletes
- **B** shows students how to follow rules
- **C** teaches kids to win by hurting others
- **D** helps students let out their aggressions

6 When Reilly says "You mean there's weak in the world?" it is an example of —
- **A** a rhetorical question
- **B** a leading question
- **C** an ethical appeal
- **D** a loaded term

What to the Slave Is the Fourth of July?

Speech by Frederick Douglass

What does INDEPENDENCE mean to you?

In the United States, we celebrate Independence Day on the 4th of July every year. The holiday commemorates our independence from England and the birth of our nation. But what does independence mean to you?

DISCUSS With a group, discuss what being independent means to students your age. Make a list of things you can do or ideas you can have as an independent person. For example, perhaps to you independence means being able to choose your own friends or listen to music your parents might not enjoy. Maybe it means mastering a skill all on your own. Then consider what independence means in a larger sense—what does it mean to be free?

Text Analysis: Speech

A **speech** is a talk or public address in which the speaker presents proposals, beliefs, or ideas. In speeches, you will often encounter rhetorical devices such as

- **rhetorical questions**—questions that do not require a reply, such as "What to the slave is the Fourth of July?" Speech writers use these to prompt listeners to think about an issue or to suggest that the answer is obvious.

- **repetition**—the use of the same word, phrase, or sound over and over. Repetition can help a speaker emphasize certain words and ideas and momentum that seizes a crowd's attention.

As you read the following speech, notice how Frederick Douglass uses rhetorical questions and repetition to stress his ideas.

Independence means ...

- *choosing my own friends*

What freedom means ...

Reading Skill: Evaluate Evidence

Distinguish between factual claims and commonplace assertions to evaluate whether supporting evidence for an argument is adequate.

- **Factual claims** can be proved by observation, an expert, or reliable sources. There should be evidence to back them up.
  "Statistics show that students who clean their own school are less likely to litter."

- **Opinions** are statements of personal belief, feeling, or thought, which do not require proof.
  "It's wrong to make students clean the school."

- **Commonplace assertions** are statements that many people assume to be true but are not necessarily so.
  "One bad apple can spoil the bunch."

As you read Douglass's speech, record examples of factual claims, commonplace assertions, and opinions in a chart like the one below. Then decide whether he provides enough solid evidence to be convincing.

Factual Claim	*Slaves are men.*
Commonplace Assertions	
Opinions	

Vocabulary in Context

Note: Words are listed in the order in which they appear in the speech.

disparity (dĭ-spăr′ĭ-tē) *n.* the condition or fact of being unequal; difference
  *The **disparity** between a slave and a free person was immense.*

prosperity (prŏ-spĕr′ĭ-tē) *n.* the condition of having success; flourishing
  *An enslaved person's chances for **prosperity** were nonexistent.*

grievous (grē′vəs) *adj.* causing grief, pain, or anguish
  *Enslaved people faced **grievous** discrimination.*

entitled (ĕn-tīt′ld) *v.* given the right to have or do something
  *All people are **entitled** to basic human rights.*

sham (shăm) *n.* something false or empty that is presented as genuine; a fake
  *The idea of freedom in America was a **sham** to enslaved people.*

fraud (frôd) *n.* a deception deliberately practiced to secure unfair or unlawful gain; a trick
  *Holidays such as the 4th of July seemed to be a **fraud** to them.*

SET A PURPOSE FOR READING

As you read, consider the differences between life for whites and life for enslaved blacks in 1852.

What to the Slave Is the Fourth of July?

Speech by

FREDERICK DOUGLASS

BACKGROUND Frederick Douglass endured 21 years of slavery before he escaped to freedom. There he became an outspoken abolitionist, or antislavery activist. He wrote and delivered speeches against slavery throughout his lifetime. Douglass delivered this speech on July 5, 1852, nine years before the beginning of the Civil War. It was not until the 13th Amendment was ratified, or approved, in 1865, that slavery was finally abolished.

Ⓐ SPEECH
Douglass opens his speech with a series of **rhetorical questions**. What point is he trying to make?

_____

_____

_____

disparity (dĭ-spăr′ĭ-tē) *n.* the condition or fact of being unequal; difference

Fellow citizens—Pardon me, and allow me to ask, why am I called upon to speak here today? What have I, or those I represent, to do with your national independence? Are the great principles of political freedom and of natural justice, embodied in that Declaration of Independence, extended to us? And am I, therefore, called upon to bring our humble offering to the national altar, and to confess the benefits, and express devout gratitude for the blessings, resulting from your independence to us? . . . Ⓐ

10   . . . [S]uch is not the state of the case. I say it with a sad sense of the **disparity** between us. I am not included within the pale[1] of this glorious anniversary! Your high

---

1. **within the pale:** within the limits of law or decency.

independence only reveals the immeasurable distance between us. The blessings in which you this day rejoice, are not enjoyed in common. The rich inheritance of justice, liberty, <u>prosperity</u>, and independence, bequeathed by your fathers, is shared by you, not by me. The sunlight that brought life and healing to you, has brought stripes[2] and death to me. This Fourth of July is *yours*, not mine. You may rejoice, I must mourn. . . .

Fellow citizens, above your national, tumultuous joy, I hear the mournful wail of millions, whose chains, heavy and <u>grievous</u> yesterday, are today rendered more intolerable by the jubilant shouts that reach them. . . .

My subject, then, fellow citizens, is "American Slavery." I shall see this day and its popular characteristics from the slave's point of view. Standing there, identified with the American bondman,[3] making his wrongs mine, I do not hesitate to declare, with all my soul, that the character and conduct of this nation never looked blacker to me than on this Fourth of July. . . . **B**

What point in the anti-slavery creed[4] would you have me argue? On what branch of the subject do the people of this country need light? Must I undertake to prove that the slave is a man? That point is conceded already. Nobody doubts it. The slaveholders themselves acknowledge it in the enactment of laws for their government. They acknowledge it when they punish disobedience on the part of the slave. There are seventy-two crimes in the state of Virginia, which, if committed by a black man (no matter how ignorant he be), subject him to the punishment of death; while only two of these same crimes will subject a white man to the like punishment. What is this but the acknowledgement that the slave is a moral, intellectual, and responsible being[?] **C**

prosperity (prŏ-spĕr′ĭ-tē) *n.* the condition of having success; flourishing

grievous (grē′vəs) *adj.* causing grief, pain, or anguish

B **EVALUATE EVIDENCE**
Underline the statement Douglass makes in the last sentence in this paragraph. Is this a **factual claim** or an **opinion**? How do you know?

_____
_____
_____
_____
_____
_____
_____
_____

C **SPEECH**
Circle the word Douglass repeats in lines 36–45. What idea is he emphasizing by repeating this word?

_____
_____
_____
_____
_____
_____

---

2. **stripes:** the marks left on the body after a whipping.
3. **bondman:** someone who is enslaved.
4. **creed:** belief.

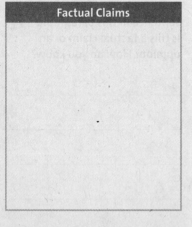

D EVALUATE EVIDENCE
When Douglass says, "The manhood of the slave is conceded" in line 46, is he making a factual claim or expressing an opinion? Add your answer to the appropriate section of the chart.

Factual Claims

Commonplace Assertions

Opinions

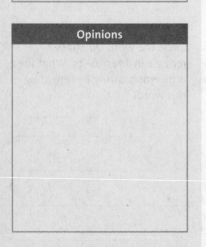

entitled (ĕn-tīt′l) *v.* given the right to have or do something

The manhood of the slave is conceded. It is admitted in the fact that Southern statute[5] books are covered with enactments[6] forbidding, under severe fines and penalties, the teaching of the slave to read or write. When you can
50 point to any such laws, in reference to the beasts of the field, then I may consent to argue the manhood of the slave. When the dogs in your streets, when the fowls of the air, when the cattle on your hills, when the fish of the sea, and the reptiles that crawl, shall be unable to distinguish the slave from a brute, then will I argue with you that the slave is a man!

For the present, it is enough to affirm the equal manhood of the Negro race. Is it not astonishing that, while we are plowing, planting, and reaping, using all kinds of
60 mechanical tools, erecting houses, constructing bridges, building ships, working in metals of brass, iron, copper, silver, and gold; that, while we are reading, writing, and ciphering,[7] acting as clerks, merchants, and secretaries, having among us lawyers, doctors, ministers, poets, authors, editors, orators,[8] and teachers; that, while we are engaged in all manner of enterprises common to other men—digging gold in California, capturing the whale in the Pacific, feeding sheep and cattle on the hillside, living, moving, acting, thinking, planning, living in families as husbands,
70 wives, and children, and, above all, confessing and worshiping the Christian's God, and looking hopefully for life and immortality beyond the grave—we are called upon to prove that we are men! **D**

Would you have me argue that man is **entitled** to liberty? That he is the rightful owner of his own body? You have already declared it. Must I argue the wrongfulness

---

5. **statute:** law.
6. **enactments:** authorized pieces of legislation; laws.
7. **ciphering:** doing arithmetic; working with sums.
8. **orators:** speakers.

of slavery? Is that a question for republicans?[9] Is it to be settled by the rules of logic and argumentation, as a matter beset with great difficulty, involving a doubtful application of the principle of justice, hard to be understood? . . . To do so, would be to make myself ridiculous, and to offer an insult to your understanding. There is not a man beneath the canopy of heaven that does not know that slavery is wrong for *him*. Ⓔ

What! Am I to argue that it is wrong to make men brutes, to rob them of their liberty, to work them without wages, to keep them ignorant of their relations to their fellow men, to beat them with sticks, to flay their flesh with the lash,[10] to load their limbs with irons,[11] to hunt them with dogs, to sell them at auction, to sunder their families, to knock out their teeth, to burn their flesh, to starve them into obedience and submission to their masters? Must I argue that a system, thus marked with blood and stained with pollution, is wrong? No; I will not. I have better employment for my time and strength than such arguments would imply. . . .

At a time like this, scorching irony, not convincing argument, is needed. . . .

What to the American slave is your Fourth of July? I answer, a day that reveals to him, more than all other days in the year, the gross injustice and cruelty to which he is the constant victim. To him, your celebration is a <u>sham</u>; your boasted liberty, an unholy license;[12] your national greatness, swelling vanity; your sounds of rejoicing are empty and heartless; your denunciations of tyrants, brass-fronted impudence; your shouts of liberty and equality, hollow mockery; your prayers and hymns, your sermons

---

9. **republicans:** people who believe in social equality and oppose aristocracy and privilege.
10. **flay . . . lash:** to strip skin off with a whip.
11. **irons:** metal shackles.
12. **license:** lack of restraint; excessive freedom.

Ⓔ **EVALUATE EVIDENCE**
A **commonplace assertion** is a statement that many people assume is true but is not necessarily true. When you come across such an assertion, ask yourself if it is really true for most people. Underline the commonplace assertion in lines 82–84. Is this assertion probably true for most people? Explain your response.

_____

_____

_____

_____

_____

_____

_____

_____

_____

_____

_____

_____

_____

_____

_____

sham (shăm) *n.* something false or empty that is presented as genuine; a fake

fraud (frôd) *n.* a deception deliberately practiced to secure unfair or unlawful gain; a trick

PAUSE & REFLECT

Has Douglass argued his position well? Do you think his listeners were convinced? Give reasons for your answers.

_____

_____

_____

_____

_____

_____

_____

_____

_____

_____

_____

_____

_____

_____

_____

_____

_____

and Thanksgivings, with all your religious parade and solemnity, are to him mere bombast,[13] <u>fraud</u>, deception, impiety, and hypocrisy—a thin veil to cover up crimes which would disgrace a nation of savages. There is not a nation on the earth guilty of practices more shocking and bloody, than are the people of these United States, at this very hour. . . . **PAUSE & REFLECT**

---

13. **bombast:** high-sounding words.

Text Analysis: Speech

In the chart below, give two examples of repeated words or phrases and rhetorical questions that Douglass uses in his speech. Explain how each example helps Douglass emphasize an idea or make a point.

"What to the Slave Is the Fourth of July?"	
Repetition	Idea Emphasized or Point Made
Rhetorical Question	Idea Emphasized or Point Made

Reading Skill: Evaluate Evidence

List three examples of evidence (facts, assertions, or opinions) that Douglass uses to support his claim. Explain why each piece of evidence is effective.

Claim: To the American slave, the Fourth of July holiday is a cruel sham.

↓

Evidence:	Why It Is Effective:

What does INDEPENDENCE mean to you?

How might Frederick Douglass's answer to this question have been different from your answer? Explain your thoughts.

_____

_____

_____

Vocabulary Practice

Tell whether each pair of words are synonyms or antonyms.

1. disparity / equality _____

2. prosperity / poverty _____

3. grievous / terrible _____

4. entitled / denied _____

5. sham / genuine _____

6. fraud / deception _____

Academic Vocabulary in Writing

accurate	bias	contrast	convince	logic

Do you think Douglass's listeners would have trusted Douglass to provide a fair and **accurate** account of the lives of slaves and the laws that govern them? In a paragraph, use at least one Academic Vocabulary word to explain how listeners might have regarded Douglass. Definitions of these words are on page 459.

_____

_____

_____

Assessment Practice

DIRECTIONS Use "What to the Slave Is the Fourth of July?" to answer questions 1–6.

1 Who are the "millions" that Douglass refers to in line 22?

- (A) citizens
- (B) enslaved people
- (C) Americans
- (D) his listeners

2 How does Douglass feel about America?

- (A) proud
- (B) worried
- (C) ashamed
- (D) confused

3 What law does Douglass cite to support his position that slaves are men?

- (A) enactments forbidding the teaching of the slave to read or write
- (B) laws allowing runaways to be hunted with dogs
- (C) statutes that regulate slaves' occupations
- (D) laws that sunder families

4 The statement "At a time like this, scorching irony, not convincing argument, is needed" is an example of —

- (A) a commonplace assertion
- (B) a rhetorical question
- (C) a factual claim
- (D) an opinion

5 Why does Douglass ask the rhetorical question: "[W]hy am I called upon to speak here today?"

- (A) to find out why he has been asked to speak
- (B) to point out that he is upset about speaking
- (C) to question the morals and intentions of all of his listeners
- (D) to emphasize the irony of a former slave speaking at a July 4th celebration

6 Douglass calls the July 4th holiday —

- (A) a fraud
- (B) discrimination
- (C) a double standard
- (D) a form of pure malice

Resources

The Glossary of Academic Vocabulary in this section is an alphabetical list of the Academic Vocabulary words found in this textbook. Use this glossary just as you would use a dictionary—to find out the meanings of words used in your literature class, to talk about and write about literary and informational texts, and to talk about and write about concepts and topics in your other academic classes.

For each word, the glossary includes the pronunciation, syllabication, part of speech, and meaning. A Spanish version of each word and definition follows the English version. For more information about the words in this glossary, please consult a dictionary.

accurate (ăk′yər- ĭt) *adj.* without error, factual; correct and exact
> **preciso** *adj.* sin errores, objetivo; correcto y exacto

affect (ə-fĕkt′) *v.* to have an effect on, to bring about a change
> **afectar** *v.* tener un efecto en algo, provocar un cambio

achieve (ə-chēv′) *v.* to accomplish or to succeed
> **lograr** *v.* alcanzar un objetivo o tener éxito

appropriate (ə-prō′prē-ĭt) *adj.* fitting for the purpose; suitable
> **apropiado** *adj.* adecuado para el propósito; conveniente

assess (ə-sĕs′) *v.* to determine value or significance
> **evaluar** *v.* determinar el valor o la importancia

attitude (ăt′ĭ-tŏŏd′) *n.* a state of mind or feeling
> **actitud** *sust.* estado de ánimo o sentimiento

bias (bī′əs) *n.* a preference for something or someone that prevents fair decision-making
> **parcialidad** *sust.* preferencia por algo o alguien que impide tomar decisiones de manera justa

circumstance (sûr′kəm-stăns′) *n.* an event or fact having some bearing on a particular situation; a determining factor
> **circunstancia** *sust.* suceso o hecho que tiene relación con una situación en particular; factor determinante

comment (kŏm′ĕnt) *n.* to make a remark, written or spoken
> **comentario** *sust.* observación escrita u oral

communicate (kə-myŏŏ′nĭ-kāt) *v.* to pass along information about; to make known
> **comunicar** *v.* transmitir información; dar a conocer algo

community (kə-myŏŏ′nĭ-tē) *n.* all people living in the same location under the same government
> **comunidad** *sust.* todas las personas que viven en un mismo lugar bajo el mismo gobierno

conclude (kən-klŏŏd′) *v.* to reach a decision
> **concluir** *v.* tomar una decisión

contrast (kŏn′trăst′) *v.* to show differences in one or more things when compared to each other
> **contrastar** *v.* mostrar las diferencias entre una o más cosas al compararlas entre sí

contribute (kən-trĭb′yŏŏt) *v.* to give something for a common purpose, to give to an organization
> **contribuir** *v.* dar algo para un propósito común, dar a una organización

convince (kən-vĭns′) *v.* to persuade; to cause one to feel sure about something
> **convencer** *v.* persuadir; hacer sentir seguro de algo

create (krē-āt′) *v.* to cause to exist; to make, form, or bring into being
> **crear** *v.* hacer existir; hacer, formar o dar vida

criteria (krī-tîr′ē-ə) *n.* standards or rules by which something can be judged; a measure of value
    criterio *sust.* norma o estándar según el cual se puede juzgar algo; medida de valor

culture (kŭl′chər) *n.* a society's way of life, including behavior, arts, beliefs, and all other products of work and thought
    cultura *sust.* modo de vida de una sociedad, que incluye las conductas, el arte, las creencias y los demás productos del trabajo y el pensamiento

emerge (ĭ-mûrj′) *v.* to appear, to come into view or existence
    surgir *v.* aparecer, hacerse visible o comenzar a existir

emphasis (ĕm′fə-sĭs) *n.* special attention or effort directed toward something to make it stand out
    énfasis *sust.* atención o esfuerzo especial dirigido hacia algo para lograr que se destaque

evident (ĕv′ĭ-dənt) *adj.* easily seen or understood
    evidente *adj.* fácil de ver o comprender

focus (fō′kəs) *n.* any center of interest or activity
    foco *sust.* centro de interés o actividad

challenge (chăl′ənj) *n.* a test of one's abilities
    desafío *sust.* prueba de las habilidades de una persona

imply (ĭm-plī′) *v.* to express indirectly
    implicar *v.* expresar de manera indirecta

income (ĭn′kŭm) *n.* money one receives as wages, salary, or by other means of profit
    ingreso *sust.* dinero que una persona recibe en forma de salario, sueldo u otro medio de compensación

individual (ĭn′də-vĭj′oo-əl) *adj.* single; relating to one human being or thing
    individual *adj.* simple; relativo a una persona o cosa

initial (ĭ-nĭsh′əl) *adj.* first; happening at the beginning
    inicial *adj.* primero; que ocurre al principio

intelligence (ĭn-tĕl′ə-jəns) *n.* the ability to learn, understand, and solve problems
    inteligencia *sust.* capacidad de aprender, comprender y resolver problemas

interpret (ĭn-tûr′prĭt) *v.* to explain the meaning of
    interpretar *v.* explicar el significado de algo

investigate (ĭn-vĕs′tĭ-gāt) *v.* to examine in detail; to learn the facts
    investigar *v.* examinar en detalle; aprender los datos

job (jŏb) *n.* a position in which one is employed
    trabajo *sust.* puesto laboral que ocupa una persona

logic (lŏj′ĭk) *n.* correct reasoning; a system of reasoning
    lógica *sust.* razonamiento correcto; sistema de razonamiento

mental (mĕn′tl) *adj.* of or related to the mind
    mental *adj.* de la mente o relacionado con ella

method (mĕth′əd) *n.* a systematic way of doing something; a process
    método *sust.* manera sistemática de hacer algo; proceso

motive (mō′tĭv) *n.* emotion, desire, or need that compels one to take a certain action
    motivo *sust.* emoción, deseo o necesidad que lleva a una persona a realizar una acción determinada

perceive (pər-sēv′) *v.* to become aware of something through one of the senses; to understand
    percibir *v.* tomar conciencia de algo por medio de uno de los sentidos; comprender

perspective (pər-spĕk′tĭv) *n.* a certain point of view; a subjective view of a particular issue
    perspectiva *sust.* punto de vista determinado; visión subjetiva de una cuestión en particular

predominant (prĭ-dŏm′ə-nənt′) *adj.* to have great importance, influence, or power
    predominante *adj.* tener gran importancia, influencia o poder

publish (pŭb'lĭsh) *v.* to prepare printed material for sale or to give out
> **publicar** *v.* preparar material impreso para su venta o distribución

rely (rĭ-lī') *v.* to be dependent on for help or support; to have confidence in
> **confiar** *v.* depender de alguien para recibir ayuda o apoyo; tener confianza en alguien

research (rĭ'-sûrch) *n.* close, careful study
> **investigación** *sust.* estudio detallado y preciso

role (rōl) *n.* a character or part played by a performer; a function or position
> **papel** *sust.* personaje o rol que representa un actor; función o posición

similar (sĭm'ə-lər) *adj.* the same, but not identical
> **similar** *adj.* el mismo pero no idéntico

source (sōrs) *n.* the point at which something comes into being; the point of origin
> **fuente** *sust.* punto en el que algo comienza a existir; punto de origen

style (stīl) *n.* the unique way in which something is said, done, expressed, or performed
> **estilo** *sust.* manera especial en que se dice, hace, expresa o representa algo

technical (tĕk-nĭ-kəl) *adj.* having special skill or knowledge, especially in a mechanical or scientfic way
> **técnico** *adj.* que tiene habilidades o conocimientos especiales, particularmente en el área de la mecánica o las ciencias

technique (tĕk-nēk) *n.* a systematic or especially organized way of completing a task; special skill related to completion of a task
> **técnica** *sust.* manera sistemática o especial de realizar una tarea; destreza especial relacionada con la realización de una tarea

technology (tĕk-nŏl'ə-jē) *n.* science as it is applied to practical use and work
> **tecnología** *sust.* ciencia aplicada a la práctica y el trabajo

trend (trĕnd) *n.* the general direction in which something tends to move; current style
> **tendencia** *sust.* dirección general en la que algo tiende a moverse; estilo actual

undertake (ŭn'dər-tāk') *v.* to take upon oneself; enter into
> **asumir** *v.* tomar para sí; comprometerse

Pronunciation Key

Symbol	Examples	Symbol	Examples	Symbol	Examples
ă	at, gas	m	man, seem	v	van, save
ā	ape, day	n	night, mitten	w	web, twice
ä	father, barn	ng	sing, hanger	y	yard, lawyer
âr	fair, dare	ŏ	odd, not	z	zoo, reason
b	bell, table	ō	open, road, grow	zh	treasure, garage
ch	chin, lunch	ô	awful, bought, horse	ə	awake, even, pencil,
d	dig, bored	oi	coin, boy		pilot, focus
ĕ	egg, ten	ŏŏ	look, full	ər	perform, letter
ē	evil, see, meal	ōō	root, glue, through		
f	fall, laugh, phrase	ou	out, cow	**Sounds in Foreign Words**	
g	gold, big	p	pig, cap	KH	German ich, auch;
h	hit, inhale	r	rose, star		Scottish loch
hw	white, everywhere	s	sit, face	N	French entre, bon, fin
ĭ	inch, fit	sh	she, mash	œ	French feu, cœur;
ī	idle, my, tried	t	tap, hopped		German schön
îr	dear, here	th	thing, with	ü	French utile, rue;
j	jar, gem, badge	th	then, other		German grün
k	keep, cat, luck	ŭ	up, nut		
l	load, rattle	ûr	fur, earn, bird, worm		

Stress Marks

' This mark indicates that the preceding syllable receives the primary stress. For example, in the word *language*, the first syllable is stressed: lăng'gwĭj.

' This mark is used only in words in which more than one syllable is stressed. It indicates that the preceding syllable is stressed, but somewhat more weakly than the syllable receiving the primary stress. In the word *literature*, for example, the first syllable receives the primary stress, and the last syllable receives a weaker stress: lĭt'ər-ə-chŏŏr'.

Adapted from *The American Heritage Dictionary of the English Language,* fourth edition. Copyright © 2000 by Houghton Mifflin Company. Used with the permission of Houghton Mifflin Company.

High-Frequency Word List

Would you like to build your word knowledge? If so,

the word lists on the next six pages can help you.

These lists contain the 600 most common words in the

English language. The most common words are on the

First Hundred Words list; the next most common are on

the Second Hundred Words list; and so on.

Study tip: Read through these lists starting with the

First Hundred Words list. For each word you don't know,

make a flash card. Work through the flash cards until

you can read each word quickly.

FIRST HUNDRED WORDS

the	he	go	who
a	I	see	an
is	they	then	their
you	one	us	she
to	good	no	new
and	me	him	said
we	about	by	did
that	had	was	boy
in	if	come	three
not	some	get	down
for	up	or	work
at	her	two	put
with	do	man	were
it	when	little	before
on	so	has	just
can	my	them	long
will	very	how	here
are	all	like	other
of	would	our	old
this	any	what	take
your	been	know	cat
as	out	make	again
but	there	which	give
be	from	much	after
have	day	his	many

SECOND HUNDRED WORDS

saw	big	may	fan
home	where	let	five
soon	am	use	read
stand	ball	these	over
box	morning	right	such
upon	live	present	way
first	four	tell	too
came	last	next	shall
girl	color	please	own
house	away	leave	most
find	red	hand	sure
because	friend	more	thing
made	pretty	why	only
could	eat	better	near
book	want	under	than
look	year	while	open
mother	white	should	kind
run	got	never	must
school	play	each	high
people	found	best	far
night	left	another	both
into	men	seem	end
say	bring	tree	also
think	wish	name	until
back	black	dear	call

THIRD HUNDRED WORDS

ask	hat	off	fire
small	car	sister	ten
yellow	write	happy	order
show	try	once	part
goes	myself	didn't	early
clean	longer	set	fat
buy	those	round	third
thank	hold	dress	same
sleep	full	tell	love
letter	carry	wash	hear
jump	eight	start	eyes
help	sing	always	door
fly	warm	anything	clothes
don't	sit	around	through
fast	dog	close	o'clock
cold	ride	walk	second
today	hot	money	water
does	grow	turn	town
face	cut	might	took
green	seven	hard	pair
every	woman	along	now
brown	funny	bed	keep
coat	yes	fine	head
six	ate	sat	food
gave	stop	hope	yesterday

High-Frequency Word List

FOURTH HUNDRED WORDS			
told	yet	word	airplane
Miss	true	almost	without
father	above	thought	wear
children	still	send	Mr.
land	meet	receive	side
interest	since	pay	poor
feet	number	nothing	lost
garden	state	need	wind
done	matter	mean	Mrs.
country	line	late	learn
different	large	half	held
bad	few	fight	front
across	hit	enough	built
yard	cover	feet	family
winter	window	during	began
table	even	gone	air
story	city	hundred	young
I'm	together	week	ago
tried	sun	between	world
horse	life	change	kill
brought	street	being	ready
shoes	party	care	stay
government	suit	answer	won't
sometimes	remember	course	paper
time	something	against	outside

FIFTH HUNDRED WORDS

hour	grade	egg	spell
glad	brother	ground	beautiful
follow	remain	afternoon	sick
company	milk	feed	became
believe	several	boat	cry
begin	war	plan	finish
mind	able	question	catch
pass	charge	fish	floor
reach	either	return	stick
month	less	sir	great
point	train	fell	guess
rest	cost	fill	bridge
sent	evening	wood	church
talk	note	add	lady
went	past	ice	tomorrow
bank	room	chair	snow
ship	flew	watch	whom
business	office	alone	women
whole	cow	low	among
short	visit	arm	road
certain	wait	dinner	farm
fair	teacher	hair	cousin
reason	spring	service	bread
summer	picture	class	wrong
fill	bird	quite	age

SIXTH HUNDRED WORDS

become	themselves	thousand	wife
body	herself	demand	condition
chance	idea	however	aunt
act	drop	figure	system
die	river	case	line
real	smile	increase	cause
speak	son	enjoy	marry
already	bat	rather	possible
doctor	fact	sound	supply
step	sort	eleven	pen
itself	king	music	perhaps
nine	dark	human	produce
baby	whose	court	twelve
minute	study	force	rode
ring	fear	plant	uncle
wrote	move	suppose	labor
happen	stood	law	public
appear	himself	husband	consider
heart	strong	moment	thus
swim	knew	person	least
felt	often	result	power
fourth	toward	continue	mark
I'll	wonder	price	voice
kept	twenty	serve	whether
well	important	national	president

Acknowledgments

Unit 1

Random House: "Raymond's Run," from *Gorilla, My Love* by Toni Cade Bambara. Copyright © 1971 by Toni Cade Bambara. Used by permission of Random House, Inc.

Sterling Lord Literistic: "Clean Sweep" by Joan Bauer, from *Shelf Life, Stories by the Book* edited by Gary Paulsen. Copyright © 2003 by Joan Bauer. Reprinted by permission of SLL/Sterling Lord Literistic, Inc.

Unit 2

Miriam Altshuler Literary Agency: "The Treasure of Lemon Brown" by Walter Dean Myers, *Boys' Life*, March 1983. Copyright © 1983 by Walter Dean Myers. Reprinted by permission of Miriam Altshuler Literary Agency, on behalf of Walter Dean Myers.

G.P. Putnam's Sons: "Rules of the Game," from *The Joy Luck Club* by Amy Tan. Copyright © 1989 by Amy Tan. Used by permission of G.P. Putnam's Sons, a division of Penguin Group (USA) Inc.

Virginia Driving Hawk Sneve: "The Medicine Bag" by Driving Hawk, from *Boy's Life*, March 1975. Copyright © 1975 by Virginia Driving Hawk Sneve. Used by permission of the author.

Scholastic: "Who Are You Today, Maria?" from *Call Me Maria* by Judith Ortiz Cofer. Copyright © 2004 by Judith Ortiz Cofer. Published by Scholastic Inc./Orchard Books. Reprinted by permission.

Unit 3

The Estate of Isaac Asimov: "Hallucination" by Isaac Asimov, from *Gold, The Final Science Fiction Collection*. Copyright © 1995 by Nightfall Inc./The Estate of Isaac Asimov. All rights reserved. Reprinted by permission of the Estate of Isaac Asimov.

The Estate of Isaac Asimov: Excerpt from "Ellis Island and I," from *The Tyrannosaurus Prescription and 100 Other Essays* by Isaac Asimov (Amherst, NY: Prometheus Books.) Copyright © 1989 by Isaac Asimov. Reprinted by permission of the Estate of Isaac Asimov.

The Wylie Agency: Excerpts from "Leaving Desire, The Ninth Ward after the Hurricane" by Jon Lee Anderson, from *The New Yorker*, September 19, 2005. Copyright © 2005 by Jon Lee Anderson. Reprinted with permission of The Wylie Agency LLC.

Arte Público Press: "Mi Madre," from *Chants* by Pat Mora. Copyright © 1985 by Arte Público Press—University of Houston. Reprinted with permission from the publisher.

Simon J. Ortiz: "Canyon de Chelly" by Simon J. Ortiz, originally published in *Woven Stone*, University of Arizona Press, Tucson, AZ. Copyright © 1992 by Simon J. Ortiz. Reprinted by permission of the author.

Unit 4

Rowman & Littlefield: "Pandora. . . The Fateful Casket," from *Firebringer and Other Great Stories, Fifty-Five Legends That Will Live Forever* by Louis Untermeyer. Copyright © 1968 by Louis Untermeyer. Reprinted by permission of Rowman & Littlefield Publishers, Inc.

Fulcrum Publishing: "Loo-Wit, the Fire-Keeper," from *Native American Stories* by Joseph Bruchac. Copyright © 1991 by Joseph Bruchac. Reprinted by permission of Fulcrum Publishing.

Little Simon: "The Old Grandfather and His Little Grandson," from *Twenty-Two Russian Tales for Young Children* by Leo Tolstoy, translated by Miriam Morton. Translation copyright © 1969 Miriam Morton. Reprinted with the permission of Little Simon, an imprint of Simon & Schuster Children's Publishing Division.

Bancroft Library: "The Wise Old Woman," from *The Sea of Gold and Other Tales from Japan* adapted by Yoshiko Uchida. Copyright © 1965 by Yoshiko Uchida. Courtesy of the Bancroft Library, University of California, Berkeley.

Random House: From *The Diary of Anne Frank* by Frances Goodrich and Albert Hackett. Copyright © 1956 by Albert Hackett, Frances Goodrich Hackett and Otto Frank. Used by permission of Random House, Inc.

Acknowledgments

UNIT 5

Marian Reiner: "Simile: Willow and Gingko," from *It Doesn't Always Have to Rhyme* by Eve Merriam. Copyright © 1964 Eve Merriam. Copyright renewed 1992 Eve Merriam. Used by permission of Marian Reiner.

University of Arkansas Press: "Introduction to Poetry," from *The Apple That Astonished Paris* by Billy Collins. Copyright © 1988 by Billy Collins. Reprinted by permission of The University of Arkansas Press.

Brooks Permissions: "Speech to the Young: Speech to the Progress-Toward," from *Blacks* by Gwendolyn Brooks. Copyright © Gwendolyn Brooks. Reprinted by consent of Brooks Permissions.

Alfred A. Knopf: "Mother to Son," from *The Collected Poems of Langston Hughes* by Langston Hughes. Copyright © 1994 by The Estate of Langston Hughes. Used by permission of Alfred A. Knopf, a division of Random House, Inc.

Special Rider Music: "Boots of Spanish Leather" by Bob Dylan. Copyright © 1963 by Warner Bros. Inc. Copyright renewed 1991 by Special Rider Music. All rights reserved. International copyright secured. Reprinted by permission.

UNIT 6

The New York Times: Adaptation of "Behind Monty Hall's Doors: Puzzle, Debate and Answer?" by John Tierney, *The New York Times*, July 21, 1991. Copyright © 1991 The New York Times. All rights reserved. Used by permission and protected by the Copyright Laws of the United States. The printing, copying, redistribution, or retransmission of the Material without express written permission is prohibited.

UNIT 7

Barbara S. Kouts Literary Agency: "The Snapping Turtle" by Joseph Bruchac, from *When I Was Your Age*, Vol. Two, Candlewick Press, 1999. Copyright © 1999 by Joseph Bruchac. Reprinted by permission of Barbara S. Kouts Literary Agency.

HarperCollins Publishers: "Out of Bounds," from *Out of Bounds: Seven Stories of Conflict and Hope* by Beverley Naidoo. Copyright © 2001 by Beverley Naidoo. Used by permission of HarperCollins Publishers.

UNIT 8

National Geographic Society: "The Spider Man Behind Spider-Man" by Bijal P. Trivedi, from *National Geographic Today*, May 2, 2002. Copyright © 2002 National Geographic Society. Reprinted by permission of National Geographic Society.

The New York Times: Excerpt from "Robo-Legs" by Michael Marriott, from *The New York Times*, June 20, 2005. Copyright © 2005 The New York Times. All rights reserved. Used by permission and protected by the Copyright Laws of the United States. The printing, copying, redistribution, or retransmission of the Material without express written permission is prohibited.

Chedd-Angier-Lewis Production Company: Excerpt from "Eureka: Scientific Twists of Fate" from *Scientific American Frontiers* Web site. Copyright © Chedd-Angier-Lewis Production Company, Inc. Reprinted by permission of Chedd-Angier-Lewis Production Company, Inc.

UNIT 9

Rob Laidlaw: "Zoos: Myth and Reality" by Rob Laidlaw. Copyright © Rob Laidlaw. Reprinted by permission of the author.

Song Hutchins: "Zoos Connect Us to the Natural World" by Michael Hutchins, *The Boston Globe*, November 2, 2003. Copyright © 2003 Michael Hutchins. Reprinted by permission of Song Hutchins.

NASPE: *Position on Dodgeball in Physical Education* (2006) by NASPE. Reprinted with permission from the National Association for Sport and Physical Education (NASPE), 1900 Association Drive, Reston, VA 20191-1599.

Sports Illustrated: Excerpts from "The Weak Shall Inherit the Gym" by Rick Reilly, from *Sports Illustrated*, May 14, 2001. Copyright © 2001 by Time Inc. Reprinted courtesy of Sports Illustrated. All rights reserved.

RESOURCES

From *Elementary Reading Instruction* by Edward Fry. Copyright © 1977 by McGraw-Hill compaines, Inc. All rights reserved. Reprinted by permission of the publisher.

COVER

(tc) Brooklyn Museum/Corbis; (tr) Civil War Archive/Bridgeman Art Library; (bc) © Getty Images; (c) Henri Georgi/All Canada Photos/Corbis; (bl) Ken Kinzie/HMH Publishers.

HOW TO USE THIS BOOK

xiii–xiv © Photos.com/Jupiterimages Corporation; **xiii** © Timothy Geiss/ShutterStock.

UNIT 1

2 © Digital Vision/PunchStock; **6–16** © Photos.com/Jupiterimages Corporation; **6** © Timothy Geiss/ShutterStock; **10** © Lise Gagne/istockphoto.com; **22–34** © Ales Nowak/ShutterStock; **22** © James Steidl/ShutterStock; **40–52** © Comstock Images/Jupiterimages Corporation; **40** © Brand X Pictures/Jupiterimages Corporation; **58–64** © Thinkstock Images/Jupiterimages Corporation; **58** © PhotoObjects/Jupiterimages Corporation.

UNIT 2

68 © Masaaki Toyoura/Taxi/Getty Images; **72–84** © PhotoDisc/PunchStock; **72** © Datacraft/Age Fotostock America, Inc.; **90–104** © Houghton Mifflin Harcourt; **90** © Lorraine Kourafas/ShutterStock; **110–121** © A. Paterson/ShutterStock; **110** Photo by Sharon Hoogstraten; **122–124** © Photos.com/Jupiterimages Corporation; **122** © Rob Cousins/Robert Harding Picture Library/Age Fotostock America, Inc.

UNIT 3

128 © Walter Hodges/The Image Bank/Getty Images; **132–158** © istockphoto.com; **132** © Brand X Pictures/PunchStock; **134** © Ryan McVay/Photodisc/Getty Images; **157** © Douglas Kirkland/Corbis; **164–176** © liquidlibrary/Jupiterimages Corporation; **166** © John Beatty/Stone/Getty Images; **182** © Arnold Genthe/Bettmann/Corbis; **191** © Bettmann/Corbis; **194** © Shawn Alladio; **212–216** © AbleStock.com/Jupiterimages Corporation; **214** © Aimin Tang/istockphoto.com.

UNIT 4

220 © Vimas/ShutterStock; **224–228** © Digital Vision/Getty Images; **224** © PhotoObjects/Jupiterimages Corporation; **229–232** © photostogo.com; **229** © istockphoto.com; **238** © PhotoObjects.net/Jupiterimages Corporation; **239–244** © Jamey Ekins/ShutterStock; **239** © freelanceartist/ShutterStock; **250–292** © Image Source Ltd.; **250** © Anne Frank Fonds-Basel/Anne Frank House-Amsterdam/Getty Images.

UNIT 5

296 © Digital Vision/PunchStock; **300–301** © Jim Jurica/istockphoto.com; **300** © Vincenzo Lombardo/Photographer's Choice/PunchStock; **302–303** © AbleStock.com/Jupiterimages Corporation; **302** © Ingram Publishing; **308** *top* © Thinkstock Images/Jupiterimages Corporation; *bottom* © Inti St. Clair/Blend Images/PunchStock; **309** *top* © Comstock Images/Jupiterimages Corporation; *bottom* © Hisom Silviu/ShutterStock; **314** *top* © PhotoDisc/Getty Images; *bottom* © Corbis; **315–316** © PhotoDisc/Getty Images; **315** © Andy Sotiriou/The Image Bank/Getty Images; **322–323** © Photos.com/Jupiterimages Corporation; **322** © 1971yes/ShutterStock; **324–329** © dinadesign/ShutterStock; **324** © Houghton Mifflin Harcourt.

UNIT 6

332 © Rehan Khan/epa/Corbis; **336–344** © Pixland/Jupiterimages Corporation; **336** © PhotoDisc/Getty Images; **349** *Let's Make a Deal*, host Monty Hall, 1963–1976 © Courtesy Everett Collection; **356–362** © Lorenzo Colloreta/istockphoto.com; **356** © Visual Language/PunchStock; **368–370** © Christine Glade/istockphoto.com; **368** Library of Congress, Prints and Photographs Division [LC-DIG-ppmsca-19301]; **370** © Joseph Sohm/Digital Vision/Getty Images.

UNIT 7

374 © UpperCut Images/PunchStock; **378–392** © Photos.com/Jupiterimages Corporation; **378** © Leo Blanchette/ShutterStock; **381** © Betsy Cullen/Photonica/Getty Images; **398–414** © Photos.com/Jupiterimages Corporation; **398** © Madeleine Openshaw/ShutterStock; **400** Marriage necklace or Thali (1800). India (Madras). Golden pendants on black thread. (CT17149). Victoria & Albert Museum, London. © Victoria & Albert Museum, London/Art Resource, New York.

UNIT 8

418 © Mike Agliolo/Corbis; **422** Photo by Michael Caulfield/AP/Wide World Photos; **434** Courtesy of Hanger Prosthetics & Orthotics, Inc. – www.hanger.com; **436** © Dith Pran/The New York Times; **439** © Science Source/Photo Researchers, Inc.; **447–455** Illustrations by David Ballard.

UNIT 9

458 © Michelle D. Bridwell/PhotoEdit; **462** © Stephen Chernin/Getty Images; **469** © Ali Burafi/AFP/Getty Images; **473** Photo by Michael Dwyer/AP/Wide World Photos; **480** © Chris Clinton/Taxi/Getty Images; **484** © John W. McDonough/Sports Illustrated/Getty Images; **492** Library of Congress, Prints and Photographs Division [LC-USZ62-15887].

Index of Authors & Titles